Fundamentals
of Flexible
Compensation

Fundamentals of Flexible Compensation

Dale L. Gifford and Christine A. Seltz
Editors

JOHN WILEY & SONS

New York • Chichester • Brisbane • Toronto • Singapore

This publication is designed to provide accurate and
authoritative information in regard to the subject
matter covered. It is sold with the understanding that
the publisher is not engaged in rendering legal, accounting,
or other professional service. If legal advice or other
expert assistance is required, the services of a competent
professional person should be sought. *From a Declaration
of Principles jointly adopted by a Committee of the
American Bar Association and a Committee of Publishers.*

Library of Congress Cataloging-in-Publication Data:
Fundamentals of flexible compensation / Hewitt Associates : editors,
  Christine A. Seltz, Dale L. Gifford.

    p.   cm.
    Bibliography: p.
    ISBN 0-471-85796-3
    1. Compensation management—United States.   I. Seltz, Christine,
1950–   .   II. Gifford, Dale L., 1950–   .   III. Hewitt Associates.

HF5549.5.C67f56 1988
658.3'22—dc19   87-28564

                                                    CIP

Printed in the United States of America

10 9 8 7 6 5 4 3 2 1

Foreword

Circumstances have propelled three waves of change in the private employee benefit field. The first was set in motion at the bargaining table in the late 1940s and early 1950s when pensions and other benefits were negotiated by unions and subsequently extended to other employee groups. The second wave saw the flourishing of the private benefit movement in the 1960s and 1970s. This was the era of expansion in terms of types and levels of coverage provided, and in terms of government involvement in ensuring that the private benefit system fulfilled public policy expectations. This second wave crested in the early 1980s and broke on the rocks of rapidly escalating health care costs, foreign competition, changing demographics, and a deep recession.

Today, the third wave in employee benefits is just beginning to form. In substance, it bears some resemblance to the second wave, except that its shape is flexible.

This book is about the shaping of that third wave in employee benefits—flexible compensation. As of this writing, 27 percent of the Fortune 100 Industrials and 16 percent of the Fortune 500 have flexible compensation programs in effect. On the service side, 20 percent of the Fortune 500 Service companies have implemented programs, including 44 percent of the 100 largest commercial banks, 26 percent of the 50 largest life insurers, 22 percent of the 50 largest utilities, and 12 percent of the 50 largest savings institutions. Hundreds of smaller to mid-size companies also have moved toward choice making in employee benefits.

This new wave, however, is about more than choices among benefits; it is about differences in the way total compensation is delivered to employees. A flexible approach places benefit dollars on the same level as compensation dollars. It creates a system under which the employer determines the total amount of compensation to be provided, while the individual determines the form and structure of that compensation amount. This is important because it changes the traditional view of employee benefit financing. No longer is the employer locked in to the cost of providing a particular configuration of benefits. Instead, the employer's commitment is to a given level of expenditure, which employees may use to meet individual needs and circumstances. Therein also lies the potential for controlling benefit costs while delivering greater value to employees.

Flexible compensation as a concept is challenging and intriguing. This book was written to inform those who need to know about its origins, structure, and mechanics of operation. The book is not intended as a final treatise, for the wave of flexible compensation is still taking shape, still gathering momentum, still formulative.

Each of the authors is expert in the subject matter, having worked individually and collectively on the creation and development of hundreds of flexible compensation programs now in effect. Hopefully, the knowledge they have to share will prove invaluable in creating understanding of this emerging tidal wave of change.

THOMAS E. WOOD*

Bannockburn, Illinois

*Editors' Note: Thomas E. Wood was one of the originators of flexible compensation and is a retired partner of Hewitt Associates.

Preface

This book is intended to serve as a comprehensive reference on flexible compensation—one of the fastest growing design approaches for the delivery of employee benefits and compensation.

The book is intended to be useful to both the novice and the expert in employee benefit matters. Within the text are answers to some of the most frequently asked questions about flexible programs. For example, what alternatives exist for the design of a flexible program? In which benefit areas is choice making most often introduced? How can the cost impact of a flexible program be measured? Also included is detailed treatment of the more technical activities involved with a flexible program implementation—the generating of flexible credits and the pricing of benefit options, establishing the administrative apparatus for individual elections, and testing for nondiscrimination.

The book is organized in seven parts. Part I provides an overview of flexible compensation, including discussion of the major forces influencing the growth and development of flexible programs, review of the alternatives available for flexible program design, and a summary of the steps involved in starting a program.

Part II concentrates on the legal and regulatory environment. Included is background on the origins and development of the legal framework for flexible programs and an explanation and illustration of the new rules established by the Tax Reform Act of 1986.

Part III focuses on the design of flexible programs. The section is organized by benefit area—health (including medical, dental, vision, and hearing); death and disability coverages; flexible spending accounts; vacation and other time off with pay arrangements; and retirement options.

Part IV examines the structure and financing of flexible programs in terms of options and prices. Also included is a discussion of the insurance and risk aspects of flexible program choices.

Parts V and VI explain the steps involved in communicating and administering flexible compensation programs.

Part VII focuses on the financial analysis of flexible programs. This section includes also a model for performing a cost/benefit analysis of a proposed program.

It should be noted that throughout this book, the text refers to flexible *compensation*. Some readers may question whether the reference ought to be flexible *benefits*. But the choice of terminology is deliberate. Benefits represent a form of compensation, even though provided to the employee indirectly in the form of employer contributions for medical or other coverages, pension benefits, and the like. Moreover, given the significant sums involved—approaching 40 percent of payroll in some organizations—the direction today is toward increased recognition of employee benefits as a component of total compensation. Finally, choice-making programs further blur once-distinct lines between benefits and compensation as employees often are able to convert unused benefits to cash, or conversely, to divert a portion of pay to the purchase of benefits on a tax-favored basis.

In compiling this book, the editors have drawn on the accumulated experience of numerous members of Hewitt Associates. The contributors were invaluable in sharing both their technical knowledge and practical insights into the many different aspects of flexible program operation. Hewitt Associates as a whole was most gracious in its support of the time devoted to developing the manuscript.

DALE L. GIFFORD
CHRISTINE A. SELTZ

The Woodlands, Texas
Lincolnshire, Illinois
April 1988

Contributors

Ablin, Marlene J., Fellow of the Society of Actuaries
Boyle, Jean E., Communication Consultant
Brackey, Marianne G., Fellow of the Society of Actuaries
Brandorff, Perry O., Fellow of the Society of Actuaries
Butterworth, Thomas C., Attorney
Certain, Stephanie L., Communication Consultant
Georgemiller, Denise, Research Consultant
Hasbargen, Donald W. Jr., Benefit Design Consultant
Hoos, John O., Attorney
Howlett, Catherine M., Communication Consultant
Irwin, Barbara Jane, Attorney
Jeffay, Jason, Benefit Design Consultant
Jones, Michael B., Benefit Design Consultant
Kenney, Suzanne M., Communication Consultant
McKee, Gail E., Benefit Design Consultant
Robb, Marybeth C., Attorney
Roof, Timothy C., Fellow of the Society of Actuaries
Schmitt, Kyle A., Systems Consultant
Steinberg, Allen T., Attorney
Tucker, Larry J., Group Insurance Consultant

About the Editors

D ale Gifford and Christine Seltz are partners with Hewitt Associates. Hewitt Associates pioneered the concept of flexible compensation and is one of the largest management consulting firms in the world specializing in employee benefits and compensation.

Mr. Gifford has designed and implemented flexible compensation programs for a wide variety of employers. Ms. Seltz has written for Hewitt Associates on a broad range of employee benefit and compensation issues. Together, the editors have written extensively on flexible compensation, including a 1982 booklet for the American Management Association entitled "Flexible Compensation: A Forward Look."

Contents

PART FOUR   STRUCTURE AND FINANCING

PART SEVEN   EXPERIENCE

20. Financial Analysis   **461**

Part One

Overview

One

Origins and Objectives

Not long ago, the concept of flexible compensation was viewed as an innovative, leading-edge approach to delivering benefits and compensation. Proponents touted employee involvement in compensation and benefit decisions as the way of the future. Detractors proclaimed the notion right for academic discussion but unfit for practical application. Until recently, management held back, uncomfortable with an idea that was both novel and different.

Today all of that has changed. As Figure 1.1 illustrates, over 800 organizations, representing most industries and all employer sizes, have implemented flexible compensation programs, with most of the activity occurring in recent years. More significant, evidence is mounting that choice making will replace fixed approaches as the "norm" for delivering employee benefits and compensation in the future.

For many years, the concept of choice has existed within benefit programs. For instance, employees have long had the opportunity to purchase supplemental life insurance beyond employer-provided levels or to pay higher contributions for more valuable medical coverage. The essential difference between that type of choice and the creation of a *choice-making* program, however, is that employees have the opportunity to determine (within certain limits) how employer dollars for benefits are spent on their behalf. Conceptually, a flexible approach recognizes that a certain portion of total compensation will be provided by

Figure 1.1
Flexible Compensation Programs among Major U.S. Employers

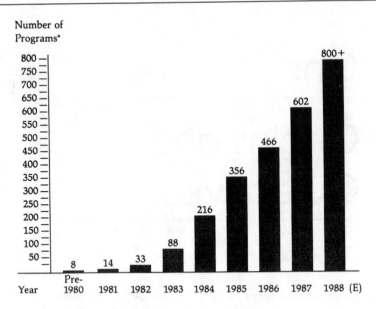

Source: Hewitt Associates
*Excludes premium conversion only

the employer in the form of employee benefits, but how that pool of funds is spent—in terms of types and levels of benefits—essentially is a matter of individual employee determination. These are largely the types of programs tabulated in the preceding figure.

§ 1.1 ENVIRONMENT FOR FLEXIBLE COMPENSATION

Why has interest in flexible compensation increased, particularly in the latter half of the 1980s?

Changes in employee benefits do not occur in a vacuum. Instead, change occurs in response to specific stimuli. In the case of flexible compensation, the environment for employee benefits was turned upside down by developments in the 1980s. Among major employers, who tend to set the pattern, employee benefits had evolved to a point of maturity. A recession focused attention on finding ways to control costs, and the demographics of the workforce had changed dramatically from decades earlier when benefit programs still were in their infancy. Meanwhile, the same pressures that led to a fundamental rethinking of benefit programs stimulated developments on two other fronts—namely, in Washington where revisions to the tax code enhanced the ability of employers to offer employee choice, and in computer technology which made it easier to administer programs with choices.

Understanding the environment for flexible programs helps clarify that these arrangements developed less as a "gimmick" of the 1980s than as a rational response to complex, emerging issues.

(a) EVOLUTION OF EMPLOYEE BENEFITS

Before the introduction of social security in 1935, responsibility for meeting security needs rested primarily with the individual. Certain major industries (e.g., railroads, utilities, mining companies, and banks) had established modest pension plans, but the payments typically were funded out of current operating income. Companies in isolated industries such as timber or oil exploration sometimes provided medical care through physicians and facilities provided by the industry. To some extent unions also had made limited progress on establishing wage replacement or other arrangements for their own members who became ill, injured, or disabled. However, the Great Depression of the 1930s, which bankrupt entire industries and produced massive unemployment, decimated even these early attempts at employee benefit provision, and wiped out personal savings as the last resort of the individual as well.

The 1940s produced dramatic changes. High wartime taxes on corporate income, including an excess-profits tax, rekindled employer interest in the deductibility of retirement plan contributions. (Concern over the potential for abuse led to establishment of the first nondiscrimination standards and limits on employer deductions for retirement plans in the Revenue Act of 1942.) Wage stabilization programs in place during World War II (and later the Korean conflict) increased union receptivity to other forms of compensation provided by the employer—namely, fringe benefits. Later in the decade, court decisions made pension and welfare benefits a matter for collective bargaining. Finally, advances in medical technology not only increased the efficacy of medical care but also raised the price, making it difficult for individuals to afford the cost except on a group basis.

The result of these changes was a major shift in responsibility for security from the individual to the employer and widespread availability of employee benefit coverage. By the 1970s, the typical large corporation provided a final-average pay pension plan, with most also offering a supplemental savings plan. Medical coverage included basic hospitalization and surgical benefits and major medical coverage with a $100 deductible. Company-paid life insurance provided at least one year's salary. Long-term disability benefits replaced 50 percent of pay inclusive of social security.

Today the configuration of employee benefit programs is even more complete. Among 812 major employers surveyed in 1986, the prevalence and characteristics of benefit programs for salaried employees appear as follows:

- 91 percent maintain a *defined benefit pension plan* that typically bases benefits on the employee's highest five-year earnings and requires no employee contributions.

- 96 percent offer one or more *defined contribution* vehicles that enable the employee to accumulate capital, usually as a supplement to retirement income. The most common defined contribution arrangements include company savings plans (85 percent of employers) that typically match 50 cents (or more) on each dollar contributed by the employee up to certain limits; deferred profit sharing plans (19 percent of employers); and company stock ownership arrangements (64 percent of employers).

- All of the surveyed employers provide *medical* coverage. Deductibles usually apply, but the amount generally is limited to $200 or less. For employees, overall out-of-pocket costs are capped each year, usually at $1000 or less. In about one-quarter of plans coverage is noncontributory, although more companies are moving toward requiring employee contributions at least for dependent coverage.

  In addition, 89 percent of employers provide *dental* coverage, 21 percent provide *vision* care, and 6 percent cover *hearing* expenses.

- The vast majority of employers also offers protection in the event of death or disability. *Group life insurance* is universally provided, with one to two times pay provided on a company-paid basis, and as much as four to five times pay provided in total from company-paid and contributory coverages. In addition, almost half of the surveyed companies make available at group rates the purchase of life insurance for dependents of an employee.

Again, disability coverage is universally provided. On *short-term disability*, majority practice is to continue all or a portion of salary for some period of time before commencement of long-term disability benefits (e.g., six months). In the event of *permanent disability*, companies replace typically 60 percent or more of salary inclusive of social security, with the income usually continuing until retirement.

- All companies provide paid *vacations* and *holidays*. Vacation time usually relates to the employee's length of service—for example, two weeks off after one year, three weeks after five years, grading up to five or more weeks after 30 years of service. In addition, most companies provide 10–12 paid holidays per year.

(b) RISE IN COSTS

As the prevalence of benefit plans has grown, so too has the cost. According to statistics compiled by the U.S. Chamber of Commerce, employee benefit costs as a percent of payroll climbed 22 percent between 1955 and 1965. Then between 1965 and 1975, costs began to skyrocket, shooting up over 43 percent. This was the period when benefits were being "improved" and new plans such as dental and savings were being added. The rate of growth in costs as a percent of payroll dropped significantly between 1975 and 1985, growing a more modest 6 percent.

Two factors account for the recent slowdown in cost increases. One has been recognition by employers that benefits had reached a saturation point. Security needs were already being met, or even exceeded for many employees, particularly in the larger organizations. Second, the early 1980s represented a period of severe recession for many employers which underscored the need to cut benefit costs, or at a minimum, to slow the rate of escalation. As a result, many employers started to cut

Table 1.1
Employer Payment for Benefits as Percent of Payroll

Type of Program	1955	1965	1975	1985
Legally required payments	3.6%	4.9%	8.0%	9.5%
Welfare and retirement plans	8.2	9.6	13.7	15.3
Paid time off	8.5	10.2	13.7	12.9
Total	20.3%	24.7%	35.4%	37.7%

Source: U.S. Chamber of Commerce, Employee Benefits: Historical Data 1951–1979; and Employee Benefits: 1985.

back some benefit areas (medical in particular) or otherwise halt improvements, which contributed to the slowdown in aggregate cost increases.

Today, action on the cost containment front is far from over. One of the most significant reasons is the continued climb in the cost of health care. Inflation in the medical component of the Consumer Price Index (CPI) has tended to outdistance the overall rise in consumer prices, even in years when the CPI has been relatively flat. In 1987, for example, consumer prices rose 4.4 percent, while the medical component posted a 5.8 percent gain.

In addition to the rising cost of medical services, another factor driving the upward escalation in health care costs is higher rates of utilization. Simply stated, more people are making more use of more medical services, and as a result, very high growth rates have occurred in annual expenditures for health care. According to figures compiled by the Department of Health and Human Services, the rate of growth in annual expenditures for medical care pushed 16 percent in the early 1980s, dropping to a more moderate rate of around 10 percent by the middle of the decade.

The combined effect of more costly services and higher rates of utilization is larger medical plan costs to employers. While few employers will be able to exert much control over external factors such as the cost of medical technology, many will be attempting to influence internal factors such as utilization. Influencing utilization through plan design and employee communication, for example, holds significant potential for helping to curb the rate of escalation in an employer's health care costs.

(c)   CHANGES IN DEMOGRAPHICS

Changes in the demographics of the workforce have been well documented. Today more women are entering and remaining in the workforce. The proportion of traditional households—employed male with dependent spouse and children—is declining. The proportion of single- and dual-income households has increased. Greater diversity in the workforce has created significant pressure on employers to recognize and accommodate the variety in employee needs for benefits, both today and as those needs change over time.

For example, child care represents one of the newer areas of need for many employees. Fewer households today—whether supported by one income or two—have the family network in place to care for young children. As a result, many employers are feeling increased pressure to "do something" to accommodate the needs of working parents. However, under sustained pressure to control benefit costs, few have been willing to shoulder the entire obligation for another new—and expensive—coverage area.

Another issue arising out of the change in demographics is an increase in the number of households with duplicate sources of employee benefit protection. Many employers as well as employees question the usefulness of two sources of coverage (e.g., medical) or high levels of protection when the need for such coverage may be minimal (e.g., death benefits for households without dependents).

Related to the issue of diversity within the workforce is growing recognition that the needs, priorities, and values people have for benefits change over time. The need for security coverages, for example, tends to be high during the child-rearing years but less so once children are grown. Retirement income is an important priority—but usually later in a working career. Life events such as marriage, saving for home purchase or education of children, loss of employment by a spouse, and so forth, occasion reevaluation of benefit coverages. In effect, these differences set up a sort of "moving target" for employee benefit programs to meet.

(d)   ENABLING LEGISLATION

Although the basic framework of rules and regulations for employee benefits has been in place for a long time, only recently have revisions been made to the tax code to enhance the viability of flexible programs. Two changes had significant impact on the environment for flexible compensation.

The first change involved legislative amendment of the code to permit choice making in benefits involving taxable and nontaxable options. It was the revenue act of 1978 that created the "twin pillars" of flexible compensation—Section 401(k) and Section 125. Section 401(k) permitted trade-offs between cash and deferral of compensation into a retirement income vehicle. Section 125 permitted choice making between taxable and nontaxable benefits. (Later both sections were linked to permit choice making among all forms of compensation—cash, welfare benefits, and deferred compensation.) Psychologically, the legislation had major impact on the growth in flexible programs in that a previously "gray area" within the tax code was clarified, providing a firm legal basis for choice-making programs.

The second change arose through regulation. In 1981, the IRS issued implementing regulations for Section 401(k) arrangements. Included within the regulations was a key provision permitting *individuals* to make the determination to defer a portion of salary into a retirement income vehicle. (Although employers had long had authority to mandate salary reduction unilaterally, previous rules were unclear on the permissibility of *employees* electing to defer compensation.) Shortly after release of the Section 401(k) regulations, salary reduction also came to be used for the purchase of other employee benefits, beyond deferral into a 401(k) plan. In effect, employee contributions for benefits were treated as *employer* payments, and escaped federal income and most state and local taxes. The result was that for the first time, employees had a tax *efficient* means of paying for benefits. Later the Tax Reform Act of 1986 confirmed through legislation the use of salary reduction for benefit purchases.

(e) ADMINISTRATIVE SOLUTIONS

Another factor influencing the environment for flexible compensation has been the relatively recent advent of computerized solutions to handle day-to-day flexible program operation. Many aspects of conventional employee benefit administration have been automated for some time. However, accommodation of choice-making programs, with their individual elections, annual reenrollments, and often special claims and payment recordkeeping requirements, placed new demands on administrative systems and procedures. Until the late 1970s and early 1980s, the obstacles associated with administering a flexible program largely were viewed as insurmountable—unless an employer was willing to commit significant resources to the design and programming of an internal system.

Eventually, however, demand led to the proliferation of automated solutions developed specifically for flexible program administration. Today personal computer systems, mainframe software, time-sharing services, and third-party approaches to administration are readily available from consulting firms, insurers, third-party administrators, and software vendors. Even though some organizations may still choose to develop administrative and recordkeeping systems in-house, alternative software solutions are available to meet the needs of both large and small organizations.

§ 1.2   KEY PURPOSES FOR FLEXIBLE COMPENSATION

The first flexible compensation programs were introduced in the early 1970s and under relatively unusual circumstances. In 1973, a West Coast division of TRW, Inc. adopted a choice-making arrangement for the principal purpose of meeting diverse employee needs. The division employed a large group of highly educated engineers and technicians who wanted more control over benefit decisions. TRW implemented a program that permitted employees to opt "up or down" from previous life and medical coverages. If the employee chose less valuable coverage, the difference was paid in cash. If the employee elected more valuable coverage, the difference in price was paid for through after-tax payroll deductions.

At about the same time, Educational Testing Service (ETS) in Princeton, New Jersey, adopted a different type of flexible approach. A benefit study indicated that ETS lagged behind other organizations in the competitiveness of their program. The organization decided to enrich its program—but allow employees to decide individually how the new funds should be spent on various benefit options.

These earliest "social experiments" proved tremendously successful. Employees appreciated the opportunity to make benefits more useful, and the employers received high marks (and considerable outside interest) for innovating on essentially a new frontier. However, both situations were pigeonholed as small and unique employee environments. Not until 1978, when the former American Can Company (now known as Primerica) implemented a flexible program, did the barrier to the broader business community collapse.

American Can's primary interest in flexible compensation was as a means of slowing the rate of growth in benefit costs and breaking a lockstep with union-driven benefits. The company also was in the process of diversifying its business and needed to be able to compete more effectively for talented employees. American Can set up a program that carved the existing package into two pieces. The first layer represented a cutback to a core level of benefits uniformly applicable to all employees. The next layer provided the flexible benefit options. Employees could arrange the flexible options to suit individual circumstances.

The American Can experience represented a breakthrough in several ways. First, the company demonstrated that a flexible approach could work in a large company environment. Second, their experience showed that an existing program could be split so that choice making need not be an "add-on" or require additional employer funding. Finally, American Can introduced the concept that a flexible approach contained the potential to control future increases in benefit costs. By dividing an existing program into core and options, some of the built-in escalation in benefit costs could be curbed. If the cost of the flexible options increased, the company could make a conscious decision to add more money, or pass along the cost to employees in the form of higher price tags.

Although considerable refinement has occurred since then, much about these early programs looks familiar in flexible program practices today.

(a) APPEAL TO DIVERSE EMPLOYEE NEEDS

Fundamentally, flexible compensation is an alternative *delivery* mechanism for compensation and benefits. Under a conventional program, an employer provides a package of benefits to all employees. Little discretion exists for the individual to shape or rearrange coverages to suit individual needs or circumstances.

In contrast, the distinguishing characteristic of a flexible approach is the opportunity for the individual to make choices about the uses of employer-provided benefit funds. Under a flexible program, the employee decides among *types* of benefits and *levels* of coverage. In addition, the employee determines the *form* of compensation in terms of whether to spend the employer contribution on benefits, to receive some portion of the allocation in cash, or to save some or all of the allocation for use at a later date (e.g., retirement). In effect, a flexible approach recognizes the different needs employees have for benefits at different points in time.

But the appeal of a flexible program is not entirely one-sided; the employer gains from the process as well. From the employer perspective, choice making is an opportunity that employees appreciate, which leads to raised perceptions of a benefit program, even in the absence of higher employer contributions for benefits or the introduction of new plans. Moreover, benefit options generally must include some recognition of "price" for employees to review and compare in making choices. Assigning a price tag to a benefit tends to give it a value that employees previously may not have recognized. Finally, to make choices, employees must understand their benefits. The process of becoming more familiar with benefits creates an active—rather than passive—interest in benefit coverages.

(b) CONTROL BENEFIT COSTS

A flexible approach allows an employer to set in place a more clearly defined mechanism for reducing or controlling costs over the long term. With a conventional program, cost management can be achieved, but largely in terms of cutting back coverages or passing along higher costs to employees. A flexible approach introduces a third option— namely, allowing employees to trade off among coverages. Consider some examples.

First, if an employer needs to reduce benefit costs immediately (as many employers did in the 1980s) a flexible program can be introduced to "soften the blow" to employees. Perhaps the prior "rich" coverages are made available *if* employees are willing to pay a larger proportion of the cost or to accept lower benefits in another area. Perhaps another "less rich" level of coverage is made available at little or no employee cost. Instead of a unilateral decision either to reduce coverage or to increase contributions, the employer allows individual employees to decide how the necessary cost containment efforts will affect them.

Second, a flexible program can provide employees with incentive to select lower levels of coverage—even in the absence of a reduction in employer contributions. In medical, plans that require *more* employee cost sharing in the delivery of services (i.e., deductibles and copayment amounts) tend to experience *lower* utilization. When the employee must pay a higher proportion of the cost of services, smarter health care utilization tends to result.

Finally, a flexible approach allows the employer to separate decisions on the *cost* of compensation from decisions on the *form* of compensation. The employer determines each year how much funding should occur in the benefit program. Employees then determine how that amount should be allocated among the various options available.

This enables the employer to avoid the automatic, inflation-driven escalation characteristic of conventional programs. In effect, the employer has introduced a *defined contribution* approach to paying for indemnity plan coverages. For example, if the cost of medical options rises faster than the employer's willingness to spend, employer contributions to the program can be held at a predetermined level, in which case employees will be required either to pay more for the same level of coverage or to select a lower-valued option. Again, the employer keeps costs at acceptable levels while individual employees determine how limitations on the benefit dollar will affect them.

(c)   DELIVER COMPENSATION TAX EFFECTIVELY

Tax efficiency became a motivation for flexible programs shortly after individual salary reduction was sanctioned. The timing also coincided with employer needs to pass along a portion of benefit program costs to employees. Many employers who needed to introduce or raise employee contributions allowed those payments to be made on a *pretax* basis, thus minimizing out-of-pocket costs to employees. By electing to use salary reduction, employees save federal and most state and local income taxes. Further, unlike 401(k) salary reduction contributions, social security taxes are not payable on amounts contributed to other benefit programs. So employees can be asked to share more of the cost for benefits, often with no impact on take home pay.

Salary reduction also proved useful in another way. Most employers have been unwilling to support expansion of employee benefit coverages into new areas—child care, personal legal, or presently noncovered health care. Using salary reduction, the employer can offer the employee the opportunity to pay for these types of coverages on a tax-advantageous basis. (This type of approach is known as a "flexible spending account.") In concept, the employer need not contribute funds, but in practice many companies do so as a relatively inexpensive means of "doing something" while avoiding the entire obligation for a new benefit area.

(d)   MEET COMPETITIVE PRESSURE

Organizations implementing flexible programs tend to be regarded as "innovative," "responsive," or "leading-edge" employers. Indeed, some companies are beginning to view flexible compensation as a means of differentiating themselves, particularly in markets with strong competition for highly qualified employees.

To some extent, also, flexible programs have moved sufficiently into the mainstream of employee benefits to set the standard for "competitive practice." Increasingly, flexibility is being regarded as a "benefit"—the lack of which can work to lower the perceived value of even a generous conventional program.

§ 1.3   EMERGING OBJECTIVES FOR FLEXIBLE COMPENSATION

The major movement toward flexible compensation in the 1980s was born of the need to contain costs and supported by the logic of meeting diverse employee needs, maximizing the perceived value of benefits, and delivering compensation tax effectively. Certainly these objectives will remain important long into the future.

But some newer objectives are emerging today that will expand the uses for flexible compensation. Consider some examples.

- **Merging benefit programs.** Flexible compensation provides a mechanism for combining benefit programs of merged or acquired organizations. Instead of continuing separate programs (thereby facilitating ongoing comparison of the different structures) or merging programs into a whole (which often leads to "cherry picking" the richest plans from each entity), a flexible approach allows the employer to offer benefit options that may resemble but not duplicate prior coverages. That way employees can come close to reconstructing earlier coverages without saddling the employer with a prior program.

- **Allowing cost variations by geographic location or business unit.** Even companies with a common benefit structure across the organization may want to introduce company cost variations. The reason may be to reflect differences in cost by geographic location or differences in acceptable overhead among various lines of business within the organization. For example, a diversified company may need to maintain lower compensation costs in labor-intensive operations (such as branch banking or restaurant operations) but have a competitive need to maintain high benefit levels in other businesses. Such an employer may be able to maintain an identical flexible program for all business units while varying the flexible credit allowance (or option price tags) based on the business unit's cost constraints.

- **Varying benefit contributions based on business performance.** Many organizations need to minimize their fixed costs, while being able to tolerate greater fluctuations in variable costs. Their inclination would be to spend labor dollars in ways that will motivate employees to be more productive. These management needs have resulted in recent revisions to direct pay systems—more emphasis on incentives such as bonuses and restructuring of salary programs so that performance becomes a more important factor. To a certain extent, fixed cost constraints have also affected the retirement area, with some employers shifting new money *away* from defined benefit pensions and into capital accumulation vehicles that do not represent the permanent, fixed commitment of a pension plan.

A few employers also are exploring the use of flexible compensation to allow variations in the funding of indemnity plan coverages based on company performance. Certainly, none are suggesting that an employee's entire benefit allocation should be subject to the whims of profitability. However, some employers are investigating the possibility of providing a fixed credit amount that will purchase a "safety net" of coverage as well as providing an additional variable contribution determined each year based upon business performance. Employees can use the variable amount to purchase benefits, defer the amount into a tax-favored savings plan, or take the amount as taxable cash.

- **Reducing compensation inequities.** Most organizations currently pay some employees more than others through the benefit program. For example, employees who cover dependents in a group health plan typically receive more value, in the form of a higher employer subsidy, than employees with no dependents. Moreover, older employees receive more value from a life insurance program than younger employees. To some organizations, these additional subsidies are appropriate and consistent with long-term security goals for employees. Others, however, have concluded that this differentiation by employee—driven not by performance or service, but by the life circumstances of the employee—is no longer appropriate.

   A few employers are using flexible compensation to reduce or eliminate differences in treatment among employees, either immediately upon introduction of the program or gradually over a period of years. The objective is to equalize employer-provided contributions for benefits, regardless of the employee's age or number of dependents.

- **Encouraging a total compensation perspective.** Such motivations as changing the fixed nature of employer contributions for welfare benefits, introducing performance-based contributions, maximizing employee perceptions of benefits, and reducing "compensation" inequities often reflect a more fundamental objective: to promote a total compensation perspective among employees, so benefit dollars appear more similar to direct pay and therefore more "real" to employees. By expressing employer contributions for benefits as dollars and allowing employees to decide how those dollars are to be spent, the line between direct pay and benefits becomes less distinct. Employees see their compensation as one amount in pay, another in flexible credits plus any other nonflexible benefit amounts, the entirety of which represents *total compensation*.

   From management's perspective, the total compensation viewpoint also reinforces the concept that benefit costs, like direct pay costs, can and should be controlled.

Two

Elements of Flexible Compensation

§ 2.1 INTRODUCTION

A flexible approach involves opening up a benefit and compensation program to individual choice. However, the degree of flexibility offered varies substantially, depending on the type of program adopted. For example, a program allowing employees to use salary reduction to convert contributions for benefits from an after-tax to a pretax basis provides more limited flexibility. In contrast, a choice-making program that permits employees to decide among types of benefits, levels of coverage, and form of compensation (cash, savings, or benefit purchase) provides a relatively high degree of flexibility. In the medium range are flexible spending accounts which offer employees the opportunity to pay for certain expenses on a tax-efficient basis. In practice, however, the different approaches overlap with companies combining some or all of these elements.

§ 2.2 PREMIUM CONVERSION

(a) IN GENERAL

One of the simplest approaches to flexible compensation can be implemented using the salary reduction or "conversion" concept. Basically, salary reduction allows employees to pay their share of benefit plan premiums on a before-tax basis. The concept is similar to deferral of salary into a 401(k) plan, except that in this case, the employee is using salary reduction amounts to pay benefit plan premiums. The salary reduction amounts escape federal and most state and local income taxes and, unlike 401(k), also social security taxes. When contributions are converted from an after-tax payroll deduction basis to a before-tax salary reduction payment method, the employee comes out ahead in terms of take-home pay.

Salary reduction for premium payment most typically is used in the health care area—for medical, dental, or other health-related contributions. Most employers mandate that the employee's share of premiums be paid in before-tax dollars. However, because of concern over possible reduction in social security benefits, a few employers permit employees to choose between pretax or after-tax premium payment. (The effect of salary reduction on social security benefits will be discussed later in this chapter.)

Premiums for group-term life insurance also may be paid through salary reduction. However, the value of employer-provided life insurance in excess of $50,000 is taxable to the employee. Since salary reduction technically constitutes an employer contribution, some of the advantage in using pretax premium payment for coverage over $50,000 is lost. Still, few employers permit a choice over method of premium payment because the tax advantages of pretax payment tend to outweigh the disadvantages.

Employee contributions for disability benefits also may be made on a before-tax basis. If salary reduction is used, however, an issue arises over the taxability of benefit payments in the event of an employee's disablement. For federal tax purposes, benefit payments from an employer-provided long-term disability program represent income to the recipient. On the other hand, benefit payments from a plan paid for by the employee with after-tax dollars are exempt from federal income taxes. For this reason, a few employers choose not to mandate pretax premium payment for long-term disability coverage.

Another use for premium conversion is to cushion the impact of increased cost sharing with employees. While the concept applies to any benefit where the employer and employee share costs, health care is where this approach most often is used. If employee contribution levels are increased but employees are allowed to pay the higher contributions on a before-tax basis, there may be little or no effect on take-home pay due to the tax savings inherent in salary reduction. If salary reduction is introduced, absent any changes in contribution levels, employees will recognize an increase in take-home pay.

Example 2.1 illustrates the effect of changing a $100 per month medical contribution from an after-tax to a before-tax payment method. The conversion to a before-tax basis, with its tax savings, allows the employee to experience an increase in take-home pay.

The salary reduction concept also extends beyond before-tax payment of benefit plan premiums. Flexible spending accounts, which will be discussed later in this chapter and in greater detail in a separate chapter, offer another opportunity for employees to pay certain expenses on a before-tax basis. These accounts allow employees to save on taxes when salary reduction amounts are set aside to pay various health, dependent care, and personal legal expenses.

Whether salary reduction is used to pay premiums or to fund a flexible spending account, the mechanics of the process are similar. For simplicity in explaining the mechanics, however, consider the case of an employee choosing to use salary reduction to pay medical plan contributions on a pretax basis.

Example 2.1
Illustration of Premium Conversion

	Payment Method	
	After-Tax	Before-Tax
Monthly salary	$2,000	$2,000
Salary reduction	0	100
Taxable pay	$2,000	$1,900
Taxes*	401	366
After-tax contribution	100	0
Take-home pay	$1,499	$1,534
Change in take-home pay		+ $35

*Assumes 1988 federal income and social security taxes. State income taxes excluded. Single, one exemption, standard deduction.

First, the employee signs an election form agreeing to the salary reduction. (This is equivalent to the employee agreeing to receive less pay and in return having the employer pay the cost of medical coverage.) Second, gross pay is reduced by the medical contribution before taxes are withheld. Third, the salary reduction amount is passed along to the insurance carrier, trust, and so forth, in the same way as after-tax contributions. Finally, the employee's paycheck is modified to reflect the new payment method.

Despite the simplicity of using salary reduction to convert employee premiums from an after-tax to a before-tax payment basis, it should be noted that premium conversion requires a formal plan document. Premium conversion is considered a type of flexible compensation program and, as such, must be established by a formal legal document. (See also the discussion of documentation in Chapter Four.)

(b) TAX CONSIDERATIONS

Salary reduction amounts receive special tax treatment. As is the case with deferrals under Section 401(k), salary reduction amounts under Section 125 are not taxable for federal income tax purposes. Further, because state income tax law tends to be patterned after federal law, salary reduction amounts generally are not considered taxable income for most state income tax purposes. There are a few exceptions, however, and these include Alabama, New Jersey, and Pennsylvania. Similarly, salary reduction amounts are typically excluded from most municipal taxes; however, exceptions include:

Kansas City, Missouri	Dayton, Ohio
St. Louis, Missouri	Erie, Pennsylvania
Canton, Ohio	Philadelphia, Pennsylvania
Cincinnati, Ohio	Pittsburgh, Pennsylvania
Columbus, Ohio	

(See also Chapter Eleven on retirement plans for discussion of the tax treatment of salary reduction under Section 401(k). The listing of states and municipalities differs for Section 401(k) salary deferrals.)

Unlike Section 401(k) deferrals, however, both the employer and the employee also avoid payment of social security (FICA) taxes on Section 125 salary reduction amounts. From the employer's perspective, the tax savings is usually small, but it may help offset the initial start-up and administrative costs involved with a flexible program.

Generally, the greater the number of employees earning less than the social security wage base, the greater the tax savings will be to the organization.

Salary reduction amounts also are generally exempt from federal unemployment payroll taxes (FUTA). However, the treatment for state unemployment taxes varies considerably from state to state and is still evolving.

(c) EFFECT ON SOCIAL SECURITY BENEFITS

Because salary reduction amounts under Section 125 are not subject to employer or employee social security taxes, these amounts are not considered as earned wages when calculating social security benefits. As a result, an individual who pays for benefits with before-tax dollars could receive smaller social security payments at retirement than if these costs had been paid on an after-tax basis.

In practice, however, the effect at retirement is minimal, as is illustrated in Table 2.1. In most cases, had the individual invested only a portion of the social security tax savings, the resulting accumulations would more than offset the benefit shortfall. (Note that the illustration does not address other social security benefits such as survivor and disability benefits.)

(d) EFFECT ON OTHER BENEFITS

Nearly all companies with flexible compensation programs involving salary reduction choose to base pay-related benefits on pay prior to salary reduction. Using the earlier illustration as an example, a person earning $24,000 annually ($2,000 per month), reducing salary by $1,200, and covered by a company-paid life insurance program equal to two times pay, would receive a full $48,000 in coverage—not $45,600. Similarly, pay-related disability and retirement programs are typically based on pay prior to salary reduction.

In certain limited situations, however, the Internal Revenue Code does not allow any latitude in defining pay. The most important area is that of the Section 415 limits. For purposes of calculating an employee's maximum retirement plan contribution and benefit limits under Section 415 of the tax code, pay *after* salary reduction must be used. (This issue is discussed in more detail in Chapter Eleven on retirement.)

Table 2.1
Effect of Level Pay Reductions Beginning in
1988 on Primary Social Security Benefits at Age 65

Employee		Social Security Benefits if NO Pay Reduction		Reduction in Social Security Benefits if Annual Pay Reduction Beginning in 1988 Is:			
1988 Pay	1988 Age	Annual Amount	Percent of FAP*	$500	$1,000	$2,500	$5,000
				Annual Social Security Reduction AMOUNT			
$15,000	25	$35,664	39.0%	$276	$ 528	$1,308	$2,604
	35	24,060	42.9	144	300	744	1,488
	45	15,228	44.2	72	132	324	648
	55	10,416	49.2	24	36	84	132
$25,000	25	$49,752	32.6%	$132	$ 252	$612	$1,224
	35	33,984	36.3	84	144	360	708
	45	21,648	37.7	48	96	228	444
	55	14,760	41.9	24	48	180	384
$35,000	25	$57,456	26.9%	$132	$ 264	$ 624	$1,236
	35	39,096	29.8	84	180	444	900
	45	24,576	30.6	60	120	300	600
	55	16,140	32.7	24	48	132	252
				Social Security Reduction PERCENTAGE			
$15,000	25			.8%	1.5%	3.7%	7.3%
	35			.6	1.2	3.1	6.2
	45			.5	.9	2.1	4.3
	55			.2	.3	.8	1.3
$25,000	25			.3%	.5%	1.2%	2.5%
	35			.2	.4	1.1	2.1
	45			.2	.4	1.1	2.1
	55			.2	.3	1.2	2.6
$35,000	25			.2%	.5%	1.1%	2.2%
	35			.2	.5	1.1	2.3
	45			.2	.5	1.2	2.4
	55			.1	.3	.8	1.6

Assumptions:

1. Future cost-of-living increases: 4% each year.
2. Future increases in average national earnings: 4.5% each year.
3. Future pay increases: 5% each year.
4. Past pay increases: at average national earnings rate.
5. All Social Security benefits are assumed to begin at age 65 (even for those born after 1937 for whom *un*reduced benefits may not be available until as late as age 67).
6. Annual pay reductions shown are *level* amounts contributed each year beginning in 1988 and continuing until retirement at age 65.

*Final average pay = last 5 years before age 65.

§ 2.3   CHOICE MAKING

(a)   IN GENERAL

Choice making continues to be one of the principal design approaches for a flexible compensation program. In allowing employees to trade off among benefits, employers can accommodate diverse employee needs, offer greater variety in benefits, and increase the perceived value of benefit expenditures. Although the approaches used to introduce choice making vary considerably from one employer to the next, conceptually, the funds used to drive a choice making system are generated in three ways: rearrangement of existing benefit dollars, cutback from existing levels, or introduction of new money.

The rearrangement approach allows employees to reduce or increase coverage levels in various benefit areas. By electing coverage levels lower than current company-paid levels, funds or credits are generated for use in other benefit areas. Election of higher-than-current coverage in one area requires trading down in another benefit area or increased employee contributions.

The cutback approach is useful when current benefits are more valuable than all employees need (or the employer can afford to support). The employer may offer lower or "core" levels of benefits, or even permit employees to waive coverage entirely in some areas. All or a portion of the difference in value between current benefit levels and the core benefit levels would provide the funds or flexible credits for employees to construct a new program or to "buy back" the former coverages, if desired. In practice, although a buy-back option is psychologically appealing, few employees actually reconstruct the prior arrangement.

The last approach relies on the introduction of new money, either employee or employer money. Employee money is introduced and used to provide additional funds or credits in a flexible program, usually through the process of salary reduction. Employer money can be introduced and used to fund a flexible program in several ways: a percentage of the employee's pay, a flat-dollar amount, or a combination of these two approaches. Flat-dollar allocations have the advantage of not inflating with increases in pay, and any change in the flat-dollar allocation can be communicated as a benefit improvement. Sometimes a credit formula can be based on service; however, in such cases, employers must be careful to avoid a discriminatory allocation pattern, in that longer-service employees tend to be higher-paid employees. Employers need not "lock in" to an allocation of additional employer dollars each year. A profit-related or gain-sharing technique can also be used to provide additional flexible credits based on financial performance of the employer. Such an approach reduces fixed costs because additional allocations are made only in years when the allocation can be justified by performance.

The differences between the three approaches—rearrangement, cutback, and new money—are illusory at best. Most plans incorporate elements of each approach in the overall design of the program. For example, cutting back to a core level of coverage might be coupled with introduction of salary reduction, and trade-offs permitted across benefit hazard areas.

(b)   AREAS OF CHOICE

Certain benefits accommodate choice making better than others. Defined benefit pension plans represent an area where choice making is not easily introduced because the value of any benefit trade-off varies significantly by the age and pay of the employee. Another reason is that deferral into a 401(k) defined contribution arrangement is the only type of retirement vehicle sanctioned within Section 125. Still, as will be discussed in a subsequent chapter, some employers have accomplished a measure of choice making in the retirement area, even though the actual design and legal structure may exist outside the flexible program.

The areas that more readily accommodate choice making include indemnity plan coverages (health care, group-term life insurance, and disability) and time off with pay. Each of these areas, however, presents unique challenges.

In health care, most companies structure options around a comprehensive medical approach, with differences occurring only in areas such as the deductible and maximum out-of-pocket payment amounts. Items such as coinsurance, lifetime maximums on plan benefits, and covered expenses usually are kept constant from option to option. The chief exception for variability in type of care involves health maintenance organizations (HMOs) or other alternative delivery mechanisms. Even within alternative delivery systems, however, usually only the incidentals (such as per-visit charges) vary from one provider to the next—not the type of care provided.

Key issues to settle in medical will include the appropriate levels of deductibles and out-of-pocket limits, the minimum level of required coverage (if any), and the degree to which employer subsidies of dependent coverage should continue.

Within group-term life insurance, there are several key considerations related to the degree of choice to be offered. For example, in
addition to deciding what total amounts of insurance to offer, an employer must also decide the increments of coverage (e.g., multiples of
$10,000 or multiples of pay). Existing practice as well as administrative
convenience will usually influence this decision. Moreover, the employer must decide the method of credit generation and the price tags
to be used—age-related (which reflects true cost) or a flat rate to all
employees. Finally, decisions also must be made regarding the levels of
coverage an employee may pay for with before-tax dollars, recognizing
that employees are taxed on the value of amounts in excess of $50,000 if
paid for through salary reduction.

Structuring appropriate levels of choice in the long-term disability
area can be challenging as well. Some employers offer employees only
an "in-or-out" decision. Others offer several alternative pay replacement levels or benefit duration periods. The key issues in the disability
area include the appropriateness of letting employees waive coverage,
the impact of before-tax versus after-tax contributions on the taxability
(and resulting adequacy) of disability income, and the most appropriate
levels of pay replacement if options are offered.

Finally, the area of time off with pay will require some special decisions. Increasingly, employers are including vacation time as a choice
area within a flexible program, offering employees both the buying and
selling aspects of a vacation choice. But some organizations limit the
choice to a one-way decision. For example, some organizations limit employee choice to the *selling* of vacation days only (i.e., receiving more pay
in return for fewer vacation days). Within these organizations, concern
often centers on the potential for scheduling conflicts when employees
are permitted more time off. Other employers offer employees only the
choice of *buying* vacation days (i.e., receiving less pay in return for more
vacation days). Existing carry-over policies and the potential impact on
cash flow are key influences on decisions to include buying and/or selling
of vacation time. As with most areas of flexible compensation, there are
no right or wrong approaches. Each design area needs to be evaluated
against the employer's own circumstances and environment.

In terms of the overall design of a choice-making program, many
employers initially are tempted to restrict the types and levels of
choice offered as a means of simplifying decisions for employees. Experience shows, however, that employees feel comfortable with even
the most complex flexible program—provided the choices are communicated well. Conversely, even the simplest program can generate

confusion if the communication effort is slighted. So while there are often good reasons to restrict choice (i.e., to provide minimum levels of protection or to minimize adverse selection), concern about employee understanding of a flexible program need not dictate the degree of choice available.

(c) SPECIAL CONSIDERATIONS

Two topics related to choice making have yet to be discussed: adverse selection and waivers of coverage. Like other aspects of choice making, these two topics are complex and will be dealt with in greater detail in other chapters. To round out this discussion, however, brief mention will be made here.

(1) Adverse Selection

All voluntary benefit plans contain an element of employee selection. Employees participate because they know they will use the benefit (e.g., dental) or because they know they will need the benefit if an unforeseen event occurs (medical emergency, death, or disability).

Adverse selection occurs when employees can accurately anticipate their use of benefits and choose the option that provides the most coverage at the least cost. For example, an employee facing open-heart surgery can know that the highest level of medical coverage is a "good buy," even if the benefit price tags are high. In most situations, however, employees cannot accurately project their benefit use, particularly for a family. In fact, many employees will choose the highest available level of medical coverage just in case a major expense occurs.

The potential for adverse selection can be controlled through the design of a flexible program. Various techniques enable employers to offer a wide range of choices without running much risk of greater-than-expected claims. These techniques will be discussed at length in a subsequent chapter. In brief, however, the approaches include:

- Restricting the employee's ability to increase coverage levels dramatically from one year to the next
- Subsidizing the price tags for certain options to encourage broad participation
- Providing a less-than-full-value "rebate" to employees waiving coverage
- Grouping coverages for more predictable expenses (e.g., prescription drugs) with less predictable expenses (e.g., other health care)

- Encouraging use of flexible spending accounts as an alternative to insuring more predictable types of expenses (e.g., vision).

Each of these techniques can help control adverse selection. The "price" that an employer pays by utilizing some of these techniques, however, is reduced choice making to the employee. The practitioner needs to recognize that the objectives of maximum flexibility in choice making and elimination of adverse selection are often in conflict.

(2)   Waivers of Coverage

Some plans allow employees to elect no coverage in certain benefit areas, which constitutes a "waiver of coverage." Whether such a waiver is allowed, and in which benefit areas, is a matter of employer discretion—and different employers will decide the issue in different ways. Some will refuse to allow employees to elect coverage below certain minimal core levels. Others will permit waivers only in certain benefit areas. Still others are comfortable allowing employees the complete freedom to opt out entirely.

Employers often are more concerned about employees going without medical and disability income benefits than dental coverage, for example. However, experience has shown that employees who waive medical coverage are not "going bare." Instead, they typically have health coverage from another source such as their spouse's employer.

Like adverse selection, restrictions on an employee's ability to waive coverage can often conflict with the objective of providing maximum flexibility through choice making.

§ 2.4   FLEXIBLE SPENDING ACCOUNTS

(a)   IN GENERAL

A flexible spending account is an individual employee account that provides reimbursement of certain eligible benefit expenses—health, dependent care, or personal legal expenses. At the start of the plan year, the employee determines whether to establish any or all of the accounts and how much money to contribute. When an expense is incurred, the employee submits a request for reimbursement to the employer who issues payment from the account. Payments from the flexible spending account represent nontaxable income to the employee, just as though he or she had incurred a medical or other nontaxable benefit claim.

The only "catch" with a flexible spending account is that expenses must be anticipated very carefully. Under the tax rules for flexible spending accounts, any monies left on deposit at year-end are forfeited by the employee and revert to the employer.

Despite this potential handicap, flexible spending accounts represent one of the most versatile and popular elements included in flexible compensation programs. Companies offering a choice-making program often include one or more types of spending accounts as another benefit option. But flexible spending accounts can also be adopted on a stand-alone basis in the absence of any other choices within an employer's benefit program.

The popularity of this element of a flexible program is attributable to several motivations, including:

- To expand the types of benefits offered employees with little or no additional employer cost (e.g., day care, vision care)
- To encourage employees to "self-insure" predictable or budgetable expenses that are subject to adverse selection (e.g., vision care, cosmetic surgery)
- To deliver compensation tax effectively.

(b)   SOURCES OF FUNDS

Flexible spending accounts attached to a choice-making program are more apt to be funded from a variety of sources: employer contributions, employee salary reduction contributions, and dollars "freed up" from trade-offs in other benefit areas. In contrast, stand-alone spending accounts are often funded by employee salary reduction only.

When salary reduction is a source of funds, deposits normally are spread proportionately throughout the year. This avoids a major drain on the employee's income at any one point during the year. Employer contributions and benefit trade-off dollars also may be spread uniformly throughout the year or deposited in blocks (e.g., at the end of each quarter) to reduce the recordkeeping effort.

(c)   TYPES OF BENEFITS

Funds generated from the sources identified earlier can be used to pay eligible expenses in several benefit areas. Flexible spending accounts for reimbursement of expenses related to health care, dependent care, and personal legal services are often found as benefit options in flexible programs. Following is a brief summary of the characteristics of each type of flexible spending account. (For a more extensive review, refer to Chapter Nine.)

Under a health care spending account, employees can be reimbursed for health-related expenses not covered by the employer's other health plans. In general, any health-related expense which could be used to meet requirements for deductibility on an employee's income tax return is eligible for reimbursement. For example, deductible and copayment amounts may be reimbursed for both medical and dental benefits, along with the cost of procedures not covered by the underlying medical and dental plans (well-baby care, physical exams, orthodontia, etc.).

Under a dependent care spending account, employees can be reimbursed for certain work-related dependent care expenses for: children under age 15 who qualify as dependents on the employee's federal income tax return; other dependents for income tax purposes who are physically or mentally incapable of self-care regardless of age, such as an elderly parent whom the employee supports; and a disabled spouse who is physically or mentally incapable of self-care.

Most types of dependent care expenses are covered, including care in the employee's home or in a day-care center. As a general rule, if the employee is married, both the employee and the employee's spouse must be employed in order to be reimbursed for dependent child or parent care expenses. Also, the employee cannot be reimbursed for expenses that exceed the employee's taxable income or the taxable income of the employee's spouse, whichever is lower.

A separate provision of the tax code provides a tax credit for dependent care expense. However, the tax credit may be claimed only on expenses paid for with after-tax dollars. Expenses reimbursed under a spending account cannot be applied toward the tax credit and vice versa. For families with income below $24,000, the tax savings from the credit generally will be greater than those generated through before-tax contributions to a spending account.

Spending accounts for legal services * allow employees to be reimbursed for personal legal services performed by or under the supervision of a lawyer. These services may be related to divorce, adoption, will preparation, personal bankruptcy, and sale or purchase of a personal residence. Legal expenses are *not* covered if they pertain to a trade or business of the participant or the management, conservation, or preservation of property held by the participant for commercial purposes. Often the employer chooses not to reimburse expenses related to representation in criminal proceedings and proceedings involving the employer.

---

*The tax exclusion for group legal expired in 1987 and as of this writing has not been reinstated. (See also Chapters Five and Nine.)

(d) MECHANICS OF THE PROCESS

The mechanics of the election/enrollment process and the reimbursement of expenses are fairly straightforward.

Employees decide whether to deposit funds in each type of flexible spending account at the *beginning* of a plan year. These funds may arise from any of the sources identified earlier. The category of benefit for which the funds will be used must be identified at the start of the year. Under the law, it is not acceptable to maintain a "general reimbursement fund" from which all health, dependent care, and personal legal services expenses are reimbursed.

Once made, the elections cannot be changed for any reason during the year unless the employee has a change in family status. Addition or loss of a dependent and a change in a spouse's employment status are examples of family status changes that generally would allow an employee to change elections during the year.

With the elections in place, the employer creates individual book accounts for each flexible spending account in which the employee has elected to participate. No formal segregation of assets takes place, and no monies are deposited in trust. (An exception is legal where a "conduit trust" is required, as will be discussed in a subsequent chapter.) Instead, the accounts are carried on the books of the employer who tracks both debits (reimbursements) and credits (accruals).

When an employee incurs an eligible expense under one of the spending accounts, the employee completes a reimbursement claim form and submits it along with a copy of the bill or proof of payment (e.g., cancelled check) to the plan administrator for reimbursement. The administrator, after reviewing the claim, reimburses the employee with a check for the amount of the claim.

After the end of the year, employers typically allow employees a few months to submit claims incurred during the prior plan year. Once this process is completed, all unused deposits or accruals are forfeited by the employee and revert to the employer. (In practice, most employees take care to estimate expenses with enough precision to avoid forfeiture.) Disposition of forfeitures is a matter of employer discretion. Some allocate funds back to spending account participants on a per capita basis (i.e., unrelated to the employee's actual amount of forfeiture). Some use forfeitures to reduce employer benefit costs in a subsequent year. A few have adopted practices unrelated to the benefit program such as donating the funds to charity.

Three

Starting a Flexible Program

The impetus to investigate flexible compensation can originate within an organization in any number of ways. Employees may have lobbied the employer for greater involvement in benefit decisions or for expansion of the existing program into new benefit areas. A comparative analysis might have revealed disparities in the current program significant enough to warrant management concern over trailing competitive practice. Business conditions might be such as to require a cutback in employee benefit costs or significant levelling of the rate of escalation in costs. Whatever the motivations, the next step involves determining whether a flexible program would meet the needs of the organization, and if so, what type of program would make the most sense, and then organizing to accomplish the implementation.

The purpose of this chapter is to provide a framework or model for organizing the start-up effort and to preview the steps involved in a flexible program implementation. Many of the functions involved in developing a flexible program are technical or substantive in nature and are dealt with at length in subsequent chapters of the book. This material focuses on the process for launching the start-up and implementation effort.

§ 3.1   OVERVIEW OF THE PROCESS

One of the few universal "truths" about a flexible compensation undertaking is that it usually is broader in scope and reach than almost any other modification an organization might make to the structure and nature of compensation and benefits. As a result, most organizations set high expectations for the outcome of a flexible program—and expect to achieve them, or few would commit the energy and resources necessary to set a program in place.

The complexity of the undertaking stems largely from the multidisciplinary nature of the effort. For example, employees are asked to make decisions in areas where they previously had little involvement, so communication plays a more extensive role than in almost any other prior benefit communication. The choicemaking mechanism requires tracking of individual elections and/or accounting for the flow of funds under flexible spending accounts. So administrative considerations exert considerable influence on the feasibility and type of flexible program undertaking. In many organizations, a decision to go with a flexible approach hinges on cost considerations so that in a sense, a flexible program is more "price sensitive" than a conventional program. Careful attention is paid to establishing the financial structure of a flexible program to achieve the organization's objectives in the first and subsequent years of operation.

Figure 3.1 provides a model of the process many organizations have followed for moving a flexible program from inception through implementation. Most organizations find it useful to divide the development process into two phases. One is creating the preliminary design, determining its feasibility, and generally planning the steps involved in an implementation. The other is actually executing the plan: finalizing the program design and cost structure, developing the communication materials, building an administration system or selecting a vendor to handle the administration, and otherwise readying the program for first-time enrollment of employees.

Although the figure separates the various activities into distinct stages, in reality many of the steps overlap. For example, design of the program rarely occurs independently from the pricing of options or the determination of systems constraints. The primary purpose of the figure is to illustrate the different types of functions that need to be performed to launch a program and only secondarily to show the progression or order of the various steps.

Figure 3.1
Steps in Starting a Flexible Program

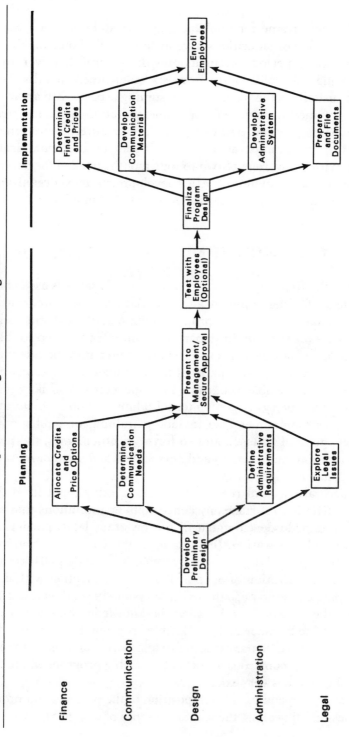

33

The time frame for implementing a flexible program varies by employer. A few organizations have installed full choice making programs in as short a period as four months. In general, however, implementation time schedules range from six to eighteen months. The systems effort usually is the most time-consuming aspect, with an average of six to eight months required for implementation of administrative software. (Longer time frames usually are required for internal development of an administrative solution.) Employee communication ranks next, with an average of two to four months needed for development of communication materials. After development, most organizations allow between four and six weeks for enrollment of employees.

§ 3.2   GETTING STARTED

One of the first steps an organization usually takes is assembling a project team for development and installation of the program. The core team usually consists of a project leader and others from within human resources or the benefit department. An effective step to take early in the process, however, is expansion of the team to include input or representation from other parts of the organization that will be most affected by a flexible program. In some cases, this is primarily staff roles—namely, systems or internal administration, corporate communications (sometimes also including training or public relations), finance, general counsel, and so forth. In other cases, the project team includes line managers to add perspective and another view of benefits and compensation issues.

There are several reasons for seeking early input from these other areas. One is to surface any constraints or limitations that could hamper or impede development of the program later, particularly in the area of administration. (For example, the current payroll system may have been pieced together to accommodate Section 401(k) salary deferral, but the addition of Section 125 salary reduction with different tax calculations could push the existing system beyond its limits.)

Another reason is to broaden the knowledge base for decisions that will need to be made about a flexible program. Participation from those closest to a particular issue will yield better and more informed judgments on the numerous aspects of a flexible program where few "right" or "obvious" answers exist.

Finally, expanding the composition of the project team promotes consensus-building along the way and a sense of ownership or responsibility for the outcome. Involvement in the process produces not only better decisions but a broader group of people who understand the reasons and rationale underlying the decisions. That shared understanding will help increase the sense of purpose people feel when carrying out the developmental tasks required to unveil a new program—and produce substantial dividends when many of these same specialists later are called upon to explain the merits of the new approach to employees.

No magic combination exists for either the size or composition of the project team. In general, a two- or three-person team may be too small to assure adequate input, while fifteen to twenty may impede effective decision making. Depending on the size of the organization, six to eight members may constitute a workable project team—large enough to ensure breadth of perspective while small enough to facilitate decision making.

Within the special project team, it often makes sense to combine "doers" and "decision makers." For example, an overall project leader might have day-to-day responsibility for coordinating the specialized tasks that need to be performed and for keeping the team on its assigned time schedule. Meanwhile, senior decision makers with an otherwise full schedule would be freed to concentrate on policy issues or to steer the process through appropriate channels within the organization.

Many organizations use people outside the company (or the benefit area) both in the preliminary planning and later stages of implementation. The role performed may be that of serving as a technical resource (for information on what can be done, how other organizations have handled a similar matter, the impact of particular decisions, etc.); as a process facilitator (to identify key issues, bring the project team to consensus, etc.); or as organizers (to scope out what needs to be done, advise on efficient means of accomplishing a particular task, etc.). This type of assistance may come from an independent consulting firm, a brokerage or insurance company consultant, or even from another internal person operating in the capacity of advisor or consultant.

§ 3.3   PLANNING THE PROGRAM

The sample framework described here for planning the program includes (1) determining the preliminary design (benefit areas to be included, development of specific options, decisions on option prices and credit allocation, use of salary reduction, and overall cost impact); (2) analyzing the implementation effort (required tasks, potential constraints, likely alternatives, budget and staffing requirements); (3) securing management approval to proceed, and, as an optional but often useful step, (4) testing the proposed program with a sample of employees. Although the model incorporates all of these steps under the phase "planning the program," in some instances the steps are viewed as covering two phases: "preliminary design" (including management approval and employee testing) and "planning for implementation."

Regardless of how the effort is categorized or how formal or informal is the process, the following steps generally are taken when planning a flexible compensation program.

(a) DEVELOP PRELIMINARY DESIGN

Each organization is unique. The size and characteristics of the employee workforce, the provisions of the current benefit program, the objectives for exploring a flexible compensation program, the financial and administrative constraints, the current employee relations environment, and the viewpoints of those responsible for benefit and compensation planning, all come together as input into designing a program that is the best "fit" for that organization. In the same way that no two traditional benefit programs are exactly alike, no two flexible programs are identical.

The project team can use a number of approaches to narrow the wide range of available design alternatives and, ultimately, to determine the most appropriate program design. An approach which has worked well for many firms, however, involves three components: data collection, objective setting, and development of design. Following this progression produces an approach which has a high likelihood of reflecting the uniqueness of the organization, its attitudes, and its employees, and of meeting the organization's objectives (i.e., being viewed as successful by management and employees).

- **Data Collection.** The data collection substep ensures that the project team knows as much as it can before starting to design the program. Although what is needed and what level of depth is required will vary considerably, the following list may be helpful:

  Employee data (number, types, demographic characteristics)
  Current benefits (types, eligibility requirements, benefit levels, employee contributions)

Current benefit costs (costs by benefit area—per employee, as a percent of pay, per $1,000 of coverage—broken down as appropriate or available)

Employee attitudes concerning benefits (optional but an often helpful step, undertaken either through a survey or a more informal collection process)

Competitive benefit information (another optional but generally helpful step as competitive positioning is often important)

Flexible compensation approaches and issues (what can be done, what others are doing, etc. in order to bring the project team to a common level of knowledge).

- **Objective Setting.** The design process is typically streamlined by identifying at the front end how management views certain key issues. Examples of the types of issues helpful to identify, discuss, and reach consensus on can include:

  What are the primary objectives for considering the implementation of a flexible compensation program?

  What are the financial goals and/or constraints for the program?

  How should responsibility for the financial security of employees be allocated between the organization and the employee?

  What minimum level of coverage (if any) should be required of employees in each benefit area?

  Should benefits be viewed primarily as a source of protection or as a part of total compensation?

  Should (or must) the current plan be maintained as an option in each benefit area?

  What concerns or problems exist with the current benefit plans (from the company or employee perspective)?

- **Development of Design.** With the foundation of knowledge gained from the data-collection stage and the objective-setting process, the project task force is prepared to develop alternative design approaches, consider the relative merits of each, and select the design that best fits the organization.

  The types of decisions which need to be made in this stage include:

Which benefit areas should be opened to employee choice?

What range of choice is appropriate (from low option to high option)?

How many options should be made available?

Which design features should vary between the options?

Should flexible spending accounts be introduced? If so, which types?

The project team will generally be able to reach a consensus on most issues, but it may decide to leave open one or two difficult decisions for additional input such as from senior management. For example, should employees be permitted to opt out of medical? Or, should vacation choices be incorporated into the program?

(b) ALLOCATE CREDITS AND PRICE OPTIONS

Once the basic design structure of the flexible program has been determined, an organization needs to analyze the expected impact on company and employee costs to develop the approximate level of flexible credits (if credits are to be an element of the program), the approach for allocating these credits to individual employees, and the prices which will be assigned (or charged to employees) for the various options.

The desired short-term impact on company costs will typically be discussed in the objective-setting phase. Often, the objective is to maintain the same level of cost which would have been produced by the prior program in the initial year of the flexible program, but gain added control over the rate of increase in future years. In other situations, the objective is to produce an immediate short-term savings in benefit costs. This may be defined as a specific dollar amount, a specific percentage of medical costs or overall benefit costs, or an amount of savings resulting from a particular aspect of the new program (e.g., FICA taxes on Section 125 salary reductions). Decisions on the amount of credits and the option prices in combination with other aspects of the program will determine the resulting impact on the organization's costs.

The intended impact on employee costs will also help dictate the decisions on credit amount, credit allocation, and option pricing. In some situations, all employees must be allowed to buy back their previous coverage with no change in net contributions (prices less credits). In other cases, prices are being modified—for example, to move from a flat-rate basis to an age-related basis in group life, or to increase medical contributions—thereby creating an expectation that the implementation of the new program will create some "winners" and "losers" among employees. An analysis of these winners and losers under alternative credit and pricing strategies is typically an important aspect of decision making in this area.

(c)   DETERMINE COMMUNICATION NEEDS

Introduction of any flexible compensation program requires explanation of the decisions employees will be asked to make. However, the context of the basic communication message (concept and mechanics of choice making) will be influenced by the specific circumstances of the employer. For example, is the new flexible program primarily a "good news" message for employees (e.g., nobody loses under the program, company costs will remain the same at least in the first year, significant new benefit opportunities are being incorporated)? Or does the flexible program represent a vehicle for accomplishing certain other employer objectives (e.g., some immediate reduction in costs, phaseout of dependent or other subsidies, introduction of cost management features in medical)? Most flexible program introductions contain elements of each; however, how much of each will be a critical influence on the tone, themes, and messages used in the communication effort.

This contextual backdrop will largely have been established in the preliminary design and financial structuring discussions, but the viewpoint reflected so far, has been primarily that of the company. The next step involves working with the tentative program design and structure to gauge how the program will "play" with employees.

Here environment plays a critical role. For example, have employees been lobbying for changes in benefits, so that even a cutback in certain areas would be viewed as a reasonable trade-off for the opportunity to exercise choice elsewhere in the program? What is the general mood or trust level in the employer? For example, have employees experienced changes in other areas so that the timing of a flexible program implementation might raise suspicions? What are employee perceptions of the business conditions of the employer, and how might these perceptions influence the packaging or "look" of communication materials?

Once the context has been established, the specifics of the communication effort need to be defined at least in enough reasonable detail to develop preliminary budgets for implementation. Also, the project team needs to focus on the assignment and staffing of communication responsibilities: How much and which elements of the communication effort can be accomplished internally? In terms of developing the preliminary communication plan, consideration should focus on the following kinds of issues:

- Types of communication channels through which to reach employees (newsletters, booklets, audiovisual presentations, mailings to the employee's home, etc.)
- Quantity and quality of communication materials
- Characteristics of the workforce or environment that might require special attention (e.g., diverse education levels, non-English-speaking employees, work areas with limited space for storing materials)
- Logistics of distributing and receiving communication materials
- Timing of the release of information to employees, including the staffing of training sessions, benefit "hotlines," and so forth.

It also may be helpful to review communication samples from other organizations where flexible programs have been introduced. However, while useful for the gleaning of ideas, few prototypes exist for adoption by other organizations. Every flexible program is different—the communication materials will reflect those differences as well as the unique environment of the particular employer introducing the program.

(d)   DEFINE ADMINISTRATIVE REQUIREMENTS

Basically the objective of this step is to determine what needs to be done to administer the flexible program and to identify how administration will be accomplished. Much of the project team's efforts in this area will be focused on information gathering: assessing current capabilities, defining new requirements of the flexible program, and evaluating alternatives for handling administration.

In this regard, it is often most useful to begin with an audit of existing systems and procedures. How well (or poorly) is benefit administration currently accomplished? What is the capability of existing payroll and human resource information systems? What computer and people resources presently are available? Part of the audit process might also involve uncovering any plans for upgrading or modifying existing systems and procedures. Looking forward a few years may aid the project team in evaluating whether any present constraints are likely to pose a temporary versus more permanent barrier to either the flexible program's design or administration.

Next, most organizations develop a checklist of administrative requirements. The focus here is on identifying which procedures and tasks already are being performed as well as what new requirements will be needed to accomplish flexible program administration (e.g., calculating individual credits and prices, performing tax calculations on Section 125 salary reductions, processing spending account contributions and reimbursements). Definition of systems requirements establishes criteria for determining the direction to take for flexible program administration.

A subsequent step usually involves evaluating externally developed administrative solutions. Here the project team is concentrating on narrowing the range of possibilities: internal development, installation of a software package, or third-party administration. Even if an organization has available the resources and capability to develop its own system, a review of the systems alternatives available on the outside may be a useful part of the process. Flexible programs require unique and specialized knowledge within the area of benefits and human resource information management, so interviewing technical specialists from provider organizations often will yield helpful information.

Another step involves exploring staffing considerations and planning the training of flexible program administrators. Depending on the type of flexible program under consideration, the administrative work load may be handled with existing resources or may require some additional staffing. Either way, however, the people responsible for administering the program on an ongoing basis will need training in the requirements and operation of the new system.

Once these steps have been completed, the project team will be in a reasonably good position to determine the magnitude of the effort and costs involved in implementing an administrative system. At this point, however, the cost figures remain preliminary in that finalization of certain details of the program design may yet influence the ultimate cost of administration.

(e)   EXPLORE LEGAL ISSUES

As soon as preliminary design has been established, many organizations involve their legal counsel to research or investigate any potential legal issues. Although most design questions have been clarified through legislation and regulations released in recent years, a few gray areas still exist in which management may want to have an opinion from legal counsel before proceeding. An organization's legal counsel may also seek additional guidance or input from outside attorneys specializing in employee benefit issues.

(f) PRESENT TO MANAGEMENT/SECURE APPROVAL

By this point in the process, the project team has completed the staff work necessary to enable management to make an informed "go/no go" decision. How formal or informal the decision-making process is depends on the organization and the extent of management involvement in the developmental phases of the program. Although a flexible program is not generally viewed as requiring approval of the Board of Directors, most organizations take measures to inform at least the Compensation Committee of the Board of the status of a flexible program undertaking.

One of the reasons formalized management approval occurs at this stage of the process (rather than earlier) is to minimize the possibility of making decisions based on insufficient information. The project team needs to make sufficient progress in the areas identified earlier to provide management a complete grasp of the issues involved—impact on company cost, impact on employees, time frame, administrative ramifications, and so forth. Also, until this point, the project team has committed largely time (rather than significant dollars) to determining the feasibility of a flexible program. From this point forward, the organization usually will be committing hard dollars to the implementation effort, and the budgets usually need to be established and approved in advance.

In presenting the program to management, organizations typically include information on the following:

- Objectives for the program
- Scope and design of the flexible program
- Cost/benefit analysis
- Communication considerations
- Administrative and systems considerations
- Legal and tax issues
- Timetable for implementation
- Implementation budgets and costs.

(g) TEST WITH EMPLOYEES

While not a mandatory step in a flexible program implementation, many organizations find it useful to gather employee input. Some of the reasons for pretesting a program with employees include the following:

- To collect employee reactions and attitudes toward the concept of flexible compensation and the specifics of the particular flexible program design
- To test the types of choices employees will be likely to make, and as a result, identify whether assumptions about option pricing, adverse selection, and so forth, are on target
- To identify any differences in attitudes or information needs by employee subgroups
- To test the content or approach to be used in the communication effort
- To build some employee "ownership" into the flexible program.

§ 3.4 IMPLEMENTING THE PROGRAM

The following framework or model focuses on completing the steps involved in a flexible program installation: finalizing the program design and financial structure, developing communication and enrollment materials, building or implementing an administrative system as well as developing day-to-day operating procedures, and completing the necessary legal documents.

Note that one of the most important steps the project team can take is to assign responsibilities and completion dates for each of the various tasks and then monitor progress against the overall time schedule. All of the different subgroups will be working on separate tasks within the implementation effort, but the "whole" needs to come together at the end for enrollment of employees. Coordination becomes critical because not one of the subgroup's undertakings is an optional part of the implementation. Delay (or derailment) of any one of the independent tasks will affect (or postpone) the outcome of the entire project.

(a) FINALIZE PROGRAM DESIGN

The preliminary program design might undergo some changes (either modest or substantive) as a result of management input received during the approval stage, or as a result of employee feedback if the program was tested with employees.

Irrespective of these changes, however, the preliminary design needs to be brought to a finer level of detail. This level of detail generally is not required earlier in the process (to evaluate the overall impact on company or employee costs, administrative requirements, and so forth), but it is necessary at this point to develop the actual administrative system and employee communication materials. Here the project team will be concentrating on issues such as the following:

- How (if at all) will pay changes during the year affect coverage amounts and/or employee contributions?
- What is the minimum claim amount that can be submitted for the issuing of a reimbursement check from the flexible spending account?
- When does an employee transferring from one division to another become eligible to make elections?
- How long does coverage continue after an employee terminates?

(b) DETERMINE FINAL CREDITS AND PRICES

The option prices and flexible credit allowances developed for the preliminary design may have been based on sketchy cost data or tentative decisions on allocation methodology to minimize the investment of time and effort required in the early stages of developing the program.

However, once the program has been approved and final design decisions made, it is typical practice to reevaluate the pricing and credit structure. Additional (and more current) experience data may be available. Given the passage of time, an organization's insurer or third-party administrator may be able to produce a better breakdown of recent claims. The new data will be helpful for taking a second look at the impact of the proposed financial structure.

In many cases, the prices for certain options will be identical to the rates charged by the carrier or service provider (e.g., HMOs). However, a change in carriers or the addition of a provider usually will result in some last minute pricing changes.

(c) DEVELOP COMMUNICATION MATERIAL

The reason for developing communication material is essentially twofold: to help employees understand the nature of the flexible program and options available to them and to enroll employees in the program (preferably with as few errors as possible). To accomplish these goals, different types of communication materials are needed.

One type of material is largely informational. This includes announcement brochures; special newsletters or mailings; articles in company magazines or newspapers; audiovisual, videotape, or overhead presentations; and descriptive booklets or handbooks. How elaborate the communication effort is depends on the organization and the circumstances surrounding the flexible program introduction. Some organizations have chosen to create a "splash" with the new program, complete with a name and special logos, high-quality graphics and paper stock, and numerous collateral materials (buttons, pins, coffee mugs, posters, tent cards, etc.). Others have adopted a more low-key approach. Regardless of production values or the extent of collateral materials, most organizations find that communicating using a variety of media is necessary to assure a high level of employee understanding.

Another type of material concentrates on getting employees enrolled in the flexible program. Enrollment material generally includes a booklet or folder describing the program, some type of worksheet or workbook for employees to use in making their elections, and an election form that once completed will be used by administrators to enroll employees in the program. Some organizations have provided employees with sophisticated "tools" to make their elections: personalized statements showing available options, option price tags, and credit allowances, or even computer programs to allow employees to model their elections under various scenarios. To aid in the enrollment process, many organizations also produce confirmation statements that recap employee elections before the options become effective.

A different aspect of the communication process is aimed at meeting leaders and flexible program administrators. These people usually are involved in employee meetings or other one-on-one interface with employees. It is often most helpful if they can have available to them meeting leader guides, training programs, and so forth, that prepare them for the roles they will play in the unveiling and eventual operation of the flexible program.

(d)   DEVELOP ADMINISTRATIVE SYSTEM

Procedures and recordkeeping systems will need to be developed to handle administration of the program. The degree to which the system is automated depends on the size of the employee group, the nature and structure of the program, and the computer and personnel resources available. In general, administrative systems and procedures need to be able to accomplish the following:

- Determine participant eligibility
- Compute flexible credit allowances and option price tags (if credits and prices are part of the design)
- Enroll employees in their benefit choices (including editing employee elections)
- Process interim coverage for new employees (if appropriate), and coverage changes for employees with a change in family status during the year
- Maintain flexible spending account balances and process claims (if spending accounts are part of the program)
- Report to management (and/or carriers and administrators) on various aspects of the program such as use of flexible credits or salary reduction, enrollment in each benefit area, utilization by coverage category, and so forth.

To avoid any last minute surprises, most organizations work into the time schedule for implementation a period of time during which to test the administrative system before the initial enrollment. That way any potential problems can be corrected before the flood of first-time enrollments.

(e)   PREPARE AND FILE DOCUMENTS

A formal legal document will be required for the flexible program if it falls under Section 125 of the Internal Revenue Code. This document must set forth the terms and conditions of the program and fulfill the requirements of the Section 125 regulations. (This requirement applies even if the only "benefit" provided to employees is pretax premium payment.)

At present, the Section 125 plan document does not need to be filed with any government agency or submitted to the Internal Revenue Service for their approval.

Depending on the design of the program it may be necessary to modify other plan documents (e.g., the 401(k) plan or the pension plan to clarify that the definition of pay includes any amounts reduced from salary under Section 125) or to submit other documents (e.g., a plan document for Section 120 if a spending account for legal services is implemented).

§ 3.5 ENROLLING EMPLOYEES

At this point, everything the project team has worked so hard to accomplish will come together. Employees will understand the new flexible program and make choices based on individual needs. The administrative system will record the elections and be ready to handle the activities involved in ongoing administration. And the project team will feel a tremendous sense of accomplishment over a job well done.

After the pace of the initial enrollment has subsided, the project team usually reassembles for a "debriefing." The purpose is to incorporate any lessons learned from the first enrollment into planning for subsequent years. This might involve identifying areas on the election form where employees or administrators had difficulty entering elections or uncovering common themes in the questions employees asked about the program that might be addressed in subsequent communication. It might also involve reevaluating any options which were elected by only a very small percentage of employees and generally looking for ways to streamline or improve any aspect of the flexible program's operation in later years.

Part Two

Rules and Regulations

Four

Legal Framework

---

§ 4.1 INTRODUCTION

Like any other employee benefit plan, there is a legal framework or set of rules within which a flexible compensation program must operate. Part of this framework is old and well established. It is made up of rules and regulations that have existed and been refined over a long period of time.

Flexible compensation means basically that employees are allowed to choose among different forms and levels of benefits. Each of the separate benefits included within a flexible program must comply with the set of rules applicable to that particular benefit. For example, if a profit sharing plan is included as one of the choices in a flexible program, the profit sharing plan will be subject to the same IRS qualification process that would be the case for a stand-alone plan. Similarly, if group-term life insurance is a choice, laws governing maximums on plan benefits must be reflected. The point is that a separate set of rules applies to each separate benefit within a flexible compensation program.

Another part of the framework governs choices between taxable and nontaxable benefits. The rules permitting this kind of choice making comprise a relatively new part of the legal framework and apply to the flexible compensation program as a whole, rather than to the separate benefit components within the program. This portion of the legal framework establishes the conditions under which choices between taxable and nontaxable benefits may be made.

This portion of the legal framework is only applicable if the flexible compensation program permits choices between taxable and nontaxable benefits. If the program permits choices between *nontaxable* benefits only, or between *taxable* benefits only, no special legal framework is applicable to the choice making mechanism. (In these situations, however, the rules applicable to each separate benefit need to be considered.) Choices between taxable and nontaxable benefits normally would trigger a tax doctrine called "constructive receipt." Essentially, the doctrine of constructive receipt provides that if an employee has the *right* to income, the employee will be taxed as if the employee actually received that income, whether or not the right is exercised. The legal framework governing the choice between taxable and nontaxable benefits allows employees to make a choice between these different types of benefits and establishes the rules which must be met to avoid triggering the doctrine of constructive receipt.

Consider the doctrine of constructive receipt as it would otherwise apply to a choice between cash and medical benefits. The doctrine would require that even though the employee chooses medical benefits (which are not taxable), the employee is taxed because of the *right* to receive cash (which is taxable). This doctrine has been used by the IRS for a number of years, especially in the employee benefit area, to minimize or limit the potential for tax deferment and tax loss.

In the absence of the doctrine of constructive receipt, the compensation and benefits area would provide numerous opportunities for tax deferment and tax loss. An example of tax *deferment* is a qualified pension or profit sharing plan. The employer receives a tax deduction at the time a contribution is made to the plan. The employee is not taxed until such time as a benefit is distributed from the plan. Thus taxes on the employer contributions are deferred from the time they are paid to the plan until the time they are paid to the participant. An example of tax *loss* occurs in the area of medical benefits. The employer receives a tax deduction at the time the coverage is purchased. The employee is exempted from taxation—both at the time the coverage is purchased and at the time benefits are paid from the plan.

The Treasury views both tax deferments and losses as "tax expenditures"—monies owed the government except that legislation exempts their collection. In order to tolerate the tax expenditures that occur when the doctrine of constructive receipt is waived, flexible compensation programs must be seen as satisfying certain social policy goals.

The triumph of flexible compensation legislation was to exempt trade-offs made within a flexible program from application of the doctrine of constructive receipt. Employers can make available an attractive range of choices—taxable benefits, including cash, and nontaxable benefits—with the employee taxed only to the extent that taxable options are selected. It is possible to have some flexibility in compensation and benefits without any special flexible compensation legislation. For example, a program can be structured to allow only taxable benefits or only nontaxable benefits. In either of these cases, the doctrine of constructive receipt has no effect on the program. However, the limits inherent in the structure of such a program have, historically, also served to limit their usefulness and popularity.

§ 4.2 LEGISLATIVE HISTORY

As long as the doctrine of constructive receipt has existed, employers have sought to provide employees with flexibility regarding the receipt of benefits without triggering constructive receipt. The Internal Revenue Service created a specific exception to the doctrine of constructive receipt with release of Revenue Ruling 56–497 in 1956. The ruling involved a profit sharing arrangement where profits were allocated among employees in proportion to annual salaries. Prior to the close of each calendar year, employees were required to make an irrevocable election whether to take their share of the current year's profits in cash or have that amount deferred into a profit sharing plan for future distribution. After the close of the year, cash payments were made to the employees electing cash, and the balance was contributed to a trust for the benefit of employees who elected deferral. Under the ruling, the profit sharing plan would remain qualified as long as the contributions actually made to the trust did not discriminate in favor of highly compensated employees. In effect, the ruling permitted a choice between cash and deferred compensation, without application of the doctrine of constructive receipt.

In the late 1960s, the IRS began permitting contributions to qualified plans on a salary reduction basis. The employee could agree to reduce salary or forego a salary increase in return for which the employer would make a contribution (equal to the salary reduction) to a qualified plan.

In both areas, however, IRS practice was inconsistent. Exceptions to the constructive receipt doctrine were permitted on a case-by-case basis and usually only if there was some showing of nondiscrimination.

In 1972, the IRS proposed regulations that would have eliminated salary reduction plans and also have called into question the future of profit sharing plans containing a cash option. However, the regulations were never finalized.

In 1974, Congress enacted the Employee Retirement Income Security Act (ERISA). Section 2006 of ERISA put a freeze on any type of plan permitting a choice between taxable and nontaxable benefits. Included were qualified plans permitting the employer contribution to be derived from salary reduction, cash-option profit sharing plans, and welfare benefit plans involving a choice of taxable benefits.

Section 2006 also prohibited the Internal Revenue Service from issuing final regulations in this area, which prevented adoption of the 1972 proposed regulations. Existing plans with taxable options could continue under the provisions of old law, but new plans were not permitted. The freeze was to last until enactment of the Revenue Act of 1978.

It should be noted that, even under the freeze, a program involving only nontaxable benefit choices could operate. Such a program is not hampered by the doctrine of constructive receipt. (After all, the doctrine assumes the employee elected to receive the highest taxable amount available, and that amount is "nothing" in a program involving only nontaxable benefits.)

The Revenue Act of 1978 created the twin pillars of flexible compensation, namely, Section 401(k) of the Internal Revenue Code and Section 125 of the Internal Revenue Code. Section 401(k) reestablished cash-or-deferred profit sharing arrangements, in effect permitting a choice between cash and deferred compensation, without application of constructive receipt. (Welfare benefits, however, were not permitted to be part of a plan established under Section 401(k).) Section 125 permitted the establishment of "cafeteria plans" and permitted choices between taxable benefits, including cash, and nontaxable benefits, such as medical benefits, without causing the entire amount to be recognized as taxable income under the doctrine of constructive receipt. (Deferred compensation, however, was not permitted to be part of a cafeteria plan.)

Interest in flexible compensation immediately after passage of the 1978 Revenue Act was somewhat dampened by the fact that choices among cash, deferred compensation, and welfare benefits could not be provided in the same program. A choice between cash and deferred compensation could be provided through a 401(k) plan. A choice between cash and welfare benefits could be provided through a Section 125 plan. A program including choices in all three plan areas, however, was not permissible because Section 401(k) prohibited the inclusion of welfare benefits, and Section 125 prohibited the inclusion of deferred compensation. Furthermore, it was unclear whether either Section 401(k) or Section 125 permitted salary reduction elections on an individual basis rather than at employer direction.

During this period, the design of flexible programs involved the establishment of two tandem but mutually exclusive programs. One permitted a choice between cash and deferrals, and the other permitted a choice between cash and welfare benefits. Flexible dollars or credits were generated either by employer contributions or across-the-board salary reductions. The latter approach involved the employer unilaterally reducing the salary of covered participants and, in lieu thereof, contributing an equivalent dollar amount to the flexible compensation program. In practice, however, use of unilateral salary reduction was relatively uncommon.

The Miscellaneous Revenue Act of 1980 expanded flexible compensation beyond the tandem-plan approach by amending Section 125 to permit inclusion of deferred compensation as a choice as long as the deferred compensation met the requirements of Section 401(k). Thus for the first time, a three-way choice among cash, deferred compensation, and welfare benefits became permissible. This relatively minor amendment removed a significant impediment to the logical design of flexible compensation programs.

A year later much of the uncertainty surrounding individual salary reduction was removed. In 1981, the Internal Revenue Service issued proposed regulations establishing that individual salary reduction elections were permissible under Section 401(k). In effect, under a cash-or-deferred arrangement, an employee could choose to transfer some otherwise taxable compensation to a profit sharing or savings plan and the deferred amount would escape federal and most state and local income taxes until distributed from the plan. The transferred amount would be treated as an employer contribution to the plan, even though the employee made the election to reduce his or her compensation. The proposed regulations generated tremendous interest in allowing employees to save for retirement on a tax-favored basis.

By analogy, the concept was soon expanded to include the purchase of benefits under Section 125. The theoretical justification was the similarity between Sections 125 and 401(k). Under Section 401(k), the employee could choose between cash or deferral of that amount as an employer contribution into a retirement vehicle. Under Section 125, the employee would be deciding between cash or treating that amount as an employer contribution applied to the purchase of welfare benefits. The chief difference was permanent avoidance of income taxes on Section 125 salary reduction amounts. Taxation of employer contributions for retirement benefits is deferred until distribution from the plan, while employer contributions for welfare benefits remain exempt from taxation at both the purchase of coverage and the payment of benefits.

At the same time, other technical issues regarding the operation of flexible compensation programs began to be resolved. The Social Security Amendments Act of 1983 addressed the taxation of salary reduction amounts for social security purposes. Specifically, the Act subjected salary reduction contributions under Section 401(k) to social security taxes, but the final legislation was silent on salary reductions under Section 125. The Committee Reports on the amendments, however, indicated that Section 125 salary reductions would not be subject to social security payroll tax withholding.

In 1984, the IRS acted to clarify the status of salary reduction under Section 125. The first step was an Information Release aimed at prohibiting use of salary reduction on a prospective basis (i.e., electing to reduce salary going forward from the point of incurring an expense). The next step was the issuance, later in 1984, of proposed regulations governing the application of Section 125. The thrust of the proposed regulations was to limit the perceived potential for abuse of Section 125 by adding an element of risk to the use of salary reduction under Section 125, particularly as a funding source for flexible spending accounts.

Under the proposed regulations, salary reduction and flexible spending accounts were permissible—but subject to certain conditions. The principal condition was that employees should not have the opportunity to recoup unused funds during a year or be allowed to roll over funds to a subsequent year. Instead, funds held pursuant to a salary reduction for premium payment or in a flexible spending account should be subject to the risk of loss, just as premiums paid for insurance coverage might never be recovered if the insured risk never occurs.

The proposed regulations imposed three major restrictions on the design of flexible benefit programs to incorporate the insurance concept of risk and to restrict the potential for abuse. First, neither the flexible program nor the separate spending accounts may allow more frequent than annual election of the sources and uses of funds contributed. Second, within spending accounts, the funds may be used only for payment of health care, dependent care, or personal legal expenses. Finally, flexible spending account funds must be exhausted for expenses incurred during the calendar year, or the funds will be forfeited (the "use-it-or-lose-it" requirement).

The Deficit Reduction Act (DEFRA), also enacted in 1984, subsequently confirmed the substance of the proposed regulations on Section 125. In addition, the Act (together with implementing regulations) established reporting requirements for Section 125 programs and

Table 4.1
Microhistory of Flexible Compensation

1956	Revenue Ruling 56-497 exempts profit sharing plans containing a cash-or-deferred option from constructive receipt.
1960s	Private letter rulings permit individual salary reduction.
1972	Proposed regulations would ban cash-option profit sharing. (Never finalized.)
1974	Educational Testing Services and TRW Systems Group install first flexible compensation programs. The Employee Retirement Income Security Act (ERISA) is passed. Section 2006 bans further introduction of choice-making programs containing taxable options.
1978	American Can Company tests flexible program offering nontaxable benefit choices with pilot group of employees. (Extended to all salaried employees in 1979.) The Revenue Act of 1978 adds Section 401(k) and Section 125 to the Internal Revenue Code. Section 401(k) allows tradeoffs between cash or deferral into a profit sharing or savings plan. Section 125 permits choices between cash and welfare benefits.
1980	The Miscellaneous Revenue Act of 1980 links Section 401(k) and Section 125, thereby permitting three-way tradeoffs among cash, welfare benefits, and deferral into a profit sharing or savings plan.
1981	The Internal Revenue Service releases proposed regulations on Section 401(k) which among other things permit individual salary reduction elections.
1982	FMC, Honeywell and Quaker Oats install Section 401(k) salary reduction plans.
1983	Salary reduction is used under Section 125 for funding of flexible spending accounts and pre-tax premium payment. Early adopters include Quaker Oats, Brown and Root, Toro Corporation, and Bank of America
1984	IRS Information Release 84-22 and proposed regulations on Section 125 ban prospective salary reduction; introduce annual designation of sources and uses of flexible spending acount monies; and implement use-it-or-lose-it (forfeiture) requirement. Deficit Reduction Act of 1984 further defines rules governing flexible compensation programs.
1986	The Tax Reform Act of 1986 reaffirms flexible compensation programs; confirms exemption of Section 125 salary reduction amounts from social security taxation; and proposes new nondiscrimination standards for all employee benefit programs (effective in 1989).

detailed the types of benefits that could and could not be made available under a Section 125 choice-making arrangement.

Under DEFRA, a Section 125 program could offer employees a choice between cash and (with certain exceptions) those nontaxable benefits that are excluded from employees' income by reason of an express provision in the Internal Revenue Code. These benefits include accident and health plans, group-term life insurance, dependent care, and legal expenses. On the other hand, a Section 125 program could not include such benefits as scholarships and fellowships under Code Section 117, vanpooling under Section 124, educational assistance under Section 127, meals and lodging under Section 119, and any "fringe benefits" specified under Section 132.

In 1986, the Tax Reform Act effectively completed the current legal framework for flexible compensation programs. The Act confirmed the permissibility of flexible spending accounts and salary reduction under Section 125, and it also reaffirmed the exemption of Section 125 deferrals from social security taxation.

Table 4.1 summarizes the history of flexible compensation.

§ 4.3   CURRENT FRAMEWORK

The 1978 enactment of Section 401(k) and Section 125 clearly involved tax expenditures. In return for permitting choice making on a tax-favored basis, the Treasury took the position that there should be something in return; that is, the assurance that tax-favored benefits would be provided on a nondiscriminatory basis. As a result, both Section 401(k) and Section 125 include nondiscrimination rules to ensure that low-paid as well as high-paid employees receive tax-favored benefits. Thus nondiscrimination became the price tag for the new favorable tax treatment of choice making under flexible compensation programs. In 1986, the Tax Reform Act took a fresh look at the issue of nondiscrimination in all employee benefit plans, promulgated new rules for Section 401(k) plans (effective in 1987), and extensively increased nondiscrimination standards in the welfare plan area. The new nondiscrimination rules for welfare benefits, including those offered under a Section 125 arrangement, generally take effect for plan years beginning in 1989.

(a)   SECTION 401(k)

Section 401(k) represents an exception to the doctrine of constructive receipt. It permits the employee to choose between contributing to a capital accumulation plan (such as a profit sharing plan) or receiving the contribution directly in cash. Under most plans today, the individual has an election to reduce salary in return for which the employer will make a contribution to the plan equal to the salary reduction. Thus an individual salary reduction election is equivalent to providing a choice between cash and deferred compensation. The doctrine of constructive receipt is not applicable and, therefore, the individual is taxed currently only to the extent that cash is elected.

To take advantage of Section 401(k), the plan must meet specific nondiscrimination tests. First, the plan must meet the coverage requirements applicable to all qualified plans. In other words, the employee group covered by the plan must cover a minimum percentage of employees or a nondiscriminatory cross section of employees (as determined on the basis of compensation). (These rules will be revised and made stricter beginning in 1989.) Second, there is a special test applicable to 401(k) plans called the Actual Deferral Percentage Test. The thrust of this latter test—both as passed in 1978 and as revamped under the 1986 tax act—is to ensure that higher-paid employees do not elect to defer too much more of their compensation into the plan than do lower-paid employees. Beginning in 1987, the definition of "highly paid" is determined precisely. Under the definition, a highly paid employee is any employee who in a year:

- Received pay in excess of $50,000 (indexed after 1987) and was in the top-paid 20 percent of all employees
- Received pay in excess of $75,000 (indexed after 1987)
- Was an officer and received pay in excess of $45,000 (indexed starting at a later date), or
- Was a 5 percent owner.

For purposes of determining the relative amounts of deferral, the measure is the percentage of an employee's compensation actually deferred.

The Actual Deferral Percentage (ADP) for an individual employee is equal to the percentage of that employee's compensation actually deferred or contributed to the plan. In turn, the ADP for a group of employees is the average of the ADPs of the individuals in that group. A 401(k) plan must meet one of two tests in order to be considered nondiscriminatory. To meet the first test, the ADP for the highly paid cannot exceed 125 percent of the ADP for the lower paid. To meet the second (and alternative) test, the ADP for the highly paid cannot be more than two percentage points greater than the ADP for the lower paid, and also cannot exceed 200 percent of the ADP for the lower paid.

For example, assume that the ADP for the lower paid is 1 percent and the ADP for the highly paid is 3 percent. The first test is that the ADP for the highly paid cannot be more than 125 percent of the ADP for the lower paid. Since 3 percent is 300 percent of 1 percent, the first test is failed. The second test is that the ADP for the highly paid cannot be more than two percentage points higher than the ADP for the lower paid and, in addition, cannot exceed 200 percent of the ADP for the lower paid. While the 3 percent for the highly paid is two percentage points higher than the 1 percent of the lower paid, it still is greater than 200 percent of the 1 percent ADP of the lower paid. Thus the second test also is failed. Given an ADP of 1 percent for the lower paid, the maximum that the highly paid can defer and still pass the test is 2 percent.

The following chart illustrates the maximum ADP for the highly paid, given different ADPs for the lower paid:

Average Deferral of Lower-Paid (%)	Maximum Average Deferral for Highly-Paid (%)
1	2
2	4
3	5
4	6
5	7
6	8
7	9
8	10
9	11.25
10	12.5

A comparable test must be passed covering any after-tax employee contributions and company contributions to a Section 401(k) or other defined contribution plan.

Three other requirements apply to amounts deferred into a 401(k) plan. First, elective deferrals must be immediately 100 percent vested. Second, the amounts cannot be withdrawn during employment unless the employee suffers a financial hardship or attains the age of $59^1/_2$. (However, loans on money in the plan are permissible.) Finally, amounts deferred are limited to $7,000 per calendar year (indexed after 1987).

Contributions for the highly paid in excess of the allowable ADP limits are subject to a 10 percent excise tax on the employer unless the excess (plus earnings) is distributed within $2^1/_2$ months after the end of the plan year. Contributions in excess of the allowable ADP limits will not disqualify the 401(k) plan if the excess (plus earnings) is distributed before the close of the next plan year. Alternatively, excess deferrals may be recharacterized as after-tax employee contributions to the extent this recharacterization is permitted by IRS regulations.

Following are additional rules that will apply uniquely to 401(k) plans (effective for plan years beginning in 1989):

- The plan may require only one year of service for participation
- Earnings on 401(k) deferrals may not be withdrawn on account of hardship, although withdrawal of the 401(k) contribution amount (only) will continue to be permitted
- Employer matching on contributions is the only benefit that can be conditioned upon an employee's elective deferral.

(b)   SECTION 125 RULES

Section 125 permits a choice between taxable cash and nontaxable welfare benefits in a flexible compensation program. Although the employee may choose cash or, in the case of salary reduction, has the option not to reduce salary, the employee will be taxed only if in fact the cash is chosen or the salary is kept whole. Again, in order to take advantage of this exception to the doctrine of constructive receipt, the flexible compensation program must meet very specific nondiscrimination tests. If the tests are not met, the highly compensated participants realize taxable income on the value of the benefits chosen. There is no taxable income for those who are not in the highly compensated group.

The same definition of highly compensated that governs the Section 401(k) tests is used for purposes of Section 125—essentially employees who earn in excess of $50,000 per year.

As stated earlier, a Section 125 program may include deferred compensation as one of the choices under the plan, but the deferred compensation must take the form of elective deferrals under a 401(k) plan. This connection with a 401(k) plan provides the only opportunity for the three-way choice between cash, deferred compensation, and welfare benefits. Any money elected to be deferred into a 401(k) plan under the Section 125 arrangement must meet the nondiscrimination tests of Section 401(k).

Section 125 contains separate nondiscrimination tests regarding the group of employees covered and the benefits provided by the plan. Regarding the group covered by the plan, the plan must cover an adequate cross section of employees by pay level. This is essentially the same coverage test that has been applied to qualified pension and profit sharing plans for many years.

The test is applied by placing employees in pay brackets (typically, in $5,000 increments) and then breaking down each bracket into those that are covered by the plan and those that are not covered. To pass the test, the plan must cover employees in all pay brackets and in more than "nominal" numbers. The determination of how many employees constitute a nominal number is largely subjective, but longstanding pension regulations provide some guidance. The regulations allow for a reasonable differential between the ratio of highly paid employees benefitted by the plan to all such highly paid employees, and the ratio of lower paid employees benefitted by the plan to all lower paid employees. If this coverage test is not satisfied, highly paid employees must include, as taxable income, amounts which the employee could have taken as cash but elected to use toward the purchase of benefits under the plan.

Regarding the benefits provided, "key employees" may not receive benefits that exceed 25 percent of the total benefits provided to all employees under the plan. The definition of key employee includes officers earning more than $45,000, five-percent owners, and one-percent owners having an annual compensation in excess of $150,000. If the 25 percent concentration test is not met, it is only the key employees (as opposed to highly compensated employees) that must include, in their gross income for the taxable year, amounts contributed to the plan instead of taken in cash.

Only certain plans (e.g., those maintained pursuant to a collective-bargaining agreement) are exempt from the nondiscrimination rules.

Prior to the Tax Reform Act of 1986, flexible programs needed to satisfy general nondiscrimination tests regarding the benefits provided under the plan. The Tax Reform Act of 1986 repealed the more general rules and, in lieu thereof, imposed specific tests applicable to each type of benefit. Thus there are separate tests applicable to medical benefits, group-term life insurance, dependent care programs, and so forth. The result is that when these benefits are offered within a Section 125 program, each benefit must meet the specific nondiscrimination test applicable to it. Also, the Section 125 plan as a whole must meet the two tests discussed earlier.

(c) BENEFITS UNDER A SECTION 125 PROGRAM

Any benefit that is part of a flexible compensation program must also meet statutory requirements applicable to that particular benefit.

(1) Medical Benefits. Perhaps the most significant benefit offered under most flexible compensation programs is medical coverage. In addition to hospital and surgical expenses, the medical coverage available under a flexible compensation program may include medical insurance premiums or employer charges under a self-insured medical plan, HMO premiums, and reimbursement of miscellaneous health-related expenses. The rules governing medical benefits are set forth in Sections 105 and 106 of the Internal Revenue Code. Another requirement is that the plan meet the continuing coverage requirements of Section 162(k) of the Internal Revenue Code, added to the Code by the Consolidated Omnibus Budget Reconciliation Act of 1985 (COBRA). The requirement for continuing coverage is that each "qualified beneficiary" who loses coverage under the plan as a result of a "qualifying event" (such as termination of employment or death) is entitled to elect continuation coverage under the plan and pay the applicable premium costs.

Effective in 1989, the nondiscrimination rules covering medical benefits are defined in Section 89 of the Code. Under Section 89, medical benefits must meet two nondiscrimination tests—one with respect to coverage and one with respect to benefits. The coverage test has three parts and requires that at least 50 percent of the employees eligible to participate must be lower-paid employees, at least 90 percent of the lower paid must be eligible for benefits worth at least 50 percent of the highest value available to any highly paid employee, and no provision in the plan relating to eligibility may discriminate in favor of highly paid employees. Under the benefits test, the value of the average benefit to the lower paid (for all medical or health plans) must be worth at least 75 percent of the value of the average benefit provided to highly paid employees. Note that this test aggregates all other health plans of the employer, including any plans that are not part of the flexible compensation program. If these nondiscrimination tests are failed, highly paid employees must include in their gross income for income tax purposes the value of the benefits in excess of the amount that could have been provided on a nondiscriminatory basis. These requirements are discussed at greater length in the next chapter.

(2) Life Insurance. In addition to medical benefits, flexible compensation programs often provide group-term life insurance benefits. Group-term life insurance benefits are subject to the provisions of Section 79 and 89 of the Internal Revenue Code. Under Section 79, a group-term life insurance plan is discriminatory if it fails the tests contained in Section 89. Under Section 89, a group-term life insurance plan must meet the three-pronged eligibility test (at least 50 percent of the employees eligible must be lower paid, 90 percent of lower-paid employees must have a benefit worth at least 50 percent of the highest benefit value provided to a highly paid employee, and there can be no discriminatory provision relating to eligibility) and the benefits test (the value of the average benefit provided to the lower paid is at least 75 percent of the value of the average benefit provided to the highly paid).

While amounts of group-term life insurance in excess of $50,000 are taxable to the employee, such amounts still are permissible choices in a Section 125 flexible compensation program. In other words, amounts in excess of $50,000 can be provided through a Section 125 program, although coverage in excess of $50,000 results in taxable income to the employee.

(3) Disability. Disability coverage also is includible in a flexible compensation program. The value of this coverage, when provided to an employee by an employer, is excludable from gross income under Section 106 of the Code. However, if the employer pays for the coverage, any benefits payable to the employee are taxable income. On the other hand, if the employee pays for the coverage (with after-tax dollars), the employee does not recognize any taxable income on the benefits attributable to employee contributions. Furthermore, no specific nondiscrimination rules apply to disability.

(4) Dependent Care Expenses. Dependent care expenses, such as day care expenses, can also be provided under a flexible compensation program. The maximum permitted benefit that can be provided to an employee in a single year is $5,000 ($2,500 in the case of a married person filing a separate tax return). Employees who incur dependent care expenses are faced with a choice of a tax credit under Section 21 of the Internal Revenue Code or payment of these benefits through a dependent care assistance plan under Section 129. The latter is subject to nondiscrimination rules contained in Section 129 of the Internal Revenue Code. However, an employer may elect, in lieu thereof, to have dependent care covered by the nondiscrimination rules of Code Section 89. Dependent care benefits are generally provided under a flexible spending account, and the nondiscrimination rules applicable to dependent care are described in the portion of this chapter covering flexible spending accounts.

(5) Legal Services. Group legal services plans, like dependent care, are subject to alternative nondiscrimination tests, at the election of the

employer. Group legal services are ordinarily subject to special nondiscrimination tests under Section 120 of the Internal Revenue Code. However, at the election of the employer, group legal services can be tested
for nondiscrimination under Section 89 of the Code. Group legal services
are usually provided through flexible spending accounts, and the nondiscrimination tests covering group legal services are described in the section of this chapter covering flexible spending accounts.

(6) Vacation Time.   Vacation or time off is sometimes included as
a benefit under a flexible compensation program. Vacation or time off
is not covered by any specific set of rules under a section of the Internal
Revenue Code and, therefore, is not subject to any special nondiscrimination rules. However, vacation that is elected in a flexible compensation program cannot be carried forward to a future year; this would
violate the prohibition of deferred compensation within a cafeteria
plan (other than that allowed under Section 401(k)). Further, any vacation used by the employee is considered first to be any vacation that is
not "elective" under the flexible compensation program. (These rules
are explained in more detail in Chapter Ten on time off.) In effect, vacation or time off is subject to the general rules applied to Section 125
programs.

(d)   FLEXIBLE SPENDING ACCOUNTS

Flexible spending accounts allow employees to direct contributions under a flexible compensation program to an account for payment of various categories of expenses, such as medical care or dependent care.
Flexible spending accounts are not governed by separate rules within
the Internal Revenue Code. Instead, they are treated as part of a Section
125 program, and as such they are subject to the nondiscrimination
rules of Section 125. Also, to the extent that a flexible spending account
is established to provide a category of benefits covered by another,
more specific nondiscrimination test, the flexible spending account
(along with the other benefits in the same area maintained by the employer) is also subject to those specific requirements.

For example, if a flexible compensation program includes a health
care spending account, the provisions of Section 89 of the Internal Revenue Code must be met to prevent the medical reimbursements from
being taxable income to highly compensated employees. As described
earlier, compliance involves passing two nondiscrimination tests—one
with respect to coverage and another with respect to benefits.

If a flexible compensation program includes a flexible spending account for dependent care expenses, the requirements of Code Section 129 must be met. However, for the nondiscrimination tests, the employer may elect either to meet the Section 89 rules discussed earlier in relation to flexible spending accounts for health care or the specific rules contained in Section 129.

The Section 129 rules provide that the contributions or benefits may not discriminate in favor of highly paid employees, and the benefit must be available to a group of employees constituting an adequate cross section of all employees by pay level. In addition, the average benefits provided to lower-paid employees must be at least 55 percent of the average benefits provided to highly paid employees. For purposes of this latter test, in the case of any benefit provided through salary reduction, any employee whose net compensation is less than $25,000 may be disregarded. Whichever set of tests is elected, the plan must not provide benefits to five-percent owners that during any plan year exceed 25 percent of the benefits provided to all employees.

A flexible compensation program may also include a spending account for legal services. Legal services plans are subject to rules under Section 120 of the Code.* Section 120 provides that amounts paid to an employee by an employer for certain legal services under a legal services plan are not included in the employee's gross income as long as certain requirements are met.

These requirements parallel the nondiscrimination requirements applicable to flexible spending accounts for dependent care. There is the same choice of either meeting the Section 89 rules or meeting the rules specifically applicable to group legal services in Section 120. Under Section 120, contributions or benefits may not discriminate in favor of highly paid employees, and the benefit must be available to a group of employees constituting an adequate cross section of all employees by pay level. Regardless of which set of rules is elected, not more than 25 percent of the amount contributed by the employer may be provided through the plan to five-percent owners.

Unlike health and dependent care spending accounts, however, reimbursements under a legal services spending account must be made through a trust meeting the conditions of Section 501(c)(20) of the Internal Revenue Code. A 501(c)(20) trust is a tax-exempt trust that exists for the sole purpose of providing reimbursement for legal services. While the trust must exist and be submitted to the Internal Revenue

---

*The tax exclusion was allowed to expire in 1987. (See also Chapter Five, § 5.5.)

Service for a determination of tax-exempt status, the trust typically is run as a "dry" or "conduit" trust. That is, there is no advance funding of the trust or, for that matter, assets of any degree. As claims are submitted by the employee, the employer typically writes a check to the trust and, in turn, a check is drawn on the trust in an identical amount and paid to the employee.

§ 4.4 DOCUMENTATION, REPORTING, AND DISCLOSURE

(a) DOCUMENTATION

Every flexible compensation program must be established by a formal legal document. This requirement applies to broad cafeteria plans with choices in many benefit areas as well as to plans which simply convert employee medical contributions to a pretax basis. Section 89(k) of the Code requires that a plan be in writing and that the employee's rights under the plan be legally enforceable. This requirement necessitates a formal legal document under which the sponsoring company assumes a legal obligation. This takes the form of a legal document executed by authorized representatives of the sponsoring company. The requirement of Section 89(k) applies to every benefit that is permitted in a Section 125 flexible compensation program as well as to the overall Section 125 program.

The basic legal document for a flexible compensation program under Section 125 is a relatively short document which establishes the framework for the operation of the program and the underlying benefits. This document is often referred to as the cafeteria plan. The document will set out the name of the sponsoring employer and the effective date of the plan. The document will then define in very specific terms the group of employees who are eligible to participate in the plan, what they must do to enroll in the plan, the manner in which contributions or credits under the plan will be generated, and the events upon which participation in the plan will terminate. The source of flexible credits is an important part of the document. Flexible credits can be generated from employer contributions, salary reduction, after-tax employee contributions, or any combination of these sources of funds.

The plan document also will set forth the choices available within the flexible compensation program. The choices available will be described either by reference to the benefit and a separate plan document through which it will be provided or by describing in the flexible compensation plan document itself the rules governing how the underlying benefit will be provided. Most benefits will be incorporated by reference to other plan documents, but it is very common to document the rules governing how flexible spending accounts will be provided as part of the basic Section 125 cafeteria plan. The cost of the various options or choices within the flexible compensation program will either be specifically set forth in the plan document, or the employer will be authorized to announce such costs prior to each plan year. The latter has become more the norm because it avoids the necessity of amending the plan document each time the price structure of the choices is changed.

As noted, most of the benefits that constitute the choices within a flexible compensation program are documented in separate legal documents. A typical example is a group-term life insurance benefit. The Section 125 program will simply refer to the employee's ability to choose a level of group-term life insurance and further refer to the plan name pursuant to which the benefit will be provided. The group-term life insurance benefit provisions will then be documented in a separate group-term life insurance contract with an insurance company.

For a flexible compensation program offering choices between medical, long-term disability, group-term life insurance, a health care spending account, and a dependent care expense account, there would normally be a basic plan document for the Section 125 cafeteria program and separate legal documents for the group-term life benefit, the long-term disability, and the medical plan. The two flexible spending accounts typically would be documented as part of the Section 125 arrangement.

If a legal services spending account is part of the flexible compensation program, a separate trust document is required. This is usually a trust agreement between the sponsoring employer and a bank having trust powers.

If the flexible compensation program offers deferred compensation as one of the choices, a separate profit sharing plan meeting the requirements of Code Section 401(a) and 401(k) is required. It is standard practice to submit the 401(k) plan document to the IRS and request a determination letter that the plan meets applicable requirements of the Internal Revenue Code. Further, the 401(k) plan will require a trust document that meets the requirements for tax exemption under Section 501 of the Code. The trust is usually a trust agreement between the sponsoring employer and a bank having trust powers, but it can also be an agreement between the sponsoring employer and individual trustees. In the latter case, the individual trustees are customarily employees of the sponsoring employer.

(b) GOVERNMENT REVIEW

As previously mentioned, some portions of a flexible compensation program can be submitted to the IRS for an advance determination of compliance with requirements of the Code. A request for such a determination for a 401(k) plan is submitted to the IRS using Form 5301 (if covered employees are not covered by collective bargaining) together with various required attachments. The trust that forms part of the 401(k) plan would be submitted at the same time and using the same Form 5301. The IRS will then issue a determination letter that the plan satisfies the applicable requirements of the Code and that the trust is tax-exempt under the Code.

If a legal services expense account is part of a flexible compensation program, the trust must be submitted to the IRS. The employer would request an IRS determination that the trust is tax-exempt under Section 501(c)(20) of the Code. While this results in a determination that the trust is tax-exempt, it provides no assurance that the plan (as opposed to the trust) meets the requirements of Section 120 of the Code.

There is no similar advance determination process available either for the flexible compensation program (in the form of the cafeteria plan) or for the other benefits that constitute the choices available within the flexible compensation program. The fact that there is no advance determination process in place for most of a flexible compensation program means that specific issues relating to the component code sections will be raised only as part of an IRS field audit. The employer, therefore, has the burden of maintaining the plan in compliance with the law.

(c) REPORTING REQUIREMENTS

Under ERISA, employee benefit plans that provide various enumerated benefits must file annual reports on IRS Form 5500. Thus an annual Form 5500 is required to be filed with the IRS for the separate benefits that are normally included in a flexible compensation program that are subject to ERISA. This includes medical benefits, life insurance, disability, and legal services. So if a flexible program offers choices between medical, group-term life insurance, and long-term disability, a separate Form 5500 filing would be made for each of the three benefits. Under ERISA, it is generally not considered necessary to file a separate Form 5500 for the flexible compensation program itself as long as the separate choices are benefits for which a Form

5500 is filed. This is because the flexible benefit program is really a mechanism, or conduit, for providing benefits that are subject to the Form 5500 requirement. But the flexible program is not, by itself, subject to this requirement.

Section 6039D of the Internal Revenue Code also requires that an annual report be made by the employer to the IRS with respect to any of the following plans:

- Section 125 Cafeteria Plan
- Section 79 Group-Term Life Insurance
- Section 105 and 106 Accident and Health Plans
- Section 120 Group Legal Services Plan
- Section 127 Education Assistance Plan, and
- Section 129 Dependent Care Assistance Plan.

This requirement is also satisfied by submission of an IRS Form 5500.

Depending on the legal reason that a plan is subject to the Form 5500 filing requirement, different items on the Form 5500 must be completed. Also, in the case of a Section 125 cafeteria plan (a flexible compensation program) which includes various benefits (each of which is, by itself, subject to the Form 5500 requirement), the reporting requirement may be met by filing one Form 5500 for the cafeteria plan and describing the component benefits.

(d) DISCLOSURE REQUIREMENTS

As with the reporting requirements, ERISA imposes a disclosure requirement with respect to certain of the separate benefits contained in a flexible compensation program. Thus a summary plan description is normally required with respect to each such separate benefit. Methods of compliance, however, will vary. For instance, a health care spending account contained in a flexible compensation program will sometimes be described in the summary plan description dealing with the employer's basic medical plan. Some benefits, like life insurance, will already have a summary plan description applicable to it and will not, therefore, need any further disclosure. Alternatively, this can be accomplished by preparing a summary plan description for the flexible benefit program and including in it all of the underlying benefits that are subject to the requirements regarding summary plan descriptions. With a Section 401(k) plan, the deferrals made by a participant during a calendar year must be reported to the participant. This disclosure must be included on the Form W-2 provided to the employee.

Similarly, under a dependent care expense account, there is also a legal requirement that the total amount of reimbursement provided to a participant during a calendar year must be disclosed in writing to the participant by January 31 of the following year. This enables the individual to calculate the amount of the dependent care credit available when preparing the individual federal income tax return.

Appendix

Statutes and Regulations

(a) INTERNAL REVENUE CODE

(1) SECTION 125 (AS AMENDED BY THE TAX REFORM ACT OF 1986)

→Caution: **Code Sec. 125, below, as amended by P.L. 99-514, generally applies to years beginning after the later of December 31, 1987, or the earlier of three months after the issuance of regulations implementing Code Sec. 89 or December 31, 1988.**←

Sec. 125 [1986 Code]. (a) GENERAL RULE.—In the case of a cafeteria plan—

(1) amounts shall not be included in gross income of a participant in such plan solely because, under the plan, the participant may choose among the benefits of the plan, and

(2) if the plan fails to meet the requirements of subsection (b) for any plan year—

(A) paragraph (1) shall not apply, and

(B) notwithstanding any other provision of part III of this subchapter, any qualified benefits received under such cafeteria plan by a highly compensated employee for such plan year shall be included in the gross income of such employee for the taxable year with or within which such plan year ends.

(b) PROHIBITION AGAINST DISCRIMINATION AS TO ELIGIBILITY TO PARTICIPATE.—

(1) HIGHLY COMPENSATED EMPLOYEES.—A plan shall be treated as failing to meet the requirements of this subsection unless the plan is available to a group of employees as qualify under a classification set up by the employer and which the Secretary find not to be discriminatory in favor of highly compensated employees.

(2) KEY EMPLOYEES.—In the case of a key employee (within the meaning of section 416(i)(1)), a plan shall be treated as failing to meet the requirements of this subsection if the qualified benefits provided to key employees under the plan exceed 25 percent of the aggregate of such benefits provided for all employees under the plan. For purposes of the preceding sentence, qualified benefits shall be determined without regard to the last sentence of subsection (e).

(3) EXCLUDABLE EMPLOYEES.—For purposes of this subsection, there may be excluded from consideration employees who may be excluded from consideration under section 89(h).

(c) CAFETERIA PLAN DEFINED.—For purposes of this section—

(1) IN GENERAL.—The term "cafeteria plan" means a plan which meets the requirements of section 89(k) and under which—

(A) all participants are employees, and

(B) the participants may choose—

(i)   among 2 or more benefits consisting of cash and qualified benefits, or

(ii)   among 2 or more qualified benefits.

(2) DEFERRED COMPENSATION PLANS EXCLUDED.—

(A) In General.—The term "cafeteria plan" does not include any plan which provides for deferred compensation.

(B) Exception for Cash and Deferred Arrangements.—Subparagraph (A) shall not apply to a profit-sharing or stock bonus plan which includes a qualified cash or deferred arrangement (as defined in section 401(k)(2)) to the extent of amounts which a covered employee may elect to have the employer pay as contributions to a trust under such plan on behalf of the employee.

(C) Exception for Certain Plans Maintained by Educational Institutions.—Subparagraph (A) shall not apply to a plan maintained by an educational organization described in section 170(b)(1)(A)(ii) to the extent of amounts which a covered employee may elect to have the employer pay as contributions for post-retirement group life insurance if—

(i)   all contributions for such insurance must be made before retirement, and

(ii)   such life insurance does not have a cash surrender value at any time.

For purposes of section 79, any life insurance described in the preceding sentence shall be treated as group-term life insurance.

(d) Highly Compensated Employee.—For purposes of this section, the term "highly compensated employee" has the meaning given such term by section 414(q).

(e) Qualified Benefits Defined.—For purposes of this section—

(1) In general.—The term "qualified benefit" means any benefit which, with the application of subsection (a), is not includible in the gross income of the employee by reason of an express provision of this chapter (other than section 117, 124, 127, or 132).

(2) Certain benefits included.—The term "qualified benefits" includes—

(A) any group-term life insurance which is includible in gross income only because it exceeds the dollar limitation of section 79, and

(B) any other benefit permitted under regulations.

(f) Collectively Bargained Plan Not Considered Discriminatory.—For purposes of this section, a plan shall not be treated as discriminatory if the plan is maintained under an agreement which the Secretary finds to be a collective bargaining agreement between employee representatives and one or more employers.

(g) Cross References.—

For reporting and recordkeeping requirements, see section 6039D.

(2) SECTION 401(k) (AS AMENDED BY THE TAX REFORM ACT OF 1986)

(k) CASH OR DEFERRED ARRANGEMENTS.—

(1) GENERAL RULE.—A profit-sharing or stock bonus plan, a pre-ERISA money purchase plan, or a rural electric cooperative plan shall not be considered as not satisfying the requirements of subsection (a) merely because the plan includes a qualified cash or deferred arrangement.

(2) QUALIFIED CASH OR DEFERRED ARRANGEMENT.—A qualified cash or deferred arrangement is any arrangement which is part of a profit-sharing or stock bonus plan, a pre-ERISA money purchase plan, or a rural electric cooperative plan which meets the requirements of subsection (a)—

(A) under which a covered employee may elect to have the employer make payments as contributions to a trust under the plan on behalf of the employee, or to the employee directly in cash;

→Caution: Code Sec. 401(k)(2)(B), below, prior to amendment by P.L. 99-514, applies generally to years beginning before January 1, 1989. For special rules, see amendment notes in the Code Volumes.←

(B) under which amounts held by the trust which are attributable to employer contributions made pursuant to the employee's election may not be distributable to participants or other beneficiaries earlier than upon retirement, death, disability, or separation from service (or in the case of a profit sharing or stock bonus plan, hardship or the attainment of age 59½) and will not be distributable merely by reason of the completion of a stated period of participation or the lapse of a fixed number of years; and

→Caution: Code Sec. 401(k)(2)(B), below, as amended by P.L. 99-514, applies generally to years beginning after December 31, 1988. However, subclauses II, III, and IV, below, apply to distributions after 1984. For special rules, see amendment notes in the Code Volumes.←

(B) under which—

(i) amounts held by the trust which are attributable to employer contributions made pursuant to the employee's election may not be distributable to participants or other beneficiaries earlier than—

(I) separation from service, death, or disability,

(II) termination of the plan without establishment of a successor plan,

(III) the date of the sale by a corporation of substantially all of the assets (within the meaning of section 409(d)(2)) used by such corporation in a trade or business of such corporation with respect to an employee who continues employment with the corporation acquiring such assets,

(IV) the date of the sale by a corporation of such corporation's interest in a subsidiary (within the meaning of section 409(d)(3)) with respect to an employee who continues employment with such subsidiary,

(V)   in the case of a profit-sharing or stock bonus plan, the attainment of age 59½, or

(VI) in the case of contributions to a profit-sharing or stock bonus plan to which section 402(a)(8) applies, upon hardship of the employee, and

(ii) amounts will not be distributable merely by reason of the completion of a stated period of participation or the lapse of a fixed number of years;

(C) which provides that an employee's right to his accrued benefit derived from employer contributions made to the trust pursuant to his election is nonforfeitable, and

→**Caution: Code Sec. 401(k)(2)(D), below, as added by P.L. 99-514, applies generally to years beginning after December 31, 1988. For special rules, see amendment notes in the Code Volumes.**←

(D) which does not require, as a condition of participation in the arrangement, that an employee complete a period of service with the employer (or employers) maintaining the plan extending beyond the period permitted under section 410(a)(1) (determined without regard to subparagraph (B)(i) thereof).

→**Caution: Code Sec. 401(k)(3), below, prior to amendment by P.L. 99-514, applies generally to years beginning before January 1, 1987. For special rules, see amendment notes in the Code Volumes.**←

(3) APPLICATION OF PARTICIPATION AND DISCRIMINATION STANDARDS.—

(A) A cash or deferred arrangement shall not be treated as a qualified cash or deferred arrangement unless—

(i)   those employees eligible to benefit under the arrangement satisfy the provisions of subparagraph (A) or (B) of section 410(b)(1), and

(ii) the actual deferral percentage for highly compensated employees (as defined in paragraph (4)) for such year bears a relationship to the actual deferral percentage for all other eligible employees for such plan year which meets either of the following tests:

(I)   The actual deferral percentage for the group of highly compensated employees is not more than the actual deferral percentage of all other eligible employees multiplied by 1.5.

(II)   The excess of the actual deferral percentage for the group of highly compensated employees over that of all other eligible employees is not more than 3 percentage points, and the actual deferral percentage for the group of highly compensated employees is not more than the actual deferral percentage of all other eligible employees multiplied by 2.5.

If 2 or more plans which include cash or deferred arrangements are considered as 1 plan for purposes of section 401(a)(4) or 410(b), the cash or deferred arrangements included in such plans shall be treated as 1 arrangement for purposes of this subparagraph.

If an employee is a participant under 2 or more cash or deferred arrangements of the employer, for purposes of determining the deferral percentage with respect to such employee, all such cash or deferred arrangements shall be treated as 1 cash or deferred arrangement.

(B) For purposes of subparagraph (A), the actual deferral percentage for a specified group of employees for a plan year shall be the average of the ratios (calculated separately for each employee in such group) of—

(i)   the amount of employer contributions actually paid over to the trust on behalf of each such employee for such plan year, to

(ii)   the employee's compensation for such plan year.

For purposes of the preceding sentence, the compensation of any employee for a plan year shall be the amount of his compensation which is taken into account under the plan in calculating the contribution which may be made on his behalf for such plan year.

(C) A cash or deferred arrangement shall be treated as meeting the requirements of subsection (a)(4) with respect to contributions if the requirements of subparagraph (A)(ii) are met.

→Caution: Code Sec. 401(k)(3), below, as amended by P.L. 99-514, applies generally to years beginning after December 31, 1986. For special rules, see amendment notes in the Code Volumes.←

(3) APPLICATION OF PARTICIPATION AND DISCRIMINATION STANDARDS.—

(A) A cash or deferred arrangement shall not be treated as a qualified cash or deferred arrangement unless—

(i)   those employees eligible to benefit under the arrangement satisfy the provisions of section 410(b)(1), and

(ii)   the actual deferral percentage for highly compensated employees (as defined in paragraph (5)) for such year bears a relationship to the actual deferral percentage for all other eligible employees for such plan year which meets either of the following tests:

(I)   The actual deferral percentage for the group of highly compensated employees is not more than the actual deferral percentage of all other eligible employees multiplied by 1.25.

(II)   The excess of the actual deferral percentage for the group of highly compensated employees over that of all other eligible employees is not more than 2 percentage points, and the actual deferral percentage for the group of highly compensated employees is not more than the actual deferral percentage of all other eligible employees multiplied by 2.

If 2 or more plans which include cash or deferred arrangements are considered as 1 plan for purposes of section 401(a)(4) or 410(b), the cash or deferred arrangements included in such plans shall be treated as 1 arrangement for purposes of this subparagraph.

If any highly compensated employee is a participant under 2 or more cash or deferred arrangements of the employer, for purposes of determining the deferral percentage with respect to such employee, all such cash or deferred arrangements shall be treated as 1 cash or deferred arrangement.

(B) For purposes of subparagraph (A), the actual deferral percentage for a specified group of employees for a plan year shall be the average of the ratios (calculated separately for each employee in such group) of—

(i)   the amount of employer contributions actually paid over to the trust on behalf of each such employee for such plan year, to

(ii)   the employee's compensation for such plan year.

(C) A cash or deferred arrangement shall be treated as meeting the requirements of subsection (a)(4) with respect to contributions if the requirements of subparagraph (A)(ii) are met.

(C) [(D)] For purposes of subparagraph (B), the employer contributions on behalf of any employee—

(i)   shall include any employer contributions made pursuant to the employee's election under paragraph (2), and

(ii)   under such rules as the Secretary may prescribe, may, at the election of the employer, include—

→Caution: Code Sec. 401(k)(3), below, as amended by P.L. 99-514, applies generally to years beginning after December 31, 1986. For special rules, see amendment notes in the Code Volumes.←

(I)   matching contributions (as defined in section 401(m)(4)(A)) which meets the requirements of paragraph (2)(B) and (C), and

(II)   qualified nonelective contributions (within the meaning of section 401(m)(4)(C)).

→Caution: **Code Sec. 401(k)(4), below, as added by P.L. 99-514, applies generally to years beginning after December 31, 1988. For special rules, see amendment notes in the Code Volumes.←**

(4) OTHER REQUIREMENTS.—

(A) BENEFITS (OTHER THAN MATCHING CONTRIBUTIONS) MUST NOT BE CONTINGENT ON ELECTION TO DEFER.—A cash or deferred arrangement of any employer shall not be treated as a qualified cash or deferred arrangement if any other benefit provided by such employer is conditioned (directly or indirectly) on the employee electing to have the employer make or not make contributions under the arrangement in lieu of receiving cash. The preceding sentence shall not apply to any matching contribution (as defined in section 401(m)) made by reason of such an election.

(B) STATE AND LOCAL GOVERNMENTS AND TAX-EXEMPT ORGANIZATIONS NOT ELIGIBLE.—A cash or deferred arrangement shall not be treated as a qualified cash or deferred arrangement if it is part of a plan maintained by—

(i)   a State or local government or political subdivision thereof, or any agency or instrumentality thereof, or

(ii)   any organization exempt from tax under this subtitle.

(C) COORDINATION WITH OTHER PLANS.—Except as provided in section 401(m), any employer contribution made pursuant to an employee's election under a qualified cash or deferred arrangement shall not be taken into account for purposes of determining whether any other plan meets the requirements of section 401(a) or 410(b). This subparagraph shall not apply for purposes of determining whether a plan meets the average benefit requirement of section 410(b)(2)(A)(ii).

→Caution: **Code Sec. 401(k)(4)(prior to redesignation), below, prior to amendment by P.L. 99-514, applies generally to years beginning before January 1, 1987. For special rules, see amendment notes in the Code Volumes.←**

(4) HIGHLY COMPENSATED EMPLOYEE.—For purposes of this subsection, the term "highly compensated employee" means any employee who is more highly compensated than two-thirds of all eligible employees, taking into account only compensation which is considered in applying paragraph (3).

→Caution: **Code Sec. 401(k)(5)(as redesignated), below, as amended by P.L. 99-514, applies generally to years beginning after December 31, 1986. For special rules, see amendment notes in the Code Volumes.←**

(5) HIGHLY COMPENSATED EMPLOYEE.—For purposes of this subsection, the term "highly compensated employee" has the meaning given such term by section 414(q).

(6) PRE-ERISA MONEY PURCHASE PLAN.—For purposes of this subsection, the term "pre-ERISA money purchase plan" means a pension plan—

(A) which is a defined contribution plan (as defined in section 414(i)),

(B) which was in existence on June 27, 1974, and which, on such date, included a salary reduction arrangement, and

(C) under which neither the employee contributions nor the employer contributions may exceed the levels provided by the contribution formula in effect under the plan on such date.

(7) RURAL ELECTRIC COOPERATIVE PLAN.—For purposes of this subsection, the term "rural electric cooperative plan" means any pension plan—

(A) which is a defined contribution plan (as defined in section 414(i)), and

(B) which is established and maintained by a rural electric cooperative (as defined in section 457(d)(9)(B)) or a national association of such rural electric cooperatives.

→**Caution: Code Sec. 401(k)(8) and (9), below, as added by P.L. 99-514, applies generally to years beginning after December 31, 1986. For special rules, see amendment notes in the Code Volumes.**←

(8) ARRANGEMENT NOT DISQUALIFIED IF EXCESS CONTRIBUTIONS DISTRIBUTED.—

(A) IN GENERAL.—A cash or deferred arrangement shall not be treated as failing to meet the requirements of clause (ii) of paragraph (3)(A) for any plan year if, before the close of the following plan year—

(i) the amount of the excess contributions for such plan year (and any income allocable to such contributions) is distributed, or

(ii) to the extent provided in regulations, the employee elects to treat the amount of the excess contributions as an amount distributed to the employee and then contributed by the employee to the plan.

Any distribution of excess contributions (and income) may be made without regard to any other provision of law.

(B) EXCESS CONTRIBUTIONS.—For purposes of subparagraph (A), the term "excess contributions" means, with respect to any plan year, the excess of—

(i) the aggregate amount of employer contributions actually paid over to the trust on behalf of highly compensated employees for such plan year, over

(ii) the maximum amount of such contributions permitted under the limitations of clause (ii) of paragraph (3)(A)(determined by reducing contributions made on behalf of highly compensated employees in order of the actual deferral percentages beginning with the highest of such percentages).

(C) METHOD OF DISTRIBUTING EXCESS CONTRIBUTIONS.—Any distribution of the excess contributions for any plan year shall be made to highly compensated employees on the basis of the respective portions of the excess contributions attributable to each of such employees.

(D) ADDITIONAL TAX UNDER SECTION 72(t) NOT TO APPLY.—No tax shall be imposed under section 72(t) on any amount required to be distributed under this paragraph.

(E) CROSS REFERENCE.—

For excise tax on certain excess contributions, see section 4979.

(9) COMPENSATION.—For purposes of this subsection, the term "compensation" has the meaning given such term by section 414(s).

(3)   SECTION 6039D (AS AMENDED BY THE TAX REFORM ACT OF 1986)

[¶ 5069ZA] RETURNS AND RECORDS WITH RESPECT TO CERTAIN FRINGE BENEFIT PLANS

Sec. 6039D [1986 Code]. (a) IN GENERAL.—Every employer maintaining a specified fringe benefit plan during any year beginning after December 31, 1984, for any portion of which the applicable exclusion applies, shall file a return (at such time and in such manner as the Secretary shall by regulations prescribe) with respect to such plan showing for such year—

(1) the number of employees of the employer,

(2) the number of employees of the employer eligible to participate under the plan,

(3) the number of employees participating under the plan,

(4) the total cost of the plan during the year, and

(5) the name, address, and taxpayer identification number of the employer and the type of business in which the employer is engaged.

→**Caution: Code Sec. 6039D(a)(6), below, as added by P.L. 99-514, is effective generally for the later of: (1) plan years beginning after 1987, or (2) the earlier of plan years beginning at least three months following the issuance of regulations or after 1988. See ¶ 899ZW.←**

(6) the number of highly compensated employees among the employees described in paragraphs (1), (2), and (3).

(b) RECORDKEEPING REQUIREMENT.—Each employer maintaining a specified fringe benefit plan during any year shall keep such records as may be necessary for purposes of determining whether the requirements of the applicable exclusion are met.

→**Caution: Code Sec. 6039(D)(c), below, prior to amendment by P.L. 99-514.←**

(c) ADDITIONAL INFORMATION WHEN REQUIRED BY THE SECRETARY.—Any employer—

(1) who maintains a specified fringe benefit plan during any year for which a return is required under subsection (a), and

(2) who is required by the Secretary to file an additional return for such year,

shall file such additional return. Such additional return shall be filed at such time and in such manner as the Secretary shall prescribe and shall contain information as the Secretary shall prescribe.

→Caution: Code Sec. 6039D(c), below, as added by P.L. 99-514, is effective generally for the later of: (1) plan years beginning after 1987, or (2) the earlier of plan years beginning at least three months following the issuance of regulations or after 1988. See ¶ 899ZW.←

(c) ADDITIONAL INFORMATION WHEN REQUIRED BY THE SECRETARY.—Any employer—

(1) who maintains a specified fringe benefit plan during any year for which a return is required under subsection (a), and

(2) who is required by the Secretary to file an additional return for such year,

shall file such additional return. Such additional return shall be filed at such time and in such manner as the Secretary shall prescribe and shall contain information as the Secretary shall prescribe. The Secretary may require returns under this subsection only from a representative group of employers.

→Caution: Code Sec. 6039(D)(d), below, prior to amendment by P.L. 99-514.←

(d) DEFINITIONS.—For purposes of this section—

(1) SPECIFIED FRINGE BENEFIT PLAN.—The term "specified fringe benefit plan" means—

(A) any qualified group legal services plan (as defined in section 120),

(B) any cafeteria plan (as defined in section 125), and

(C) any educational assistance plan (as defined in section 127).

(2) APPLICABLE EXCLUSION.—The term "applicable exclusion" means—

(A) section 120 in the case of a qualified group legal services plan,

(B) section 125 in the case of a cafeteria plan, and

(C) section 127 in the case of an educational assistance plan.

→Caution: Code Sec. 6039D(d), below, as added by P.L. 99-514, is effective generally for the later of: (1) plan years beginning after 1987, or (2) the earlier of plan years beginning at least three months following the issuance of regulations or after 1988. See ¶ 899ZW.←

(d) DEFINITIONS.—For purposes of this section—

(1) SPECIFIED FRINGE BENEFIT PLAN.—The term "specified fringe benefit plan" means any plan under section 79, 105, 106, 120, 125, 127, or 129.

(2) APPLICABLE EXCLUSION.—The term "applicable exclusion" means, with respect to any specified fringe benefit plan, the section specified under paragraph (1) under which benefits under such plan are excludable from gross income.

(b) INTERNAL REVENUE SERVICE REGULATIONS

(1) TEMPORARY REGULATIONS ON CAFETERIA PLANS

● **Temporary Regulations**

[¶ 1197SA] § 1.125-2T. **Question and answer relating to the benefits that may be offered under a cafeteria plan. (Temporary)**

Q-1: What benefits may be offered to participants under a cafeteria plan?

A-1: (a) Generally, for cafeteria plan years beginning on or after January 1, 1985, a cafeteria plan is a written plan under which participants may choose among two or more benefits consisting of cash and certain other permissible benefits. In general, benefits that are excludable from the gross income of an employee under a specific section of the Internal Revenue Code may be offered under a cafeteria plan. However, scholarships and fellowships under section 117, vanpooling under section 124, educational assistance under section 127 and certain fringe benefits under section 132 may not be offered under a cafeteria plan. In addition, meals and lodging under section 119, because they are furnished for the convenience of the employer and thus are not elective in lieu of other benefits or compensation provided by the employer, may not be offered under a cafeteria plan. Thus, a cafeteria plan may offer coverage under a group-term life insurance plan of up to $50,000 (section 79), coverage under an accident or health plan (sections 105 and 106), coverage under a qualified group legal services plan (section 120), coverage under a dependent care assistance program (section 129), and participation in a qualified cash or deferred arrangement that is part of a profit-sharing or stock bonus plan (section 401(k)). In addition, a cafeteria plan

→Caution: Reg. § 1.125-2T, below, does not reflect amendments to Code
Sec. 125 made by P.L. 99-514.←

may offer group-term life insurance coverage which is includible in gross income only because it is in excess of $50,000 or is on the lives of the participant's spouse and/or children. In addition, a cafeteria plan may offer participants the opportunity to purchase, with after-tax employee contributions, coverage under a group-term life insurance plan (section 79), coverage under an accident or health plan (section 105(e)), coverage under a qualified group legal services plan (section 120), or coverage under a dependent care assistance program (section 129). Finally, a cafeteria plan may offer paid vacation days if the plan precludes any participant from using, or receiving cash for, in a subsequent plan year, any of such paid vacation days remaining unused as of the end of the plan year. For purposes of the preceding sentence, elective vacation days provided under a cafeteria plan are not considered to be used until all nonelective paid vacation days have been used.

(b) Note that benefits that may be offered under a cafeteria plan may or may not be taxable depending upon whether such benefits qualify for an exclusion from gross income. However, a cafeteria plan may not offer a benefit that is taxable because such benefit fails to satisfy any applicable eligibility, coverage, or nondiscrimination requirement. Similarly, a plan may not offer a benefit for purchase with after-tax employee contributions if such benefit would fail to satisfy any eligibility, coverage, or nondiscrimination requirement that would apply if such benefit were designed to be provided on a nontaxable basis with employer contributions. Also, note that section 125(d)(2) provides that a cafeteria plan may not offer a benefit that defers the receipt of compensation (other than the opportunity to make elective contributions under a qualified cash or deferred arrangement) and may not operate in a manner that enables participants to defer the receipt of compensation. [Temporary Reg. § 1.125-2T.]

.10 **Historical Comment:** Adopted 1/29/86 by T.D. 8073.

(2) PROPOSED REGULATIONS ON CAFETERIA PLANS

¶ 20,137Q

Proposed regulations: Tax treatment of cafeteria plans.—Reproduced below are proposed regulations on the tax treatment of cafeteria plans set forth in a question and answer format. Note: Q&A-21 has been replaced by a new Q&A-21 in proposed regulations at ¶ 20,137R. Additional Q&As providing transition rules in accordance with changes made by the Tax Reform Act of 1984 also appear at that paragraph.

The proposed regulations were published in the Federal Register on May 7, 1984 (49 FR 19321).

Back references: ¶ 4252, 4951—4594, and 7930.

DEPARTMENT OF THE TREASURY

Internal Revenue Service

26 CFR Part 1

[EE-16-79]

Tax Treatment of Cafeteria Plans

AGENCY: Internal Revenue Service, Treasury.

ACTION: Notice of proposed rulemaking.

SUMMARY: This document contains proposed regulations relating to the tax treatment of cafeteria plans. Changes to the applicable tax law were made by the Revenue Act of 1978, by the Technical Corrections Act of 1979 and by the Miscellaneous Revenue Act of 1980. The proposed regulations would provide the public with the guidance needed to comply with those Acts and would affect employees who participate in cafeteria plans.

DATES: Written comments and requests for a public hearing must be delivered or mailed by July 6, 1984. The regulations are generally proposed to be effective for plan years beginning after December 31, 1978, except with respect to certain provisions set forth in Q&A-21 which would be effective as of September 4, 1984. In addition, transitional relief is provided with respect to employer contributions made before June 1, 1984, pursuant to certain "flexible spending arrangements" that satisfy specified conditions. Also, the provision relating to qualified cash or deferred arrangements would be effective for plan years beginning after December 31, 1980.

ADDRESS: Send comments and requests for a public hearing to: Commissioner of Internal Revenue, Attention: CC:LR:T (EE-16-79), Washington, D. C. 20224.

FOR FURTHER INFORMATION CONTACT:

Harry Beker of the Employee Plans and Exempt Organizations Division, Office of the Chief Counsel, Internal Revenue Service, 1111 Constitution Avenue, NW., Washington, D. C. 20224 (Attention: CC:EE) (202-566-6212) (not a toll-free call).

SUPPLEMENTARY INFORMATION:

Background

This document contains proposed Income Tax Regulations (26 CFR Part 1) under section 125 of the Internal Revenue Code of 1954. These proposed regulations are to be issued pursuant to section 134 of the Revenue Act of 1978 (92 Stat. 2763), section 101 of the Technical Corrections Act of 1979 (92 Stat. 2227), section 226 of the Miscellaneous Revenue Act of 1980 (94 Stat. 3529) and under the authority contained in section 7805 of the Code (68A Stat. 917, 26 U. S. C. 7805).

Format

These proposed regulations are presented in the form of questions and answers. The questions and answers do not address various issues regarding the application of the discrimination standards under section 125. Written comments are requested specifically with respect to the application of these discrimination standards. In particular, comments are requested regarding tests that a plan may use to determine whether it is nondiscriminatory, methods by which to value benefits, appropriate safe harbors from discrimination, and tests to assure that the pricing of benefits under a cafeteria plan is not discriminatory.

The guidance provided by these questions and answers may be relied upon to comply with provisions of section 125 and will be applied by the Internal Revenue Service in resolving issues arising under cafeteria plans and related Code sections. However, pending the issuance of final regulations, advance determinations and rulings regarding whether a cafeteria plan is or is not discriminatory will not be issued; determinations regarding discrimination will be made only on audit.

If final regulations are more restrictive than the guidance in this Notice, the regulations will not be applied retroactively. No inference, however, should be drawn regarding issues not expressly raised that may be suggested by a particular question or answer or by the inclusion or exclusion of certain questions.

Nonapplicability of Executive Order 12291

The Treasury Department has determined that this Regulation is not subject to review under Executive Order 12291 or the Treasury and Office of Management and Budget implementation of the Order dated April 28, 1982.

Regulatory Flexibility Act

Although this document is a notice of proposed rulemaking which solicits public comments, the Internal Revenue Service has concluded that the regulations proposed herein are interpretative and that the notice and public procedure requirements of 5 U. S. C. 553 do not apply. Accordingly, these proposed regulations do not constitute regulations subject to the Regulatory Flexibility Act (5 U. S. C. chapter 6).

Comments and Requests for a Public Hearing

Before adopting these proposed regulations, consideration will be given to any written comments that are submitted (preferably seven copies) to the Commissioner of Internal Revenue. All comments will be available for public inspection and copying. A public hearing will be held on a date announced in the notice of public hearing appearing elsewhere in this *Federal Register*.

Drafting Information

The principal author of these proposed regulations is Harry Beker of the Employee Plans and Exempt Organizations Division of the Office of Chief Counsel, Internal Revenue Service. However, personnel from other offices of the Internal Revenue Service and Treasury Department participated in developing the regulations, both on matters of substance and style.

List of Subjects in 26 CFR Parts 1.61-1—1.281-4

Income taxes, Taxable income.

PART 1—[AMENDED]

Proposed Amendments to the Regulations

Accordingly, it is proposed to amend the Income Tax Regulations, 26 CFR Part 1, by adding the following new section:

§ 1.125-1 Questions and answers relating to cafeteria plans.

Q-1: What does section 125 of the Internal Revenue Code provide?

A-1: Section 125 provides that a participant in a nondiscriminatory cafeteria plan will not be treated as having received the taxable benefits offered under the plan solely because the participant has the opportunity, before the benefits become currently available to the participant, to choose among the taxable and nontaxable benefits offered under the plan.

Q-2: What is a "cafeteria plan" under section 125?

A-2: A "cafeteria plan" is a separate written benefit plan maintained by an employer for the benefit of its employees, under which all participants are employees and each participant has the opportunity to select the particular benefits that he desires. A cafeteria plan may offer participants the opportunity to select among various taxable benefits and nontaxable benefits, but a plan must offer at least one taxable benefit and at least one nontaxable benefit. For example, if participants are given the opportunity to elect only among two or more nontaxable benefits, the plan is not a cafeteria plan.

Q-3: What must the written cafeteria plan document contain?

A-3: The written document embodying a cafeteria plan must contain at least the following information: (i) A specific description of each of the benefits available under the plan, including the periods during which the benefits are provided (i.e., the periods of coverage), (ii) the plan's eligibility rules governing participation, (iii) the procedures governing participants' elections under the plan, including the period during which elections may be made, the extent to which elections are irrevocable, and the periods with respect to which elections are effective, (iv) the manner in which employer contributions may be made under the plan, such as by salary reduction agreement between the participant and the employer or by nonelective employer contributions to the plan, (v) the maximum amount of employer contributions available to any participant under the plan, and (vi) the plan year on which the cafeteria plan operates.

In describing the benefits available under the cafeteria plan, the plan document need not be self-contained. For example, the plan document may include by reference benefits established under other "separate written plans," such as coverage under a qualified group legal services plan (section 120) or under a dependent care assistance program (section 129), without describing in full the benefits established under these other plans. But, for example, if the plan offers different maximum levels of coverage under a dependent care assistance program, the descriptions must specify the available maximums. In addition, an arrangement under which a participant is provided with coverage under a dependent care assistance program for dependent care expenses incurred during the period of coverage up to a specified amount (e.g., $500) and the right to receive, either directly or indirectly in the form of cash or any other benefit, any portion of the specified amount that is not reimbursed for such expenses will be considered a single benefit and must be fully described as such in the plan document. This also is the case with other benefits, such as coverage under an accident or health plan and coverage under a qualified group legal services plan. See Q&A-17 and Q&A-18 regarding the taxability of such benefit arrangements.

Q-4: What does the term "employees" mean under section 125?

A-4: The term "employees" includes present and former employees of the employer. All employees who are treated as employed by a single employer under subsections (b), (c), or (m) of section 414 are treated as employed by a single employer for purposes of section 125. The term "employees" does not, however, include self-employed individuals described in section 401(c) of the Code. Even though former employees generally are treated as employees, a cafeteria plan may not be established predominantly for the benefit of former employees of the employer.

In addition, even though the spouses and other beneficiaries of participants may not be participants in a cafeteria plan, a plan may provide benefits to spouses and beneficiaries of participants. For example, the spouse of a participant may not be permitted to participate actively in a cafeteria plan (i.e., the spouse may not be given the opportunity to select or purchase benefits offered by the plan), but the spouse of a participant may benefit from the participant's selection of family medical insurance coverage or of coverage under a dependent care assistance program. A participant's spouse will not be treated as actively participating in a cafeteria plan merely because the spouse has the right, upon the death of the participant, to select among various settlement options available with respect to a death benefit selected by the participant under the cafeteria plan or to elect among permissible distribution options with respect to the deceased participant's benefits under a cash or deferred arrangement that is part of the cafeteria plan.

Q-5: What benefits may be offered to participants under a cafeteria plan?

A-5: With the exception of benefits that defer the receipt of compensation (see Q&A-7), a cafeteria plan may offer participants the opportunity to select among certain taxable benefits and nontaxable benefits described in the plan document. The term "taxable benefit" means cash, property, or other benefits attributable to employer contributions that are currently taxable to the participant under the Internal Revenue Code upon receipt by the participant. The term "nontaxable benefit" means any benefit attributable to employer contributions to the extent that such benefit is not currently taxable to the participant under the Internal Revenue Code upon receipt of the benefit. Thus, a cafeteria plan may offer participants the following benefits, which will be nontaxable when provided in accordance with the applicable provisions of the Internal Revenue Code: group-term life insurance up to $50,000 (section 79), coverage under an accident or health plan (section 106), coverage under a qualified group legal services plan (section 120), and coverage under a dependent care assistance program (section 129). Also, amounts received by participants under one of these benefits may or may not be taxable depending upon whether such amounts qualify for an exclusion from gross income. See Q&A-17 and Q&A-18 regarding the inclusion of an accident or health plan, dependent care assistance program, or qualified group legal services plan in a cafeteria plan. Also, see Q&A-7 regarding the inclusion of deferred compensation benefits in a cafeteria plan.

In addition, a cafeteria plan may offer benefits that are nontaxable because they are attributable to after-tax employee contributions. For example, a cafeteria plan may offer participants the opportunity to purchase, with after-tax employee contributions, coverage under an accident or health plan providing for the payment of disability benefits. A participant's receipt of coverage under such an accident or health plan would not trigger taxable income because the coverage would be purchased with after-tax employee contributions. Similarly, any amounts paid to a participant under such an accident or health plan on account of disability incurred during the year of coverage may be nontaxable under section 104(a)(3).

Q-6: May employer contributions to a cafeteria plan be made pursuant to a salary reduction agreement between the participant and employer?

A-6: Yes. The term "employer contributions" means amounts that have not been actually or constructively received (after taking section 125 into account) by the participant and have been specified in the plan document as available to a participant for the purpose of selecting or "purchasing" benefits under the plan. A plan document may provide that the employer will make employer contributions, in whole or in part, pursuant to salary reduction agreements under which participants elect to reduce their compensation or to forgo increases in compensation and to have such amounts contributed, as employer contributions, by the employer on their behalf. A salary reduction agreement will have the effect of causing the amounts contributed thereunder to be treated as employer contributions under a cafeteria plan only to the extent the agreement relates to compensation that has not been actually or constructively received by the participant as of the date of the agreement (after taking section 125 into account) and, subsequently, does not become currently available to the participant. In addition, a plan document also may provide that the employer will make employer contributions on behalf of participants equal to specified amounts (or specified percentages of compensation) and that such nonelective contributions will be available to participants for the selection or purchase of benefits under the plan.

Q-7: May a cafeteria plan offer a benefit that defers the receipt of compensation?

A-7: No. A cafeteria plan does not include any plan that offers a benefit that defers the receipt of compensation, with the exception of the opportunity for participants to make elective contributions under a qualified cash or deferred arrangement defined in section 401(k). Thus, employer contributions made at a participant's election to a profit-sharing plan containing a qualified cash or deferred arrangement will be treated as nontaxable benefits under a cafeteria plan.

In addition, a cafeteria plan does not include a plan that operates in a manner that enables participants to defer the receipt of compensation. Generally, a plan that permits participants to carry over unused benefits or contributions from one plan year to a subsequent plan year operates to enable participants to defer the receipt of compensation. This is the case regardless of whether the plan permits participants to convert the unused contributions or benefits into another benefit in the subsequent plan year. For example, a plan that offers participants the opportunity to purchase vacation days (or to receive cash or other benefits under the plan in lieu of vacation days) will not be a cafeteria plan if participants who purchase the vacation days for a plan year are allowed to use any unused days in a subsequent plan year. This is the case even though the plan does not permit the participant to convert, in the subsequent plan year, the unused vacation days into any other benefit. In determining whether a plan permits participants to carry over unused vacation days, a participant will be deemed to have used his nonelective vacation days (i.e., the vacation days with respect to which the participant had no election under the plan) before his elective vacation days. For example, assume that an employer provides a participant with three weeks of vacation for a year and, under the plan, the participant is permitted to receive cash or other benefits in lieu of one of these three weeks. Assume that the participant elects not to exchange the one elective week of vacation for another benefit. If the participant uses two weeks of vacation during the year, he will be treated as having used the two nonelective weeks of vacation. Thus, if the participant is permitted to carry the one unused week over to the next year, the plan will be treated as operating to enable participants to defer the receipt of compensation. Thus, the plan will fail to be a cafeteria plan and the section 125 exception to the constructive receipt rules will not apply.

In addition, a plan that allows participants to use employer contributions for one plan year to purchase a benefit that will be provided in a subsequent plan year operates to enable participants to defer the receipt of compensation.

Q-8: What requirements apply to participants' elections under a cafeteria plan?

A-8: A plan is not a cafeteria plan unless the plan requires that participants make elections among the benefits offered under the plan. A plan may provide that elections may be made at any time. However, benefit elections under a cafeteria plan should be made in accordance with certain guidelines (see Q&A-15) in order for participants to qualify for the protections of the section 125 exception to the constructive receipt rules. An election will not be deemed to have been made if, after a participant has elected and begun to receive a benefit under the plan, the participant is permitted to revoke the election, even if the revocation relates only to that portion of the benefit that has not yet been provided to the participant. For example, a plan that permits a participant to revoke his election of coverage under a dependent care assistance program or of coverage under an accident or health plan after the period of coverage has commenced will not be a cafeteria plan. However, a cafeteria plan may permit a participant to revoke a benefit election after the period of coverage has commenced and to make a new election with respect to the remainder of the period of coverage if both the revocation and new election are on account of and consistent with a change in family status (e.g., marriage, divorce, death of spouse or child, birth or adoption of child, and termination of employment of spouse).

Q-9: What is the tax treatment of benefits offered under a nondiscriminatory cafeteria plan?

A-9: A participant in a nondiscriminatory cafeteria plan will not be treated as having received taxable benefits offered under the plan and thus will not be required to include the benefits in gross income solely because the plan offers the participants the opportunity, before the benefits become currently available to the participant, to elect to receive or not to receive the benefits. Section 125 thus provides an exception to the constructive receipt rules that apply with respect to employee elections among nontaxable and taxable benefits (including cash). These constructive receipt rules generally provide that an individual will be required to include in gross income the taxable benefits that he could have elected to receive if the individual had the opportunity to elect to receive or not to receive the benefits even though both the opportunity to make this election occurs and the actual election is made before the benefits become currently available to the individual. Section 125 does not, however, alter the application of the constructive receipt rules to a situation in which benefits become currently available to an individual even though the individual elects not to receive and does not actually receive the benefits. Thus, if taxable benefits become currently available to a participant in a nondiscriminatory cafeteria plan, the participant will be taxable on the benefits, even though the participant has elected or subsequently elects not to receive the benefits and does not actually receive the benefits.

Q-10: What is the tax treatment of benefits offered under a discriminatory cafeteria plan?

A-10: The section 125 exception to the constructive receipt rules is not available to the highly compensated participants in a cafeteria plan that is discriminatory for a plan year. Thus, a highly compensated participant in a cafeteria plan that is discriminatory for a plan year will be taxable on the combination of the taxable benefits with the greatest aggregate value that he could have selected for the plan year. The section 125 exception to the constructive receipt rules remains available to participants who are not highly compensated without regard to whether the cafeteria plan is discriminatory.

Q-11: How are the amounts taxable to a highly compensated participant because a cafeteria plan is discriminatory for a plan year to be allocated among the benefits actually selected by the participant for the plan year?

A-11: A highly compensated participant in a discriminatory cafeteria plan is taxable on the maximum taxable benefits that he could have selected for the plan year. For example, assume that a cafeteria plan provides a highly compensated participant with the opportunity to select, for a plan year, benefits costing $1300 from among the following: up to $300 in cash, coverage under an accident or health plan providing medical expense reimbursement (cost of $600), coverage under an accident or health plan providing disability benefits (cost of $200), coverage under a qualified legal services plan (cost of $400), and coverage under a dependent care assistance program (cost of $400). For the plan year in question, the participant elects to receive $100 in cash, coverage under both the accident or health plans ($600 and $200), and coverage under the dependent care assistance program ($400). If the cafeteria plan is discriminatory for the plan year, the participant will be taxable on the $100 cash benefit actually selected and on the $200 cash benefit that the participant could have selected. This $300 will be allocated, first, to the taxable benefits actually selected by the participant and, second, on a pro rata basis to the nontaxable benefits actually selected by the participant. Thus, $100 is allocated to the $100 cash benefit actually received and the $200 is allocated as employee contributions among the nontaxable benefits actually selected as follows: $100 to coverage under the accident or health plan for medical care, $33.33 to the coverage under the accident or health plan for disability benefits, and $66.67 to the coverage under the dependent care assistance program. This allocation would not affect the nontaxable status of any of these benefits—the purchase of coverage under any of these plans with employee contributions would not trigger taxable income—but it may affect the taxability of amounts received under any of the plans. In addition, depending upon whether other conditions are satisfied, the participant may be able to deduct under section 213 some or all of the employee cost of the coverage under the accident or health plan for medical care. Thus, reimbursements received by the participant for medical care expenses incurred during the year of coverage may be nontaxable under either section 104(a)(3) or section 105(b), depending upon whether the reimbursements are attributable to after-tax employee or pre-tax employer contributions. Also, if the participant became disabled during the year of coverage, benefits provided under the accident or health plan would be nontaxable to the participant under section 104(a)(3) to the extent that the benefits were attributable to the portion of the coverage purchased with the after-tax employee contributions. Finally, any reimbursements received under the dependent care assistance program for the year of coverage will be nontaxable under section 129 if the requirements of that section are satisfied.

Q-12: When must a highly compensated participant in a discriminatory cafeteria plan include in gross income amounts attributable to the taxable benefits that the participants could have selected, but did not in fact select?

A-12: Amounts required to be included in gross income by a highly compensated participant because a cafeteria plan does not satisfy the applicable nondiscrimination standards for a plan year will be treated as received or accrued in the participant's taxable year within which ends the plan year with respect to which an election was or could have been made.

Q-13: Who are highly compensated participants under section 125?

A-13: The term "highly compensated participant" means a participant who is an officer, a shareholder owning more than 5 percent of the voting power or value of all classes of stock of the employer, or highly compensated. The classification of a participant as highly compensated for this purpose will be made on the basis of the facts and circumstances of each case. A spouse or a dependent (within the meaning of section 152) of any such "highly compensated participant" will be treated as highly compensated.

Q-14: When will a benefit be treated as currently available to a participant in a cafeteria plan?

A-14: A benefit is treated as currently available to a participant if the participant is free to receive the benefit currently at his discretion or the participant could receive the benefit currently if an election or notice of an intent to receive the benefit were given. A benefit will not be treated as not currently available merely because of a requirement that the participant must elect or give notice of intent to receive the benefit in advance of receipt of the benefit. However, a benefit is not currently available to a participant if there is a substantial limitation or restriction on the participant's receipt of the benefit. A benefit will not be treated as currently available if the participant may under no circumstances receive the benefit before a particular time in the future and there is a substantial risk that, if the participant does not fulfill specified conditions during the period preceding this time, the participant will not receive the benefit.

Q-15: What procedures with respect to benefit elections should a cafeteria plan adopt in order to assure that participants are not subject to tax, under the constructive receipt rules, on taxable benefits that the participants have elected not to receive?

A-15: Generally, in order for participants to avoid constructive receipt with respect to taxable benefits offered under a cafeteria plan, the taxable benefits must at no time become currently available to the participants. Thus, a cafeteria plan should require participants to elect the specific benefits that they will receive before the taxable benefits become currently available. A benefit will not be treated as currently available as of the time of the election if the election specifies the future period for which the benefit will be provided and the election is made before the beginning of this period.

In addition, after the beginning of the specified period for which the benefits are provided, the taxable benefits must not become currently available to the participants. After the commencement of this period, taxable benefits will be treated as currently available if participants have the right to revoke their elections of nontaxable benefits and instead to receive the taxable benefits for such period, without regard to whether the participants actually revoke their elections. For example, assume that a cafeteria plan offers each participant the opportunity to elect, for a plan year, between coverage under a dependent care assistance program for up to $2000 of the dependent care expenses incurred by the participant during the plan year or a cash benefit of $2000 for the year. If the plan requires participants to elect between these benefits before the beginning of the plan year and, after the year has commenced, the participants are prohibited from revoking their elections, participants who elected coverage under the dependent care assistance program will not be taxable on the cash benefit of $2000. But if, after the beginning of the plan year, participants have the right to revoke their elections of coverage under the dependent care assistance program and thereby to receive the cash benefit, the participants will be treated as having received the $2000 in cash even though they do not revoke their elections. The same result would obtain even though the cash benefit is not payable until the end of the plan year. See Q&A-8, however, regarding the revocation of elections on account of changes in family status.

Q-16: Do the rules of section 125 affect whether any particular benefit offered under a cafeteria plan is a taxable or nontaxable benefit?

A-16: Generally, no. A benefit that is nontaxable under its Internal Revenue Code when offered separately is treated as a nontaxable benefit under a cafeteria plan only if the rules providing for the exclusion of the benefit from gross income continue to be satisfied when the benefit is offered under the cafeteria plan. For example, if $50,000 in group-term life insurance is offered under a cafeteria plan and the rules under section 79(a) governing the exclusion of the cost of this benefit from gross income are satisfied, the rules of section 79(d) still apply to determine the status of the benefit as taxable or nontaxable for key employees who participate in the plan. See Q&A-17 and Q&A-18, however, regarding the inclusion of coverage under an accident or health plan, dependent care assistance program, or qualified group legal services plan in a cafeteria plan.

Similarly, if a cafeteria plan offers benefits that are nontaxable under the Internal Revenue Code when offered outside of a cafeteria plan, but are prohibited from inclusion in a cafeteria plan, the benefits will be treated as taxable benefits under the cafeteria plan. Thus, coverage under a qualified transportation plan (section 124) and coverage under an educational assistance program (section 127) will be treated as taxable benefits if offered under a cafeteria plan. Also, any benefits (either reimbursement for expenses or in kind benefits) received by a participant under a qualified transportation plan or an educational assistance program will be taxable if the benefits are provided under a cafeteria plan.

Finally, if a benefit that is taxable under the Internal Revenue Code when offered separately is offered under a cafeteria plan, the benefit will continue to be a taxable benefit under the cafeteria plan. For example, if a cafeteria plan offers a participant the opportunity to direct the employer to make charitable contributions or contributions to an individual retirement account on behalf of the participant, such contributions must be included in the participant's gross income for income and employment tax purposes without regard to whether the plan satisfies section 125 and without regard to whether the contributions are deductible by the participant.

Q-17: How are the specific rules of section 105, providing an income exclusion for amounts received as reimbursement for medical care expenses under an accident or health plan, to be applied when coverage under an accident or health plan is offered as a benefit under a cafeteria plan?

A-17: Section 105(b) provides an exclusion from gross income for amounts that are paid to an employee under an employer-funded accident or health plan specifically to reimburse the employee for certain medical care expenses incurred by the employee during the period for which the benefit is provided to the employee, i.e., the period during which the employee is covered under the accident or health plan. Section 105(h) provides that the exclusion provided by section 105(b) is not available with respect to certain amounts received by a highly compensated individual (as defined in section 105(h)(5)) under a discriminatory self-insured medical reimbursement plan. Several rules are of particular importance when coverage under an accident or health plan is a benefit offered under a cafeteria plan.

First, in order for medical care reimbursements paid to a participant under a cafeteria plan to be treated as nontaxable under section 105(b), the reimbursements must be paid pursuant to an employer-funded "accident or health plan," as defined in section 105(e) and § 1.105-5. This means that, although the reimbursements need not be provided under a commercial insurance contract, the reimbursements must be provided under a benefit that exhibits the risk-shifting and risk-distribution characteristics of insurance. A benefit will not exhibit the required risk-shifting and risk-distribution characteristics, even though the benefit is provided under a commercial insurance contract, if the ordinary actuarial risk of the insurer is negated either under the terms of the benefit or by any related benefit or arrangement (including arrangements formally outside of the cafeteria plan).

Second, a cafeteria plan benefit under which a participant will receive reimbursements of medical expenses is a benefit within sections 106 and 105(b) only if, under the benefit, reimbursements are paid specifically to reimburse the participant for medical expenses incurred during the period of coverage. Amounts paid to a participant as reimbursement are not treated as paid specifically to reimburse the participant for medical expenses, if, under the benefit, the participant is entitled to the amounts, in the form of cash (e.g., routine payment of salary) or any other taxable or nontaxable benefit, irrespective of whether or not he incurs medical expenses during the period of coverage, even if the participant will not receive the amounts not used for expense reimbursement until the end of the period. A benefit under which participants will receive reimbursement for medical expenses up to a specified amount and, if they incur no expenses, will receive cash or any other benefit in lieu of the reimbursements is not a benefit that qualifies for the exclusions under sections 106 and 105(b). See § 1.105-2. This is the case without regard to whether the benefit was purchased with contributions made at the employer's discretion, at the participant's discretion (such as pursuant to a salary reduction agreement), or pursuant to a collective bargaining agreement. For example, if a cafeteria plan offers participants coverage under an employer-funded plan that provides for the reimbursement of medical expenses incurred during the plan year up to a specified amount (e.g., $1,000) and the participants are entitled to receive, in the form of any other taxable or nontaxable benefits (including deferrals under a cash or deferred arrangement), any portion of the specified amount that is not paid as reimbursement for medical expenses, the employer contributions used to purchase the coverage will not qualify for the section 106 exclusion and any reimbursements paid to participants for expenses incurred during the year of coverage will not be eligible for the section 105(b) exception. Arrangements formally outside of the cafeteria plan that provide for the adjustment of a participant's compensation or a participant's receipt of any other benefits on the basis of the expenses incurred or reimbursements received by the participant will be considered in determining whether the reimbursements are provided under a benefit eligible for the exclusions under sections 106 and 105(b).

Third, the medical expenses that are reimbursed under an accident or health plan must have been incurred during the period for which the participant is actually covered by the accident or health plan in order for the reimbursements to be excluded from gross income under section 105(b). For purposes of this rule, expenses are treated as having been incurred when the participant is provided with the medical care that gives rise to the medical expenses, and not when the participant is formally billed, charged for, or pays for the medical care. Also, for purposes of this rule, medical expenses that are incurred before the later of the date the plan is in existence and the date the participant is enrolled in the plan will not be treated as having been incurred during the period for which the participant is covered by the plan. Thus, in order for reimbursements to be excluded from gross income under section 105(b), the accident or health plan must provide a participant the right to reimbursement for medical expenses incurred during a specified period of plan coverage. Reimbursements of expenses incurred prior to or after the specified period of coverage will not be excluded under section 105(b). However, the actual reimbursement of covered medical care expenses may be made after the applicable period of coverage.

Fourth, in order for reimbursements under an accident or health plan to qualify for the section 105(b) exclusion, the cafeteria plan may not operate in a manner that enables participants to purchase coverage under the accident or health plan only for periods during which the participants expect to incur medical care. For example, if a cafeteria plan permits participants to purchase coverage under an accident or health plan on a month-by-month or an expense-by-expense basis, reimbursements under the accident or health plan will not qualify for the section 105(b) exclusion. If, however, the period of coverage under an accident or health plan offered in a cafeteria plan is twelve months (or, in the case of a cafeteria plan's initial plan year, at least equal to the plan year) and the plan does not permit a participant to select specific amounts of coverage, reimbursement, or salary reduction for less than twelve months, the cafeteria plan will be deemed not to operate to enable participants to purchase coverage only for periods during which medical care will be incurred. See Q&A-8 regarding the revocation of elections during a period of coverage on account of changes in family status.

Fifth, in order for reimbursements to a highly compensated individual under a self-insured accident or health plan to be treated as nontaxable under a cafeteria plan, the discrimination rules of section 105(h) must be satisfied. For purposes of these rules, coverage under a self-insured accident or health plan offered by a cafeteria plan will be treated as an optional benefit (even if only one level and type of coverage is offered) and, for purposes of the optional benefit rule in § 1.105-11(c)(3)(i), employer contributions will be treated as employee contributions to the extent that taxable benefits are offered by the plan. In addition, the accident or health plan offered by the cafeteria plan must provide for the nondiscriminatory reimbursement of expenses on a per capita basis, rather than as a proportion of compensation.

Q-18: How are the specific rules of section 129, providing an income exclusion for dependent care assistance provided under a dependent care assistance program, to be applied when coverage under a dependent care assistance program is offered as a benefit under a cafeteria plan?

A-18: Section 129(a) provides an employee with an exclusion from gross income both for employer-funded coverage under a dependent care assistance program and for amounts paid or incurred by the employer for dependent care assistance provided to the employee if the amounts are paid or incurred under a dependent care assistance program. A program under which participants receive reimbursements of dependent care expenses up to a specified amount and are entitled to receive, in the form of any other taxable or nontaxable benefits, any portion of the specified amount not used for reimbursement is to be treated as a single benefit that is not a dependent care assistance program within the scope of section 129. Thus, dependent care assistance provided under a cafeteria plan will be treated as provided under a dependent care assistance program only if, after the participant has elected coverage under the program and the period of coverage has commenced, the participant does not have the right to receive amounts under the program other than as reimbursements for dependent care expenses. This is the case without regard to whether coverage under the program was purchased with contributions made at the employer's discretion, at the participant's discretion, or pursuant to a collective bargaining agreement. For example, assume a cafeteria plan allows participants to elect to receive, for a particular plan year, either the right to reimbursements of dependent care expenses incurred during the year up to $2,000 or a cash benefit of $2,000. If the participant elects the right to receive reimbursements of dependent care expenses, the reimbursements will not be treated as made under a dependent care assistance program if, after the period of coverage has commenced, the participant has the right to revoke his election of this benefit and instead to receive the cash or if, under the terms of the program itself, the participant is entitled to receive, in the form of cash (e.g., routine payment of salary) or any other benefit, any amounts not reimbursed for dependent care provided during the period of coverage. Arrangements formally outside of the cafeteria plan that provide for the adjustment on a participant's compensation or a participant's receipt of any other benefits on the basis of the assistance or reimbursements received by the participants will be considered in determining whether a dependent care benefit is a dependent care assistance program under section 129.

Moreover, in order for dependent care assistance to be treated as provided under a dependent care assistance program eligible for the section 129 exclusion, the care must be provided to or on behalf of the participant during the period for which the participant is covered by the program. For example, if a participant elects coverage for a plan year under a dependent care assistance program that provides for the reimbursement of dependent care expenses, only reimbursements for dependent care expenses incurred during that plan year will be treated as having been provided under a dependent care assistance program within the scope of section 129. For purposes of this rule, dependent care expenses will be treated as having been incurred when the dependent care is provided, and not when the participant is formally billed, charged for, or pays for the dependent care. Also, for purposes of this rule, expenses that are incurred before the later of the date the program is in existence and the date the participant is enrolled in the program will not be treated as having been incurred during the period for which the participant is covered by the program. Similarly, if the dependent care assistance program furnishes the dependent care in kind (e.g., under an employer-maintained child care facility), only dependent care provided during the plan year of coverage will be treated as having been provided under a dependent care assistance program within scope of section 129.

In addition, in order for dependent care assistance under a cafeteria plan to be treated as provided under a dependent care assistance program eligible for the section 129 exclusion, the plan may not operate in a manner that enables participants to purchase coverage under the program only for periods during which the participants expect to receive dependent care assistance. If the period of coverage under a dependent care assistance program offered by a cafeteria plan is twelve months (or, in the case of a cafeteria plan's initial plan year, at least equal to the plan year) and the plan does not permit a participant to select specific amounts of coverage, reimbursement, or salary reduction for less than twelve months, the plan will be deemed not to operate to enable participants to purchase coverage only for periods during which dependent care assistance will be received. See Q&A-8 regarding the revocation of elections during the period of coverage on account of changes in family status.

Finally, if coverage under a dependent care assistance program is a benefit offered under a cafeteria plan, the rules of section 129 will determine the status of the benefit as a taxable or nontaxable benefit. As a result, coverage under a dependent care assistance program in a cafeteria plan will be nontaxable for a plan year only if, among other requirements, the principal shareholder and owner discrimination test contained in section 129(d)(4) is satisfied with respect to employer contributions actually used to provide participants with dependent care assistance during the plan year. In addition, amounts paid or incurred by the employer under a dependent care assistance program are excludable from gross income only to the extent that these amounts do not exceed the lesser of the participant's earned income or the participant's spouse's earned income.

Rules similar to the rules applicable to dependent care assistance program apply with respect to coverage under a qualified group legal services plan (section 120) offered as a benefit under a cafeteria plan.

Q-19: What are the rules governing whether a cafeteria plan is discriminatory?

A-19: The applicable discrimination rules under section 125 provide that, in order to be treated as nondiscriminatory for a plan year, a cafeteria plan must not discriminate in favor of highly compensated participants as to benefits and contributions for that plan year. Generally, this discrimination determination will be made on the basis of the facts and circumstances of each case. Section 125(c) provides that a cafeteria plan does not discriminate where either (i) total nontaxable benefits and total benefits or (ii) employer contributions allocable to total nontaxable benefits and employer contributions allocable to total benefits do not discriminate in favor of highly compensated participants. A cafeteria plan must satisfy section 125(c) with respect to both benefit availability and benefit selection. Thus, a plan must give each participant an equal opportunity to select nontaxable benefits, and the actual selection of nontaxable benefits under the plan must not be discriminatory, i.e., highly compensated participants do not disproportionately select nontaxable benefits while other participants select taxable benefits.

In addition to not discriminating as to either benefit availability or benefit selection, a cafeteria plan must not discriminate in favor of highly compensated participants in actual operation. A plan may be discriminatory in actual operation if the duration of the plan (or of a particular nontaxable benefit offered under the plan) coincides with the period during which highly compensated participants utilize the plan (or the benefit).

Q-20: May nontaxable benefits provided under a cafeteria plan be counted as "compensation" under section 401(a)(5) for purposes of determining whether a qualified pension, profit-sharing, or stock bonus plan discriminates under section 401(a)(4), or under section 415 for purposes of the limitations contained in that section?

A-20: A qualified pension, profit-sharing, or stock bonus plan will not be treated as discriminatory within the meaning of section 401(a)(4) merely because, for purposes of allocating contributions to the participant or calculating the participant's benefit under the plan, the plan considers nontaxable benefits provided to a participant as compensation. For example, if a participant in a cafeteria plan elects coverage under an accident or health plan, the value of such coverage may be considered as compensation under a qualified plan for purposes of calculating the participant's allocation or benefit under the qualified plan. Nontaxable reimbursements under the accident or health plan, however, generally may not be treated as compensation under a qualified plan. Similarly, the value of coverage under a dependent care assistance program may be counted as compensation under a qualified plan for allocation and benefit purposes, but nontaxable reimbursements of dependent care expenses under the program generally may not be treated as compensation for these purposes. On the other hand, a qualified plan will not be treated as discriminatory under section 401(a)(4) merely because the plan does not consider nontaxable benefits, such as coverage under an accident or health plan or coverage under a dependent care assistance program, as compensation for allocation or benefit purposes under the plan.

For purposes of section 415, "compensation" does not include amounts that are excluded from gross income, such as premiums for group-term life insurance under section 79 or employer contributions to an accident or health plan excluded under section 106.

→**Caution: Q&A-21 have been replaced by a new Q&A-21 in proposed regulations at ¶ 20,137R.←**

Q-21: What are the effective dates of the rules contained in these questions and answers?

A-21: These rules contained in questions and answers relating to section 125 generally shall apply to plan years of cafeteria plans beginning after December 31, 1978. However, a cafeteria plan that failed to satisfy one or more of the following rules for plan years beginning before May 7, 1984 will not be deemed thereby to have failed to satisfy section 125 for such plan years if, by September 4, 1984, the plan is amended to operate in accordance with these rules: (i) the rules requiring certain information to be included in the cafeteria plan document (Q&A-3), (ii) the rules governing the active participation of a participant's spouse in a cafeteria plan (Q&A-4), (iii) only in the case of a plan under which participants were permitted neither to carry over unused benefits for more than one plan year nor to convert, into any other benefits, any unused benefits that had been carried over to a subsequent plan year, the rules prohibiting the carryover of any unused contribution or benefit from one plan year to a subsequent plan year (Q&A-7), and (iv) the rules limiting the revocability of benefit elections (Q&A-8). A cafeteria plan may treat the portion of its current plan year remaining after September 4, 1984 as a new period of coverage for purposes of satisfying the rules governing benefit elections (Q&A-8). Also, a benefit offering participants the opportunity to make elective contributions under a qualified cash or deferred arrangement may be included in a cafeteria plan only in plan years beginning after December 31, 1980.

The rules contained in Q&A-17 governing the taxability of coverage and benefits under an accident or health plan relate specifically to sections 105 and 106 and thus generally are effective with respect to all taxable years beginning after December 31, 1953. The rules contained in Q&A-18 governing the taxability of coverage and benefits under a dependent care assistance program relate specifically to section 129 and thus generally are effective with respect to all taxable years beginning after December 31, 1981. The rules contained in Q&A-18 governing the taxability of coverage and benefits under a qualified group legal services plan relate specifically to section 120 and thus generally are effective with respect to all taxable years beginning after December 31, 1976. However, if coverage under an accident or health plan, dependent care assistance program, or qualified group legal services plan was offered as a benefit under a cafeteria plan and such benefit failed to satisfy, before May 7, 1984, the rule prohibiting a plan from operating to enable a participant to elect coverage under an accident or health plan, a dependent care assistance program, or a qualified group legal services plan only for periods during which the participant expects to receive medical care, dependent care, or legal services (Q&A-17 and Q&A-18), such benefit will not be deemed solely on account of such failure to have failed to satisfy the statutory rules providing for the income exclusion of such coverage or of any benefits provided thereunder, if, by September 4, 1984, the cafeteria plan is amended to operate in accordance with such election of coverage rule. A cafeteria plan may treat the portion of its current plan year remaining after September 4, 1984 as a new period of coverage and as an initial plan year for purposes of satisfying the rule prohibiting a plan from operating to enable participants to elect coverage under an accident or health plan, dependent care assistance program, or qualified group legal services plan only for periods during which they expect to receive medical care, dependent care, or legal services (Q&A-17 and Q&A-18).

In addition, if the conditions set forth below are satisfied, employer contributions (including elective and nonelective contributions) made before June 1, 1984, under an arrangement described in the next sentence which is part of a cafeteria plan, will not be treated as having been made to an accident or health plan, dependent care assistance program, or qualified group legal services plan that fails to satisfy the rules contained in the second and third paragraphs of Q&A-17 and the first paragraph of Q&A-18, merely because, for a plan year, a participant was entitled to receive, in the form of cash or any other taxable or nontaxable benefit, amounts available for reimbursement under the arrangement without regard to whether covered expenses are incurred. An arrangement is described in this sentence only if, under the arrangement,

(i)   An account was actually established on behalf of the participant by the employer, by an entry on the employer's books or in similar fashion, prior to the beginning of the plan year (or prior to the date on which an individual first becomes eligible to participate under the arrangement in the case of an individual who first becomes eligible to participate, on account of years of employment, during the plan year);

(ii)   The amount (or specific rate) of contributions to the account under the arrangement was fixed prior to the beginning of the plan year;

(iii) Neither the participant nor the employer possessed the right to increase or decrease contributions to the account during the plan year (but a plan may provide that contributions could be terminated during the year on account of the participant's (a) separation from service or (b) cessation of participation under the arrangement for the remainder of the plan year);

(iv) Contributions were actually deposited in or credited to the account before being made available for reimbursement; and

(v)   Distributions were not available for reasons other than reimbursement of covered expenses until the end of the plan year (but a plan may provide that a single distribution of the unreimbursed balance may be made on account of the participant's (a) separation from service or (b) cessation of participation under the arrangement for the remainder of the plan year).

A cafeteria plan may operate on a plan year other than the calendar year for purposes of this transitional rule, so long as terms of the plan permit contributions to a plan to be fixed only once during, and a distribution of the unreimbursed amount to be received, only once for any plan year, provided that contributions may be fixed for a short plan year of the plan's first period of operation. This transitional rule does not affect or alter the requirement of Q&A-17 and -18 that expenses that are reimbursed under an arrangement must have been incurred during the period for which the participant actually is covered by the arrangement.

Roscoe L. Egger, Jr.,
Commissioner of Internal Revenue.
[FR Doc. 84-12263 Filed 5-2-84; 2:49 pm]

(3)   AMENDMENTS TO PROPOSED REGULATIONS ON CAFETERIA PLANS

[¶ 8957]

Proposed Regulations (EE-16-79), published in the Federal Register on December 26, 1984.

Employee benefits: Cafeteria plans.—Amendments of proposed Reg. § 1.125-1, relating to the tax treatment of cafeteria plans, have been proposed. Back reference: ¶ 1197S.

AGENCY: Internal Revenue Service, Treasury.

ACTION: Amendment of notice of proposed rulemaking.

SUMMARY: This document contains proposed amendments to a notice of proposed rulemaking which was published in the Federal Register on May 7, 1984 (49 F.R. 19321). That notice contained proposed regulations relating to the tax treatment of cafeteria plans. Changes to the applicable tax law necessitating the proposed amendments were made by section 531(b)(5) of the Tax Reform Act of 1984. The proposed amendments relate to general and special transition relief under the proposed regulations and provide the public with the guidance needed to comply with that Act.

DATES: Written comments and requests for a public hearing must be delivered or mailed by January 30, 1985. The proposed regulations are generally to be effective for plan years beginning after December 31, 1978, but are subject to the general and special transition rules.

ADDRESS: Send comments and requests for a public hearing to: Commissioner of Internal Revenue, Attention: CC:LR:T (EE-16-79), Washington, D.C. 20224.

FOR FURTHER INFORMATION CONTACT:

Harry Beker of the Employee Plans and Exempt Organizations Division, Office of the Chief Counsel, Internal Revenue Service, 1111 Constitution Avenue, N.W., Washington, D.C. 20224 (Attention: CC:EE)(202-566-6212)(not a toll-free call).

SUPPLEMENTAL INFORMATION:

Background

This document contains proposed amendments to the notice of proposed rulemaking under section 125 of the Internal Revenue Code of 1954. On May 7, 1984, the Federal Register published proposed regulations relating to the tax treatment of cafeteria plans (49 FR 19321). The regulations in this document are being proposed in order to replace portions of those earlier proposed regulations which have been rendered obsolete by section 531(b)(5) of the Tax Reform Act of 1984 (98 Stat. 494). The proposed regulations are issued under the authority contained in section 7805 of the Internal Revenue Code of 1954 (68A Stat. 917, 26 U.S.C. 7805).

On February 10, 1984, the Internal Revenue Service issued a news release (IR-84-22) which stated that so-called "flexible spending arrangements" do not provide employees with nontaxable benefits under the Code because, under such arrangements, employees are assured of receiving the benefit of what they would have received had no covered expenses been incurred.

On May 7, 1984, proposed regulations in question and answer form were published in the Federal Register. Q&A-21 provided that the proposed regulations were generally to be effective for cafeteria plan years beginning after December 31, 1978. However, as to particular rules in the proposed regulations, a cafeteria plan could be amended by September 4, 1984, to meet those particular rules and thus the requirements of the proposed regulations. In addition, as to benefits provided under a flexible spending arrangement which was part of a cafeteria plan, if such arrangement met specified conditions, the benefits (funded by employer contributions made before June 1, 1984) qualified for the statutory exclusion notwithstanding that a cash-out of unused contributions was available at the end of the plan year.

General Rules

The Tax Reform Act of 1984 renders Q&A-21 obsolete and provides both general and special transition relief from certain of the rules in the proposed regulations for certain cafeteria plans and flexible spending arrangements. First, as to plans and arrangements which were in existence on or before February 10, 1984 (or for which substantial implementation costs had been incurred before such date) and which failed on or before such date and continued to fail thereafter to satisfy the proposed regulations, general transition relief is provided until January 1, 1985, provided that the plans or arrangements are not modified after February 10, 1984, to allow additional benefits.

Second, as to flexible spending arrangements which qualify for general transition relief through December 31, 1984, under which an employee must fix the amount of contributions before the beginning of the period of coverage and under which unused contributions generally are not available to the employee before July 1, 1985, special transition relief is available until July 1, 1985, provided there are no modifications after December 31, 1984, which allow for additional benefits.

Section 7805(b) Relief for Amended and Suspended Plans and Benefits

Section 531(b)(5)(A) of the Tax Reform Act grants general transition relief only to cafeteria plans and benefits (including benefits that are provided through flexible spending arrangements) that failed on or before February 10, 1984, and "continued to fail thereafter" to satisfy the rules in the proposed regulations. In addition, general transition relief is available only until the effective date, after February 10, 1984, "of any modification to provide additional benefits."

A plan or benefit that has been modified (by amendment or otherwise) after February 10, 1984, so that the plan or benefit no longer continues to fail one or more of the rules of the proposed regulations (a "conforming modification") does not "continue to fail thereafter" and therefore does not meet the requirement of the statute for continued general transition relief with respect to the rule or rules in question. For example, if contributions or reimbursements (or both) under a flexible spending arrangement have been suspended, the benefit provided through the flexible spending arrangement does not satisfy the statute for continued relief. Furthermore, a modification to restore a plan or benefit to its condition before a conforming modification (e.g., a reactivation of contributions or reimbursements or both under a suspended flexible spending arrangement) would be a "modification to provide additional benefits." Therefore, as to a plan or benefit which, after February 10, 1984, was modified so that it no longer failed to satisfy one or more of the rules in the proposed regulations, general transition relief is available only until the effective date of the modification but not thereafter with respect to the rule or rules in question. These statutory requirements are reflected in Q&A-25.

The Internal Revenue Service has determined, however, that participants in plans or benefits that were modified, after February 10, 1984, so that they no longer fail to satisfy one or more of the rules in the proposed regulations should not be disadvantaged because of such conforming modifications. In order to limit any adverse effect upon those participants, the Internal Revenue Service has determined to grant such plans and benefits relief under section 7805(b) of the Internal Revenue Code (See Q&A-26). Accordingly, the rules delineated in Q&A-27 generally do not become effective with respect to such plans or benefits until January 1, 1985.

Pursuant to the grant of section 7805(b) relief, a plan or benefit that has been modified, after February 10, 1984, so that it no longer fails to satisfy one or more of the rules in the proposed regulations may be further modified and continue in operation until December 31, 1984, but only under the same terms that applied immediately before the conforming modification. However, because such modified plans or benefits do not qualify for general transition relief through December 31, 1984, special transition relief is not available to such plans or benefits.

In addition, pursuant to the grant of section 7805(b) relief, certain relief is available, as set forth in Q&A-29, for cafeteria plans or benefits that were eligible for transition relief under the regulations proposed on May 7, 1984, but are not eligible for general transition relief under Q&A-25.

Nonapplicability of Executive Order 12291

The Treasury Department has determined that this Regulation is not subject to review under Executive Order 12291 or the Treasury and Office of Management and Budget implementation of the Order dated April 29, 1983.

Regulatory Flexibility Act

Although this document is a notice of proposed rulemaking which solicits public comment, the Internal Revenue Service has concluded that the regulations proposed herein are interpretative and that the notice and public procedure requirements of 5 U.S.C. 533 do not apply. Accordingly, these proposed regulations do not constitute regulations subject to the Regulatory Flexibility Act (5 U.S.C. chapter 6).

Comments and Request for A Public Hearing

Before adopting these proposed regulations, consideration will be given to any written comments that are submitted (preferably seven copies) to the

Commissioner of Internal Revenue. All comments will be available for public inspection and copying. A public hearing will be held upon request to the Commissioner by any person who has submitted written comments. If a public hearing is held, notice of the time and place will be published in the Federal Register.

Drafting Information

The principal author of these proposed regulations is Harry Beker of the Employee Plans and Exempt Organizations Division of the Office of Chief Counsel, Internal Revenue Service. However, personnel from other offices of the Internal Revenue Service and Treasury Department participated in developing the regulations, both on matters of substance and style.

List of Subjects in 26 CFR §§ 1.61-1—1.281-4

Income Taxes, Taxable income.

Proposed amendments to the regulations

The proposed amendments to 26 CFR Part 1 are as follows:

Paragraph 1. Q&A-21 of proposed § 1.125-1 as published in the Federal Register on May 7, 1984 (43 FR 19328-19329) is removed.

Par. 2. New Qs & As of proposed § 1.125-1 are substituted to read as follows: [Reproduced at ¶ 1197S.]

(4) PROPOSED REGULATIONS ON SECTION 401(k)

¶ 20,142C

Proposed regulations—Qualified cash or deferred arrangements— Contributions made by employers to cash or deferred arrangements at an employee's election—Deferral of taxation.—Reproduced below is the text of proposed regulations relating to amounts that employees elect to defer under qualified cash or deferred arrangements. The proposed regulations were published in the Federal Register on November 10, 1981 (46 FR 55544).

Back reference: ¶ 2437A.

26 CFR Part 1
[EE-169-78]
Certain Cash or Deferred Arrangements Under Employee Plans

AGENCY: Internal Revenue Service, Treasury.

ACTION: Notice of proposed rulemaking.

SUMMARY: This document contains proposed regulations relating to certain cash or deferred arrangements under employee plans. Changes in the applicable tax law were made by the Revenue Act of 1978. The regulations would provide the public with the guidance needed to comply with the Act and would affect employees who are entitled to make elections under certain cash or deferred arrangements.

DATES: Written comments and requests for a public hearing must be delivered or mailed by January 11, 1982. The amendments are generally proposed to be effective for plan years beginning after December 31, 1979.

ADDRESS: Send comments and requests for a public hearing to: Commissioner of Internal Revenue, Attention: CC:LR:T, Washington, D.C. 20224.

FOR FURTHER INFORMATION CONTACT:

Charles M. Watkins of the Employee Plans and Exempt Organizations Division, Office of the Chief Counsel, Internal Revenue Service, 1111 Constitution Avenue, N. W., Washington, D.C. 20224 (Attention: CC:EE)(202-566-3430)(not a toll-free number).

SUPPLEMENTARY INFORMATION:

Background

This document contains proposed amendments to the Income Tax Regulations (26 CFR Part 1) under section 401(k) and section 402(a)(8) of the Internal Revenue Code of 1954. These amendments are proposed to conform the regulations to section 135 of the Revenue Act of 1978 (92 Stat. 2785) and are to be issued under the authority contained in section 7805 of the Internal Revenue Code of 1954 (68A Stat. 917; 26 U. S. C. 7805).

History

Prior to 1972, the Internal Revenue Service treatment of tax-qualified plans where employees had the option of receiving direct cash payments or having employers contribute an equal amount to the plans was illustrated in Revenue Ruling 56-497 (1956-2 C. B. 284), Revenue Ruling 63-180 (1963-2 C. B. 189), and Revenue Ruling 68-89 (1968-1 C. B. 402). Generally, employer contributions to these plans were not considered constructively received by the employees. Therefore, employees were not presently taxed on these contributions. If the plans met the other requirements for qualification, and if the cash or deferred arrangements with respect to the contributions made to the trusts forming part of the plans met the enumerated tests of these rulings, they would be considered qualified.

On December 6, 1972, the Internal Revenue Service issued proposed regulations which called into question the tax treatment of contributions made at the direction of employees under cash or deferred arrangements to these qualified plans. In order for Congress to have time to study this area, section 2006 of the Employee Retirement Income Security Act of 1974 (Pub. L. 93-406, 88 Stat. 992)("ERISA") was enacted. That section provided that for those qualified plans in existence on or before June 27, 1974, the three above-mentioned revenue rulings would be controlling through December 31, 1976. Further, for plans coming into existence after June 27, 1974, contributions made at the direction of employees under cash or deferred arrangements were considered employee contributions and thus were presently taxable to the employee.

The status-quo treatment of ERISA section 2006 was extended through December 31, 1979, by section 1506 of the Tax Reform Act of 1976 (Pub. L. 94-455, 90 Stat. 1739) and by section 5 of the Foreign Earned Income Act of 1978 (Pub. L. 95-615, 92 Stat. 3097).

New Law—In General

For plan years beginning after December 31, 1979, section 135 of the Revenue Act of 1978 (Pub. L. 95-600, 92 Stat. 2785) provides two new rules relating to amounts that employees elect to defer under qualified cash or deferred arrangements.

First, the section specifically provides that if amounts deferred at an employee's election meet certain requirements relating to nonforfeitability and withdrawal, the deferred amounts will not be treated as made available to the employee or as employee contributions to the plan. The nonforfeitability requirement provides that amounts deferred under the arrangement, and the earnings on those amounts, must be nonforfeitable. The withdrawal limitation requires that no amounts may be distributed earlier than death, disability, retirement, separation from service, the attainment of age $59^{1}/_{2}$ or upon a finding of hardship. In service distributions or withdrawals by reason of the completion of a stated period of participation or the lapse of a fixed number of years are prohibited.

Second, the new section adds detailed, mechanical antidiscrimination rules for cash or deferred arrangements. Under these rules, both the eligibility requirements in section 410(b)(1) and the antidiscrimination requirements in section 401(a)(4) are satisfied with respect to those eligible employees who actually participate if the class of employees eligible to elect deferrals under the arrangement satisfies one of the tests in section 410(b)(1) and the ratios of the amounts deferred, as a percentage of compensation, by eligible employees are within the two standards enumerated in new Code section 401(k).

In general, the two deferral ratio tests involve a comparison of the amounts deferred by the highest paid one-third of eligible employees, as a percentage of compensation, to the amounts deferred by the remainder of the eligible employees.

Under one standard, the antidiscrimination requirement is satisfied if the average deferral by the highest paid one-third is not more than 1.5 times the average deferral by the other employees. For example, if lower paid employees elected to defer an average of 10 percent of their compensation, this standard would be satisfied if the highest paid one-third deferred an average of not more than 15 percent of their compensation.

The second standard involves a comparison of average deferral percentages in two steps. First, the average deferral for the highest paid one-third may not be more than three percentage points greater than the average deferral by the remainder of employees. Second, the average deferral for the highly paid cannot be more than 2.5 times the average deferral of the remainder of employees. For example, if the lower paid employees elected to defer an average of two percent of their compensation, then the second standard would be satisfied if the highest paid employees elected to defer an average of five percent of pay since (A) five percent is not more than three percentage points greater than two percent, and (B) five percent is not greater than 2.5 times the average deferral of the lower paid.

For purposes of determining these average deferral percentages, only those deferred amounts which satisfy the nonforfeitability and withdrawal rules applied under the qualified cash or deferred arrangement definition may be taken into account. Employer contributions under the Federal Insurance Contribution Act may not be taken into account for purposes of determining the deferral percentages.

Fail Safe Device

Neither the Revenue Act of 1978 nor the legislative history of the provision which became section 135 of that Act (H. R. Rep. No. 95-1445, 95th Cong., 2d Sess. 65 (1978); S. Rep. No. 95-1263, 95th Cong., 2d Sess. 76 (1978); H. R. Rep. No. 95-1800, 95th Cong., 2d Sess. 206 (1978)) require a provision for fail-safe devices or other mechanisms that will assure compliance with the antidiscrimination requirements applied to qualified cash or deferred arrangements. However, the proposed regulations incorporate a special rule which recognizes the need for an administrable and automatic procedure that satisfies the new requirements.

This rule allows employer contributions which were not subject to any employee election to be used in satisfying the deferral percentage tests. However, in order to be consistent with the principles of the cash or deferred provisions, only employer contributions which satisfy the nonforfeitability and withdrawal limitations applied to elect deferrals may be used in computing the percentage. This rule enables a plan sponsor to assure that one of the antidiscrimination tests always is satisfied. For example, if an employer contributes 5 percent of compensation of each eligible employee to a plan and also allows each eligible employee to elect to defer all or part of an additional 2.5 percent of compensation, then, assuming the classification of eligible employees satisfies section 410(b)(1) and all employer contributions satisfy the nonforfeitability and withdrawal requirements, the plan will always satisfy the antidiscrimination standard because even if all of the highest paid one-third elect deferral and all of the remainder of employees elect current cash, the average deferrals for the high paid (7.5 percent) cannot be more than 1.5 times the average deferrals for the other employees (5 percent).

Comments are requested as to any additional fail-safe devices that plans could utilize to satisfy the nondiscrimination requirements.

Scope of Deferral Rules

While the proposed regulations allow employer contributions made without an employee's election to be included in computing the deferral percentages, this device may not be used to circumvent the basic antidiscrimination rules applied to qualified profit sharing and stock bonus plans. Thus, the proposed regulations prohibit any arrangement attempting to take advantage of the mechanical antidiscrimination tests in section 401(k)(3) from providing a discriminatory level of contributions. For example, a plan could not use the antidiscrimination tests to provide a contribution, without election, equal to 10 percent of the compensation of rank and file employees while providing a contribution of 15 percent of compensation to the highly paid employees.

The proposed regulations indicate that an important element of a qualified cash or deferred arrangement is the total amount subject to deferral. Thus, as long as the total amount subject to deferral is nondiscriminatory, the plan will be allowed to apply the mechanical antidiscrimination tests. For example, a plan provides that the highly paid one-third may elect to have all or a portion of 15 percent of their compensation paid in cash or deferred. The plan also provides that the remainder of employees will have 10 percent of their compensation contributed without being subject to an election, and that an additional five percent will be subject to the cash or deferred election. If the 10 percent contributed on behalf of the lower paid employees satisfies the nonforfeitability and withdrawal rules applied to elected deferrals, the plan will satisfy the antidiscrimination tests in section 401(k)(3) and will not be deemed to be discriminatory merely because of the difference in the amounts subject to the election.

Finally, the proposed regulations provide that the antidiscrimination tests, which are effectively safe harbors, apply only to amounts which satisfy the nonforfeitability and withdrawal requirements for elected deferrals. For example, additional employer contributions which "match" amounts used in computing deferral percentages but which are not fully vested and subject to withdrawal limitations would not be entitled to protection under the antidiscrimination tests in section 401(k)(3).

Salary Reduction

The proposed regulations specifically recognize that a qualified cash or deferred arrangement may be in the form of a salary reduction agreement. Under such an agreement an employee could elect, for example, to reduce his or her current compensation or to forgo an increase in compensation, and to have the forgone amounts contributed to the plan on his or her behalf.

Failure to Satisfy Requirements

The consequences of not satisfying the new requirements include the present inclusion of employer contributions deferred at the employee's election under the cash or deferred arrangement in the income of the employee, even if the rest of the plan remains qualified. Also, the special nondiscrimination rules may not be used if the other new requirements are not satisfied.

Regulatory Flexibility Act

Although this document is a notice of proposed rulemaking which solicits public comment, the Internal Revenue Service has concluded that the regulations proposed herein are interpretative and that the notice and public procedure requirements of 5 U. S. C. 553 do not apply. Accordingly, these proposed regulations do not constitute regulations subject to the Regulatory Flexibility Act (5 U. S. C. chapter 6).

Comments and Requests for a Public Hearing

Before adopting these proposed regulations, consideration will be given to any written comments that are submitted (preferably six copies) to the Commissioner of Internal Revenue. All comments will be available for public inspection and copying. A public hearing will be held upon written request to the Commissioner by any person who has submitted written comments. If a public hearing is held, notice of the time and place will be published in the *Federal Register*.

Drafting Information

The principal author of these proposed regulations was Leonard S. Hirsh of the Employee Plans and Exempt Organizations Division of the Office of the Chief Counsel, Internal Revenue Service. However, personnel from other offices of the Internal Revenue Service and Treasury Department participated in developing the regulation, both on matters of substance and style.

Proposed Amendments to the Regulations

The proposed amendments to 26 CFR Part 1 are as follows:

PART 1—INCOME TAX; TAXABLE YEARS BEGINNING AFTER DECEMBER 31, 1953

Paragraph 1. The following new § 1.401(k)-1 is added immediately after § 1.401(j)-6:

§ 1.401(k)-1 Certain cash or deferred arrangements.

(a) *In general.*

(1) *General rule.* Any profit-sharing or stock bonus plan shall not fail to satisfy the requirements of section 401(a) merely because the plan includes a qualified cash or deferred arrangement. For purposes of this section, a cash or deferred arrangement is any arrangement which is part of a profit-sharing or stock bonus plan under which an eligible employee may elect to have the employer contribute an amount to a trust under the plan or to have the amount paid to the employee in cash. The arrangement may also be in the form of a salary reduction agreement between an eligible employee and the employer

under which a contribution will be made only if the employee elects to reduce his compensation or to forgo an increase in his compensation. The eligible employee may be given the option under the arrangement to have a portion of the amount that is subject to the election contributed to a trust under the plan and a portion of the amount paid to the eligible employee in cash. The plan of which the arrangement is a part may provide for contributions, both employer and employee, other than those subject to the election.

(2) *Treatment of contributions under the qualified arrangement.* Employer contributions to a plan under a qualified cash or deferred arrangement are not includible in the employee's gross income; see § 1.402(a)-1(d).

(3) *Nonqualified arrangement.* A profit-sharing or stock bonus plan that includes a cash or deferred arrangement that is not qualified may, nevertheless, be a qualified plan under section 401(a). Even if the plan satisfies the requirements of section 401(a), contributions to the plan made at the election of the employee for the plan year are includible in the employee's gross income; see § 1.402(a)-1(d).

(4) *Qualified arrangement.* A qualified cash or deferred arrangement is an arrangement which is part of a plan satisfying the requirements of section 401(a) and the additional requirements set forth in paragraphs (b), (c) and (d) of this section.

(b) *Coverage and discrimination requirements —*

(1) *Arrangement alone.* This paragraph applies if a plan consists only of elective contributions. This plan shall satisfy this paragraph for a plan year if the plan satisfies either the general rules in paragraph (b)(3) or the special rules in paragraph (b)(4) of this section, for such plan year.

(2) *Combined plan.* This subparagraph applies if a plan consists of both elective contributions and non-elective contributions. This plan shall satisfy this paragraph if it satisfies either paragraph (b)(2)(i), (ii), or (iii) of this section.

(i)   The combined elective and non-elective portions of the plan satisfy the general rules in paragraph (b)(3) of this section.

(ii)   The non-elective portion of the plan satisfies the general rules in paragraph (b)(3) of this section and the elective portion of the plan satisfies the special rules in paragraph (b)(4) of this section.

(iii) The non-elective portion of the plan satisfies the general rules in paragraph (b)(3) of this section and the combined elective and non-elective portions of the plan satisfy the special rules in paragraph (b)(4) of this section.

(iv)   In applying the test in paragraph (b)(2)(iii) of this section the non-elective portion of the plan may only be considered in applying the special rules to the extent that such contributions satisfy the requirements in paragraphs (c) and (d) of this section.

(3) *General cash or deferred discrimination rules.* A plan (or portion of a plan) will satisfy these rules if it satisfies the requirements of section 410(b)(1) and section 401(a)(4). In testing whether the requirements of section 410(b)(1) are satisfied, the employees who benefit from the plan may be

either (i) the eligible employees or (ii) the covered employees. In testing for discrimination under section 401(a)(4), the eligible or covered employees will be considered depending on the group used to satisfy section 410(b)(1).

(4) *Special cash or deferred discrimination rules.* A plan (or portion of a plan) will satisfy these rules if the eligible employees satisfy section 410(b)(1) and the contributions satisfy one of the alternative actual deferral percentage tests in paragraph (5). For purposes of this subparagraph, in applying section 410(b)(1), all eligible employees are considered to benefit from the plan.

(5) *Actual deferral percentage test.*

(i) The actual deferral percentage test is satisfied if either of the tests specified in paragraph (b)(5)(ii) or (iii) of this section is satisfied.

(ii) The actual deferral percentage for the eligible highly compensated employees (top $1/3$) is not more than the actual deferral percentage of all other eligible employees (lower $2/3$) multiplied by 1.5.

(iii) The excess of the actual deferral percentage for the top $1/3$ over the lower $2/3$ is not more than three percentage points, and the actual deferral percentage for the top $1/3$ is not more than the actual deferral percentage of the lower $2/3$ multiplied by 2.5.

(6) *Nondiscriminatory deferrals.* A plan will not satisfy this paragraph unless the total amounts subject to deferral on behalf of both the higher and lower paid employees is nondiscriminatory.

(7) *Time when contributions credited.* For purposes of applying the discrimination rules in paragraphs (b)(3) and (4) of this section for a particular plan year, a contribution will be considered for that plan year if it is allocated to the participant's account under the terms of the plan as of any date within that plan year. A contribution may be considered allocated as of any date within a plan year only if—

(i) Such allocation is not dependent upon participation in the plan as of any date subsequent to that date,

(ii) The non-elective contribution is actually made to the plan no later than the end of the period described in section 404(a)(6) applicable to the taxable year with or within which the particular plan year ends, and

(iii) The elective contribution is actually made to the plan no later than 30 days after the end of the plan year.

(8) *Definitions.* For purposes of this section the following definition shall apply:

(i) *Eligible employee.* In any year, eligible employees are those employees who are eligible for employer contributions under the plan for that year.

(ii) *Covered employee.* In any year, covered employees are those employees whose accounts are credited with a contribution under the plan for that year.

(iii) *Non-elective contribution.* Non-elective contributions are those which were not subject to the cash or deferred election.

(iv) *Elective contribution.* Elective contributions are those which were subject to the cash or deferred election and which were deferred.

(v) *Actual deferral percentage.* The actual deferral percentage for the top $1/3$ and lower $2/3$ for a plan year is the average of the ratios, calculated separately for each employee in such group, of the amount of employer contributions paid under the plan on behalf of each such employee for such plan year, to the employee's compensation for such plan year.

(vi) *Employee compensation.* An employee's compensation is the amount taken into account under the plan prior to calculating the contribution made on behalf of the employee under the deferral election. However, if such amount has the effect of discriminating against the lower $2/3$, a nondiscriminatory definition shall be determined by the Commissioner. It is permissible for a plan to calculate plan compensation other than on a plan year basis if it is calculated on a reasonable and consistent basis.

(vii) *Highly compensated employee.* For purposes of the actual deferral percentage test, a highly compensated employee is any eligible employee who receives, with respect to the compensation taken into account for that plan year, more compensation than two-thirds of all other eligible employees. Both $1/3$ and $2/3$ of all the eligible employees shall be rounded to the nearest integer.

(9) *Examples.* The provisions of this paragraph are illustrated by the following examples:

Example (1). (i) Employees A, B, and C are the eligible employees and earn $30,000, $15,000 and $10,000 a year respectively. These salary figures are used by the employer in determining contributions up to 10% of compensation to a profit-sharing plan under a qualified cash or deferred arrangement. Under the arrangement, each eligible employee may elect either to receive, in whole or in part, a direct cash payment of his allocated contribution, or to have the amount contributed by the employer to the plan. For a plan year A, B, and C make the following elections:

Employee	Compensation	Elected contribution to plan	Cash election
A	$30,000	$2,000	$1,000
B	15,000	750	750
C	10,000	400	600

(ii) The ratios of employer contributions to the trust on behalf of each eligible employee to the employee's compensation for the plan year (calculated separately for each employee) are:

Employee	Ratio of contribution to compensation	Individual's actual deferral percentage
A	2,000/30,000	6.7
B	750/15,000	5
C	400/10,000	4

(iii) The actual deferral percentage for the top $1/3$ is 6.7 percent (2,000/30,000), and the actual deferral percentage for the lower $2/3$ is 4.5 percent

$$\frac{5\% + 4\%}{2}$$

Because 6.7 percent is less than 6.75 percent (4.5 percent multiplied by 1.5) the first percentage test is satisfied.

Example (2). (i) Employees 1 thru 9 are the eligible employees who earn compensation as indicated in the table below. Employer A contributes to a profit-sharing plan. Employer A makes elective contributions as well as non-elective contributions. Under the plan Employer A contributes on behalf of each employee a non-elective contribution equal to three percent of compensation. Under the cash or deferred arrangement, each employee may elect either to receive up to six percent of compensation as a direct cash payment or to have that amount contributed by Employer A to the plan. For a plan year employees 1 thru 9 make the following elections:

Employee	Compensation	Nonelective contribution to plan	Elective contribution elected to be deferred under cash or deferred arrangement
1	$100,000	$3,000	$6,000
2	80,000	2,400	4,800
3	60,000	1,800	3,600
4	40,000	1,200	1,200
5	30,000	900	900
6	20,000	600	600
7	20,000	600	600
8	10,000	300	300
9	5,000	150	150

(ii) For the plan year under the cash or deferred arrangement the ratios of Employer A's contributions on behalf of each employee to the employee's compensation are:

Employee	Ratio of elective contribution to compensation	Individual's actual deferral percentage
1	6,000/100,000	6
2	4,800/80,000	6
3	3,600/60,000	6
4	1,200/40,000	3
5	900/30,000	3
6	600/20,000	3
7	600/20,000	3
8	300/10,000	3
9	150/5,000	3

(iii) The actual deferral percentage for the top $1/3$ (1, 2, 3) is 6% and the actual deferral percentage for the lower $2/3$ (4 thru 9) is 3%. Because

6% is greater than 4.5% (3% multiplied by 1.5), the first percentage test is not satisfied. However, because 6% is not more than 3 percentage points greater than 3% and 6% is less than 7.5% (3% × 2.5), the second percentage test is satisfied.

Example (3). Employer B has a qualified profit-sharing plan which includes a qualified cash or deferred arrangement. The qualified cash or deferred arrangement in operation produces an actual deferral percentage for the top 1/3 of 5%. The actual deferral percentage for the lower 2/3 is 2%. This arrangement does not satisfy the first percentage test because 5% is greater than 3% (2% multiplied by 1.5). However, this arrangement does satisfy the second percentage test because the actual deferral percentage for the top 1/3 is not more than 3 percentage points in excess of the actual deferral percentage for the lower 2/3 (5% − 2%) and 5% is not greater than 5% (2% multiplied by 2.5).

Example (4). Employer C has a stock bonus plan which includes a qualified cash or deferred arrangement. The cash or deferred arrangement in operation produces an actual deferral percentage for the top 1/3 of 12%. The actual deferral percentage for the lower 2/3 is 8%. This arrangement does not satisfy the second percentage test because 12% is more than three percentage points above 8%. However, this arrangement does satisfy the first percentage test because 12% for the top 1/3 is not greater than 12% (8% for the lower 2/3 multiplied by 1.5).

Example (5). (i) Employees 1 thru 9 are the only employees of Employer D. Employer D maintains and contributes to a profit-sharing plan the following amounts:

(A) Six percent of each employee's compensation, where such amounts do not satisfy paragraphs (c) and (d).

(B) Two percent of each employee's compensation, where such amounts do satisfy paragraphs (c) and (d), and

(C) Up to three percent of each employee's compensation which the employee may elect to receive as a direct cash payment or to have that amount contributed to the plan.

(ii) For a plan year, employees 1 thru 9 received compensation and deferred contributions as indicated in the table below:

Employee	Compensation	6 percent non-elective contribution	2 percent non-elective contribution	Elective contribution elected to be deferred
1	$100,000	$6,000	$2,000	$3,000
2	80,000	4,800	1,600	2,400
3	60,000	3,600	1,200	1,800
4	40,000	2,400	800	0
5	30,000	1,800	600	0
6	20,000	1,200	400	0
7	20,000	1,200	400	0
8	10,000	600	200	0
9	5,000	300	100	0

(iii) In this case, the eligible employees are all the employees of Employer D, and the eight percent non-elective contributions are made for every eligible employee. Thus, the non-elective portion of the plan satisfies the general rules in subparagraph (3).

(iv) However, the elective portion of the plan does not satisfy the special rules in subparagraph (4) because the actual deferral percentage for the top $1/3$ is 3 percent and the actual deferral percentage for the lower $2/3$ is zero. Nevertheless, as allowed by subparagraph (2)(iii) the 2 percent non-elective contributions may also be taken into account in applying the special rules because such contributions satisfy paragraphs (c) and (d).

(v) If these contributions are considered the actual deferral percentage for the top $1/3$ is 5 percent and the actual deferral percentage for the lower $2/3$ is 2 percent. Because 5 percent is not more than 3 percentage points greater than 2 percent and not more than 2 percent multiplied by 2.5, the alternative actual deferral percentage test in subparagraph (5) is satisfied. Thus, this plan satisfies paragraph (b).

(c) *Nonforfeitability*—(1)*General rule.* A cash or deferred arrangement is not qualified unless the employee's rights to the accrued benefit derived from elective contributions made on or after the effective date of this section and non-elective contributions considered under paragraph (b)(2)(iv) of this section—

(i) Are nonforfeitable within the meaning of section 411, without regard to section 411(a)(3),

(ii) Are disregarded, for purposes of applying section 411(a) to other contributions, and

(iii) Remain nonforfeitable, even if there are other plan years in which there were no qualified deferrals under a cash or deferred arrangement.

(2) *Example.* This paragraph may be illustrated by the following example:

Example. Employee A is covered by X Company's qualified stock bonus plan and trust. The plan includes a qualified cash or deferred arrangement. Under the plan, an employer contribution equal to 3% of A's compensation is automatically contributed. A further amount equal to 2% of A's compensation is subject to A's election under the qualified cash or deferred arrangement. Those amounts up to 2% which A elects to have contributed by X Company to the trust under the qualified cash or deferred arrangement, adjusted pursuant to paragraph (e)(2), must be nonforfeitable at all times. The employer contribution of 3% of compensation, not subject to the election under the arrangement, is treated as an employer contribution for purposes of applying the vesting rules of section 411. Furthermore, in accordance with paragraph (c)(1)(ii), for purposes of applying the vesting requirements of section 411(a) to these non-elective contributions, an employee's right to the accrued benefit attributable to the contributions under the qualified cash or deferred arrangement must be disregarded.

(d) *Distribution limitation*—(1) *General rule.* A cash or deferred arrangement is not qualified unless amounts attributable to elective contributions made on or after the effective date of this section or non-elective contributions considered under paragraph (b)(2)(iv) of this section are not distributable earlier than upon one of the following events:

> (i) The participant's retirement, death, disability, separation from service, or attainment of age 59 1/2; or

> (ii) The participant's hardship.

(2) *Definitions.* For purposes of this section, a distribution will be on account of hardship if the distribution is necessary in light of immediate and heavy financial needs of the employee. A distribution based upon financial hardship cannot exceed the amount required to meet the immediate financial need created by the hardship and not reasonably available from other resources of the employee. The determination of the existence of financial hardship and the amount required to be distributed to meet the need created by the hardship must be made in accordance with uniform and non-discriminatory standards set forth in the plan.

(3) *Impermissible distributions.* Elective contributions and non-elective contributions under paragraph (b)(2)(iv) of this section cannot be distributed merely by reason of completion of a state period of plan participation or by the lapse of a fixed period of time.

(e) *Other rules* —(1)*General rule.* All amounts held under a plan that has qualified cash or deferred arrangement (including amounts contributed for plan years beginning prior to January 1, 1980, contributions made other than on account of a deferral election, and contributions made for years when the cash or deferred arrangement is qualified) will be deemed to be attributable to contributions made pursuant to the employee's deferral election and therefore subject to the requirements of paragraphs (c) and (d) unless the requirements of paragraph (e)(2) of this section are satisfied.

(2) *Separate accounting.* The portion of an employee's accrued benefit that is subject to the requirements of paragraph (c) and (d) of this section determined by an acceptable separate accounting between such portion and any other benefits, by allocating investment gains and losses on a reasonable pro rata basis, and by adjusting account balances for withdrawals and contributions. The separate accounting is not acceptable unless gains, losses, withdrawals, forfeitures and other credits or charges are separately allocated to the accrued benefits subject to paragraphs (c) and (d) of this section and other benefits on a reasonable and consistent basis. A plan may allow for the designation of accounts when making withdrawals or the plan must specify from which accounts withdrawals will be made if there is no designation.

(f) *Effective date* —(1) *In general.* This section shall apply to plan years beginning after December 31, 1979.

(2) *Transitional rule.* In the case of cash or deferred arrangements in existence on June 27, 1974, see § 1.402(a)-1(d)(3) for transitional rule applicable to such arrangements.

Five

Tests for Nondiscrimination

§ 5.1   INTRODUCTION

The Tax Reform Act of 1986 (Tax Reform) included a sweeping overhaul of federal laws regulating pay-based discrimination in flexible benefit plans and in the welfare benefits most frequently offered through flexible programs: health care, group-term life insurance, and dependent care reimbursement. The new rules are expected to be effective for calendar year plans on January 1, 1989.

This chapter explains the key concepts behind each of these rules in nontechnical terms. It also provides a guide for applying the rules in the ongoing operation of group benefit plans and flexible compensation programs.

Nondiscrimination rules are a tool of federal tax policy meant to induce employers to provide essential benefits to low- and middle-income employees who may not otherwise secure these benefits on their own. The inducement takes the form of a "carrot and stick" approach.

The "carrot" has remained essentially the same for many years—employees generally are not taxed on the value of health care, group-term life insurance, and dependent care benefits provided by their employers. This means that compensating an employee with these benefits provides greater value per employer dollar than if the dollar were taxable to the employee.

For health care, there is no fixed cap on the tax preference. For group-term life insurance, the tax preference continues to be limited to the value of $50,000 of coverage. Only for dependent care has Tax Reform imposed a new cap—the greatest nontaxable benefit per family is now $5,000.

The "stick" is that highly paid employees (generally those making at least $50,000 per year) can receive welfare benefits tax-free only if comparable benefits are available to—and elected by—nonhighly paid employees. To the extent availability and/or actual coverage is not comparable for the nonhighly paid group, the tax preference for the highly paid is shaved back accordingly.

Under prior law, the stick of taxing highly paid employees on discriminatory benefits was used infrequently because the rules were vague and full of loopholes. The main impact of Tax Reform in this area has been to sharpen the stick with more precise technical rules that are more likely to support enforcement in the future.

Each new rule has its own complicated mechanics, but the basic theme is always the same. The first step is to identify the employer-provided benefits received by (or available to) nonhighly paid employees. The second step is to plug that data into a formula to determine whether the benefits received by highly paid employees are excessive in comparison to the benefits of nonhighly paid employees. Benefits are excessive if they exceed the highest level of nontaxable benefits permitted for highly paid employees. Each test has its own formula for determining this highest permitted benefit level.

Technically, the label *discriminatory* applies to a plan where a highly paid employee receives benefits in excess of the highest amount permitted. In most cases, the practical significance of this is merely that the employer must report the excess value as taxable income on the employee's W-2 statement.

The following sections describe the specific tests applicable to health care plans, group-term life insurance, dependent care, and group legal services plans. The next section then focuses on a separate, additional test that must be applied to most flexible programs. The chapter concludes with a discussion of various other issues, including the categories of employees who may be excluded from the tests, the aggregation of plans in certain instances for testing purposes, and the special rules for testing by lines of business or operating units.

Complete understanding of the actual mechanics of the new nondiscrimination rules will have to await IRS regulations. In the meantime, this chapter sets forth current understanding of the mechanics apparently intended by Congress. The discussion is based on the provisions of the Tax Reform Act of 1986 as originally enacted, the proposed technical corrections, and explanations of these provisions prepared by the staff of the Joint Committee on Taxation (the Blue Book). In some cases, detailed examples are provided. However, the reader should understand that the information contained herein may require modification to reflect forthcoming regulations.

§ 5.2   DISCRIMINATION TESTS FOR HEALTH CARE

All types of employer-sponsored health care plans must be taken into account in applying the health care discrimination tests under Section 89 of the Internal Revenue Code. This includes traditional medical plans, health maintenance organizations, vision plans, dental plans, health care spending accounts, and physical exam plans.

The Internal Revenue Code definition of health plan also appears to include accidental death and dismemberment, although the precise treatment of the separate value of the accidental death component awaits clarification by the IRS.

Health care benefits are subject to tests that measure the benefits made available to different groups of employees (eligibility tests) and a test that measures the benefits actually provided to employees (a benefits test).

(a)   ELIGIBILITY TESTS

Health care plans are subject to three eligibility tests: a 50-Percent Test, a 90/50 Test, and a Plan-Provision Test. All three of these tests must be satisfied except in limited situations where the Alternative 80-Percent Test is met.

(1)   The 50-Percent Test

(i)   In General.   A plan is nondiscriminatory under this test if, on each day of the testing period, at least 50 percent of those eligible to participate are not highly paid employees. This test is satisfied easily where all benefits are available to all employees, through a company-wide flexible benefit program or otherwise. The test will be a problem only in cases where special plans are available to select groups consisting primarily of highly paid employees.

Tax Reform provides a specific definition of highly paid employees, which is discussed in some detail in Chapter Four. Employees earning more than $50,000 generally are considered to be highly paid for purposes of the nondiscrimination tests.

In addition to a general description of the mechanics of the 50-Percent Test, this discussion demonstrates the impact of the test on a problem case—the supplemental executive-only medical plan. This example was selected because it is relatively common for employers to offer such plans as an overlay to a flexible program and because the mechanics of the test are best understood by focusing on a problem case.

(ii)   Definition of Plan.   A special definition of the term *plan* applies for purposes of the 50-Percent Test. Health benefits are divided into separate plans to reflect distinctions in the terms of coverage, the amount of employee contributions, the organizations providing services (e.g., each HMO is a separate plan), or the family members covered. Thus if an employer offers "employee plus one family member" coverage, and "employee plus full family" coverage, three plans are involved—one for the employee, one for one additional family member, and one for the remaining family members. The 50-Percent Test is meant to ensure that each of these separate plans must be available to at least as many nonhighly paid employees as highly paid employees.

(iii)   Aggregation.   A plan that separately does not satisfy the 50-Percent Test can be aggregated with another health care plan that does satisfy the test, as long as the employer-provided value available under the "helper" plan is at least 95 percent of the employer-provided value available under the flunking plan. The value of a plan for this purpose is to be determined from IRS tables and will not necessarily be based on the actual cost of the plan.

Aggregation could be used, for example, where a particular medical plan is available only to a pocket of employees at a company's headquarters office, the majority of whom are highly paid. Taken alone, the plan violates the 50-Percent Test. If, however, the plan is aggregated with a comparable health care plan which is available to a broader group of nonhighly paid employees at another facility, the 50-Percent Test is satisfied.

One early question was whether an executive-only supplemental medical plan could be made to pass the 50-Percent Test by aggregating it with the basic health care plan provided to the rank and file. Under proposed technical corrections legislation, the Secretary of Treasury would be authorized to clarify in regulations that aggregation could be used to demonstrate nondiscrimination in such a case only if the value of the helper plan (or plans) is comparable to the combined value of all plans (i.e., base plus supplemental) available to employees who are eligible for the flunking plan.

An example of this aggregation concept is a case where all of a company's employees are covered by a flexible benefit program under which they can elect full-family medical coverage worth $3,000, full-family dental coverage worth $600, and $2,400 of coverage under a medical spending account, for a combined maximum value of $6,000. In addition, executives are covered by a supplemental plan valued at $2,000. Regulations can be expected to provide that aggregation could not be used to fully eliminate the discriminatory effect of the supplemental plan because the difference in value between the $8,000 amount available to executives and the $6,000 amount available to other employees is too great to meet the 95-percent comparability test.

An example where the aggregation approach is likely to be useful in demonstrating compliance involves an HMO which is available only in a particular geographic area in which predominantly highly paid employees reside. In many cases it will be easy to identify another plan (an HMO or an indemnity plan) of comparable value covering a group consisting primarily of nonhighly paid employees. The test would be passed by aggregating the health care plans covering the two groups.

(iv) Sanction. When the 50-Percent Test is failed, the employer must determine the highest level permitted of nontaxable benefits for highly paid employees. Effectively, this is the cap on nontaxable benefits which, if imposed on highly paid employees, would allow the plans to pass the 50-Percent Test and would prevent discrimination from occurring. Each highly paid employee is then taxed on the amount by which the actual value of employer-provided health care coverages exceeds this level.

In the example just described, it appears that if the nontaxable benefits provided by the employer through the supplemental executive-only medical plan were reduced to $315 in value, the combined health care benefits available to executives would be comparable in value to the combined benefits available to other employees, and the 50-Percent Test would be satisfied. This is because the $6,000 value available to all employees is at least 95 percent of the $6,315 maximum value that would have been available to executives if the $315 cap had been applied to the supplemental plan.

(v) *Testing Period.* The 50-Percent Test apparently is to be applied on each day in the testing period. In general, the testing period is the plan year of the health care plan being tested, but regulations are expected to provide a method for establishing a common testing period (e.g., the calendar year) in cases of health care plans with multiple plan years.

Regulations should clarify the consequences of failing to satisfy the 50-Percent Test for only part of the testing period. In a case where the test is satisfied for half of the testing period, it is reasonable to expect that the sanction would be only half as much as in a case where the test is not satisfied at any point during the testing period.

(vi) *Coping with Potential Discrimination.* Several strategies may be available to an employer who maintains a potentially discriminatory plan such as a supplemental executive-only medical plan. The first strategy would be to do away with the plan to avoid the inconvenience of having to cope with the consequences of flunking the 50-Percent Test. Another strategy would be to limit the employer subsidy under the supplemental plan to the highest benefit permitted ($315 in the previous example), and require the executive to pay the balance with after-tax contributions. A third strategy would be to continue the present structure, with the likely result that additional taxable income would have to be reported on W-2 statements for employees whose actual aggregate coverage value exceeds the highest benefit level permitted. Regulations should clarify whether in the example just described the "worst-case" result would merely be the taxation of benefits exceeding the highest benefit level permitted ($6,315) or whether the full value of the executive-only plan would be taxable in all cases.

An executive-only plan may be so comprehensive as to provide coverage for any health care claim not reimbursable under the basic plan. Or it may be as simple as an arrangement allowing executives to participate in a health care plan immediately from their date of hire (through a flexible program or otherwise), while other employees have a waiting period of a month or more. The coverage available during such an early eligibility period appears to be a separate plan which, if available only to executives, would fail to satisfy the 50-Percent Test. Regulations should clarify whether and how aggregation may be available to demonstrate compliance with the 50-Percent Test in such cases.

As noted earlier, the 50-Percent Test is likely to be satisfied easily by employers who do not provide additional coverages, earlier participation, or lower contribution rates to groups consisting primarily of highly paid employees.

(2)   The 90/50 Test

(i)   In General.   This test is satisfied if on each day of the testing period, 90 percent of nonhighly paid employees are eligible for a package of health care benefits with a value equal to at least 50 percent of the value of the health care benefit package available to the highly paid employee with the richest available health care benefits.

Before demonstrating the operation of the 90/50 Test, four special rules should be noted.

First, all employees working in a group of corporations under common control are included in the 90/50 Test with two exceptions. The employer may exclude employees working in separate lines of business or separate operating units under rules described later in this chapter. Also, the employer may exclude certain employees, such as seasonal hires and part-time employees working less than 17 1/2 hours a week, under rules also described in more detail later in this chapter. Thus the 90/50 Test requires that some health care coverage must be available on each day during the testing period to 90 percent of the group of nonhighly paid employees who are in the same line of business and who are "nonexcludables" on that day.

Second, the value of a health care benefit is not considered to include amounts payable either with pretax salary reduction or with flexible credits which could have been taken as cash. Thus the 90/50 Test focuses on an amount that is essentially a "company subsidized value," that is, the total value of benefits less the amount of salary reduction contributions, after-tax employee contributions, and cashable flexible credits that could be used to elect the benefit.

Third, if an employee would be eligible to elect family coverage if he or she had a family, the employee is considered to be eligible for family coverage when applying the test. The actual family status of the employee is irrelevant. This provision, which would be added by technical corrections legislation, would eliminate the need to demonstrate that the subsidized value available to single, nonhighly paid employees is comparable to the subsidized value available to married, highly paid employees.

Fourth, an employer is not penalized for providing a lesser subsidized value to certain part-time employees. This policy is implemented by increasing for testing purposes the value attributed to the employer-provided value of the benefit available to certain part-time employees. Specifically, the subsidized value available to an employee who normally works less than 22 1/2 hours per week may be multiplied by 2, while the subsidized value available to an employee who normally works less than 30 hours per week (but at least 22 1/2 hours per week) may be multiplied by 1 1/3. This special adjustment for part-timers is not available to an employer unless during the year more than 50 percent of nonhighly paid employees normally work more than 30 hours per week.

(ii)   Step-by-Step Application.   The first step in applying the 90/50 Test is to identify the highly paid employees who are eligible for the package of health care benefits with the richest subsidized value. This amount is equal to the full value of the richest coverages in the aggregate, including full-family coverages when available, less amounts payable with after-tax employee contributions, salary reduction, or cashable credits.

The second step is to determine the number of nonexcludable nonhighly paid employees, under rules which will be described later. From this group the employer then can set aside up to 10 percent for whom the available subsidized value is particularly low (or nonexistent). If the remaining 90 percent have some health care coverage available, the first part of the 90/50 Test is satisfied.

The third step is to identify, from the 90 percent group of nonhighly paid employees, the employee who would generate the lowest subsidized value if he or she were to elect the richest available coverages on a full-family basis (i.e., assuming the employee has a family), taking into account any part-timer adjustments that may apply. If the subsidized value available to this "worst-off" nonhighly paid employee is at least half of the subsidized value available to the "best-off" highly paid employee, the second part of the 90/50 Test is satisfied.

(iii)   Sanction.   In the case of an employer who is unable to demonstrate that 90 percent of nonhighly paid employees are eligible for a health care benefit with some employer-subsidized value (however little), it appears that highly paid employees must be taxed on the entire value of all employer-provided health care coverages.

If the employer fails to satisfy only the 50-percent portion of the 90/50 test, the sanction is less drastic. The highest benefit permitted for highly paid employees apparently would be equal to twice the subsidized value for the worst-off nonhighly paid employee described in the previously mentioned third step. Regulations will have to specify a method for taxing highly paid employees in such a case. Under one approach, the sanction might apply only to the extent the actual subsidized value exceeds the highest benefit permitted. Or the sanction may apply to the amount by which the total value of nontaxable health care (i.e., the employer-paid portion plus pretax salary reduction or flexible credits) exceeds the highest benefit permitted.

(iv) *Example.*   Consider a flexible program covering all employees, including part-timers who normally work at least $17^1/2$ hours a week. Subsidized values available to full-time employees who elect full-family, high-option coverages are shown in Example 5.1. The "value" column indicates the full value of each option, and the "employee contribution" column indicates the amount the employee must pay for the coverage using either salary reduction or flexible credits that are available as cash under the terms of the plan.

Assume that part-timers are required to use salary reduction contributions to pay the full cost of dental coverage, as well as a portion of medical coverage based on the number of hours scheduled to be worked. Assume further that the worst-off nonhighly paid employee is a part-timer who normally works 25 hours a week who must pay $2,400 for family medical coverage, resulting in a maximum available subsidized value of $600. Applying the special part-timer adjustment rule, this employee is treated for testing purposes as having available a subsidized value of $800 ($600 × $1^1/3$).

The highest subsidy value permitted for highly paid employees in this example is $1,600 ($800 × 2). In the case of an employee who elects the richest full-family medical and dental coverages, having a subsidized value of $2,200, the discriminatory excess would appear to be $600— the amount by which the actual subsidy value exceeds $1,600, the highest benefit level permitted.

The example also demonstrates that health care spending accounts fueled only by salary reduction have no effect on the 90/50 Test, as they have no subsidized value.

Example 5.1

	Value	Employee Contribution	Subsidized Value
High-option full-family medical plan	$3,000	$1,000	$2,000
Family dental	600	400	200
Maximum flexible spending account	2,000	2,000	0
	$5,600	$3,400	$2,200

(v) Coping with Potential Discrimination.   In cases where an employer can foresee failing the 90/50 Test, it will often be advisable to make preventive adjustments before the testing period begins. For an employer who expects to fail the 90-percent part of the test, the only effective adjustment will be to broaden the group of nonhighly paid employees eligible for one or more subsidized health care plans.

If the 50-percent part of the test is expected to be violated, either of two different kinds of adjustments can be effective. One approach would be to restrict the amount of nontaxable, employer-provided health care coverage available to highly paid employees. (A possible corollary step would be to increase cash compensation, from which the highly paid employee could purchase coverage on an after-tax basis.) Another approach would be to increase the subsidized amount under the plan or plans for which nonhighly paid employees are eligible. If this subsidy is to be increased for part-time employees, the cost to the employer may be mitigated by two factors. First, the subsidy value used for testing purposes will be increased for employees who normally work less than 30 hours a week. Second, many part-timers will not actually elect coverage, even if presented with a decrease in required employee contributions.

(vi) Special Situations.   The fact that employee contributions are not taken into account for purposes of the 90/50 Test could pose difficulties in a case where a flexible program is established, but one or more highly paid employees are covered instead by a nonflexible program.

Assume, for instance, that a flexible program is established for Hospital A, one of two hospitals with work forces of comparable size operated in the same city by a common owner. Under the program, Hospital A's entire contribution to medical coverage consists of $2,000 of credits which may be used to elect health care coverage or may be taken in cash. Hospital B provides a health care plan valued at $2,000 on a nonelective basis. The worst-off nonhighly paid employees under the 90/50 Test in this case would be the participants in the Hospital A flexible program. This is because all contributions to the Hospital A health care plan are cashable and therefore have no "subsidized value" under the 90/50 Test. However, the test would not be satisfied in this situation because a subsidized value of $2,000 is available to all highly paid employees of Hospital B. This result probably was not intended by Congress, and the problem may be resolved either in technical corrections legislation or in Treasury regulations.

The scenario of some nonhighly paid employees with no subsidized value would not pose a problem if all highly paid employees were also in the flexible plan with no subsidized value. It is only the existence of a second plan under which subsidies are available which causes this issue.

(3)   The Plan-Provision Test

A plan satisfies this test if it does not contain a provision relating to eligibility to participate which discriminates in favor of highly paid employees.

This rule is intended primarily to deal with discrimination which is not quantifiable and therefore is not identified under one of the first two eligibility tests. An example would be a case where coverage for a rare disease is added solely because the chief executive or someone in his family has contracted the disease, and nonhighly paid employees are not likely to utilize the coverage. Treasury regulations will have to determine a sanction for plans not satisfying the Plan-Provision Test.

(b)   AVERAGE BENEFITS TEST

(1)   In General

In addition to satisfying all three of the eligibility tests, a health plan must satisfy the Average Benefits Test. This test is satisfied if the average value of health care benefits actually in effect for nonhighly paid employees during a testing period is at least 75 percent of the average value for highly paid employees during the same period.

The testing period generally will be the plan year, but regulations are expected to provide for the designation of a common twelve-month testing period in cases involving multiple health care plans with overlapping plan years.

The Average Benefits Test requires that employee turnover and coverage changes during the testing period be taken into account. Accordingly, employers will not be able to perform the actual test until after the close of the testing period when all data is available. This does not mean, however, that employers must wait to evaluate the likelihood that their plans will pass the test. In most cases remedial action, if any is necessary, can be taken during the testing period or before it begins.

(2) Mechanics of the Test

The Average Benefits Test is performed by setting up two fractions, one for nonhighly paid employees and another for highly paid employees.

The numerator of the nonhighly paid employee fraction includes the value—determined under IRS tables—of all health care benefits in effect for such employees, their spouses, and their dependents at any time during the testing period. In the case of an employee who is covered by a plan with an annual value of $1,000 but who works for only six months, the amount included would be $500.

Benefits taken into account in the numerator include the employer-provided portion of the indemnity-type medical and dental plans, HMOs, vision care, health spending accounts, physical exam plans, and any other type of health care benefit (other than income replacement disability plans) which is nontaxable under Section 106 of the Internal Revenue Code. Unlike the eligibility tests, here the employer-provided value of a benefit includes the amount of elective contributions made on a pretax basis. Benefit values are reduced only by the amount of any after-tax employee contributions.

The denominator of this first fraction includes each nonhighly paid employee with service during the testing period, whether or not the employee is covered by a health care plan, except for employees excluded from testing under the exclusion rules described later in this chapter. For employees working for only part of the testing period, an appropriate adjustment is made in the denominator. For example, a nonhighly paid employee working only six months would appear as one-half employee in the denominator.

Average benefits for highly paid employees are determined by using the same numerator/denominator approach as for nonhighly paid employees.

(3) Sanction

If the Average Benefits Test is not satisfied, the employer must reduce the level of nontaxable benefits to the highly paid, beginning with the individual with the highest benefit, until the average nontaxable benefit for the nonhighly paid is at least 75 percent of the average highly paid benefit. In effect, this reduction of benefits creates a cap on permitted nontaxable benefits to highly paid employees. If this cap had been imposed at the beginning of the plan year, it would have prevented discrimination from occurring. Each highly paid employee whose benefits exceed this highest benefit level permitted is taxed on the excess.

(4) Example

Consider the case of a simple flexible program established solely to allow employees to pay their share of medical plan premiums on a pretax basis. Assume that employee-only coverage is valued under IRS tables at $1,200, and the additional coverage for the employee's spouse and dependents also is valued at $1,200. Employees are required to pay part of the cost of single-employee coverage and all of the value of spouse and dependent coverage.

Assume that the employer has a static workforce of fifteen employees throughout the testing period. Of the twelve nonhighly paid employees, one elects full-family coverage (valued at $2,400), ten elect employee-only coverage, and one elects no coverage because he is covered under the plan of his spouse's employer. Of the three highly paid employees, two elect full-family coverage, and one elects employee-only coverage.

The average benefit for nonhighly paid employees in this example is $1,200 (the sum of $2,400 × 1 plus $1,200 × 10 plus 0 × 1, divided by 12). Thus the average benefit for highly paid employees may not exceed $1,600 (75 percent of $1,600 = $1,200). Accordingly, the highly paid employees electing full family-coverage must have their nontaxable benefits reduced until the average benefit is $1,600. If each highly paid employee electing full-family coverage is taxed on $600 of coverage, the benefit levels of these two highly paid employees is reduced to $1,800, bringing the average of the three highly paid employees to $1,600.

It should be noted that the employer may view the decision to provide pretax contributions as sound even though the plan fails to satisfy the Average Benefits Test. This is because all nonhighly paid employees shelter the entire amount of their contributions from federal income tax, and highly paid employees shelter a substantial portion of their contributions notwithstanding the plan's discriminatory status.

(5) Special Rule for Employees with Other Coverage

It is fairly common for an employee to elect no coverage because he or she is covered under another plan—typically the plan of a spouse's employer. A special rule was added to the Average Benefits Test to recognize that a plan should not become discriminatory for this reason alone. Unfortunately, the complexity of the steps necessary to apply the special rule may limit its attractiveness to employers.

An employer electing to apply this special "Other Coverage" rule may disregard, for purposes of the Average Benefits Test, employees who receive core health care coverage for themselves and for their spouse and dependents (if any) under a plan maintained by another employer of the employee, spouse, or dependents.

Core coverage for this purpose does not include coverage for dental, vision, psychological or orthodontia expenses, or elective cosmetic surgery. Further, it does not include salary reduction health care spending accounts or nonsalary reduction health care spending accounts with balances which under IRS regulations are considered too low to provide meaningful coverage.

The special rule contemplates that once each year the employer will collect a sworn statement (from each employee on an IRS form designed for this purpose) indicating whether the employee and his or her family have core medical coverage from another employer's plan. A review of the following three additional requirements suggests, however, that it may be necessary to collect sworn statements only from certain employees.

First, highly paid employees with health care benefits exceeding the highest benefit level permitted cannot be disregarded in the test, whether or not a sworn statement is provided. Therefore, statements from this group serve little purpose.

Second, a highly paid employee with benefits at or below the highest benefit level permitted will be disregarded unless a sworn statement indicates that the employee does not have other coverage. Thus statements should be solicited from this group each year to avoid an artificial increase in the highly paid average which would result from disregarding employees with below-average benefits.

Third, a nonhighly paid employee can be disregarded only if a sworn statement is provided which indicates that the employee has coverage elsewhere. Thus it becomes important to obtain sworn statements only from employees who actually have other coverage and who elect below-average benefits from the employer applying the test. Little is gained by collecting sworn statements from other nonhighly paid employees.

Employers with large employee groups may be able to use a sampling technique (to be spelled out in Treasury regulations) to determine the portion of each employee group with coverage under the plan of another employer. Whether sampling will be useful depends in large part on how those regulations are structured.

Applying the Other Coverage rule to the fifteen-employee company described earlier could increase the highest benefit level permitted, therefore decreasing the amount of taxable income to the highly paid employees. This is because the nonhighly paid employee electing no coverage can be disregarded (assuming that the employee provides a sworn statement evidencing that the employee and family have coverage under the spouse's plan). As a result, the average benefit for nonhighly paid employees would increase from $1,200 to $1,309, and the highest benefit permitted for highly paid employees would increase accordingly from $1,800 to $2,018.

(6)   Special Rule for Separate Testing of Family Coverage

Highly paid employees typically will have a disproportionately higher percentage of families than nonhighly paid employees. As illustrated in the earlier example, it can be difficult to satisfy the Average Benefits Test if as a result of this disparity, highly paid employees elect family medical coverage at a greater rate than nonhighly paid employees. In recognition of this problem, Congress provided a special rule under which an employer may elect to apply the Average Benefits Test separately to health care coverages for spouses and dependents.

An employer electing this rule applies two Average Benefits Tests. The first is performed by merely deleting the value of spouse and dependent coverages from the numerator of both the highly paid employee fraction and the nonhighly paid employee fraction. In many cases, this first test will be satisfied easily.

Second, the employer sets up a highly paid fraction and a nonhighly paid fraction where the numerators include only the value of spouse and dependent coverages for highly paid and nonhighly paid employees, respectively. The denominators of these fractions are intended to include the number of employees who in fact have a spouse or dependents. Annual sworn statements on a form to be provided by the IRS are necessary to identify family status for this purpose.

If each employee provides a sworn statement regarding family status, separate testing should make it much easier to satisfy the Average Benefits Test. A sampling technique to be made available by regulations also should yield favorable results if each employee in the sampling provides a sworn statement regarding family status. However, in cases where sworn statements are not collected from all employees (or all employees in the sample), Congress provided certain statutory presumptions as to family status which tend to undermine the attractiveness of the separate testing rule.

Under these statutory presumptions, in the absence of a sworn statement, a highly paid employee is presumed not to have a spouse or dependents, while a nonhighly paid employee is presumed to have a spouse or dependents. The effect of these presumptions is to increase the average value of spouse and dependent benefits for highly paid employees (because the number of employees in the denominator of that fraction is artificially lowered) and decrease the average value for nonhighly paid employees (because the number of employees in the denominator is artificially increased).

Gathering sworn statements from employees may prove quite burdensome for employers. The favorable impact on the Average Benefits Test may make the effort worthwhile—but only if sworn statements are collected annually from virtually all employees.

(7)   Special Rule for Part-Time Employees

As under the 90/50 Test, some part-time employees can be treated under the Average Benefits Test as having received more tax-free health care coverage then actually is the case. This is achieved by increasing the subsidized value (total tax-free value less salary reduction and cashable credits) actually provided. In the case of an employee who normally works less than $22^{1}/_{2}$ hours per week, the subsidized value is multiplied by 2. In the case of an employee who normally works less than 30 hours per week (but at least $22^{1}/_{2}$ hours per week), the subsidized value is multiplied by $1^{1}/_{3}$.

(c)   THE ALTERNATIVE 80-PERCENT TEST

A health care plan is considered to satisfy the 50-Percent Test, the 90/50 Test, and the Average Benefits Test if the plan covers at least 80 percent of all nonhighly paid employees in the workforce being tested. For purposes of this test, an employee is not viewed as being covered simply because he or she is eligible to participate—actual coverage is required.

The definition of plan for this purpose is the one used earlier in applying the 50-Percent Test. Thus the 80-Percent Test generally would be applied separately to each option or different benefit, and separately for employee-only and dependent coverages. Plans of comparable value could be aggregated, however.

In applying the test to contributory spouse and dependent coverages, an employer may elect to take into account only employees who on the basis of sworn statements are determined to have a spouse or dependents, applying IRS rules similar to those used for separate testing under the Average Benefits Test.

In general, the more diverse an employer's plans, the less likely it is that the 80-Percent Test would be useful. The typical health care spending account would not satisfy the 80-Percent Test, for instance, because each dollar amount of coverage employees actually elect would appear to be considered a different plan for this purpose.

The 80-Percent Test could prove useful to an employer providing a single, uniform package of noncontributory plans covering employees and their families. In such a case, it would be possible to designate a group of up to 20 percent of nonhighly paid employees as ineligible for any health care plans. This is more liberal than the 90/50 Test, which permits the exclusion of only 10 percent of nonhighly paid employees.

§ 5.3   DISCRIMINATION TESTS FOR GROUP-TERM LIFE INSURANCE

The rules for testing employer-sponsored group-term life insurance under the Tax Reform Act are covered in considerably less detail in the Blue Book and Conference Committee Report than the rules for testing health care plans. To fill in some of the blanks, information contained in this section is based on discussions with Congressional staff members as to the intended operation of the rules. While forthcoming regulations are likely to differ in some respects from the understanding presented here, the following discussion should be useful in assessing the status of life insurance programs during the period before regulations are available.

Group-term life insurance plans are subject to the same general eligibility and benefits tests as health care plans, although the specific application of the rules varies substantially.

(a)   ELIGIBILITY TESTS

(1)   The 50-Percent Test

(i)   In General.   This test is satisfied if on each day of the testing period at least 50 percent of those eligible for each separate plan are nonhighly paid employees. As with health care, benefits are divided into

separate plans to reflect differences in the amount of coverage and in the amount of employee contributions required to obtain the coverage.

An employer providing $50,000 of noncontributory coverage to salaried employees and $25,000 of noncontributory coverage to hourly employees has two plans. In most cases, the salaried plan satisfies the 50-Percent Test only if at least half of the salaried employees are non-highly paid employees.

(ii) *Pay-Related Plans.*   Under a special exception to the separate plan rules, an arrangement providing coverage which bears a uniform relationship to the compensation of employees can be treated as a single plan for testing purposes. Thus a noncontributory plan providing one times compensation would satisfy the 50-Percent Test if at least one-half the eligibles are nonhighly paid employees.

A contributory pay-related arrangement also would be considered a single plan if the employee contribution for employees in each age grouping is a uniform percentage of cost. Thus an arrangement under which each employee pays 80 percent of the cost of an option providing supplemental coverage of one times compensation could be considered a single plan.

The application of the nondiscrimination rules becomes more complicated in cases where an employer varies the subsidy percentage for different age groups. In the case of a one times compensation option in which employees under age 60 pay 80 percent of the actual age-related cost, and employees 60 and older pay only 40 percent of such cost, the option could not be treated as a single plan. This is because the subsidized (or employer-provided) portion of the benefit available to the younger group of employees provides coverage equal to only 20 percent of compensation, while the subsidized portion for older employees provides coverage equal to 60 percent of compensation. Accordingly, the arrangement for the older employees would violate the 50-Percent Test if more than one-half are highly paid employees.

Regulations should provide guidance on the compensation definition used in applying the group-term life insurance tests and on the age groupings used in determining whether employee contributions are a uniform percentage of actual cost for all eligible employees. Depending on the approach taken in final regulations, some employers may want to modify either the compensation base or the contribution schedule (or both) in order to simplify the application of the tests.

(iii) *Compensation Limit.*   The maximum amount of compensation that may be taken into account in applying the group-term life insurance tests is $200,000. The effect of this rule on the 50-Percent Test can be seen in the case of an arrangement providing coverage of one times compensation to all of a company's employees, including the chief executive, whose compensation is $210,000. This arrangement would be treated as two plans. One plan would be the portion providing all employees with one times compensation not in excess of $200,000. The other plan, providing $10,000 of coverage, would fail the 50-Percent Test because no nonhighly paid employee is eligible.

It is important to note that the nondiscrimination rules do not prohibit providing coverage (or benefits) on the basis of pay in excess of $200,000; they simply make it more likely that such excess coverage will be considered discriminatory. As a practical matter, however, such discriminatory coverages may be undesirable only if a meaningful sanction applies.

(iv) Sanction.   It appears that a highly paid employee who is covered under a separate plan that fails to satisfy the 50-Percent Test is taxed on the full value of such separate plan, less any amount paid with after-tax employee contributions. No sanction results from mere eligibility; to be taxable, the coverage must actually be in effect.

The "value" of the coverage which is included in the employee's taxable income is the greater of the actual employer cost for the coverage or the value determined under the IRS value table appearing in regulations under Section 79 of the Internal Revenue Code. (This table is reproduced in Chapter Eight.)

Tax Reform left unchanged the rule that employees are taxed on the value of group-term life insurance in excess of $50,000, whether or not provided under a discriminatory plan. As a result, the nondiscrimination rules impose additional tax for providing discriminatory plans only in two cases. The first case is where the highest benefit permitted (as a result of testing) for a highly paid employee is less than $50,000. The second case is where the employer's actual cost, determined under IRS regulations, for providing the coverage is greater than the rate determined under the Section 79 table.

(2) The 90/50 Test

(i) In General.   This test is satisfied if on each day of the testing period 90 percent of nonhighly paid employees are eligible for employer-provided life insurance coverage (expressed as a multiple of compensation) which is at least 50 percent of the employer-provided coverage (expressed as a multiple of compensation) available to the

highly paid employee to whom the highest such amount is available. As under the health care 90/50 Test, an employee's employer-provided benefit does not include any portion of the coverage which is payable with salary reduction contributions, after-tax contributions, or cashable flexible credits.

(ii) Step-by-Step Application. The following description reflects current understanding of the testing methodology set forth in the Tax Reform Act and the Blue Book. In the interest of clarity and simplicity of calculation, the steps are stated somewhat differently than in the Blue Book, but the results are the same. One step—determining value as if all employees were age 40—has been omitted because it appears superfluous except when testing group-term life insurance together with either health care or dependent care. (See later discussion on aggregation of plans.)

(1) Step One: Identify Nonexcludable Employees

The first step is to identify the group of employees to be included in the 90/50 Test. A list of excludable employees (such as those working less than 17 1/2 hours a week) is included in the later discussion of Types of Excludable Employees.

(2) Step Two: Determine the Employer-Provided Coverage Amount

The second step in applying the 90/50 Test is to determine the employer-provided portion of life insurance coverage for which each employee is eligible. For noncontributory coverage this is the entire dollar amount of coverage.

For contributory coverage, IRS regulations are expected to provide a formula for determining the employer-provided portion. One approach apparently under consideration is to multiply the dollar amount of each employee's contributory coverage by a ratio reflecting the portion of actual cost which is provided by the employer. The numerator would be the amount (if any) by which the employer's actual cost for the coverage, taking into account the employee's age, exceeds the amount of after-tax contributions, salary reduction, or cashable credits required to purchase the coverage. The denominator would be the employer's actual cost for coverage, taking into account the employee's age. For example, in the case of an employee charged 80 percent of the actual cost of $100,000 of life insurance, the employer-provided coverage amount would be $20,000.

The contribution rate charged to relatively younger employees under certain plans can exceed the actual cost of coverage for such employees. Regulations should provide whether the employer-provided coverage amount in such a case is to be treated for purposes of the 90/50 Test as zero or as a negative amount. Current regulations under Section 79 specify a method of determining actual cost for employees of various ages in particular companies, but the possibility exists that these regulations may be restructured to meet the specific needs of the Tax Reform tests.

(3)   Step Three: Express Coverage as a Multiple of Compensation

The third step is to divide the employer-provided coverage amount by the employee's compensation not in excess of $200,000. The uniform definition of compensation used for this purpose generally includes taxable pay plus, at the election of the employer, amounts which would have been included as taxable pay but for salary reduction arrangements in connection with qualified cafeteria plans or Section 401(k) cash-or-deferred plans.

IRS regulations should clarify whether, in the case of pay-related life insurance plans, it would be acceptable to apply the group-term life insurance tests on the basis of the compensation definition used to determine actual coverage under the plan (often a base-pay rate at a particular date) as opposed to Tax Reform's uniform compensation definition.

(4)   Step Four: Identify the Best-off Employee

The fourth step is to identify the highly paid employee who is eligible for employer-provided coverage providing the highest multiple of the employee's compensation not in excess of $200,000. This will not necessarily be the most highly paid employee. For plans where greater employer subsidies are provided for relatively older employees, the older employees may be the best-off employees for testing purposes.

(5)   Step Five: Determine the Nonhighly Paid Testing Group

From the group of nonexcludable nonhighly paid employees, the employer may choose to disregard for testing purposes up to 10 percent whose maximum available employer-provided coverage, expressed as a multiple of compensation, is particularly low. If the remaining 90 per-cent have some group-term life insurance coverage available, the 90-percent component of the 90/50 Test is satisfied.

(6) Step Six: Identify the Worst-off Nonhighly Paid Employee

The sixth step is to identify, from among the 90-percent group of non-highly paid employees, the employee eligible for the lowest amount of employer-provided coverage, expressed as a multiple of compensation. If this employee's employer-provided compensation multiple is at least one-half the multiple available to the best-off highly paid employee, the 50-percent component of the 90/50 Test is satisfied.

(iii) Example. As an example, assume that Company M pro-vides employees with noncontributory coverage of one times compen-sation. In addition, under the company's flexible program, employees can elect up to an additional three times compensation for which they must allocate $1 per year of salary reduction contributions for each $1,000 of coverage.

Employee A is age 30 and has $30,000 of compensation. Assume that the actual annual cost for 30-year-old employees of Company M is $1.20 per $1,000 of coverage. Applying the formula described in Step One, the amount of the employer-provided portion of the contributory coverage available to Employee A is $15,000. This is determined by subtracting the required contribution from the actual cost ($1.20 − $1.00 = $.20), dividing the result by actual cost ($.20/$1.20 = 1/6), and multiplying the total available contributory coverage by the resulting ratio ($90,000 × 1/6 = $15,000). The total employer-provided coverage for Employee A is $45,000, which is the sum of the employer-provided portion of the con-tributory coverage and the full amount of the noncontributory cover-age. This represents 150 percent of Employee A's compensation.

Employee B is age 57 and has $60,000 of compensation. Assume that the actual cost for 57-year-old employees of Company M is $10 per $1,000 of coverage. Actual cost minus employee contributions divided by the actual cost, brings the result that 9/10 of the total cost is em-ployer paid ($10 − $1 = $9; $9/$10 = 9/10). Thus the employer-provided portion of the contributory coverage is $162,000 ($180,000 × 9/10). Employee B's total employer-provided coverage, including the noncon-tributory coverage of one times compensation, is $222,000 ($60,000 + $162,000 = $222,000). This represents 370 percent of Employee B's compensation.

Assume that Employee A is the worst-off employee among the 90-percent group of nonhighly paid employees, and Employee B is the best off among the highly paid employees. The 90/50 Test would not be satisfied because the compensation multiple for Employee A (150 percent) is less than 50 percent of the compensation multiple for Employee B (370 percent).

As indicated by this example, "flat rate" contributory plans are more likely to be discriminatory than plans under which contributions increase with age, especially when increases are in proportion to age-related increases in actual cost.

(iv) Sanction. If the employer does not offer the option of group-term life insurance coverage to at least 90 percent of nonexcludable nonhighly paid employees, it appears that the entire value of the coverage (including the first $50,000) will be taxable income to highly paid employees.

If the 90-percent component is satisfied, but the 50-percent component is not, the value of coverage in excess of the highest benefit level permitted will be taxable income to the highly paid. The highest benefit permitted for this purpose would be twice the compensation multiple for the worst-off nonhighly paid employee. Under the example given earlier, the highest benefit permitted for Employee B would be 300 percent of compensation, $180,000. The discriminatory amount would be the balance of the employer-provided coverage, $42,000.

Because the discriminatory level for this employee would be $180,000, the first $50,000 of Employee B's coverage apparently will be considered part of the permitted benefit and therefore is not taxed, even though the arrangement is considered discriminatory under the 90/50 Test. The value of the next $130,000 is taxed in accordance with the Section 79 table rates—again the same treatment as for nondiscriminatory arrangements. The $42,000 discriminatory excess is taxed according to the greater of actual cost (for a 57-year-old employee) or the Section 79 table rate.

(3) The Plan-Provision Test

Like health care plans, group-term life plans are also subject to the Plan-Provision Test. This test requires that a plan not contain any provision relating to eligibility which discriminates in favor of the highly paid. This does not cover discrimination that can be quantified under the first two eligibility tests, but it is intended primarily to deal with discrimination which is not quantifiable.

(b)   AVERAGE BENEFITS TEST

(1)   In General

This test is satisfied if the average employer-provided coverage (expressed as a multiple of compensation) actually provided to nonhighly paid employees is at least 75 percent of the average employer-provided coverage (expressed as a multiple of compensation) actually provided to highly paid employees.

(2)   Mechanics of the Test

The Average Benefits Test is performed by determining the employer-provided compensation multiple for each nonhighly paid employee and computing an average of these multiples for the entire group of nonhighly paid employees. An average multiple also is computed for all highly paid employees. As with the other tests, certain part-timers and other employees can be excluded.

The process of computing the employer-provided compensation multiple is similar to that used for the 90/50 Test. The amount of employer-provided coverage is determined for each employee and then divided by the employee's compensation. There are two major differences, however, that typically will require separate calculations for group-term life insurance with elective coverage or paid through Section 125 salary reduction.

First, for elective coverages the calculation is based on what the employee actually elects, not on the maximum that could have been elected, as is done for the 90/50 Test. Second, coverage paid on a pretax basis under a flexible program is considered employer-provided. Thus the actual cost ratio used under the 90/50 Test to determine the employer-provided portion of contributory coverages is necessary under the Average Benefits Test only in the case of coverages the employee pays for with after-tax contributions.

(3)   Sanction

As with health care, if the Average Benefits Test for group-term life insurance is not passed, the employer-provided benefits provided to highly paid employees must be decreased, beginning with the employee with the greatest benefit, to a level at which the Average Benefits Test would have been satisfied if a cap on nontaxable benefits had been imposed at such level at the beginning of the year. The coverage of each highly paid employee in excess of this amount will be considered discriminatory, and its value would be taxed according to the greater of its actual cost or the amount determined under the Section 79 tables.

(c)   THE ALTERNATIVE 80-PERCENT TEST

The Alternative 80-Percent Test can be applied to group-term life insurance plans as well as health care plans. Under this test, a group-term life insurance plan is considered to satisfy the 50-Percent Test, the 90/50 Test, and the Average Benefits Test if it actually covers at least 80 percent of all nonhighly paid employees in the workforce being tested.

In general, each option and separate benefit level would be a separate plan for this purpose. However, as under the 50-Percent Test, an arrangement under which the amount of employer-provided coverage bears a uniform relationship to compensation can be considered a single plan.

The 80-Percent Test may be useful in cases where virtually all employees have the same basic coverage (one times compensation, for example) and nothing more is available. The test is not expected to be useful in the more typical situation where multiple-coverage options are available because actual coverage is required—not just eligibility to be covered.

§ 5.4   DISCRIMINATION TESTS FOR DEPENDENT CARE

Tax Reform imposes a somewhat different set of nondiscrimination rules for employer-assisted dependent care reimbursement plans. Section 129 imposes three basic tests: an eligibility test, a concentration test, and a benefits test. Alternatively, an employer may choose to apply the Section 89 eligibility and benefits tests to dependent care plans. However, the Section 129 concentration test described next would always be applied, even if the plan is tested under Section 89.

(a)   SECTION 129 NONDISCRIMINATION TESTS

(1)   The Eligibility Test

Section 129 requires that the employer-provided dependent care program must benefit employees who qualify under a classification set up by the employer which is not discriminatory in favor of highly paid employees and their dependents. Employees who can be excluded from the Section 89 tests may be excluded from this test. A similar classification test was part of Section 129 prior to Tax Reform.

(2) The Concentration Test

No more than 25 percent of the benefits paid by the plan may be provided for five-percent shareholders or owners. This test was also imposed by Section 129 prior to Tax Reform.

(3) The Average Benefits Test

The average benefit provided to nonhighly paid employees under the plan must be at least 55 percent of the average benefit provided to highly paid employees. The value of benefits for this purpose is the amount reimbursed by the plan. For this test, in the case of benefits provided through a salary reduction agreement, the employer may choose to disregard any employees whose compensation is less than $25,000. Guidance will be needed from Treasury as to how this rule will be applied to benefits which are only partially provided through a salary reduction agreement.

(4) Sanction

The sanction for failing any one of these tests is that all benefits provided under the plan are taxable income to *all* employees, not simply highly paid employees.

(b) CHOOSING THE SECTION 129 OR SECTION 89 TESTS

For many employers, the choice between whether to apply the Section 129 tests or the Section 89 tests may not be obvious. The Section 129 tests appear to be less stringent and easier to apply. However, the sanction for failure to comply is that benefits are taxable to all employees. Conversely, the Section 89 tests are more stringent and possibly more complex, but the sanction for failure to comply is taxation on the discriminatory portion of the benefit. Furthermore, as is discussed in more detail later, if the employer chooses to apply the Section 89 tests, dependent care may be aggregated with other benefit plans in applying the tests.

Guidance will also be needed from Treasury as to when the decision of testing method is to be made. Ideally, employers would be able to choose at the end of the year the testing method producing the most favorable result.

§ 5.5 DISCRIMINATION TESTS FOR GROUP LEGAL SERVICES

Under Tax Reform, Section 120 authorizing employer-sponsored group legal service reimbursement plans expired at the end of 1987. As a result, the Act does not mandate new rules for these plans. However, the Blue Book general explanation of the Act states that if Section 120 is extended, Congress anticipates that the Section 89 nondiscrimination rules will be applied to group legal service plans. The Blue Book also states that, as with dependent care, employers will have the election to test group legal service plans under the nondiscrimination rules of Section 120. In that case, the group legal plan could not be aggregated with other welfare benefit plans in applying the Section 89 tests.

§ 5.6 SPECIAL DISCRIMINATION TESTS FOR FLEXIBLE PROGRAMS

(a) IN GENERAL

Under Tax Reform, health, group-term life, dependent care, and group legal service offered as part of a flexible benefit plan are subject to the applicable nondiscrimination rules under Section 89, or in the case of dependent care and group legal, either Section 89 or the applicable Code Section. In addition, a Section 125 flexible benefit plan as a whole is subject to nondiscrimination tests under that Code Section.

Prior to Tax Reform, Section 125 imposed three nondiscrimination tests: a benefits test, an eligibility test, and a concentration test. Tax Reform eases the nondiscrimination rules somewhat, imposing only an eligibility test and the same concentration test as under prior law.

(1) The Eligibility Test

To meet the eligibility test, a Section 125 plan must be available to a group of employees that qualifies under a classification set up by the employer which the Secretary of the Treasury finds does not discriminate in favor of the highly paid. This is the fair cross-section test which was previously part of the nondiscrimination rules for self-insured medical plans and for retirement plans. Guidance will be needed as to how this rule applies specifically to Section 125 plans.

(2)   The Concentration Test

This test is identical to the concentration test previously included in Section 125. It states that no more than 25 percent of the aggregate benefits provided under the plan may go to key employees. Key employees generally include officers, the top ten employees ranked by compensation, five-percent owners, and one-percent owners earning more than $150,000.

(b)   SANCTION

If the eligibility test is not satisfied, highly paid employees will be taxed to the extent that the participant could have elected to take cash in lieu of benefits. In the original statute, Tax Reform would have taxed all employees to the extent that the benefit could have been taken as cash and would have taxed all highly compensated employees on the entire value of the benefits offered under the cafeteria plan. However, the proposed Technical Corrections Act would reduce the Tax Reform penalties to those described in the first sentence.

Similarly, under the proposed Technical Corrections Act, the penalty for failure to comply with the concentration test is imputed income to key employees on any taxable benefits. Tax Reform would impose the same stiffer sanction that it imposed if the eligibility test were not met.

§ 5.7   TYPES OF EXCLUDABLE EMPLOYEES

(a)   IN GENERAL

Under the "excluded employee" rules, employers can deny eligibility and coverage to certain employees—at least temporarily—with no adverse impact on the welfare plan nondiscrimination tests. These rules do not specifically define who must be provided with coverage; instead, they define who must be included in the testing for nondiscrimination.

(b) SPECIFIC EXCLUSIONS

(1) New Hires

Newly hired employees generally can be disregarded until they have worked for the employer for the shortest of the following periods:

- Six months of service, when applying the tests to health care plans
- One year of service, when applying the tests to group-term life insurance or dependent care assistance plans
- The shortest initial period of service required under any plan of the same type (i.e., the shortest period for any health care plan when applying the health care tests, the shortest period for any group-term life insurance plan when applying the group-term life tests, etc.), or
- For a flexible benefit program treated as a cafeteria plan under Code Section 125, the shortest period of service required under any benefit provided under the plan.

Two exceptions deserve mention. First, in cases where the tests focus in particular on noncore health care benefits, employees can be disregarded (for up to one year) during the shortest initial service period for any noncore plan, without regard to the initial service period for core health care benefits. (Noncore benefits are defined to include coverage for dental, vision, psychological and orthodontia expenses, and elective cosmetic surgery. All other health care benefits are considered core benefits for this purpose.) The second exception, involving separate testing, is discussed later.

(2) Part-Time Employees

Employees may be disregarded during any period in which they normally work less than the lesser of:

- $17^1/_2$ hours per week
- Any lesser number of hours per week used to determine eligibility for the benefits of the type being tested or under a cafeteria plan maintained by the employer.

(3) Seasonal Employees

Seasonal employees may be disregarded for any period during which they work. A seasonal employee is defined as an employee who normally works not more than the lesser of:

- Six months during any year
- A lesser period used to determine eligibility for seasonal employees for benefits of the type being tested or under a cafeteria plan maintained by the employer.

(4) Age 21 or Younger Employees

Employees can be disregarded until they attain the lower of:

- Age 21, or
- A lower age used to determine eligibility for benefits of the type being tested or under a cafeteria plan maintained by the employer.

(5) Collective Bargaining Groups

In limited situations, union-represented employees can be disregarded. However, this so-called collective-bargaining exclusion applies only if:

- There is evidence that the type of benefits provided under the plan was the subject of good-faith bargaining between employee representatives and the employer, and
- The type of benefits being tested is not provided to employees in the collective-bargaining unit.

The collective-bargaining exclusion typically will not apply in testing either health care or group-term life insurance benefits, because benefits of each such type generally are provided to collective-bargaining unit employees. The exclusion often will not apply in testing dependent care assistance plans, because such plans are not, as a matter of course, the subject of good-faith bargaining.

Given these limitations, union-represented employees and their benefit arrangements typically will have to be taken into account in testing welfare benefits provided to nonunion employees.

(6)   Nonresident Aliens

Employees may be disregarded during periods that they are nonresident aliens and receive no earned income from the employer that constitutes income from sources within the United States, whether or not they are covered under the plan being tested or any other plan of the same type.

(c)   SEPARATE TESTING RULE

Congress apparently recognized that the excludable employee rules just described contemplate a uniformity in benefit design that often does not occur with welfare plans. A company may, for example, apply a one-month waiting period for health care plans for the great majority of employees, but it may provide immediate participation for an isolated group of employees. Absent a special rule, the majority of new hires in this situation would be taken into account under the tests as uncovered employees during the one-month waiting period simply because the isolated group enjoyed immediate coverage.

The separate testing rule provides a way to avoid this result when testing health care and group-term life insurance. In the case of an employer who can demonstrate that benefits provided to newly hired employees, when tested separately from other employees, satisfy the welfare plan nondiscrimination tests, the exclusion rules can be utilized without regard to the fact that particular groups are eligible immediately, or after shorter initial service periods than others. (The rules provide a similar exception for cases where particular groups of employees are allowed to participate at lower ages than generally required.)

It is not uncommon for benefits to be provided from date of hire for certain groups such as salaried employees. In such cases it may not be possible to demonstrate that the newly hired group, when tested separately, would satisfy the tests without some further modification. One such modification would be to require certain highly paid employees to purchase benefits on an after-tax basis during the initial service period. Doing so could ensure that the separate test would be satisfied, and thus the modification would preserve the employer's ability to exclude those in the general employee group during their eligibility waiting periods. Moreover, for large companies, the group whose benefits were changed to after-tax may be quite small. This is because (under Tax Reform) employees can become highly compensated in their year of hire usually only if they are in the group of the 100 most highly paid employees.

IRS regulations should clarify the scope of the newly hired group which must be tested separately under this exception, as well as specify how the separate testing rule would apply to benefits other than health care and group-term life insurance.

§ 5.8 AGGREGATION OF PLANS

If a group-term life insurance plan or a dependent care plan does not pass the Section 89 Average Benefits test, the employer may choose to aggregate two or more types of benefits in order to pass the tests. Health care plans must pass the Average Benefits test on their own. But health care plans may help other types of plans pass the tests.

There are several special rules related to aggregation. First, the excluded employee rules apply as if the plans were of the same type. The nonexcludable employee group is determined based on the most liberal requirements of any plan being aggregated. Thus if a life insurance plan with 30-day eligibility and no age requirement is aggregated with a health plan with 90-day eligibility and an age 21 requirement, employees with at least 30 days of service must be included in the testing group with no age requirement.

Second, if a life insurance plan is aggregated with another plan, the amount tested is the value of employer-provided coverage assuming all employees are age 40 and using the Section 79 table rates. No adjustment for compensation is applied.

Third, if dependent care is to be aggregated with another plan, the dependent care plan must be tested under the Section 89 nondiscrimination rules rather than the rules under Section 129.

§ 5.9 SEPARATE TESTING FOR LINES OF BUSINESS AND OPERATING UNITS

In addition to the rules described in this chapter, there is one more issue for employers (particularly larger employers) to consider. That issue is whether all business units are to be tested as one entity or whether the tests should be applied separately to each line of business or each operating unit. A line of business is a business unit that is engaged in a different business than other business units of the same organization. An operating unit, on the other hand, is a business unit that may or may not engage in the same business as other units in the organization. (For example, two factories making the same products may be separate operating units.)

The ability to test lines of business and operating units separately is subject to several limits. A line of business or operating unit must be operated for bonafide business reasons. Also, a line of business or operating unit must have at least 50 (nonexcludable) employees. However, separate lines of business or operating units can be aggregated to meet this rule. The employer must notify the IRS that it intends to apply these tests on a line of business/operating unit basis. Finally, the employer must either meet guidelines to be established by the IRS or obtain a ruling from the IRS permitting testing on a line of business/operating unit basis. At the time of this writing, the IRS had not established any guidelines or ruling criteria.

As an alternative to meeting IRS guidelines or obtaining a ruling (but not to the other requirements) there is an automatic "safe harbor" available to an employer to prove that these tests can be applied separately to operating units or lines of business. Under this safe harbor, the employer's highly paid employees (as defined in Chapter Four) must not be overrepresented or underrepresented in any single line of business or operating unit. This is to help ensure that units with rich benefit programs do not have a disproportionately high percentage of highly paid employees. Under the safe harbor, the percentage of highly paid employees within a line of business or operating unit may not comprise more than twice nor less than one-half the percentage of all employees (throughout the employer) who are highly paid. The "less than one-half" portion of the test is met if at least 10 percent of all highly paid employees (throughout the employer) perform services soley for the line of business or operating unit.

There are various other rules that limit separate testing by lines of business or operating units. The most significant rules include:

- Corporate headquarters may not be tested as a separate line of business or operating unit. Special rules will be established to "allocate" headquarters personnel to different lines of business.
- All employees within a corporation (or group of related corporations) must be included in a line of business.
- Operating units (in the same line of business) cannot be tested separately if they are located in the same geographic vicinity. Treasury regulations will be needed to clarify the meaning of "same geographic vicinity."

Appendix

Statutes and Explanations

(a) **INTERNAL REVENUE CODE**

    (1) Section 89 (As Amended by Tax Reform Act of 1986)
    (2) Section 105 (As Amended by Tax Reform Act of 1986)
    (3) Section 106 (As Amended by Tax Reform Act of 1986)
    (4) Section 120 (As Amended by Tax Reform Act of 1986)
    (5) Section 129 (As Amended by Tax Reform Act of 1986)

(b) **GENERAL EXPLANATION OF THE TAX REFORM ACT OF 1986:
TITLE XI, PART F, SECTIONS 1–6 (THE BLUE BOOK)**

(a) INTERNAL REVENUE CODE

(1) SECTION 89 (AS AMENDED BY THE TAX REFORM ACT OF 1986)

[¶ 899ZV]   BENEFITS PROVIDED UNDER CERTAIN EMPLOYEE BENEFIT PLANS

→**Caution: Code Sec. 89, below, as added by P.L. 99-514, applies to years beginning after later of 12/31/87 or earlier of date 3 months after issuance of Regs. or 12/31/88.←**

Sec. 89 [1986 Code]. (a) BENEFITS UNDER DISCRIMINATORY PLANS.—

(1) IN GENERAL.—Notwithstanding any provision of part III of this subchapter, gross income of a highly compensated employee who is a participant in a discriminatory employee benefit plan during any plan year shall include an amount equal to such employee's excess benefit under such plan for such plan year.

(2) YEAR OF INCLUSION.—Any amount included in gross income under paragraph (1) shall be taken into account for the taxable year of the employee with or within which the plan year ends.

(b) EXCESS BENEFIT.—For purposes of this section—

(1) IN GENERAL.—The excess benefit of any highly compensated employee is the excess of such employee's employer-provided benefit under the plan over the highest permitted benefit.

(2) HIGHEST PERMITTED BENEFIT.—For purposes of paragraph (1), the highest permitted benefit under any plan shall be determined by reducing the nontaxable benefits of highly compensated employees (beginning with the employees with the greatest nontaxable benefits) until such plan would not be treated as a discriminatory employee benefit plan if such reduced benefits were taken into account.

(3) PLANS OF SAME TYPE.—In computing the excess benefit with respect to any benefit, there shall be taken into account all plans of the employer of the same type.

(4) NONTAXABLE BENEFITS.—For purposes of this subsection, the term "nontaxable benefit" means any benefit provided under a plan to which this section applies which (without regard to subsection (a)(1)) is excludable from gross income under this chapter.

(c) DISCRIMINATORY EMPLOYEE BENEFIT PLAN.—For purposes of this section, the term "discriminatory employee benefit plan" means any statutory employee benefit plan unless such plan meets the—

(1) eligibility requirements of subsection (d), and

(2) benefit requirements of subsection (e).

(d) ELIGIBILITY REQUIREMENTS.—

(1) IN GENERAL.—A plan meets the eligibility requirements of this subsection for any plan year if—

(A) at least 90 percent of all employees who are not highly compensated employees—

(i) are eligible to participate in such plan (or in any other plan of the employer of the same type), and

(ii) would (if they participated) have available under such plans an employer-provided benefit which is at least 50 percent of the largest employer-provided benefit available under all such plans of the employer to any highly compensated employee,

(B) at least 50 percent of the employees eligible to participate in such plan are not highly compensated employees, and

(C) such plan does not contain any provision relating to eligibility to participate which (by its terms or otherwise) discriminates in favor of highly compensated employees.

(2) ALTERNATIVE ELIGIBILITY PERCENTAGE TEST.—A plan shall be treated as meeting the requirements of paragraph (1)(B) if—

(A) the percentage determined by dividing the number of highly compensated employees eligible to participate in the plan by the total number of highly compensated employees, does not exceed

(B) the percentage similarly determined with respect to employees who are not highly compensated employees.

(e) BENEFIT REQUIREMENTS.—

(1) IN GENERAL.—A plan meets the benefit requirements of this subsection for any plan year if the average employer-provided benefit received by employees other than highly compensated employees under all plans of the employer of the same type is at least 75 percent of the average employer-provided benefit received by highly compensated employees under all plans of the employer of the same type.

(2) AVERAGE EMPLOYER-PROVIDED BENEFIT.—For purposes of this subsection, the term "average employer-provided benefit" means, with respect to highly compensated employees, an amount equal to—

(A) the aggregate employer-provided benefits received by highly compensated employees under all plans of the type being tested, divided by

(B) the number of highly compensated employees (whether or not covered under such plans). The average employer-provided benefit with respect to employees other than highly compensated employees shall be determined in the same manner as the average employer-provided benefit for highly compensated employees.

(f) SPECIAL RULE WHERE HEALTH OR GROUP-TERM PLAN MEETS 80-PERCENT COVERAGE TEST.—If at least 80 percent of the employees who are not highly compensated employees are covered under a health plan or group-term life insurance plan during the plan year, such plan shall be treated as meeting the requirements of subsections (d) and (e) for such year. The preceding sentence shall not apply if the plan does not meet the requirements of subsection (d)(1)(C) (relating to nondiscriminatory provisions).

(g) OPERATING RULES.—

(1) AGGREGATION OF COMPARABLE HEALTH PLANS.—In the case of health plans maintained by an employer—

(A) IN GENERAL.—An employer may treat a group of comparable plans as 1 plan for purposes of applying subsections (d)(1)(B), (d)(2) and (f).

(B) COMPARABLE PLANS.—For purposes of subparagraph (A), a group of comparable plans is any group (selected by the employer) of plans of the same type if the smallest employer-provided benefit available to any participant in any such plan is at least 95 percent of the largest employer-provided benefit available to any participant in any such plan.

(2) SPECIAL RULES FOR APPLYING BENEFIT REQUIREMENTS TO HEALTH PLANS.—

(A) ELECTION.—For purposes of determining whether the requirements of subsection (e) are met with respect to health plans, the employer may elect—

(i) to disregard any employee if such employee and his spouse and dependents (if any) are covered by a health plan providing core benefits maintained by another employer, and

(ii) to apply subsection (e) separately with respect to coverage of spouses or dependents by such plans and to take into account with respect to such coverage only employees with a spouse or dependents who are not covered by a health plan providing core benefits maintained by another employer.

(B) SWORN STATEMENTS.—Any employer who elects the application of subparagraph (A) shall obtain and maintain, in such manner as the Secretary may prescribe, adequate sworn statements to demonstrate whether individuals have—

(i) a spouse or dependents, and

(ii) core health benefits under a plan of another employer.

The Secretary shall provide a method for meeting the requirements of this subparagraph through the use of valid sampling techniques.

(C) PRESUMPTION WHERE NO STATEMENT.—In the absence of a statement described in subparagraph (B)—

(i) an employee who is not a highly compensated employee shall be treated—

(I) as not covered by another plan of another employer providing core benefits, and

(II) as having a spouse and dependents not covered by another plan of another employer providing core benefits, and

(ii) a highly compensated employee shall be treated—

(I)   as covered by another plan of another employer providing core benefits, and

(II)   as not having a spouse or dependents.

(D) CERTAIN INDIVIDUALS MAY NOT BE DISREGARDED.—In the case of a highly compensated employee who receives employer-provided benefits under all health plans of the employer which are more than 133¹/₃ percent of the average employer-provided benefit under such plan for employees other than highly compensated employees, the employer may not disregard such employee, or his spouse or dependents for purposes of clause (i) or (ii) of subparagraph (A).

(3) EMPLOYER-PROVIDED BENEFIT.—For purposes of this section—

(A) IN GENERAL.—Except as provided in subsection (k), an employee's employer-provided benefit under any statutory employee benefit plan is—

(i)   in the case of any health or group-term life insurance plan, the value of the coverage, or

(ii)   in the case of any other plan, the value of the benefits,

provided during the plan year to or on behalf of such employee to the extent attributable to contributions made by the employer.

(B) SPECIAL RULE FOR HEALTH PLANS.—The value of the coverage provided by any health plan shall be determined under procedures prescribed by the Secretary which shall—

(i)   set forth the values of various standard types of coverage involving a representative group, and

(ii)   provide for adjustments to take into account the specific coverage and group involved.

(C) SPECIAL RULE FOR GROUP-TERM LIFE PLANS.—

(i)   IN GENERAL.—Except as provided in clause (ii), in determining the value of coverage under a group-term life insurance plan, the amount taken into account for any employee shall be based on the cost of the insurance determined under section 79(c) for an employee who is age 40.

(ii)   EXCESS BENEFIT.—For purposes of subsection (b), the excess benefit with respect to coverage under a group-term life insurance plan shall be equal to the greater of—

(I)   the cost of such excess benefit (expressed as dollars of coverage) determined without regard to section 79(c), or

(II)   such cost determined with regard to section 79(c).

(D) SALARY REDUCTIONS.—Except for purposes of subsections (d)(1)(A)(ii) and (j)(5), any salary reduction shall be treated as an employer-provided benefit.

(4) ELECTION TO TEST PLANS OF DIFFERENT TYPES TOGETHER.—

(A) IN GENERAL.—Except as provided in subparagraph (B), the employer may elect to treat all plans of the types specified in such election as plans of the same type for purposes of applying subsection (e).

(B) EXCEPTION FOR HEALTH PLANS.—Subparagraph (A) shall not apply for purposes of determining whether any health plan meets the requirements of subsection (e); except that benefits provided under health plans which meet such requirements may be taken into account in determining whether plans of other types meet the requirements of subsection (e).

(5) SEPARATE LINE OF BUSINESS EXCEPTION.—If, under section 414(r), an employer is treated as operating separate lines of business for a year, the employer may apply the preceding provisions of this section separately with respect to employees in each such separate line of business. The preceding sentence shall not apply to any plan unless such plan is available to a group of employees as qualify under a classification set up by the employer and found by the Secretary not to be discriminatory in favor of highly compensated employees.

(6) SPECIAL RULE FOR APPLYING ELIGIBILITY REQUIREMENTS AND 80-PERCENT TEST TO HEALTH PLANS.—For purposes of determining whether the requirements of subsection (d)(1)(A)(ii) or of subsection (f) are met with respect to health plans, the employer may elect—

(A) to apply this section separately with respect to coverage of spouses and dependents by such plans, and

(B) to take into account with respect to such coverage only those employees with a spouse or dependent (determined under rules similar to the rules of paragraphs (2)(B) and (C)).

(h) EXCLUDED EMPLOYEES.—

(1) IN GENERAL.—The following employees shall be excluded from consideration under this section:

(A) Employees who have not completed 1 year of service (or in the case of core benefits under a health plan, 6 months of service). An employee shall be excluded from consideration until the 1st day of the 1st month beginning after completion of the period of service required under the preceding sentence.

(B) Employees who normally work less than $17^{1}/_{2}$ hours per week.

(C) Employees who normally work during not more than 6 months during any year.

(D) Employees who have not attained age 21.

(E) Employees who are included in a unit of employees covered by an agreement which the Secretary finds to be a collective bargaining agreement between employee representatives and 1 or more employers if there is evidence that the type of benefits provided under the plan was the subject of good faith bargaining between the employee representatives and such employer or employers.

(F) Employees who are nonresident aliens and who receive no earned income (within the meaning of section 911(d)(2)) from the employer which constitutes income from sources within the United States (within the meaning of section 861(a)(3)).

Subparagraphs (A), (B), (C), and (D) shall be applied by substituting a shorter period of service, smaller number of hours or months, or lower age specified in the plan for the period of service, number of hours or months, or age (as the case may be) specified in such subparagraph.

(2) CERTAIN EXCLUSIONS NOT TO APPLY IF EXCLUDED EMPLOYEES COVERED.—Except to the extent provided in regulations, employees shall not be excluded from consideration under any subparagraph of paragraph (1) (other than subparagraph (F)) unless no employee described in such subparagraph (determined with regard to the last sentence of paragraph (1)) is eligible under the plan.

(3) EXCLUSION MUST APPLY TO ALL PLANS.—

(A) IN GENERAL.—An exclusion shall apply under any subparagraph of paragraph (1) (other than subparagraph (F) thereof) only if the exclusion applies to all statutory employee benefit plans of the employer of the same type. In the case of a cafeteria plan, all benefits under the cafeteria plan shall be treated as provided under plans of the same type.

(B) EXCEPTION.—Subparagraph (A) shall not apply to any difference in waiting periods for core and noncore benefits provided by health plans.

(4) EXCEPTION FOR SEPARATE LINE OF BUSINESS.—If any line of business is treated separately under subsection (h)(5), then paragraphs (2) and (3) shall be applied separately to such line of business.

(5) REQUIREMENTS MAY BE MET SEPARATELY WITH RESPECT TO EXCLUDED GROUP.—Notwithstanding paragraphs (2) and (3), if employees do not meet minimum age or service requirements described in paragraph (1) (without regard to the last sentence thereof) and are covered under a plan of the employer which meets the requirements of this section separately with respect to such employees, such employees may be excluded from consideration in determining whether any plan of the employer meets the requirements of this section.

(i) STATUTORY EMPLOYEE BENEFIT PLAN.—For purposes of this section—

(1) IN GENERAL.—The term "statutory employee benefit plan" means—

(A) an accident or health plan (within the meaning of section 105(e)), and

(B) any plan of an employer for providing group-term life insurance (within the meaning of section 79).

(2) EMPLOYER MAY ELECT TO TREAT OTHER PLANS AS STATUTORY EMPLOYEE BENEFIT PLAN.—An employer may elect to treat any of the following plans as statutory employee benefit plans:

(A) A qualified group legal services plan (within the meaning of section 120(b)).

(B) An educational assistance program (within the meaning of section 127(b)).

(C) A dependent care assistance program (within the meaning of section 129(d)).

An election under this paragraph with respect to any plan shall apply with respect to all plans of the same type as such plan.

(3) PLANS OF THE SAME TYPE.—2 or more plans shall be treated as of the same type if such plans are described in the same subparagraph of paragraph (1) or (2).

(j) OTHER DEFINITIONS AND SPECIAL RULES.—For purposes of this section—

(1) HIGHLY COMPENSATED EMPLOYEE.—The term "highly compensated employee" has the meaning given such term by section 414(q).

(2) HEALTH PLAN.—The term "health plan" means any plan described in paragraph (1)(A) of subsection (i).

(3) TREATMENT OF FORMER EMPLOYEES.—Except to the extent provided in regulations, this section shall be applied separately to former employees under requirements similar to the requirements that apply to employees.

(4) GROUP-TERM LIFE INSURANCE PLANS.—

(A) IN GENERAL.—Any group-term life insurance plan shall not be treated as 2 or more separate plans merely because the amount of life insurance under the plan on behalf of employees bears a uniform relationship to the compensation (within the meaning of section 414(s)) of such employees.

(B) LIMITATION ON COMPENSATION.—For purposes of subparagraph (A), compensation in excess of the amount applicable under section 401(a)(17) shall not be taken into account.

(C) LIMITATION.—This paragraph shall not apply to any plan if such plan is combined with plans of other types pursuant to an election under subsection (g)(4).

(5) SPECIAL RULE FOR EMPLOYEES WORKING LESS THAN 30 HOURS PER WEEK.—Any health plan shall not fail to meet the requirements of this section merely because the employer-provided benefit is proportionately reduced for employees who normally work less than 30 hours per week. The preceding sentence shall apply only where the average work week of employees who are not highly compensated employees is 30 hours or more.

(6) TREATMENT OF SELF-EMPLOYED INDIVIDUALS.—In the case of a statutory employee benefit plan described in subparagraph (A), (B), or (C) of subsection (i)(2)—

(A) TREATMENT AS EMPLOYEE, ETC.—The term "employee" includes any self-employed individual (as defined in section 401(c)(1)), and the term "compensation" includes such individual's earned income (as defined in section 401(c)(2)).

(B) EMPLOYER.—An individual who owns the entire interest in an unincorporated trade or business shall be treated as his own employer. A partnership shall be treated as the employer of each partner who is treated as an employee under subparagraph (A).

(7) CERTAIN PLANS TREATED AS MEETING OTHER NONDISCRIMINATION REQUIREMENTS.—If an employer makes an election under subsection (i)(2) to have this section apply to any plan and such plan meets the requirements of this section, such plan shall be treated as meeting any other nondiscrimination requirement imposed on such plan (other than any requirement under section 120(c)(3), 127(b)(3), or 129(d)(4)).

(8) SPECIAL RULES FOR CERTAIN DISPOSITIONS OR ACQUISITIONS.—

(A) IN GENERAL.—If a person becomes, or ceases to be, a member of a group described in subsection (b), (c), (m), or (o) of section 414, then the requirements of this section shall be treated as having been met during the transition period with respect to any plan covering employees of such person or any other member of such group if—

(i) such requirements were met immediately before each such change, and

(ii) the coverage under such plan is not significantly changed during the transition period (other than by reason of the change in members of a group).

(B) TRANSITION PERIOD.—For purposes of subparagraph (A), the term "transition period" means the period—

(i) beginning on the date of the change in members of a group, and

(ii) ending on the last day of the 1st plan year beginning after the date of such change.

(9) COORDINATION WITH MEDICARE, ETC.—If a plan may be coordinated with health benefits provided under any Federal, State, or foreign law or under any other health plan covering the employee or family member of the employee, such plan shall not fail to meet the requirements of this section with respect to health benefits merely because the amount of such benefits provided to any employee or family member of any employee are coordinated in a manner which does not discriminate in favor of highly compensated employees.

(10) DISABILITY BENEFITS.—

(A) IN GENERAL.—If a plan may be coordinated with disability benefits provided under any Federal, State, or foreign law or under any other plan covering the employee, such plan shall not fail to meet the requirements of this section with respect to disability benefits merely because the amount of such benefits provided to an employee are coordinated in a manner which does not discriminate in favor of highly compensated employees.

(B) CERTAIN DISABILITY PLANS EXEMPT FROM NONDISCRIMINATION RULES.—Subsection (a) shall not apply to any disability coverage other than disability coverage the benefits of which are excludable from gross income under section 105(b) or (c).

(11) SEPARATE APPLICATION IN THE CASE OF OPTIONS.—Each option or different benefit shall be treated as a separate plan.

(k) REQUIREMENT THAT PLAN BE IN WRITING, ETC.—

(1) IN GENERAL.—Notwithstanding any provision of part III of this subchapter, gross income of an employee shall include an amount equal to such employee's employer-provided benefit for the taxable year under an employee benefit plan to which this subsection applies unless, except to the extent provided in regulations—

(A) such plan is in writing,

(B) the employees' rights under such plan are legally enforceable,

(C) employees are provided reasonable notification of benefits available in the plan,

(D) such plan is maintained for the exclusive benefit of employees, and

(E) such plan was established with the intention of being maintained for an indefinite period of time.

Such inclusion shall be in lieu of any inclusion under subsection (a) with respect to such plan.

(2) PLANS TO WHICH SUBSECTION APPLIES.—This subsection shall apply to—

(A) any statutory employee benefit plan,

(B) a qualified tuition reduction program (within the meaning of section 117(d)),

(C) a cafeteria plan (within the meaning of section 125),

(D) a fringe benefit program providing no-additional-cost services, qualified employee discounts, or employer-operated eating facilities which are excludable from gross income under section 132, and

(E) a plan to which section 505 applies.

(3) SPECIAL RULE FOR DETERMINING INCLUSION.—For purposes of paragraph (1), an employee's employer-provided benefit shall be the value of the benefits provided to the employee.

(4) PLANS TO WHICH CONTRIBUTIONS ARE MADE BY MORE THAN 1 EMPLOYER.—For purposes of paragraph (1)(D), in the case of a plan to which contributions are made by more than 1 employer, each employer shall be treated as employing employees of all other employers.

(l) REPORTING REQUIREMENTS.—

(1) IN GENERAL.—If an employee of an employer maintaining a plan is required to include any amount in gross income under this section for any plan year ending with or within a calendar year, the employer shall separately include such amount on the statement which the employer is required to provide the employee under section 6051(a) (and any statement required to be furnished under section 6051(d)).

(2) PENALTY.—

For penalty for failing to report, see section 6652(l).

(m) REGULATIONS.—The Secretary shall prescribe such regulations as may be necessary or appropriate to carry out the purposes of this section, including regulations providing for appropriate adjustments in case of individuals not employees of the employer throughout the plan year.

(2)   SECTION 105 (AS AMENDED BY THE TAX REFORM ACT OF 1986)

HEALTH PLANS

[¶ 1030]   AMOUNTS RECEIVED UNDER ACCIDENT AND HEALTH PLANS

Sec. 105 [1986 Code]. (a) AMOUNTS ATTRIBUTABLE TO EMPLOYER CONTRIBUTIONS.—Except as otherwise provided in this section, amounts received by an employee through accident or health insurance for personal injuries or sickness shall be included in gross income to the extent such amounts (1) are attributable to contributions by the employer which were not includible in the gross income of the employee, or (2) are paid by the employer.

→Caution: P.L. 98-369 (Tax Reform Act of 1984) added the last sentence of Code Sec. 105(b), effective for tax years beginning after December 31, 1984.←

(b) AMOUNTS EXPENDED FOR MEDICAL CARE.—Except in the case of amounts attributable to (and not in excess of) deductions allowed under section 213 (relating to medical, etc., expenses) for any prior taxable year, gross income does not include amounts referred to in subsection (a) if such amounts are paid, directly or indirectly, to the taxpayer to reimburse the taxpayer for expenses incurred by him for the medical care (as defined in section 213(d)) of the taxpayer, his spouse, and his dependents (as defined in section 152). Any child to whom section 152(e) applies shall be treated as a dependent of both parents for purposes of this subsection.

(c) PAYMENTS UNRELATED TO ABSENCE FROM WORK.—Gross income does not include amounts referred to in subsection (a) to the extent such amounts—

(1)   constitute payment for the permanent loss or loss of use of a member or function of the body, or the permanent disfigurement, of the taxpayer, his spouse, or a dependent (as defined in section 152), and

(2)   are computed with reference to the nature of the injury without regard to the period the employee is absent from work.

→Caution: Code Sec. 105(d), below, is repealed by P.L. 98-21, effective for taxable years beginning after December 31, 1983.←

(d) CERTAIN DISABILITY PAYMENTS.—

(1) IN GENERAL.—In the case of a taxpayer who—

(A) has not attained age 65 before the close of the taxable year, and

(B) retired on disability and, when he retired, was permanently and totally disabled,

gross income does not include amounts referred to in subsection (a) if such amounts constitute wages or payments in lieu of wages for a period during which the employee is absent from work on account of permanent and total disability."

(2) LIMITATION.—This subsection shall not apply to the extent that the amounts referred to in paragraph (1) exceed a weekly rate of $100.

(3) PHASEOUT OVER $15,000.—If the adjusted gross income of the taxpayer for the taxable year (determined without regard to this subsection and section 221) exceeds $15,000, the amount which but for this paragraph would be excluded under this subsection for the taxable year shall be reduced by an amount equal to the excess of the adjusted gross income (as so determined) over $15,000.

(4) PERMANENT AND TOTAL DISABILITY DEFINED.—For purposes of this subsection, an individual is permanently and totally disabled if he is unable to engage in any substantial gainful activity by reason of any medically determinable physical or mental impairment which can be expected to result in death or which has lasted or can be expected to last for a continuous period of not less than 12 months. An individual shall not be considered to be permanently and totally disabled unless he furnishes proof of the existence thereof in such form and manner, and at such times, as the Secretary may require.

(5) SPECIAL RULES FOR MARRIED COUPLES.—

(A) MARRIED COUPLE MUST FILE JOINT RETURN.—Except in the case of a husband and wife who live apart at all times during the taxable year, if the taxpayer is married at the close of the taxable year, the exclusion provided by this subsection shall be allowed only if the taxpayer and his spouse file a joint return for the taxable year.

(B) APPLICATION OF PARAGRAPHS (2) AND (3).—In the case of a joint return—

(i) paragraph (2) shall be applied separately with respect to each spouse, but

(ii) paragraph (3) shall be applied with respect to their combined adjusted gross income.

(C) DETERMINATION OF MARITAL STATUS.—For purposes of this subsection, marital status shall be determined under section 143(a).

(D) JOINT RETURN DEFINED.—For purposes of this subsection, the term "joint return" means the joint return of a husband and wife made under section 6013.

(6) COORDINATION WITH SECTION 72.—In the case of an individual described in subparagraphs (A) and (B) of paragraph (1) for purposes of section 72 the annuity starting date shall not be deemed to occur before the beginning of the taxable year in which the taxpayer attains age 65, or before

the beginning of an earlier taxable year for which the taxpayer makes an irrevocable election not to seek the benefits of this subsection for such year and all subsequent years.

(e) ACCIDENT AND HEALTH PLANS.—For purposes of this section and section 104—

(1) amounts received under an accident or health plan for employees, and

(2) amounts received from a sickness and disability fund for employees maintained under the law of a State, or the District of Columbia,

shall be treated as amounts received through accident or health insurance.

(f) RULES FOR APPLICATION OF SECTION 213.—For purposes of section 213(a) (relating to medical, dental, etc., expenses) amounts excluded from gross income under subsection (c) or (d) shall not be considered as compensation (by insurance or otherwise) for expenses paid for medical care.

(g) SELF-EMPLOYED INDIVIDUAL NOT CONSIDERED AN EMPLOYEE.—For purposes of this section, the term "employee" does not include an individual who is an employee within the meaning of section 401(c)(1) (relating to self-employed individuals).

→**Caution: Code Sec. 105(h), below, was repealed by P.L. 99-514 effective, generally, for tax years beginning after December 31, 1987.**←

(h) AMOUNT PAID TO HIGHLY COMPENSATED INDIVIDUALS UNDER A DISCRIMINATORY SELF-INSURED MEDICAL EXPENSE REIMBURSEMENT PLAN.—

(1) IN GENERAL.—In the case of amounts paid to a highly compensated individual under a self-insured medical reimbursement plan which does not satisfy the requirements of paragraph (2) for a plan year, subsection (b) shall not apply to such amounts to the extent they constitute an excess reimbursement of such highly compensated individual.

(2) PROHIBITION OF DISCRIMINATION.—A self-insured medical reimbursement plan satisfies the requirements of this paragraph only if—

(A) the plan does not discriminate in favor of highly compensated individuals as to eligibility to participate; and

(B) the benefits provided under the plan do not discriminate in favor of participants who are highly compensated individuals.

(3) NONDISCRIMINATORY ELIGIBILITY CLASSIFICATIONS.—

(A) IN GENERAL.—A self-insured medical reimbursement plan does not satisfy the requirements of subparagraph (A) of paragraph (2) unless such plan benefits—

→**Caution: Code Sec. 105(h), below, was repealed by P.L. 99-514.**←

(i) 70 percent or more of all employees, or 80 percent or more of all the employees who are eligible to benefit under the plan if 70 percent or more of all employees are eligible to benefit under the plan; or

(ii) Such employees as qualify under a classification set up by the employer and found by the Secretary not to be discriminatory in favor of highly compensated individuals.

(B) EXCLUSION OF CERTAIN EMPLOYEES.—For purposes of subparagraph (A), there may be excluded from consideration—

(i)   employees who have not completed 3 years of service;

(ii) employees who have not attained age 25;

(iii) part-time or seasonal employees;

(iv) employees not included in the plan who are included in a unit of employees covered by an agreement between employee representatives and one or more employers which the Secretary finds to be a collective bargaining agreement, if accident and health benefits were the subject of good faith bargaining between such employee representatives and such employer or employers; and

(v)   employees who are nonresident aliens and who receive no earned income (within the meaning of section 911(d)(2)) from the employer which constitutes income from sources within the United States (within the meaning of section 861(a)(3)).

(4) NONDISCRIMINATORY BENEFITS.—A self-insured medical reimbursement plan does not meet the requirements of subparagraph (B) of paragraph (2) unless all benefits provided for participants who are highly compensated individuals are provided for all other participants.

(5) HIGHLY COMPENSATED INDIVIDUAL DEFINED.—For purposes of this subsection, the term "highly compensated individual" means an individual who is—

(A) one of the 5 highest paid officers,

(B) a shareholder who owns (with the application of section 318) more than 10 percent in value of the stock of the employer, or

(C) among the highest paid 25 percent of all employees (other than employees described in paragraph (3)(B) who are not participants).

(6) SELF-INSURED MEDICAL REIMBURSEMENT PLAN.—The term "self-insured medical reimbursement plan" means a plan of an employer to reimburse employees for expenses referred to in subsection (b) for which reimbursement is not provided under a policy of accident and health insurance.

(7) EXCESS REIMBURSEMENT OF HIGHLY COMPENSATED INDIVIDUAL.—For purposes of this section, the excess reimbursement of a highly compensated individual which is attributable to a self-insured medical reimbursement plan is—

(A) in the case of a benefit available to highly compensated individuals but not to all other participants (or which otherwise fails to satisfy the requirements of paragraph (2)(B)), the amount reimbursed under the plan to the employees with respect to such benefit, and

(B) in the case of benefits (other than benefits described in subparagraph (A)) paid to a highly compensated individual by a plan which fails to satisfy the requirements of paragraph (2), the total amount reimbursed to the highly compensated individual for the plan year multiplied by a fraction—

(i) the numerator of which is the total amount reimbursed to all participants who are highly compensated individuals under the plan for the plan year, and

(ii) the denominator of which is the total amount reimbursed to all employees under the plan for such plan year.

In determining the fraction under subparagraph (B), there shall not be taken into account any reimbursement which is attributable to a benefit described in subparagraph (A).

(8) CERTAIN CONTROLLED GROUPS, ETC.—All employees who are treated as employed by a single employer under subsection (b), (c), or (m) of section 414 shall be treated as employed by a single employer for purposes of this section.

(9) REGULATIONS.—The Secretary shall prescribe such regulations as may be necessary to carry out the provisions of this section.

(10) TIME OF INCLUSION.—Any amount paid for a plan year that is included in income by reason of this subsection shall be treated as received or accrued in the taxable year of the participant in which the plan year ends.

→Caution: Code Sec. 105(h), below, as added by P.L. 98-76 and amended by P.L. 99-514, is applicable to amounts received after 1983 in tax years ending after 1983.←

(h) SICK PAY UNDER RAILROAD UNEMPLOYMENT INSURANCE ACT.—Notwithstanding any other provision of law, gross income includes benefits paid under section 2(a) of the Railroad Unemployment Insurance Act for days of sickness; except to the extent such sickness (as determined in accordance with standards prescribed by the Railroad Retirement Board) is the result of on-the-job injury.

(3)   SECTION 106 (AS AMENDED BY THE TAX REFORM ACT OF 1986)

[¶ 1050]   CONTRIBUTIONS BY EMPLOYER TO ACCIDENT AND HEALTH PLANS

Sec. 106 [1986 Code]. (a) IN GENERAL.—Gross income of an employee does not include employer-provided coverage under an accident or health plan.

→Caution: Code Sec. 106(b), as added by P.L. 99-272, is effective for plan years beginning after June 30, 1986.←

(b) EXCEPTION FOR HIGHLY COMPENSATED INDIVIDUALS WHERE PLAN FAILS TO PROVIDE CERTAIN CONTINUATION COVERAGE.—

(1) IN GENERAL.—Subsection (a) shall not apply to any amount contributed by an employer on behalf of a highly compensated employee (within the meaning of section 414(q)) to a group health plan maintained by such employer unless all such plans maintained by such employer meet the continuing coverage requirements of section 162(k).

(2) EXCEPTION FOR CERTAIN PLANS.—Paragraph (1) shall not apply to any—

(A) group health plan for any calendar year if all employers maintaining such plan normally employed fewer than 20 employees on a typical business day during the preceding calendar year,

(B) governmental plan (within the meaning of section 414(d)), or

(C) church plan (within the meaning of section 414(e)).

Under regulations, rules similar to the rules of subsections (a) and (b) of section 52 (relating to employers under common control) shall apply for purposes of subparagraph (A).

(3) GROUP HEALTH PLAN.—For purposes of this subsection, the term "group health plan" has the meaning given such term by section 162(i)(3).

(4)   SECTION 120 (AS AMENDED BY THE TAX REFORM ACT
OF 1986)

→**Caution: Code Sec. 120, below, is scheduled to expire with respect to
tax years ending after December 31, 1987.←**

[¶ 1191A]   AMOUNTS RECEIVED UNDER QUALIFIED GROUP LEGAL
SERVICES PLANS

Sec. 120 [1986 Code]. (a) EXCLUSION BY EMPLOYEE FOR CONTRIBUTIONS AND
LEGAL SERVICES PROVIDED BY EMPLOYER.—Gross income of an employee, his
spouse, or his dependents, does not include—

(1)   amounts contributed by an employer on behalf of an employee, his
spouse, or his dependents under a qualified group legal services plan (as
defined in subsection (b)); or

(2)   the value of legal services provided, or amounts paid for legal services, under a qualified group legal services plan (as defined in subsection
(b)) to, or with respect to, an employee, his spouse, or his dependents.

→**Caution: Code Sec. 120(b), below, prior to amendment by P.L. 99-514,
applies to years beginning before the later of January 1, 1988, or the
earlier of three months after the issuance of regulations implementing
Code Sec. 89 or January 1, 1988.←**

(b)   QUALIFIED GROUP LEGAL SERVICES PLAN.—For purposes of this section, a
qualified group legal services plan is a separate written plan of an employer for
the exclusive benefit of his employees or their spouses or dependents to provide
such employees, spouses, or dependents with specified benefits consisting of
personal legal services through prepayment of, or provision in advance for, legal fees in whole or in part by the employer, if the plan meets the requirements
of subsection (c).

→**Caution: Code Sec. 120(b), below, as amended by P.L. 99-514, applies to
years beginning after the later of December 31, 1987, or the earlier of three
months after the issuance of regulations implementing Code Sec. 89 or
January 1, 1989.←**

(b)   QUALIFIED GROUP LEGAL SERVICES PLAN.—For purposes of this section, a
qualified group legal services plan is a separate plan of an employer—

(1)   under which the employer provides specified personal legal services to employees (or their spouses or dependents) through the prepayment

of, or the provision in advance for, any portion of the legal fees for such services, and

(2)   which meets the requirements of subsection (c) and section 89(k).

(c)   REQUIREMENTS.—

→Caution: Code Sec. 120(c)(1), below, prior to amendment by P.L. 99-514, applies to years beginning before 1988.←

(1)   DISCRIMINATION.—The contributions or benefits provided under the plan shall not discriminate in favor of employees who are officers, shareholders, self-employed individuals, or highly compensated.

→Caution: Code Sec. 120(c)(1), below, as amended by P.L. 99-514, applies to years beginning after 1987.←

(1)   DISCRIMINATION.—The contributions or benefits provided under the plan shall not discriminate in favor of employees who are highly compensated employees (within the meaning of section 414(q)).

→Caution: Code Sec. 120(c)(2), below, prior to amendment by P.L. 99-514, applies to years beginning before the later of January 1, 1988, or the earlier of three months after the issuance of regulations implementing Code Sec. 89 or January 1, 1989.←

(2)   ELIGIBILITY.—The plan shall benefit employees who qualify under a classification set up by the employer and found by the Secretary not to be discriminatory in favor of employees who are described in paragraph (1). For purposes of this paragraph, there shall be excluded from consideration employees not included in the plan who are included in a unit of employees covered by an agreement which the Secretary of Labor finds to be a collective bargaining agreement between employee representatives and one or more employers, if there is evidence that group legal services plan benefits were the subject of good faith bargaining between such employee representatives and such employer or employers.

→Caution: Code Sec. 120(c)(2), below, as amended by P.L. 99-514, applies to years beginning after the later of December 31, 1987, or the earlier of three months after the issuance of regulations implementing Code Sec. 89 or December 31, 1988.←

(2)   ELIGIBILITY.—The plan shall benefit employees who qualify under a classification set up by the employer and found by the Secretary not to be discriminatory in favor of employees who are described in paragraph (1). For purposes of this paragraph, there may be excluded from consideration employees who may be excluded from consideration under section 89(h).

→Caution: Code Sec. 120, below, is scheduled to expire with respect to tax years ending after December 31, 1987.←

(3) CONTRIBUTION LIMITATION.—Not more than 25 percent of the amounts contributed under the plan during the year may be provided for the class of individuals who are shareholders or owners (or their spouses or dependents), each of whom (on any day of the year) owns more than 5 percent of the stock or of the capital or profits interest in the employer.

(4) NOTIFICATION.—The plan shall give notice to the Secretary, in such manner as the Secretary may by regulations prescribe, that it is applying for recognition of the status of a qualified group legal services plan.

(5) CONTRIBUTIONS.—Amounts contributed under the plan shall be paid only (A) to insurance companies, or to organizations or persons that provide personal legal services, or indemnification against the cost of personal legal services, in exchange for a prepayment or payment of a premium, (B) to organizations or trusts described in section 501(c)(20), (C) to organizations described in section 501(c) which are permitted by that section to receive payments from an employer for support of one or more qualified group legal services plan or plans, except that such organizations shall pay or credit the contribution to an organization or trust described in section 501(c)(20), (D) as prepayments to providers of legal services under the plan, or (E) a combination of the above.

→Caution: Code Sec. 120(d)(1), below, prior to amendment by P.L. 99-514, applies to years beginning before 1988.←

(d) OTHER DEFINITIONS AND SPECIAL RULES.—For purposes of this section—

(1) SELF-EMPLOYED INDIVIDUAL; EMPLOYEE.—The term "self-employed individual" means, and the term "employee" includes, for any year, an individual who is an employee within the meaning of section 401(c)(1) (relating to self-employed individuals).

→Caution: Code Sec. 120(d)(1), below, as amended by P.L. 99-514, applies to years beginning after 1987.←

(1) EMPLOYEE.—The term "employee" includes, for any year, an individual who is an employee within the meaning of section 401(c)(1)(relating to self-employed individuals).

(2) EMPLOYER.—An individual who owns the entire interest in an unincorporated trade or business shall be treated as his own employer. A partnership shall be treated as the employer of each partner who is an employee within the meaning of paragraph (1).

(3) ALLOCATIONS.—Allocations of amounts contributed under the plan shall be made in accordance with regulations prescribed by the Secretary and shall take into account the expected relative utilization of benefits to be

provided from such contributions or plan assets and the manner in which any premium or other charge was developed.

(4) DEPENDENT.—The term "dependent" has the meaning given to it by section 152.

(5) EXCLUSIVE BENEFIT.—In the case of a plan to which contributions are made by more than one employer, in determining whether the plan is for the exclusive benefit of an employer's employees or their spouses or dependents, the employees of any employer who maintains the plan shall be considered to be the employees of each employer who maintains the plan.

(6) ATTRIBUTION RULES.—For purposes of this section—

(A) ownership of stock in a corporation shall be determined in accordance with the rules provided under subsections (d) and (e) of section 1563 (without regard to section 1563(e)(3)(C)), and

(B) the interest of an employee in a trade or business which is not incorporated shall be determined in accordance with regulations prescribed by the Secretary, which shall be based on principles similar to the principles which apply in the case of subparagraph (A).

(7) TIME OF NOTICE TO SECRETARY.—A plan shall not be a qualified group legal services plan for any period prior to the time notification was provided to the Secretary in accordance with subsection (c)(4), if such notice is given after the time prescribed by the Secretary by regulations for giving such notice.

(e) TERMINATION.—This section and section 501(c)(20) shall not apply to taxable years ending after December 31, 1987.

(f) CROSS REFERENCE.—

For reporting and recordkeeping requirements, see section 6039D.

(5) SECTION 129 (AS AMENDED BY THE TAX REFORM ACT OF 1986)

[¶ 1199] DEPENDENT CARE ASSISTANCE PROGRAMS

→**Caution: Code Sec. 129(a), below, prior to amendment by P.L. 99-514, applies to tax years beginning before 1987.←**

Sec. 129 [1986 Code]. (a) IN GENERAL.—Gross income of an employee does not include amounts paid or incurred by the employer for dependent care assistance provided to such employee if the assistance is furnished pursuant to a program which is described in subsection (d).

→**Caution: Code Sec. 129(a), below, as amended by P.L. 99-514, applies to tax years beginning after 1986.←**

(a) EXCLUSION.—

(1) IN GENERAL.—Gross income of an employee does not include amounts paid or incurred by the employer or dependent care assistance provided to such employee if the assistance is furnished pursuant to a program which is described in subsection (d).

(2) LIMITATION OF EXCLUSION.—The aggregate amount excluded from the gross income of the taxpayer under this section for any taxable year shall not exceed $5,000 ($2,500 in the case of a separate return by a married individual).

For purposes of the preceding sentence, marital status shall be determined under the rules of paragraphs (3) and (4) of section 21(e).

(b) EARNED INCOME LIMITATION.—

(1) IN GENERAL.—The amount excluded from the income of an employee under subsection (a) for any taxable year shall not exceed—

(A) in the case of an employee who is not married at the close of such taxable year, the earned income of such employee for such taxable year, or

(B) in the case of an employee who is married at the close of such taxable year, the lesser of—

(i) the earned income of such employee for such taxable year, or

(ii) the earned income of the spouse of such employee for such taxable year.

(2) SPECIAL RULE FOR CERTAIN SPOUSES.—For purposes of paragraph (1), the provisions of section 21(d)(2) shall apply in determining the earned income of a spouse who is a student or incapable of caring for himself.

→**Caution: Code Sec. 129(c), below, prior to amendment by P.L. 99-514, applies to tax years beginning before 1987.←**

(c) PAYMENTS TO RELATED INDIVIDUALS.—No amount paid or incurred during the taxable year of an employee by an employer in providing dependent care assistance to such employee shall be excluded under subsection (a) if such amount was paid or incurred to an individual—

(1) with respect to whom, for such taxable year, a deduction is allowable under section 151(e) (relating to personal exemptions for dependents) to such employee or the spouse of such employee, or

(2) who is a child of such employee (within the meaning of section 151(e)(3)) under the age of 19 at the close of such taxable year.

→**Caution: Code Sec. 129(c), below, as amended by P.L. 99-514, applies to tax years beginning after 1986.←**

(c) PAYMENTS TO RELATED INDIVIDUALS.—No amount paid or incurred during the taxable year of an employee by an employer in providing dependent care assistance to such employee shall be excluded under subsection (a) if such amount was paid or incurred to an individual—

(1) with respect to whom, for such taxable year, a deduction is allowable under section 151(c) (relating to personal exemptions for dependents) to such employee or the spouse of such employee, or

(2) who is a child of such employee (within the meaning of section 151(c)(3)) under the age of 19 at the close of such taxable year.

(d) DEPENDENT CARE ASSISTANCE PROGRAM.—

→**Caution: Code Sec. 129(d)(1), below, prior to amendment by P.L. 99-514, applies to years beginning before the later of January 1, 1988, or the earlier of three months after issuance of regulations implementing Code Sec. 89 or January 1, 1989.←**

(1) IN GENERAL.—For purposes of this section a dependent care assistance program is a separate written plan of an employer for the exclusive benefit of his employees to provide such employees with dependent care assistance which meets the requirements of paragraphs (2) through (7) of this subsection.

→**Caution: Code Sec. 129(d)(1), below, as amended by P.L. 99-514, applies to years beginning after the later of December 31, 1987, or the earlier of three months after issuance of regulations implementing Code Sec. 89 or December 31, 1988.←**

(1) IN GENERAL.—For purposes of this section, a dependent care assistance program is a plan of an employer—

(A) under which the employer provides employees with dependent care assistance, and

(B) which meets the requirements of paragraphs (2) through (6) and section 89(k).

→Caution: Code Sec. 129(d)(2), below, prior to amendment by P.L. 99-514, applies to years beginning before 1988.←

(2) DISCRIMINATION.—The contributions or benefits provided under the plan shall not discriminate in favor of employees who are officers, owners, or highly compensated, or their dependents.

→Caution: Code Sec. 129(d)(2), below, as amended by P.L. 99-514, applies to years beginning after 1987.←

(2) DISCRIMINATION.—The contributions or benefits provided under the plan shall not discriminate in favor of employees who are highly compensated employees (within the meaning of section 414(q)) or their dependents.

→Caution: Code Sec. 129(d)(3), below, prior to amendment by P.L. 99-514, applies to years beginning before the later of January 1, 1988, or the earlier of three months after issuance of regulations implementing Code Sec. 89 or January 1, 1989.←

(3) ELIGIBILITY.—The program shall benefit employees who qualify under a classification set up by the employer and found by the Secretary not to be discriminatory in favor of employees described in paragraph (2), or their dependents. For purposes of this paragraph, there shall be excluded from consideration employees not included in the program who are included in a unit of employees covered by an agreement which the Secretary of Labor finds to be a collective bargaining agreement between employee representatives and one or more employers, if there is evidence that dependent care benefits were the subject of good faith bargaining between such employee representatives and such employer or employers.

→Caution: Code Sec. 129(d)(3), below, as amended by P.L. 99-514, applies to years beginning after the later of December 31, 1987, or the earlier of three months after issuance of regulations implementing Code Sec. 89 or December 31, 1988.←

(3) ELIGIBILITY.—The program shall benefit employees who qualify under a classification set up by the employer and found by the Secretary not to be discriminatory in favor of employees described in paragraph (2), or their dependents. For purposes of this paragraph, there may be excluded from consideration employees who may be excluded from consideration under section 89(h).

(4) PRINCIPAL SHAREHOLDERS OR OWNERS.—Not more than 25 percent of the amounts paid or incurred by the employer for dependent care assistance during the year may be provided for the class of individuals who are shareholders or owners (or their spouses or dependents), each of whom (on any day of the year) owns more than 5 percent of the stock or of the capital or profits interest in the employer.

(5) NO FUNDING REQUIRED.—A program referred to in paragraph (1) is not required to be funded.

→Caution: Code Sec. 129(d)(6), below, was struck out by P.L. 99-514, Code Sec. 129(d)(7), below, was redesignated as Code Sec. 129(d)(6), and Code Sec. 129(d)(8)[7], below, was added, all of these changes effective for years beginning after the later of December 31, 1987, or the earlier of three months after the issuance of regulations implementing Code Sec. 89 or December 31, 1988.←

(6) NOTIFICATION OF ELIGIBLE EMPLOYEES.—Reasonable notification of the availability and terms of the program shall be provided to eligible employees.

(7) STATEMENT OF EXPENSES.—The plan shall furnish to an employee, on or before January 31, a written statement showing the amounts paid or expenses incurred by the employer in providing dependent care assistance to such employee during the previous calendar year.

(8)[7]   BENEFITS.—

(A) IN GENERAL.—A plan meets the requirements of this paragraph if the average benefits provided to employees who are not highly compensated employees under all plans of the employer is at least 55 percent of the average benefits provided to highly compensated employees.

(B) SALARY REDUCTION AGREEMENTS.—For purposes of subparagraph (A), in the case of any benefits provided through a salary reduction agreement, there shall be disregarded any employees whose compensation (within the meaning of section 415(q)(7)) is less than $25,000.

(e) DEFINITIONS AND SPECIAL RULES.—For purposes of this section—

(1) DEPENDENT CARE ASSISTANCE.—The term "dependent care assistance" means the payment of, or provision of, those services which if paid for by the employee would be considered employment-related expenses under section 21(b)(2) (relating to expenses for household and dependent care services necessary for gainful employment).

(2) EARNED INCOME.—The term "earned income" shall have the meaning given such term in section 32(c)(2), but such term shall not include any amounts paid or incurred by an employer for dependent care assistance to an employee.

(3) EMPLOYEE.—The term "employee" includes, for any year, an individual who is an employee within the meaning of section 401(c)(1) (relating to self-employed individuals).

(4) EMPLOYER.—An individual who owns the entire interest in an unincorporated trade or business shall be treated as his own employer. A partnership shall be treated as the employer of each partner who is an employee within the meaning of paragraph (3).

(5) ATTRIBUTION RULES.—

(A) OWNERSHIP OF STOCK.—Ownership of stock in a corporation shall be determined in accordance with the rules provided under subsections (d) and (e) of section 1563 (without regard to section 1563(e)(3)(C)).

(B) INTEREST IN UNINCORPORATED TRADE OR BUSINESS.—The interest of an employee in a trade or business which is not incorporated shall be determined in accordance with regulations prescribed by the Secretary, which shall be based on principles similar to the principles which apply in the case of subparagraph (A).

(6) UTILIZATION TEST NOT APPLICABLE.—A dependent care assistance program shall not be held or considered to fail to meet any requirements of subsection (d) merely because of utilization rates for the different types of assistance made available under the program.

(7) DISALLOWANCE OF EXCLUDED AMOUNTS AS CREDIT OR DEDUCTION.—No deduction or credit shall be allowed to the employee under any other section of this chapter for any amount excluded from the gross income of the employee by reason of this section.

→Caution: Code Sec. 129(e)(8), below, as added by P.L. 99-514, applies to tax years beginning after 1986.←

(8) TREATMENT OF ONSITE FACILITIES.—In the case of an onsite facility, except to the extent provided in regulations, the amount excluded with respect to any dependent shall be based on—

(A) utilization, and

(B) the value of the services provided.

(b)   GENERAL EXPLANATION OF THE TAX REFORM ACT OF 1986; TITLE XI, PART F, SECTIONS 1–6 (THE BLUE BOOK)

F. Employee Benefit Provisions

1. Nondiscrimination rules for certain statutory employee benefit plans (sec. 1151 of the Act, secs. 79, 105, 106, 117(d), 120, 125, 127, 129, 132, 414, 505, 6039D, and 6652, and new sec. 89 of the Code)[1]

Prior Law

Overview

Under prior and present law, certain employer-provided employee benefits are excluded from the gross income of employees if provided under certain statutorily prescribed conditions. Similar exclusions generally apply for employment tax purposes.

Among those conditions that generally applied under prior law to the exclusion of employer-provided employee benefits was the requirement that employee benefits be provided on a nondiscriminatory basis. With the exception of the exclusion for employer-provided health insurance, no employee benefit exclusion was available unless the benefit was provided on a basis that did not favor certain categories of employees who were officers, owners, or highly compensated. Failure to satisfy the applicable nondiscrimination test for a specific benefit resulted in a denial of the tax exclusion for all employees receiving the benefit or only for the employees in whose favor discrimination was prohibited, depending on the benefit.

Separate nondiscrimination rules applied with respect to each benefit. An individual in whose favor discrimination was prohibited for one benefit may or may not have been such an individual for another benefit. Also, what constituted impermissible discrimination and the consequences of such discrimination differed with respect to different benefits.

Health benefit plans

Under prior law, a nondiscrimination test was not applied as a condition of the exclusion of health benefits provided by an employer under an insured plan, or as a condition of the exclusion of medical benefits and reimbursements provided under such insurance (secs. 105 and 106). However, if an employer provided its employees with health benefits under a self-insured medical reimbursement plan (sec. 105(h)), the exclusion of a medical reimbursement under such plan was available to a highly compensated individual only to the extent that the plan did not discriminate in favor of highly compensated employees. A self-insured health

---

[1]For legislative background of the provision, see: H.R. 3838, as reported by the House Committee on Ways and Means on December 7, 1985, sec. 1151; H.Rep. 99-426, pp. 765–779; H.R. 3838, as reported by the Senate Committee on Finance on May 29, 1986, sec. 1251; S.Rep. 99-313, pp. 646–665; and H.Rep. 99-841, Vol. II (September 18, 1986), pp. 498–538 (Conference Report).

plan was discriminatory if it favored highly compensated individuals either as to eligibility to participate or as to benefits.

Group-term life insurance plans

Under prior and present law, an exclusion is provided for the cost of group-term life insurance coverage (up to $50,000) under a plan maintained by an employer (sec. 79). Under prior law, if a group-term life insurance plan was determined to be discriminatory, the exclusion of the cost of $50,000 of group-term life insurance did not apply with respect to key employees. A discriminatory plan was one that discriminated in favor of key employees as to eligibility to participate or as to the type or amount of benefits available under the plan. Group-term life insurance benefits were not considered discriminatory merely because the amount of life insurance provided to employees bore a uniform relationship to compensation.

Group legal services plans

Under prior law, the exclusion for contributions to or services provided under an employer-maintained group legal services plan was available to employees only if (1) the plan benefited a class of employees that did not discriminate in favor of employees who were officers, shareholders, self-employed individuals, or highly compensated, and (2) the contributions or benefits provided under the plan did not discriminate in favor of such employees (sec. 120). In addition, under prior and present law, the exclusion is not available if more than 25 percent of the amounts contributed during a year may be provided for 5-percent owners (or their spouses or dependents). Under prior law, the exclusion for group legal services benefits expired for taxable years ending after 1985. (See Part F.3., below.)

Educational assistance programs

Under prior and present law, the amounts paid or expenses incurred (up to $5,000 a year under prior law) for an employee under an employer-provided educational assistance program are excluded from income (sec. 127). Under prior law, the exclusion was not available if the program benefited a class of employees that was discriminatory in favor of employees who were officers, owners, or highly compensated (or their dependents). Also, under prior and present law, the exclusion is not available if more than 5 percent of the amounts paid or incurred by the employer for educational assistance may be provided for 5-percent owners (or their spouses or dependents). Under prior law, the exclusion for educational assistance benefits expired for taxable years beginning after 1985. (See Part F.3., below.)

Dependent care assistance programs

Prior and present law provides an exclusion from income for amounts paid or incurred for an employee under a dependent care assistance program (sec. 129). The exclusion was not available unless (1) the program benefited a class of employees that did not discriminate in favor of employees who were officers, owners, or highly compensated (or their dependents), and (2) the contributions or benefits provided under the plan did not discriminate in favor of such employees. In addition, under prior and present law, the exclusion is not available if more than 25 percent of the amounts paid or incurred by the employers for dependent care assistance may be provided for 5-percent owners (or their spouses or dependents).

Welfare benefit funds

A voluntary employees' beneficiary association or a group legal services fund that is part of an employer plan is not exempt from taxation unless the plan of which the association or fund is a part meets certain nondiscrimination rules (sec. 505). (These nondiscrimination rules also apply for certain other purposes, such as the deductibility of contributions to a welfare benefit fund to provide post-retirement health benefits.) Under these rules, no class of benefits may be provided to a classification of employees that is discriminatory in favor of highly compensated employees. In addition, with respect to each class of benefits, the benefits may not discriminate in favor of highly compensated employees. A life insurance, disability, severance pay, or supplemental unemployment compensation benefit will not fail the benefits test merely because the amount of benefits provided to employees bears a uniform relationship to compensation.

Cafeteria plans

Under a cafeteria plan, as defined under prior law, a participant is offered a choice between cash and one or more employee benefits. The mere availability of cash or certain taxable benefits under a cafeteria plan does not cause an employee to be treated as having received the available cash or taxable benefits for income tax purposes if certain conditions are met (sec. 125). This cafeteria plan exception to the constructive receipt rules did not apply to any benefit provided under the plan if the plan discriminated in favor of highly compensated individuals as to eligibility to participate or as to contributions and benefits. In addition, under prior and present law, no more than 25 percent of the aggregate of the statutory nontaxable benefits provided to all employees under the cafeteria plan may be provided to key employees.

Eligibility tests

Under prior and present law, for purposes of the eligibility tests applicable to the employee benefits described above, the same rules applicable to the classification test for qualified plan coverage (sec. 410(b)(1)(B)) apply.

Reasons for Change

Under prior and present law, the tax-favored treatment of employer-provided employee benefits reduces the Federal income tax base and reduces Federal budget receipts. However, Congress believed these costs are justifiable if such benefits fulfill important social policy objectives, such as increasing health insurance coverage among taxpayers who are not highly compensated and who otherwise would not purchase or could not afford such coverage.

In order to achieve these objectives, Congress believed that effective nondiscrimination rules with respect to all employee benefits, including health insurance, were necessary because they permit the exclusion from income of employee benefits only if the benefits are provided to required levels of nonhighly compensated employees. Congress was concerned that the prior-law nondiscrimination rules did not require sufficient coverage of nonhighly compensated employees as a condition of the exclusions.

Under prior law, the definition of those individuals in whose favor discrimination was prohibited generally was vague, as it was unclear, for example, who qualified as an "officer," "owner," or "highly compensated employee." Similarly, little specific guidance was provided as to whether a particular pattern of coverage discriminated in favor of such individuals.

Therefore, Congress believed that the prior-law nondiscrimination rules should be modified to expand required coverage of nonhighly compensated employees particularly with respect to health and group-term life insurance plans and to provide more consistent principles for employee benefit exclusions. As a general rule, Congress believed that, to the extent possible, the nondiscrimination rules should require employers to cover nonhighly compensated employees to an extent comparable to the coverage of highly compensated employees.

Congress recognized that employers desire flexibility in designing employee benefit programs. However, Congress believed that flexibility should be provided only to the extent not inconsistent with the nondiscrimination rules. For example, if an employer operates, for legitimate economic reasons, multiple lines of business, the employee benefit structures in each line of business may differ because of historical trends within each industry. The Act permits employers to test the new nondiscrimination rules separately with respect to each line of business. Congress is concerned, however, that the line of business exception not be administered in a manner that circumvents Congress' premise that highly compensated employees should not be permitted to exclude employee benefits unless the employer's plan benefits a nondiscriminatory group of the employer's employees.

Explanation of Provision

Overview

The Act applies new nondiscrimination rules to statutory employee benefit plans. The term "statutory employee benefit plans" includes accident or health plans and group-term life insurance plans. At the election of the employer, the term also includes qualified group legal services plans, educational assistance programs, and dependent care assistance programs.

Under the new nondiscrimination rules, a plan generally is required to satisfy 3 eligibility tests—a 50-percent test, a 90-percent/50-percent test, and a nondiscriminatory provision test—and a benefits test. Alternatively, a plan may satisfy an 80-percent coverage test, provided it also satisfies the nondiscriminatory provision test.

Generally, each different option is a separate plan for testing purposes. However, the Act provides aggregation rules that allow plans to be tested together based on their relative values.

The Secretary is to prescribe rules regarding valuation of different benefits. With respect to health coverage, the Secretary is to prescribe a table prescribing the relative values of different types of health coverage.

If a plan is discriminatory, highly compensated employees are taxable on the value of the discriminatory excess. If the employer does not report such excess in a timely manner, the employer may be subject to an employer-level sanction.

For purposes of applying the new nondiscrimination rules, the Act provides generally applicable definitions of the following: (1) highly compensated employee; (2) employer (including the employee leasing rules); (3) line of business or operating unit (as the Act permits the new nondiscrimination rules to be applied separately to separate lines of business or operating units); and (4) employees who are excluded from consideration. These definitions, other than the line of business or operating unit rule, apply generally to all employee benefit plans, not only to statutory employee benefit plans.

In addition, the Act provides a benefits test applicable to dependent care assistance programs and includes in the definition of a cafeteria plan a plan offering a choice between nontaxable benefits.

The Act also applies to employee benefit plans generally new qualification and reporting requirements.

Applicability of new nondiscrimination rules

The Act provides new nondiscrimination rules applicable to statutory employee benefit plans. The term "statutory employee benefit plans" is defined to include group-term life insurance plans and accident or health plans (whether self-insured or insured through an insurance company). In addition, an employer may elect to treat one or more of the following as statutory employee benefit plans subject to the new nondiscrimination rules: qualified group legal services plans, educational assistance programs, and dependent care assistance programs.

New nondiscrimination rules

In general

Under the new nondiscrimination rules, a statutory employee benefit plan is required to satisfy either (1) 3 eligibility tests and a benefits test, or (2) an alternative test designed for certain plans with broad coverage.

A plan maintained by an employer that has no nonhighly compensated employees is considered to satisfy the new nondiscrimination rules.[2]

Eligibility tests

The Act provides 3 eligibility tests: a 50-percent test, a 90-percent/50-percent test, and a nondiscriminatory provision test.

50-percent test.—Under the 50-percent test, nonhighly compensated employees must constitute at least 50 percent of the group of employees eligible to participate in the plan. This requirement will be deemed satisfied if the percentage of highly compensated employees who are eligible to participate is not greater than the percentage of nonhighly compensated employees who are eligible.

For example, assume that an employer has 20 employees, 15 of whom are highly compensated employees. Because more than 50 percent of its workforce is highly compensated, the employer could make all employees eligible but still not satisfy the 50-percent test. However, if all employees are eligible, the employer would be deemed to satisfy the 50-percent test because the percentage of highly compensated employees and nonhighly compensated employees who are eligible is the same (i.e., 100 percent).

---

[2]A technical correction may be needed so that the statute reflects this intent.

For purposes of satisfying the 50-percent test, comparable accident or health plans (as defined below) may be aggregated.

90-percent/50-percent test.—A plan does not satisfy the 90-percent/50-percent test unless at least 90 percent of the employer's nonhighly compensated employees are eligible for a benefit that is at least 50 percent as valuable as the benefit available to the highly compensated employee to whom the most valuable benefit is available. For purposes of this test, all plans of the same type (i.e., all benefits excludable under the same Code section) are aggregated. Thus, if an employee is eligible to participate in 2 or more plans of the same type, the employee is considered eligible for a benefit with a value equal to the sum of the values available under the plans for which the employee is eligible. On the other hand, if an employee is eligible to participate in only 1 plan, but may choose among more than 1 plan, such employee is considered eligible for a benefit with a value equal to the value of the benefit in the available plan with the most valuable benefit. In determining the highly compensated employee with the most valuable benefit available, benefits under all plans of the same type are aggregated in the same manner.

In certain situations, an employee may elect between plans of different types. For example, an employee may be able to elect (with or without a required employee contribution) to be covered under a health plan or a group-term life insurance plan, but not fully under both. In such circumstances, the value of the benefit available to an employee—determined in the manner described above—may be allocated among the different types of plans in any reasonable manner permitted by the Secretary.

For purposes of this 90-percent/50-percent test, available salary reduction[3] is not taken into account. (See "Cafeteria plans" below regarding the retention of the prior-law eligibility test for cafeteria plans generally.)

Nondiscriminatory provision test.—The third eligibility test provides that a plan may not contain any provision relating to eligibility to participate that by its terms or otherwise discriminates in favor of highly compensated employees. This third test is intended to disqualify arrangements only on the basis of discrimination that is not quantifiable. For example, if an employer maintains one health plan for its salaried employees and one health plan for its hourly employees, the fact that the hourly plan is quantifiably less valuable will not cause the salaried plan to fail the third eligibility test. On the other hand, if an employer provides unusual coverage for a rare condition to which only the owner of the employer is subject, such coverage may fail the third eligibility requirement, even if theoretically provided to all employees of the employer.

Another example of a failure to satisfy the third eligibility test occurs if, under the facts and circumstances, the employer is satisfying the other nondiscrimination tests by providing or making available to nonhighly compensated employees benefits that clearly have less value than that ascribed to them under the Secretary's valuation tables (see "Valuation" below). For example, assume that an employer that offers certain standard health coverage to its highly compensated employees satisfies the first 2 eligibility tests by

[3]See note 5, below, for a discussion of the term "salary reduction."

offering to its nonhighly compensated employees coverage for a condition that is extremely rare for individuals with the nonhighly compensated employees' characteristics, but has a substantial value under the Secretary's tables. Under these circumstances, the plans offering standard coverage to highly compensated employees would not be considered to satisfy the third eligibility test.

For a discussion of another application of the third eligibility test, see "Special accident or health plan rules—Family coverage" below.

Benefits test

Under the Act, a plan does not satisfy the benefits test unless the average employer-provided benefit received by nonhighly compensated employees under all plans of the employer of the same type (i.e., plans providing benefits excludable under the same Code section) is at least 75 percent of the average employer-provided benefit received by highly compensated employees under all plans of the employer of the same type.

For purposes of this test, the term "average employer-provided benefit" means with respect to highly compensated employees an amount equal to the aggregate employer-provided benefits received by highly compensated employees under all plans of the employer of the type being tested divided by the number of highly compensated employees of the employer (whether or not covered by any such plans). The term is defined in the same manner with respect to nonhighly compensated employees.

Alternative test

The Act also provides an alternative test that may be applied in lieu of the eligibility and benefits tests described above. If a plan benefits at least 80 percent of an employer's nonhighly compensated employees, such plan is considered to satisfy the new nondiscrimination rules. This alternative test will not apply unless the plan satisfies the nondiscriminatory provision test described above.

This alternative test applies only to insurance-type plans. Under the Act, the term "insurance-type plans" means accident or health plans and group-term life insurance plans.

For purposes of this alternative test, an individual will only be considered to benefit under a plan if such individual receives coverage under the plan; eligibility to receive coverage is not considered benefiting under the plan. Also, for purposes of this alternative test, comparable accident or health plans may be aggregated.

Definition of plan and aggregation of plans

In general

The definition of the term "plan" is relevant only for certain purposes. First, each separate plan is required to be valued separately. Second, the 50-percent test and the alternative 80-percent test are to be satisfied by each plan. However, for purposes of satisfying these two tests, comparable accident or health plans may be aggregated. See "Aggregation of accident or health plans" below.

Aside from the valuation issue, the definition of a plan is not relevant for purposes of the 90-percent/50-percent test or the benefits test because, for purposes of those tests, all plans of the same type are aggregated.

The definition of a plan also applies for purposes of the qualification requirements described below.

Separate plans

Under the Act, each option or different benefit offered is, except in the two instances described in "Single plan" below, treated as a separate plan. This means, for example, that if two types of insurance coverage vary in any way (including the amount of the employee contribution), they will be considered separate plans. Thus, in the case of health plans under which there are different levels or types of coverage, each separate level or type of health coverage is considered a separate plan under the nondiscrimination rules. Also, each health maintenance organization is considered a separate plan due to the difference in prescribed providers of services.

In addition, an employee who has available or receives coverage both for himself and his family is to be treated as having available or received 2 separate coverages: individual coverage with respect to himself, and family coverage with respect to his family. Each coverage is considered provided under a separate plan.

Also, limitations on family coverage give rise to separate plans. For example, if an employer offers "employee plus 1 family member" health coverage and "employee plus 2 or more family members" health coverage, there are 3 plans: (1) employee coverage, (2) coverage of 1 family member, and (3) coverage of additional family members.

In addition, if 2 plans of the same employer provide overlapping coverage, an employee technically eligible for or covered by both plans is not to be considered fully eligible for or covered by both. With respect to 1 of the plans, the employee is to be considered only partially eligible or covered under rules prescribed by the Secretary.

Single plan

Under the Act, 2 or more plans that are identical in all respects, except for the group of employees covered, may be treated as a single plan, even if, for example, they are established pursuant to separate written documents.

Further, for purposes of determining what constitutes a single plan, 2 exceptions are provided to the rule that insurance coverage (or available noninsurance benefits) be identical within a plan.

First, in the case of group-term life insurance, the provision of insurance coverage that varies in proportion to compensation is not to be considered as the provision of different options or benefits with respect to such varying coverage. Thus, for example, if an employer provides all employees with group-term life insurance equal to one-times compensation, such arrangement may be considered one plan. For this purpose, the definition of and limitation on compensation applicable for purposes of qualified plans applies. See Parts B.1. and D., above.

Under the second exception, if accident or health coverage available or provided to employees is identical except that the employer subsidy is proportionately reduced for employees who normally work less than 30 hours per week, such arrangement may be considered a single plan. The permissible proportionate reduction corresponds to the special rule described below for the benefits test and the 50-percent component of the 90-percent/50-percent test. If an employee normally works at least 22 1/2 hours per week but less than 30 hours per week, the second exception applies if the employer subsidy is reduced by no more than 25 percent. If the employee normally works less than 22 1/2 hours per week, the second exception applies if the employer subsidy is reduced by no more than 50 percent. If the second exception is used, it is required to be used on a uniform, nondiscriminatory basis with respect to all employees. Of course, this rule does not affect the benefit actually made available or provided for purposes of any other tests.

Assume, for example, that an employer makes 1 group health insurance policy available to all of its employees. Generally, for a $100 contribution, employees receive coverage with a value of $1,100. Under these circumstances, the employer subsidy is $1,000. Assume further that the employer employs certain individuals who normally work 20 hours per week. Under the rule described above, if the employer required a $600 contribution from these individuals—making the employer subsidy $500 (50 percent of the employer subsidy for the other employees)—such individuals may be considered eligible for the same plan as is available to the other employees, even though the required employee contribution is different.

The second exception described above does not apply in any plan year unless during such year more than 50 percent of the nonexcludable employees (determined without regard to plan provisions) normally work more than 30 hours per week. (For a discussion of which employees are nonexcludable, see below.) Also, the second exception allowing a proportionate reduction in benefits does not apply to elective contributions.

Restructuring plans

Under the Act, under rules prescribed by the Secretary, for purposes of determining what constitutes a single plan, employers may structure options in different ways as long as all coverage within a plan is identical. For example, if the deductible for all highly compensated employees is $200 and the deductible for all nonhighly compensated employees is $50, it is not necessary to classify the $200 deductible coverage as a separate plan that covers only highly compensated employees. Instead, the employer could classify the coverage as 1 plan for all employees providing coverage for expenses in excess of a $200 deductible and a second plan covering costs between $50 and $200 for only nonhighly compensated employees. Such restructuring may be helpful in demonstrating compliance with the nondiscrimination rules without resort to the aggregation rules described below.

Aggregation of accident or health plans

For purposes of satisfying the 50-percent eligibility test, 1 or more accident or health plans ("nonhelper plans") that separately do not satisfy the 50-percent test may be aggregated with 1 or more comparable accident or health "helper plans" that are not aggregated with other nonhelper plans for this purpose. A "helper plan" is any plan in the group of aggregated plans that satisfies the 50-percent test without regard to aggregation. A helper plan is considered comparable to a group of nonhelper plans if the value of the employer-provided coverage available to each eligible employee in the helper plan is at least 95 percent of the value of the employer-provided coverage available to each eligible employee in the nonhelper plan in the group of aggregated plans with the highest such value.

For purposes of the 80-percent test, the general rule is that a group of plans are comparable and may be aggregated if the value of the employer-provided coverage provided to each covered employee in the plan with the lowest such value is at least 95 percent of the value of the employer-provided coverage provided to each covered employee in the plan with the highest such value. However, if a plan with a greater value than permitted under the previous sentence satisfies section 89(d)(2) based on actual coverage provided rather than on eligibility, such plan may be aggregated with the group of less valuable plans for purposes of the 80-percent test.

Under rules prescribed by the Secretary, if an employee is eligible for or receives coverage under more than 1 accident or health plan, then, for purposes of the 50-percent test and the 80-percent test, such plans are to be considered 1 plan with respect to such employee.[4] For example, assume that an employer maintains two plans: one covering all employees with a value of $950 and a second covering only highly compensated employees with a value of $1,000. The highly compensated employees receiving benefits from both plans are to be treated for purposes of the 50-percent test and the 80-percent test as receiving $1,950 of benefits from one plan while the nonhighly compensated employees are to be treated as receiving $950 of benefits from a separate plan. Under the rules described above, these plans would not be comparable so that the plan covering the highly compensated employees would satisfy neither the 50-percent test nor the 80-percent test. For a discussion of the sanction applicable to such a plan, see "Sanction for discrimination" below.

In addition, the special part-time employee rule applicable for purposes of defining what constitutes a plan also applies for comparability purposes. Thus, if two plans that would be comparable but for the fact that under the rules described above the employer-provided benefit in both of such plans is proportionately reduced for employees who normally work less than 30 hours per week, the plans are to be considered comparable.

Valuation

In general

For purposes of the nondiscrimination rules, in the case of an insurance-type plan (i.e., an accident or health plan or a group-term life insurance plan), an employee's employer-provided benefit is the value of the coverage provided to or on behalf of such employee, to the extent attributable to contributions made by the employer. For example, the value of a health plan, whether insured or self-insured, is the value of the insurance, not the services or the amount of claims proceeds received by a particular employee. In the case of any plan other than an insurance-type plan, an employee's employer-provided benefit is defined as the value of the benefits provided to or on behalf of such employee, to the extent attributable to contributions made by the employer. Except as otherwise provided (sec. 89(g)(3)(D)) with respect to the 90-percent/50-percent test

---

[4] A technical correction may be needed so that the statute reflects this intent.

and the special part-time employee rule, employer contributions include elective contributions under a cafeteria plan.[5]

Accident or health plans

With respect to accident or health coverage, the Secretary is to promulgate tables that establish the relative values of plans with certain characteristics. Such tables may use as a reference point an identifiable standard plan. These tables are to provide the exclusive means of valuing accident or health coverage.

Such tables are to be adjusted in certain instances to take into account the specific coverage and group involved. For example, in determining the value of discriminatory coverage, the actual costs expended by the employer may be taken into account and allocated among all coverages, including the discriminatory coverage, on the basis of the relative values of such coverages, as determined under the tables. Another example is that in certain instances it may be appropriate to adjust the table value of coverage based on whether such coverage would have been provided at group rates by an insurance company. Thus, an individually designed plan may have a higher value than a group plan with the same characteristics.

Special group-term life insurance rules

Under the Act, certain special valuation rules apply for purposes of applying the nondiscrimination rules to group-term life insurance plans. Other special rules apply for purposes of valuing life insurance coverage determined to be discriminatory. In all cases, all employer-provided coverage (including coverage over $50,000) is taken into account.

In applying the benefits test and the 50-percent component of the 90-percent/50-percent test to a group-term life insurance plan, the first step in valuing the employer-provided benefit under a plan is to determine the amount of group-term life insurance coverage that is employer-provided. The next step is to determine the value of the employer-provided coverage under section 79(c) as if the insured were age 40. Except in the case where group-term life insurance plans are aggregated with plans of a different type for purposes of the benefits test (see discussion below), this value may then be adjusted depending on the compensation of the employee. The permissible adjustment is made by multiplying the amount by a fraction the numerator of which is a uniform amount for all plans and the denominator of which is the employee's compensation.

For purposes of the above rules, the definition of compensation (including the limitation on the amount that may be taken into account) applicable to qualified plans (see Part B.1. and Part D., above) applies.

In determining the value of discriminatory coverage, the special valuation rules described above—regarding the age 40 assumption and the compensation adjustment—do not apply. Instead, the value of the discriminatory coverage is the greater of the cost of the coverage under section 79(c) or the actual cost of

---

[5]The terms "elective contribution" and "salary reduction" are used interchangeably to refer to the provision of nontaxable benefits in lieu of available taxable benefits. Nontaxable benefits provided by an employer on a nonelective basis, or through a choice among nontaxable benefits only, are, of course, employer-provided benefits but are not considered elective contributions or provided through salary reduction.

the coverage. The same special rules also do not apply for purposes of determining the value of any inclusion amount attributable to a failure to satisfy the qualification requirements described below or for purposes of determining the amount subject to the employer-level sanction described below.

Other benefits

The valuation of other benefits, such as educational assistance, is to be based on general valuation principles.

Valuation unnecessary

In certain instances, employers need not value their accident or health plans or group-term life insurance plans or, alternatively, the number of plans that need to be valued can be significantly reduced.

For example, assume that an employer makes available to all of its employees a group of 10 health plans. In such a situation, it generally is not necessary to value the plans for purposes of the eligibility tests; the plans all pass. Assume further that for the entire year the percentage of nonhighly compensated employees in each plan is at least 75 percent of the percentage of highly compensated employees in the plan. Because the definition of a plan generally requires all features to be identical, each of these plans individually would pass the benefits test; thus, in the aggregate, they pass the benefits test. No valuation is necessary to make this determination.

In other situations, this approach can reduce the number of plans that have to be valued. For example, assume the same facts described above except that in 1 of the 10 plans, the percentage of nonhighly compensated employees covered is less than 75 percent of the percentage of highly compensated employees covered. The employer could aggregate with the tenth plan only so many of the other 9 plans as would be necessary to satisfy the benefits test with respect to that group of plans. Thus, only that group of plans would have to be valued to demonstrate compliance with the benefits test.

Sanction for discrimination

Inclusion in income

Under the Act, in the case of a discriminatory statutory employee benefit plan, highly compensated employees are required to include in gross income the discriminatory excess. Congress provided rules regarding the definition of the discriminatory excess, how to allocate the excess among highly compensated employees, and the year of inclusion.

The discriminatory excess is defined as the amount of the otherwise nontaxable employer-provided benefit (including benefits purchased with elective contributions) that would have to have been purchased with after-tax employee contributions by the highly compensated employees in order for all of the nondiscrimination tests to be satisfied. In applying this definition, the objective nondiscrimination tests are, except as provided by the Secretary, to be applied in the following order: the 50-percent test, the 90-percent/50-percent test, and then the benefits test. Alternatively, the definition of the discriminatory excess may be applied to the alternative 80-percent test. The determination of the discriminatory excess with respect to the third eligibility test (the nondiscriminatory provision test) is to be made under rules prescribed by the Secretary. See the discussion of these tests above.

Any discriminatory excess determined with respect to the benefits test is to be allocated to highly compensated employees by reducing the otherwise non-taxable employer-provided benefit (again including elective benefits) of highly compensated employees (beginning with the employees with the greatest such benefit) until the plan (or plans) being tested would not be discriminatory under the benefits test.

The discriminatory excess is includible in the employee's income in the employee's taxable year with or within which the plan year ends.

For purposes of determining and allocating the discriminatory excess with respect to a group-term life insurance plan, coverage over $50,000 is considered nontaxable. Thus, to the extent that the discriminatory coverage does not exceed the total coverage over $50,000, the effect of a finding of discrimination is simply the inclusion in income of the excess, if any, of the actual cost of the discriminatory coverage over the cost of such coverage under section 79(c). For example, assume an employee receives $150,000 of coverage, the $100,000 excess over $50,000 being included in income at the cost determined under section 79(c). Assume further that $25,000 of such employee's coverage is determined to be discriminatory. The effect of this finding of discrimination is that the excess, if any, of the actual cost of such $25,000 of coverage over the section 79(c) cost of such coverage is included in the employee's income (in addition to the section 79(c) cost of the $100,000 of coverage (i.e., the amount over $50,000)). See discussion above for the rule regarding valuing discriminatory group-term life insurance coverage.

An example with respect to the 50-percent test will illustrate how the excess benefit approach applies to the eligibility tests. Assume that an employer maintains 2 health plans, one (Plan A) available only to highly compensated employees and the other (Plan B) available to an equal number of nonhighly compensated employees. Under Plan A, the value of the available employer-provided coverage is $1,500; under Plan B, the value is $950. In this example, Plan A fails the 50-percent test. However, if $500 of the $1,500 in coverage available under Plan A were available on an after-tax basis, the value of available employer-provided coverage under Plan A would be $1,000 and, under the rules regarding aggregation of plans, Plan A and Plan B could then be aggregated for purposes of the 50-percent test. Aggregated, they would satisfy the test. Thus, in this example, any highly compensated employee receiving over $1,000 of employer-provided coverage is taxable on that excess as an excess benefit. No highly compensated employee is taxable merely because more than $1,000 of employer-provided coverage is available, but not provided (because, for example, the employee declines to make the required employee contribution).

Employer sanction

Except to the extent provided by the Secretary, if an employer (including an employer exempt from tax) does not report the discriminatory excess to the affected employees and the IRS on Forms W-2 by the due date (with any extension) for filing such Forms W-2, all benefits of the same type provided to such employees are subject to an employer-level sanction without regard to whether the employees report some or all of the benefits as income. Under this sanction, the employer is liable for a tax at the highest individual rate on the total value of benefits of the same type provided to employees with respect to whom the employer failed to report the discriminatory excess. With respect to group-term life insurance, the value of benefits for this purpose is the greater of the table cost (sec. 79(c)) or actual cost of all coverage.[6] This tax is not deductible and may not be offset by credits or deductions in any manner. This tax, however, does not apply if the employer can demonstrate that the failure to report was due to reasonable cause, such as a reasonable difference in the valuation of health benefits prior to the issuance of valuation rules.

This tax applies in addition to any other penalties or taxes otherwise applicable.

For a description of the general reporting requirement applicable to benefits that are includible in income due to the new nondiscrimination rules or the new qualification rules described below, see discussion below.

Special rules applicable to all tests and statutory employee benefit plans

There are four special rules applicable to all of the tests and plans described above. These four rules—

(1) provide a uniform definition of "highly compensated employee";
(2) provide a uniform definition of "employer";
(3) allow the nondiscrimination rules to apply on a line of business or operating unit basis; and
(4) define classes of employees who are excluded from consideration in applying the nondiscrimination rules.

Highly compensated employees

Under the Act, a uniform definition of the term "highly compensated employee" is provided. This definition applies for purposes of statutory employee benefit plans (including the sanction for violation of the rules regarding continuing health coverage); qualified tuition reduction programs; qualified group legal services plans; cafeteria plans; educational assistance programs; dependent care assistance programs; fringe benefit programs providing no-additional-cost services, qualified employee discounts, or employer-operated eating facilities (sec. 132); welfare benefit funds; qualified plans; and other provisions listed in the Act.

In general, an employee is treated as highly compensated with respect to a year if, at any time during the year or the preceding year, the employee (1) was a 5-percent owner of the employer (as defined in sec. 416(i)); (2) received more than $75,000 in annual compensation from the employer; (3) received more than $50,000 in annual compensation from the employer and was a member of the top-paid group of the employer during the same year; or (4) was an officer of the employer (generally as defined in sec. 416(i)). Under this definition, every employer is to have at least 1 officer treated as a highly compensated employee for any year; if necessary, this means that the compensation floor required for such status is not to apply to 1 individual. Also, the $50,000 and $75,000 thresholds are to be adjusted at the same time and in the same manner as the adjustments to the dollar limit on benefits under defined benefit pension plans.[7]

---

[6]A technical correction may be needed so that the statute reflects this intent.

[7]A technical correction may be needed so that the statute reflects this intent.

In addition, a former employee is to be treated as a highly compensated employee if such employee was highly compensated at the time of separation from service or at any time after attaining age 55.

As noted, the definition of the term "highly compensated employee" is the same as the definition used with respect to qualified plans. (For a more detailed description of the definition, see Part B.7., above.) One clarification applies to employee benefits, however, that does not apply to qualified plans. With respect to those benefits for which family coverage is treated as a benefit separate from employee coverage, such as accident or health benefits, the special rule aggregating family members is modified. In such instances, where a family member would be aggregated with a 5-percent owner or 1 of the top 10 highly compensated employees under the qualified plan rules, such family member is to be treated as a nonemployee family member under rules prescribed by the Secretary.

Definition of employer

Aggregation

The Act provides that related employers are treated as a single employer for purposes of all aspects of the employee benefit rules, including the nondiscrimination requirements (sec. 414(b), (c), (m), and (t)). In addition, leased employees are treated for the same purposes as employees of the person or organization for whom they perform services (sec. 414(n)). The qualified plan exemption from the employee leasing rules with respect to individuals covered by a safe-harbor plan (sec. 414(n)(5)) does not apply to employee benefits. For further discussion of the employee leasing rules and their applicability to employee benefits, see Part E.8. above. The Act also provides that the Secretary's general regulatory authority to prevent abuse of employee benefit requirements applies (sec. 414(o) and (t)).

Under the Act, the rules described above, which under prior law applied to qualified plans, apply also to statutory employee benefit plans, qualified tuition reduction programs, qualified group legal services plans, cafeteria plans, educational assistance programs, dependent care assistance programs, miscellaneous fringe benefits (sec. 132), continuation of health care requirements,[8] welfare benefit funds, and employee achievement awards.

Special rule for certain dispositions and acquisitions

The Act contains a special transition rule for certain dispositions or acquisitions of a business. Under the Act, if a person becomes or ceases to be a member of a controlled group (sec. 414 (b) and (c)) or affiliated service group (sec. 414(m)), the nondiscrimination rules will, with respect to a plan maintained by the person or group, be deemed satisfied during the transition period, provided that (1) the nondiscrimination rules were satisfied immediately before the acquisition or disposition, and (2) the coverage under the plan (or under another plan on which the plan relied to satisfy the nondiscrimination rules) does not change significantly during the transition period (other than by reason of the

---

[8]A technical correction may be needed so that the statute reflects this intent. Such a correction was included in the versions of H.Con.Res. 395 which passed the House and Senate in the 99th Congress.

acquisition or disposition). The transition period begins on the date of the acquisition or disposition and ends on the last day of the first plan year beginning after the transaction.

This rule is not intended to compel employers to determine if the nondiscrimination rules were satisfied immediately prior to any disposition or acquisition to which the rule could apply. For example, if an insignificant disposition or acquisition occurs during a transition period with respect to a prior disposition or acquisition, an employer might want to apply the special rule throughout the existing transition period, rather than determine if the nondiscrimination rules are actually satisfied immediately prior to the subsequent disposition or acquisition. Thus, employers may apply the nondiscrimination rules without regard to this special rule.

In addition, this special rule is to be applied under rules prescribed by the Secretary in a manner consistent with the purposes of the nondiscrimination rules. For example, this special rule is to grant relief only with respect to that part of the nondiscrimination rules affected by the disposition or acquisition. For example, if the employer applies the rules separately to separate lines of business, and the employer disposes of one of such incorporated lines of business, the effect of this rule may simply be to allow the employer to continue to apply the nondiscrimination rules separately to the other lines of business during the transition period. This result occurs because, although the disposition of 1 line of business can affect an employer's option to apply the nondiscrimination rules separately to other lines of business (e.g., by causing a plan to fail the classification test on an employer-wide basis), such disposition does not affect the application of the nondiscrimination rules to the other lines of business if such lines of business can continue to be tested separately. This assumes that the identity of the highly compensated employees is not affected by the disposition of the line of business. See the discussion below relating to lines of business or operating units.

Self-employed individuals

For purposes of all nondiscrimination rules applicable to qualified group legal services plans, educational assistance programs, and dependent care assistance programs, self-employed individuals are treated as employees. An individual who owns the entire interest in an unincorporated trade or business is treated as his own employer and a partnership is treated as the employer of each partner.

Line of business or operating unit rules

In general

Under the Act, if an employer is treated as operating separate lines of business or operating units for a year, the employer may apply the new nondiscrimination rules separately to each separate line of business or operating unit for that year. This rule does apply, however, to any plan that does not satisfy the classification test on an employer-wide basis. (For a discussion of the classification test, see Part B.1., above.)

In general, an accident or health plan that would, tested separately, fail the classification test may be aggregated with 1 or more other accident or health plans ("helper plans") for purposes of satisfying the classification test, provided that the value of the employer-provided coverage available to each eligible employee in each helper plan is at least 100 percent of the value of the employer-provided coverage available to each eligible employee in the plan that would otherwise fail the classification test. This aggregation rule is to be applied in the same manner as the aggregation rule described above with respect to the 50-percent test.

Definitions of line of business and operating unit

The Secretary is to prescribe by regulation what constitutes a separate line of business or operating unit. Congress generally intended that a line of business or operating unit include all employees necessary for the preparation of property for sale to customers or for the provision of services to customers. Thus, a headquarters or home office is not to be treated as a separate line of business or operating unit. Certain exceptions to the general rule (but not to its application to headquarters or home offices) may be established by regulation where an employer has 2 operations that are vertically integrated and that traditionally are operated by unrelated entities.

In addition, whether claimed lines of business or operating units are separate and bona fide is a facts and circumstances determination requiring examination of each particular situation. Differences and similarities between the services provided and products produced by such claimed lines of business or operating units are, of course, important considerations. Also, the manner in which the employer organizes itself is relevant. Thus, if an employer fails to treat itself as comprised of separate lines of business or operating units and treats employees from different claimed lines or units in an equivalent fashion for certain purposes, such as for coverage under an employer-wide qualified plan, it may not be appropriate to allow such activities to be treated as separate lines of business or operating units.

Notwithstanding the general rules described above, the line of business or operating unit concept is not to be used to undermine the nondiscrimination rules. Thus, for example, certain job classifications (such as hourly employees or leased employees) are not considered to be separate lines of business or operating units. Also, for example, secretaries and other support service personnel are not to be treated as in a line of business or operating unit separate from the lawyers, other professionals, or other employees for whom such personnel perform services, and nurses and laboratory personnel are not to be treated as in a line of business or operating unit separate from the medical doctors for whom they perform services. In addition, the members of an affiliated service group (sec. 414(m)) may not be treated as separate lines of business or operating units.

Also, the Act provides that an operating unit will not be recognized for purposes of these rules unless, for a bona fide business reason, it is separately operated in a geographic area significantly separate from another operating unit in the same line of business. For example, two plants in the same city would not be considered to be in significantly separate geographic areas and thus could not be considered separate operating units if both were in the same line of business.

Separate maintenance

A line of business or operating unit will generally be recognized as separate for purposes of the nondiscrimination rules if it is separately maintained for bona fide business reasons under the rules described above. However, notwithstanding those rules, a line of business or operating unit will not be treated as separate unless it also satisfies the following 3 requirements:

(1) such line of business or operating unit has at least 50 employees;

(2) the employer notifies the Secretary that such line of business or operating unit is being treated as separate; such notification is to be made annually and is to include the basis for the position that the employer is maintaining a separate line of business or operating unit; and

(3) the line of business or operating unit satisfies guidelines prescribed by the Secretary or the employer obtains a determination from the Secretary that the line of business or operating unit may be treated as separate.

Safe harbor

The Act provides a safe-harbor rule under which a separate line of business or operating unit is treated as meeting the third requirement listed in "Separate maintenance," above. A line of business or operating unit satisfies this safe-harbor rule if the "highly compensated employee percentage" of the line of business or operating unit is (1) not less than one-half ("50-percent rule"), and (2) not more than twice ("200-percent rule") the percentage of all employees of the employer who are highly compensated. For purposes of this requirement, the 50-percent rule will be deemed satisfied if at least 10 percent of all highly compensated employees of the employer are employed by the line of business or operating unit. The term "highly compensated employee percentage" means the percentage of all employees performing services for a line of business or operating unit who are highly compensated employees.

If an employer applies the nondiscrimination rules separately to a line of business or operating unit that does not fall within the safe-harbor rule, this may trigger additional reporting requirements.

Guidelines and determinations

The guidelines prescribed by the Secretary for purposes of the third requirement described in "Separate maintenance" above are intended to identify those claimed lines of business or operating units deserving of special scrutiny. For example, if a plan maintained for a claimed line of business or operating unit is significantly better or worse than plans for other lines of business or operating units, such a situation deserves special scrutiny. Also, if a disproportionate percentage of the accrued benefits under the qualified plans of a claimed line of business or operating unit is for highly compensated employees, such employer's claim of a separate line of business or operating unit is to be specially examined.

As noted, if a claimed line of business or operating unit does not satisfy the safe-harbor rule or the applicable guidelines, then the claimed line of business or operating unit will not be recognized for purposes of the nondiscrimination rules unless the employer obtains a determination from the Secretary (e.g., by determination letter or private letter ruling) that such line of business or operating unit is operated separately for bona fide business reasons.

Special rules regarding lines of business and operating units

Combining lines of business

For purposes of satisfying the 50-employee requirement or the safe-harbor rule (or the guidelines, if permitted by the Secretary), a line of business or operating unit may be combined with another line of business or operating unit. Any plan maintained for employees of one of the combined lines of business or operating units is required to satisfy the nondiscrimination rules with respect to the aggregate entity.

Excludable employees

For purposes of determining (1) the number of employees in a line of business or operating unit; (2) the highly compensated employee percentage of a line of business or operating unit; and (3) the percentage of all employees of the employer who are highly compensated, an employer is to disregard the categories of employees that are disregarded for purposes of determining which employees are highly compensated employees. (See Part B.7., above.)

Headquarters employees

The Act clarifies the proper treatment of employees of a headquarters or home office and of other employees serving more than 1 line of business or operating unit (e.g., payroll personnel). Like all other employees, these employees are to be allocated to 1 line of business or operating unit. Generally, this allocation is, under rules prescribed by the Secretary, to be made in accordance with their performance of services. Thus, if a majority of an employee's services are performed for a particular line of business or operating unit, such employee is to be allocated to that line of business or operating unit.

Other employees performing services for more than 1 line of business or operating unit are to be allocated in 1 of 2 ways. First, the employer may allocate such employees on a pro rata basis among its lines of business or operating units, under rules prescribed by the Secretary. Alternatively, such employees may be allocated to any 1 line of business or operating unit for which they perform substantial services provided that such allocation does not cause any line of business or operating unit to violate, continue to violate, or further violate the 50-percent rule or the 200-percent rule provided in the safe-harbor rule. Thus, for this purpose, the 50-percent rule and the 200-percent rule serve as substantive rules, not as safe harbors. This means, for example, that if any lines of business or operating units do not pass the 50-percent rule, highly compensated employees at the home office or headquarters who do not perform a majority of their services for any particular line of business or operating unit are to be allocated first to such lines of business or operating units. This also means that in no event may such highly compensated employees be allocated to any line of business or operating unit if after such allocation the 200-percent rule would be violated (regardless of whether it was violated prior to such allocation).

Allocation of all employees

The Act clarifies that if an employer is using the separate line of business or operating unit rule with respect to any plan, all employees are to be considered part of a line of business or operating unit. Thus, it would not be permissible to maintain that an employer has, in addition to 1 line of business with 50 employees, 10 other employees who are not part of any line of business or operating unit and who would be tested separately. The 10 other employees would have to be treated as part of 1 or more lines of business or operating units. Such lines of business or operating units would have to be aggregated with the 50-employee line of business in order to satisfy the requirement that to be tested separately, a line of business or operating unit is required to have at least 50 employees.

Attribution of benefits

The Act requires that benefits attributable to service for a line of business or operating unit are to be considered as provided by that line of business or operating unit. For purposes of these rules, an employee who performs services for more than one line of business or operating unit, but is allocated to one line of business or operating unit under the rules described above, is to be considered to perform services solely for that line of business or operating unit.

Excluded employees

In general

Under the Act, certain classes of employees are disregarded in applying the nondiscrimination rules if neither the plan, nor any other plan of the same type, is available to any employee in such class. The classes of excluded employees are (1) in the case of an accident or health plan (other than with respect to noncore benefits), employees who have not completed at least 6 months of service (or such shorter period of service as may be specified in the plan); (2) in the case of any other statutory employee benefit plan (including an accident or health plan with respect to noncore benefits), employees who have not completed 1 year of service (or such shorter period of service as may be specified in the plan); (3) employees who normally work less than 17 1/2 hours per week (or such lesser amount as may be specified in the plan); (4) employees who normally work no more than 6 months during any year (or such lesser amount as may be specified in the plan); and (5) employees who have not attained age 21 (or such lower age as may be specified in the plan). In addition, employees included in a unit of employees covered by a collective bargaining agreement are disregarded if neither the plan nor any other plan of the same type is available to any employee in that unit. Finally, nonresident aliens who receive no United States source earned income are disregarded, regardless of whether any such individuals are eligible under a plan.

Conditions for exclusions

In general. —In applying the nondiscrimination rules, an employer may exclude from consideration a category of employees only if no employee in that category is eligible under the plan being tested or any other plan of the employer of the same type. Plans are treated as being of the same type if their benefits are eligible to be excluded from income under the same section of the Code. Thus, if an employer maintains 2 group-term life insurance plans, only 1 of which excludes employees with less than a year of service, the employer is not permitted to exclude from consideration employees with less than a year of service in testing either plan for compliance with the nondiscrimination rules.

In the case of a cafeteria plan, for purposes of applying the cafeteria plan nondiscrimination rules, an employer may exclude a category of employees from consideration only if all employees in such category are excluded with respect to all options offered by the cafeteria plan.

The Act contains certain exceptions described below to the rule that if even one excludable employee is eligible under a plan, all employees who are excludable on the same basis (and on no other basis) as the eligible employee are to be taken into account in applying the nondiscrimination rules to the plan and any other plan of the same type.

Core and noncore benefits.—If a plan offering noncore accident or health benefits excludes employees with less than a year of service, the employer is not required to take into consideration employees with less than a year of service merely because another plan maintained by the employer offering core accident or health benefits has a shorter service requirement. Noncore accident or health benefits consist of coverage for dental, vision, psychological and orthodontia expenses and elective cosmetic surgery.

For purposes of the initial service rules, core accident or health benefits may be considered provided under a separate plan from noncore benefits.

Line of business.—If an employer elects to apply the nondiscrimination rules on a separate line of business or operating unit basis, the employees who are excluded from consideration are determined on a separate line of business or operating unit basis. Thus, for example, if (1) an employer maintains a statutory employee benefit plan for a line of business, (2) the nondiscrimination rules are applied to the plan on a line of business basis, and (3) all plans providing benefits of the same type to employees in that line of business exclude all employees who have not attained the age of 21, then the employer is to exclude from consideration, in applying the nondiscrimination rules to the plan, all employees in that line of business who have not attained age 21, even if the employer maintains a plan of the same type that does not impose an age requirement for employees in another line of business.

Collective bargaining agreement.—If any employee in a unit of employees covered by a collective bargaining agreement is eligible under a plan, then all employees in that unit are required to be taken into account for purposes of applying the nondiscrimination rules to all plans of the same type. However, the fact that employees in one unit must be taken into account with respect to a plan does not alone mean that employees in another unit must be taken into account with respect to the same plan.

Nonresident aliens.—Nonresident aliens with no United States source income are disregarded regardless of whether any such individuals are covered by the plan being tested or by any other plan of the same type.

Separate testing.—The Act also provides that if, for purposes of applying the nondiscrimination rules to a plan, certain employees ("excludable employees") could be excluded from consideration based on the age and service requirements but for the fact that certain of such excludable employees are covered by that plan or another plan of the same type, the excludable employees may be disregarded for purposes of testing the plan if the nondiscrimination rules are satisfied with respect to the excludable employees, treating the excludable employees as the only employees of the employer.

Under the rule described above, an employer may test all such excludable employees separately. Alternatively, an employer may elect to test 1 group of excludable employees separately without testing all excludable employees separately if such group is defined in a nondiscriminatory manner solely by reference to the age or service requirements. For example, an employer may elect to test separately all employees excludable solely on the grounds that they do not have 6 months of service, but not include in such testing group employees excluded under the other age and service rules. (Of course, in this case, the rule permitting employees to be disregarded if the separate testing requirement is satisfied only applies to employees excludable on the grounds that they do not have 6 months of service.) Also, an employer may test separately a group of employees who would pass less restrictive age or service requirements. For example, an employer could test separately all employees excludable solely on the grounds that they are not age 21, but who are at least age 18.

Supplemental employees. —Treasury regulations are to provide a limited exception to the rule that employees who otherwise are excludable as not having 6 months (or 1 year) of service or not normally working more than 6 months a year may not be excluded if any plan of the same type does not exclude such employees. The limited exception will be available if (1) substantially all employees of the employer (other than supplemental employees) generally are eligible to participate in an accident or health plan (or other employee benefit plan) within 30 days after the date of hire; (2) the employer also employs supplemental employees who generally do not work more than 6 months per year; (3) the supplemental employees generally are not rehired if they have previously been supplemental employees; and (4) the supplemental employees do not exceed 15 percent of the employer's workforce.

Under this limited exception, supplemental employees who are (1) retired employees of the employer who are covered under an accident and health plan of the employer maintained for retirees, or (2) students hired by the employer under a work-study program, may be disregarded in determining whether the employer's employee benefit plans satisfy the nondiscrimination requirements. Of course, this limited exception would not be available if any supplemental employees are eligible to participate in any employee benefit plan of the employer (other than a plan maintained for retired employees).

Initial period of service

An employer is to exclude an employee, on the grounds that such employee has not satisfied the required period of initial service, during the period prior to the first day of the calendar month immediately following the actual satisfaction of the initial service requirement. (Of course, subject to the exceptions described above, this exclusion does not apply if any employee is eligible under any plan of the same type prior to the first day of the calendar month immediately following the actual satisfaction of the initial service requirement.) For example, assume an employer required 30 days of service for participation in a health plan, but did not allow participation to begin other than on the first day of a calendar month. Assume further that the employer hires 2 employees, A on

July 2 and B on July 3. Under the terms of the employer's plan, A would be a participant on August 1 and B would be a participant on September 1. Thus, A is a participant after 30 days of service while B has to wait 60 days. Because of the special rule allowing B to be disregarded prior to the first day of the next month following satisfaction of the period of service requirement, B is not taken into account for nondiscrimination purposes until September 1, even though B would have 30 days of service after August 1.

The exclusion described above also may be applied with respect to the first day of a period of less than 31 days specified by the plan.[9] For example, assume an employer required 60 days of service for participation in a health plan, but did not allow participation to commence other than on the first day of 4-week periods. As in the prior example, such employer is to exclude employees during the period prior to the first day of the first 4-week period following satisfaction of the 60-days-of-service requirement.

The Act also clarifies that the 6-month and 1-year service requirements (or shorter service requirements of an employer) are satisfied if an employee is employed continuously for the required period without regard to the number of hours or days worked. A period during which an employee does not perform services for the employer counts toward this service requirement unless there has been a bona fide, indefinite cessation of the employment relationship.

Aggregation of plans

If an employer aggregates plans of different types for purposes of satisfying the benefits test (see discussion below), the excluded employee rules apply as if such plans were the same type. Thus, for example, the lowest age and service requirements in any plans are to apply. The lowest age requirement may come from one plan, the shortest waiting period may come from another plan, the lowest hour requirement for part-time status may come from a third plan, etc.

Special accident or health plan rules

In general

The Act provides certain rules that relate only to accident or health plans. The rules involve (1) treatment of employees or family members covered under another employer's health plan; (2) treatment of family coverage; (3) the type of coverage subject to the nondiscrimination rules; (4) permissible coordination with other accident or health plans; (5) treatment of State-mandated accident or health benefits and continuation coverage; and (6) treatment of part-time employees.

Other coverage

The Act provides that for purposes of applying the benefits test to accident or health plans, an employer may elect to disregard any employee if the employee and the employee's spouse and dependents (if any) are covered by a health plan that provides core benefits and that is maintained by another employer of the employee, spouse, or dependents. Also, in testing employee coverage only under the benefits test (see discussion in this section), an employee may be disregarded if such employee is covered by a health plan that provides core benefits

---

[9]A technical correction may be needed so that the statute reflects this intent.

and that is maintained by another employer of the employee, spouse, or dependents. An employee may not, however, be disregarded in applying the benefits test to any other type of plan, even if accident and health plans are aggregated with such other type of plan for purposes of applying the benefits test to such other type of plan. (See discussion below.)

An election to disregard employees under the rules described above is to be made under rules prescribed by the Secretary. In general, an election is to apply to all employees of the employer who could be disregarded. However, if the employer is applying the nondiscrimination rules on a separate line of business or operating unit basis, the election may be made separately with respect to any separate line of business or operating unit.

For purposes of these rules, the term "core benefits" generally has the same meaning as for purposes of determining the excluded employees (see "Excluded employees" above) except to the extent provided by the Secretary. For example, the Secretary is to except from the definition of core benefits for this purpose, any benefits attributable to a salary reduction medical reimbursement plan or a low-level nonelective medical reimbursement plan. In addition, in no event may disability coverage be considered a core benefit.

Family coverage

Under the Act, family coverage (i.e., coverage of an employee's family which under the Act is considered separate from coverage of the employee) may be considered to be available or provided to an employee despite the fact that the employee does not have a family.[10] The purpose of this rule is to relieve employers from the burden of determining which employees have families.

Congress also recognized, however, that this rule alone could produce inappropriate results in certain very limited circumstances and intended that the nondiscriminatory provision test (see discussion above) be applied to prevent such results. Thus, if, under the facts and circumstances, it is clear that the employer is, by using the above rule—allowing family coverage to be considered to be available or provided to an employee who does not have a family—evading the other nondiscrimination tests, the nondiscriminatory provision test is not to be considered satisfied with respect to the relevant plan or plans.

For example, assume that an employer had 2 highly compensated employees and 8 nonhighly compensated employees, none of whom had families. The employer provided $3,000 of employee coverage to each of the 2 highly compensated employees. For the same year, the employer provided family coverage to each of the 8 nonhighly compensated employees the value of which was $3,000 per employee under the Secretary's valuation tables. Because comparable plans may be aggregated for purposes of the alternative 80-percent test, the employer would satisfy such test. This is not the result intended by Congress, since the facts of this case clearly indicate that by using the rule allowing family coverage to be considered to be provided to employees without families the employer is avoiding providing the nonhighly compensated employees truly

---

[10]A technical correction may be needed so that the statute reflects the treatment of family coverage described below.

nondiscriminatory benefits. Thus, the nondiscriminatory provision test would not be considered satisfied with respect to the plan covering the highly compensated employees.

This application of the nondiscriminatory provision test applies not only with respect to evasion of the alternative 80-percent test, but to evasion of any of the tests. For example, the nondiscriminatory provision test would not be considered satisfied with respect to a plan maintained by the employer in the above example for its highly compensated employees if such plan satisfied the 90-percent/50-percent test by virtue of a second plan making family coverage available to the nonhighly compensated employees.

Congress also provided a special rule in recognition of the fact that in certain instances highly compensated employees will have a disproportionately high percentage of families. In such situations, if family coverage is available under a contributory plan, highly compensated employees will likely receive a disproportionate amount of the coverage. Thus, Congress permitted employers the option of applying the benefits test separately to family coverage as if the only employees of the employer were those with families. (Since this rule is elective for employers, employers not using the rule are not required to determine which employees have families.)

In addition, an employer may elect to disregard, solely for purposes of testing family coverage separately under the benefits test, employees who have a family all of whom are covered by a health plan that provides core benefits and that is maintained by another employer of the employee, spouse, or dependents. (In effect, the family is disregarded.) However, neither this rule nor the rule regarding separate testing of family coverage applies if all accident and health plans are aggregated with plans of a different type for purposes of applying the benefits test to such other plans.

An election to disregard families under the above rule is to be made under rules similar to those referred to in "Other coverage," above.

In addition, the rule permitting employers to test family coverage separately and, with respect to such family coverage, to take into account only employees with families also applies to the alternative 80-percent test. However, for this purpose, the rule permitting families to be disregarded based on other coverage does not apply.

Special rules for other coverage and family coverage

If an employee or a family is disregarded for purposes of the benefits test, any coverage actually provided to the employee or family is disregarded in determining the average employer-provided benefit, as is the existence of that employee or family. An exception to this rule provides that in no case may a highly compensated employee be disregarded if the coverage provided with respect to the highly compensated employee under all accident and health plans of the employer has a value in excess of $133^{1}/_{3}$ percent of the average employer-provided benefit provided with respect to nonhighly compensated employees.[11] If employee and family coverage are tested separately, the same rule applies to

---

[11]A technical correction may be needed so that the statute reflects this intent. Such a correction was included in the versions of H.Con.Res. 395 which passed the House and Senate in the 99th Congress.

each. Thus, with respect to family coverage, for example, the family of a highly compensated employee may not be disregarded if the coverage provided with respect to such family has a value in excess of 133 1/3 percent of the average employer-provided benefit provided with respect to families of nonhighly compensated employees.

The rules described above allowing certain employees or families to be disregarded apply only to the benefits test. Thus, for example, the fact that an employee has other core health coverage does not mean such employee may be disregarded for purposes of the eligibility tests or the alternative 80-percent test.

The Secretary is to prescribe rules, consistent with the rules described above, for the treatment of an employee who has a spouse or dependent employed by the same employer.

Statements regarding family members and other coverage

An employer who elects the optional rules described above is required to obtain and maintain, in such manner as the Secretary prescribes, adequate sworn statements to demonstrate whether individuals have spouses, dependents, or core health coverage from another employer. Congress intended that an employer who elects the application of these optional rules may not treat a nonhighly compensated employee as having other coverage (of the employee or the employee's family), as not having a family, or both unless the employer has a statement to that effect that includes, with respect to the other coverage, the name of the insurer and the employer providing the coverage. In the case of a highly compensated employee, Congress intended that the opposite presumptions are to apply. Thus, a highly compensated employee may not be treated as not having other coverage (of the employee or the employee's family), as having a family, or both, unless the employer has a sworn statement to that effect.

The statements required for purposes of these special rules are to be collected annually on forms provided by the Internal Revenue Service that indicate whether other coverage was provided (or is expected to be provided) for the entire plan year and whether the employee has a family. The statements need not be notarized.

Congress also permitted employers to secure sworn statements from a statistically valid sample of all employees and to use the results of the sample to project the facts regarding the entire workforce. Such a sampling is required to be performed by an independent third party in accordance with rules prescribed by the Secretary. If this sampling rule is used, the same rules described above apply, including the presumptions and the annual collection on IRS forms. In addition, the report by the third party is to be attached to the employer's return and is to include such facts regarding the sampling as are required by the Secretary.

For cases in which an employer avails itself of this sampling rule, the Secretary is to prescribe rules for disregarding actual coverage provided. For example, if the sampling shows that 10 percent of a group of nonexcludable employees has core health benefits from another employer, the Secretary could require that the 10 percent of the nonexcludable employees with the lowest health benefits from the employer (including those with no health benefits) are to be disregarded, subject to the 133 1/3-percent rule described above.

Coverage subject to the nondiscrimination rules

Under the Act, disability coverage attributable to employer contributions (including elective contributions) is subject to the nondiscrimination rules to the extent that benefits provided under such coverage are excludable from income (sec. 105(b) or (c)); no other disability coverage is subject to the rules. Disability coverage subject to the rules is tested for discrimination generally in the same manner in which health coverage is tested.

All plans providing medical care (as defined under sec. 213) are health plans and thus subject to the nondiscrimination rules, including, for example, plans providing ancillary benefits such as dental or vision coverage and physical examination plans.

With respect to accident or health plans, it is the value of the coverage provided, not the contributions, that is subject to the nondiscrimination rules. (Correspondingly, the Act modified the exclusion section to apply to the value of the coverage, rather than to the contributions under the plan.)

Coordination with other plans

Under the Act, an accident or health plan may be integrated (in a manner that does not favor highly compensated employees) with accident or health benefits provided under Federal, State, or foreign law, or under any other accident or health plan, provided such integration is otherwise permissible.

State-mandated benefits and continuation coverage

The Act authorizes the Secretary, in applying the nondiscrimination rules to accident or health plans, to disregard State-mandated benefits under certain circumstances. For example, in comparing the benefits of employees in one State to the benefits of employees in another State, the Secretary may disregard benefits that are mandated in one of the States but are not mandated in the other.

Congress intended, however, that only ancillary benefits may be disregarded, rather than core benefits. For example, if a State mandates an HMO option, Congress did not intend that the value of coverage under an HMO may be disregarded.

Congress further intended that, under rules prescribed by the Secretary, certain benefits provided in connection with "continuation coverage" are to be disregarded in applying the nondiscrimination rules. For example, if an employer requires that a qualified beneficiary who elects continuing health coverage pay, on an after-tax basis, the maximum amount permitted under the rules of section 162(k), any excess of the value of employer-provided coverage over the amount charged is to be disregarded in applying the nondiscrimination rules.

Part-time employee rule

In applying the benefits test and the 50-percent component of the 90-percent/50-percent test to accident or health plans, the Act provides that an employer may elect to adjust the benefits provided to certain employees. With respect to an employee who normally works less than $22\frac{1}{2}$ hours per week, an employer may deem benefits provided (or available in the case of the 90-percent/50-percent test) to have a value equal to up to double the actual value of coverage provided (or available). With respect to an employee who normally works less than 30 hours per week, an employer may deem benefits provided (or available) to have a value equal to up to $1^1/_3$ times the actual value.

If this part-time employee rule is used, it is to be used on a uniform, nondiscriminatory basis for all employees. However, the rule may not be applied for any purpose in a plan year unless during such year more than 50 percent of the nonexcludable employees (determined without regard to plan provisions) normally work more than 30 hours per week. In addition, the multiplication of the benefit under this rule does not apply to elective contributions.

Aggregation of plans for the benefits test

In applying the benefits test to a plan other than an accident or health plan, the Act provides that the employer may aggregate different types of statutory employee benefit plans. Thus, for example, an employer may aggregate benefits provided under all group-term life insurance plans and all qualified group legal services plans (if the employer elects to treat such plans as statutory employee benefit plans) in order to satisfy the benefits test with respect to all such plans. In addition, an employer may aggregate all accident and health plans with plans providing benefits excludable under 1 or more other Code sections for purposes of satisfying the benefits test with respect to plans other than accident or health plans.

In no case, however, may an employer aggregate with other plans some but not all of the plans providing benefits excludable under a Code section. Thus, an employer may not, for example, aggregate some but not all of its group-term life insurance plans with all of its qualified group legal services plans.

When plans excludable under different Code sections are aggregated for purposes of the benefits test, the definition of excluded employees (for purposes of determining the average employer-provided benefit) is to be made as if the plan benefits were excludable under the same Code section. Thus, the lowest age and service requirements from any plans apply (see "Excluded employees" above), and if members of a collective bargaining unit are not excluded for one aggregated plan, they are not excluded for the group of plans. Thus, in determining the average employer-provided benefit, the denominator is all nonexcludable employees, determined generally under the employer's most expansive definitions of such term.

Time for testing

Under the Act, the nondiscrimination rules are to be applied on the basis of the benefits available or provided during the entire year. An example will illustrate how this rule applies for purposes of the benefits test. Assume employee A becomes nonexcludable on July 1 and on that day A is covered under a health plan that provides coverage that on an annual basis has a value of $1,000. The employer's plan year is the calendar year, so for that plan year, A only receives $500 worth of benefits. That $500 goes in the numerator in determining the average employer-provided benefit. However, because A was only taken into account for half the year, A is only counted as half an employee in the denominator.

Congress also provided, for accident or health plans and group-term life insurance plans, a rule of convenience to ease the administrative burden on employers. Under this rule of convenience, an employer may, for purposes of applying the benefits test to active employees, treat employees who separate from service during the last 3 months (or a shorter period elected by the employer) of the plan year as continuing to work and receive benefits for the remainder of the plan year. For employees who separate from service earlier in the plan year, an employer may treat such employees as continuing to work and receive benefits through the end of the month in which they separate. (An employer may elect to apply this rule to periods of less than 31 days specified by the plan; for example, an employer may elect to treat employees as continuing to work and receive benefits through the end of the 4-week period in which they separate.) The effect of these rules is that employers will not have to use the exact day that employees separate in calculating the average employer-provided benefit. Instead, an employer may deem employees to have separated only on the last day of a month (or a shorter period) and in the case of employees separating in the last quarter, on the last day of the plan year.

For purposes of this rule of convenience, employees are considered to receive after separation whatever benefit they had been receiving prior to separation, provided such benefit had been provided for at least 90 days prior to separation. If there had been a change in the benefit during such 90-day period, then the benefit deemed provided during the period of separation is the average benefit provided to the employee during the period beginning on the date in the plan year on which the employee first had to be taken into account for purposes of the nondiscrimination rules and ending on the date of separation from service.

The rule illustrated by the example treating A as only half an employee for purposes of the benefits test and the rule of convenience described above do not apply to group-term life insurance plans with respect to which the employer adjusts the value of the benefit provided based on the employee's compensation or otherwise takes compensation into account. See the discussion above for a description of the adjustment.

The rule of convenience described above also applies to the alternative 80-percent test, the 90-percent/50-percent test, the 50-percent test, and the comparability rules, except that for purposes of the eligibility tests, employees who have separated from service are deemed to have available to them after separation the benefits available prior to separation. For purposes of determining the benefits available prior to separation, the same rules applicable for the benefits test apply. Other than this one difference, the rule of convenience applies in the same manner. Thus, in determining whether the tests listed above are satisfied, an employer is required to examine the entire year, but may use the rule of convenience to reduce substantially the administrative burden. For example, assume that an employee (A) who was not excludable on the first day of the plan year separated from service during the sixth month of the plan year. A may be considered to be employed through the end of the sixth month and have available or provided benefits determined under the rule of convenience described above. During the second 6 months, A is not an active employee for purposes of applying the tests.

Of course, the rule of convenience under which employees are deemed to receive or have available to them benefits after separation from service does not apply in testing benefits actually received by or available to former employees. (See discussion below.)

As is true with respect to the nondiscrimination rules applicable to qualified retirement plans, the fact that a failure to meet any of the nondiscrimination rules was attributable to unforeseen circumstances does not affect the application of the rules.

Congress also provided an additional rule of convenience for employers that do not require any initial period of service for participation in a statutory employee benefit plan. Under this second rule of convenience, an employer may, for purposes of the 90-percent/50-percent test and the benefits test, disregard benefits available or provided to an employee during the interval between the employee's commencement of employment and the first day of the first calendar month (or the first day of a period of less than 31 days specified by the plan, such as a 4-week period) following such commencement. (This rule does not apply to an employee who commences employment on the first day of a calendar month (or of the shorter period).) However, benefits available or provided during such interval that relate to any other period may not be disregarded. For example, if an employer pays for a year's worth of dependent care or provides an annual physical examination, only a proportionate part of the value of such benefit may be disregarded. This second rule of convenience applies to all statutory employee benefit plans. If an employer uses this rule of convenience, it is required to do so with respect to all employees.

Former employees

The Act provides that, except to the extent provided by the Secretary, rules similar to the nondiscrimination rules applicable to active employees are to be applied separately to former employees. In applying the rules to former employees, the Secretary is to provide certain special provisions. Under such provisions, employers generally may restrict the class of former employees to be tested to those who have retired on or after a reasonable retirement age, or to those who have separated from service due to disability. In addition, employers generally may limit the class further to employees who have, for example, retired within a certain number of years. Finally, in testing whatever class of employees is chosen, employers may make reasonable assumptions regarding mortality, so that they do not have to determine those former employees not covered by a plan who are still alive.

Benefits other than life and health

In general

As noted above, the new nondiscrimination rules apply on a mandatory basis only to accident or health plans and group-term life insurance plans.

With respect to dependent care assistance programs, the prior-law eligibility standards continue to apply, but the Act adds a special benefits test described below. The prior-law nondiscrimination rules apply to qualified tuition reduction programs, qualified group legal services plans, educational assistance programs, employee benefit programs providing no-additional-cost services, qualified employee discounts, or employer-operated eating facilities (sec. 132), and welfare benefit funds.

The reason that the new nondiscrimination rules are not mandatorily applicable to qualified group legal services plans and educational assistance programs is that these types of plans generally are scheduled to expire prior to the effective date of the new nondiscrimination rules. Congress anticipates, however, that if the qualified group legal services plans and educational assistance programs are extended to periods after the effective date of the new nondiscrimination rules, such nondiscrimination rules will be applied on a mandatory basis.

Also, as noted above, the Act permits employers to elect to treat qualified group legal services plans, educational assistance programs, and/or dependent care assistance programs as statutory employee benefit plans, and to apply the new nondiscrimination rules to them in lieu of the otherwise applicable nondiscrimination rules [though not in lieu of the applicable concentration tests (secs. 120(c)(3), 127(b)(3), and 129(d)(4))]. Such an election enables an employer to use these types of plans for purposes of satisfying the benefits test. (See the description in "Benefits test" above.)

Although the new nondiscrimination rules do not mandatorily apply to plans other than accident or health plans and group-term life insurance plans, the Act does provide certain amendments described below affecting other employee benefits.

Definitions

The following definitions applicable to statutory employee benefit plans also are applied to qualified tuition reduction programs, qualified group legal services plans, cafeteria plans, educational assistance programs, dependent care assistance programs, miscellaneous fringe benefits (sec. 132), and welfare benefit funds: (1) highly compensated employees; (2) compensation (including the limitation on the amount that can be taken into account) with respect to those plans for which compensation is relevant; (3) excluded employees; and (4) employer (including application of the employee leasing rules). These new definitions are discussed more fully in this Part, above, except for the "compensation" definition and limitation, which are discussed in Part B.1. and Part D., above.

The only plans for which compensation is relevant, other than group-term life insurance plans (which are discussed above), are plans providing life insurance, disability, severance pay, or supplemental unemployment compensation through a welfare benefit fund.

With respect to nonemployees participating in a plan that is part of a welfare benefit fund, the Secretary is to prescribe appropriate rules for determining which, if any, of such nonemployees are to be considered highly compensated employees.

Dependent care assistance programs

As noted, a special benefits test applies to dependent care assistance programs that are not treated as statutory employee benefit plans. Under this special rule, the same benefits test applicable to statutory employee benefit plans applies,[12] with two modifications.

---

[12]This benefits test was intended to apply notwithstanding the provision providing that utilization rates cannot cause a dependent care assistance program to fail to qualify. (Sec. 129(e)(6).) A technical correction may be needed so that the statute reflects this intent. Such a correction was included in the versions of H.Con.Res. 395 which passed the House and Senate in the 99th Congress.

First, the average employer-provided benefit received by nonhighly compensated employees is required to be at least 55 percent (as opposed to 75 percent) of the average employer-provided benefit received by highly compensated employees.

Second, for purposes of applying the benefits test to salary reduction amounts, employees with compensation (as defined in sec. 414(q)(7))[13] below $25,000 may be[14] disregarded. If an employer provides dependent care assistance both through salary reduction and otherwise, the treatment of the employees with compensation below $25,000 is to be determined under rules prescribed by the Secretary.

Cafeteria plans

The Act retains the prior-law eligibility test for cafeteria plans. The Act deletes the special cafeteria plan benefits tests, although the concentration test is retained. Thus, each type of benefit available or provided under a cafeteria plan is subject to its own applicable nondiscrimination rules and to any applicable concentration test. For example, group-term life insurance benefits under a cafeteria plan are required to satisfy the nondiscrimination rules applicable to group-term life insurance plans outside a cafeteria plan. As discussed above, certain aggregation of plans excludable under different Code sections is permissible for purposes of the benefits test applicable to statutory employee benefit plans.

The Act also modifies the definition of a cafeteria plan to include a plan under which an employee may only choose among qualified benefits and may not choose cash or a taxable benefit. In addition, the Act creates a new exception to the general rule that the term "cafeteria plan" does not include any plan that provides for deferred compensation. The exception applies to certain post-retirement life insurance provided under a plan maintained by an educational organization. See Part F.6., below.

Under the Act, the definition of a qualified benefit is modified so that a benefit will not fail to be a qualified benefit solely because it is includible in an employee's income under section 89.[15] Thus, for example, if a portion of the health benefits provided under a plan are discriminatory under section 89 and thus includible in income, that alone will not cause the plan to fail to be a cafeteria plan.

The Act provides that if a cafeteria plan does not satisfy the cafeteria plan eligibility or concentration test, the benefits under the plan are taxable to highly compensated employees or key employees, respectively.[16]

The Act allows employers to limit the elections of highly compensated employees to the extent necessary to comply with the applicable nondiscrimina-

---

[13]A technical correction may be needed so that the statute reflects this intent. Such a correction was included in the version of H.Con.Res. 395 which passed the House and Senate in the 99th Congress.

[14]A technical correction may be needed so that the statute reflects the intent that an employer may elect whether to disregard employees with compensation below $25,000.

[15]A technical correction may be needed so that the statute reflects this intent.

[16]A technical correction may be needed so that the statute reflects this intent.

tion rules. However, the limitations are to be applied, under rules prescribed by the Secretary, in the manner described above for allocating the discriminatory excess among highly compensated employees.

Reporting

The Act also amends the rules regarding reporting of employee benefits and extends those rules to additional benefits. These rules are discussed below.

Qualification requirements

In general

In addition to imposing new nondiscrimination rules, the Act also prescribes certain basic standards that any employee benefit plan must satisfy in order to preserve the applicable exclusion for employees.

Under the Act, except to the extent provided in regulations, the gross income of any employee, whether or not highly compensated, includes such employee's employer-provided benefit under an employee benefit plan, unless (1) the plan is in writing; (2) the employees' rights under the plan are legally enforceable; (3) employees are provided reasonable notification of benefits available under the plan; (4) the plan is maintained for the exclusive benefit of the employees; and (5) the employer established the plan with the intention of maintaining it indefinitely.

These rules apply to statutory employee benefit plans, qualified tuition reduction programs, qualified group legal services plans, cafeteria plans, educational assistance programs, dependent care assistance programs, fringe benefit programs providing no-additional-cost services, qualified employee discounts, or employer-operated eating facilities (sec. 132), and plans providing benefits through a welfare benefit fund. With respect to dependent care assistance programs, the required notification is to include a description of the dependent care credit (sec. 21) and the circumstances under which the credit is more advantageous than the exclusion.

With respect to the requirement that a statutory employee benefit plan be legally enforceable, Congress intended that a plan will generally not be considered legally enforceable if it is discretionary with the employer. For example, if a plan of the employer provides that medical expenses will be reimbursed at the employer's discretion, the plan is not legally enforceable, because the employees have no right to compel payment of benefits. A plan will not fail to satisfy the legally enforceable requirement merely because the employer has the right to terminate the plan with respect to claims not yet incurred. If, however, the employer maintains the right to terminate the plan with respect to incurred claims, those claims would not be considered legally enforceable, and payment of the claims would not be excludable. Of course, termination in some circumstances could violate the permanency requirement.

With respect to the requirement that a plan be maintained for the exclusive benefit of an employer's employees, Congress did not intend that a plan would fail to satisfy this requirement merely because benefits are provided to nonemployees whose receipt of the benefits is excludable under the Code section that excludes the same benefits when provided to employees. For example, under section 132(f)(3), use of air transportation by a parent of an employee is treated as use by the employee for purposes of determining the excludability of the air transportation. In such a situation, excludable use of air transportation by a parent of an employee under an employer's plan would not cause the plan to fail to satisfy the requirement that it be maintained for the exclusive benefit of the employer's employees.

In addition, Congress did not intend that a plan fail to satisfy the exclusive benefit rule merely because benefits are provided under the plan to nonemployees on a basis that is not tax-favored. For example, if an airline furnishes nonexcludable air transportation to its directors under the same plan maintained for employees, the plan will not fail to satisfy the exclusive benefit rule merely because taxable benefits are provided to nonemployees.

Employer-provided benefit

Notwithstanding the valuation rules for purposes of the nondiscrimination rules, if any plan fails to satisfy the qualification requirements described above, an employee's employer-provided benefit is defined as the value of the benefits provided to or on behalf of such employee, to the extent attributable to contributions made by the employer (including elective contributions). Thus, even in the case of insurance-type plans, the amount includible in an employee's income is the value of the benefits, not the coverage.

For example, in the case of a health plan failing the qualification requirements, the services provided and reimbursements made are includible in income. In addition, such amount is includible in an employee's gross income in the taxable year in which such benefits are received.

Employer sanction

The employer-level sanction applicable to a failure to report discriminatory benefits in a timely manner also applies to a failure to report income attributable to a violation of the qualification requirements. However, this sanction applies to the value of benefits in all such cases, rather than to the value of coverage. (The sanction applicable to the nondiscrimination rules applies to the value of coverage with respect to insurance-type benefits.)

Reporting requirements

The Act expanded the prior-law requirement that the employers that maintain cafeteria plans, educational assistance programs, and qualified group legal services plans file information returns in accordance with regulations (sec. 6039D). Under the Act, this requirement also applies to statutory employee benefit plans and dependent care assistance programs.

The Act also modified the reporting requirements by requiring that all employers maintaining a plan subject to the requirements report the number of highly compensated employees (1) of the employer, (2) eligible to participate in the plan, and (3) participating in the plan. Also, the Act clarifies that the requirement that certain employers file an additional return only applies to a representative sample of employers.

In addition, if benefits provided to an employee are includible in such employee's income due to a violation of the new nondiscrimination rules or of the qualification requirements, the employer is required to include such amounts separately on an employee's Form W-2. For a description of the penalty for a failure to include such an amount, see discussion above.

Effective Dates

In general

Under the Act, the general effective date is plan years beginning after the later of (1) December 31, 1987, or (2) the earlier of December 31, 1988, or the date 3 months following the issuance of Treasury regulations.

Collective bargaining agreements

A special effective date applies to plans maintained pursuant to a collective bargaining agreement.

Highly compensated employee definition

For purposes of the sanction applicable to a violation of the rules regarding continuation of health care (sec. 106), the new definition of highly compensated employee applies to years beginning after December 31, 1986. With respect to qualified tuition reduction programs, qualified group legal services plans, educational assistance programs, dependent care assistance programs, miscellaneous fringe benefits (sec. 132), and welfare benefit funds, the new definition applies to years beginning after 1987. The new definition applies to statutory employee benefit plans and cafeteria plans when the new rules described above are generally effective with respect to such plans.

Aggregation of employers for continuation of health care

The provisions aggregating related employers and applying the employee leasing rules for purposes of the continuation of health care rules apply to years beginning after December 31, 1986.[17]

Group-term life insurance plans

The Act contains an exception to the new rules for certain group-term life insurance plans. In the case of a plan described in section 223(d)(2) of the Tax Reform Act of 1984, such plan is to be treated as meeting the requirements of the new nondiscrimination rules with respect to individuals described in section 223(d)(2) of the Act. (Of course, an individual to whom section 223(d)(2)(A) does not apply because of section 223(d)(2)(B) is not considered to be described in section 223(d)(2).) In addition, an employer may elect to exclude such individuals in applying the new nondiscrimination rules.

At the election of the employer, the new rules described in this section (including the nondiscrimination rules, qualification rules, and cafeteria plan rules) are to apply to certain group-term life insurance plans in plan years beginning after October 22, 1986.[18] The plans for which this election is available are those that are maintained by educational institutions (within the meaning of sec. 170(b)(1)(A)(ii)) and that are described in "Exclusion for Post-Retirement Group-Term Life Insurance Under a Cafeteria Plan" below.

---

[17]A technical correction may be needed so that the statute reflects this intent. A correction that reflected part of this intent was included in the versions of H.Con.Res. 395 which passed the House and Senate in the 99th Congress.

[18]A technical correction may be needed so that the statute reflects this intent. Such a correction was included in the versions of H.Con.Res. 395 which passed the House and Senate in the 99th Congress.

Church plans

In addition, the Act provides a delayed effective date for church plans. Such plans are not required to comply with the new nondiscrimination rules until years beginning after December 31, 1988.

Revenue Effect

The provision is estimated to increase fiscal year budget receipts by $72 million in 1988, $128 million in 1989, $140 million in 1990, and $154 million in 1991.

2. Deductibility of health insurance costs of self-employed individuals (sec. 1161 of the Act and sec. 162 of the Code)[19]

Prior Law

Under prior and present law, an employer's contribution to a plan providing accident or health benefits is excludable from an employee's income (sec. 106). No equivalent exclusion was provided, under prior law, for self-employed individuals (sole proprietors or partners).

Benefits actually paid to an employee under an accident or health plan generally are includible in the employee's gross income to the extent attributable to employer contributions (sec. 105(a)). Reimbursements for costs incurred for medical expenses (within the meaning of sec. 213) and disability benefit payments that compensate for permanent injury and are computed without reference to the period of absence from work are excluded from gross income (secs. 105(b) and (c)).

Individuals who itemized deductions were permitted, under prior law, to deduct amounts paid during the taxable year, if not reimbursed by insurance or otherwise, for medical care of the taxpayer and of the taxpayer's spouse and dependents, to the extent that the total of such expenses exceeded five percent of adjusted gross income (sec. 213).

Reasons for Change

Congress believed the prior-law rules relating to the exclusion from income for benefits under employer accident or health plans created unfair distinctions between self-employed individuals (the owners of unincorporated businesses) and the owners of corporations. The ability to exclude health benefits of an owner to the extent provided by a corporate employer created tax incentives for incorporation that Congress believed led to inefficient tax-driven decision making.

More importantly, Congress was aware that access to employer health plans is lowest with small employers (particularly with small, self-employed employers). The need for adequate health coverage is so important that Congress believed it was essential to encourage a narrowing of the gap in health coverage. Congress concluded that a partial temporary exclusion for health plans maintained by self-employed individuals would accomplish this goal.

---

[19]For legislative background of the provision, see: H.R. 3838, as reported by the Senate Committee on Finance on May 29, 1986, sec. 1261; S.Rep. 99-313, pp. 665–667; and H.Rep. 99-841, Vol. II (September 18, 1986), pp. 538–539 (Conference Report).

However, Congress also believed this exclusion for the self-employed would not be justified unless nondiscriminatory health insurance coverage is also extended to the employees of an unincorporated employer. To facilitate implementation of these nondiscrimination rules, Congress found it desirable to direct the Secretary to provide guidance for small employers.

Explanation of Provision

The Act provides a deduction for 25 percent of the amounts paid for health insurance for a taxable year on behalf of a self-employed individual and the individual's spouse and dependents. This deduction is allowable in calculating adjusted gross income. A self-employed individual means an individual who has earned income for the taxable year (sec. 401(c)(1)). However, under the Act, no deduction is allowable to the extent the deduction exceeds the self-employed individual's earned income for the taxable year. In addition, no deduction is allowable for any taxable year for which the self-employed individual is eligible to participate (on a subsidized basis) in a health plan of an employer of the self-employed individual or of such individual's spouse.

In addition, the deduction is not allowable unless the nondiscrimination requirements (as modified by the Act) applicable to accident or health plans are satisfied with respect to each such plan tested as though all coverage for which a 25-percent deduction is allowable under this section were employer-provided.

Under the Act, the amount allowable as a deduction for health coverage for a self-employed individual is not also taken into account for purposes of determining the amount of any medical deduction to which the self-employed individual is entitled. Thus, such amounts deductible under this provision are not treated as medical expenses of the individual for purposes of determining whether the threshold for the itemized medical expense deduction (sec. 213(a)) is met.

Further, the Act provides that the amount deductible under this provision is not taken into account in computing net earnings from self-employment (sec. 1402(a)). Therefore, the amounts deductible under this provision do not reduce the income base for the self-employed individual's social security tax.[20]

The Act directs the Treasury to provide guidance to self-employed individuals to whom this deduction applies with respect to the nondiscrimination requirements applicable to accident or health plans.

Effective Date

The provision is effective for taxable years beginning after December 31, 1986. The provision does not apply to any taxable year beginning after December 31, 1989.

Revenue Effect

The provision is estimated to decrease fiscal year budget receipts by $141 million in 1987, $205 million in 1988, $227 million in 1989, and $71 million in 1990.

---

[20]A technical correction may be needed so that the statute reflects this intent.

3. Exclusions for educational assistance programs, qualified group legal services plans, and dependent care assistance programs (secs. 1162 and 1163 of the Act and secs. 120, 127, and 129 of the Code)[21]

Prior Law

Educational assistance

Under prior and present law, an employee is required to include in income for income and employment tax purposes the value of educational assistance provided by an employer to the employee, unless the cost of such assistance qualifies as a deductible job-related expense of the employee. Amounts expended for education qualify as deductible employee business expenses if the education (1) maintains or improves skills required for the employee's job, or (2) meets the express requirements of the individual's employer that are imposed as a condition of employment. Under prior law, an employee's gross income for income and employment tax purposes did not include amounts paid or expenses incurred by the employer for educational assistance provided to the employee if such amounts were paid or such expenses were incurred pursuant to an educational assistance program that meets certain requirements (Code sec. 127).

Under prior law, the maximum amount of educational assistance benefits that an employee could receive tax-free during any taxable year was limited to $5,000; thus, the excess benefits over this amount were subject to income and employment taxes. In the case of an employee who worked for more than one employer, the $5,000 cap applied to the aggregate amount of educational assistance benefits received from all employers.

The exclusion for educational assistance benefits expired for taxable years beginning after December 31, 1985.

Group legal services

Under prior law, amounts contributed by an employer to a qualified group legal services plan for employees (or their spouses or dependents) were excluded from an employee's gross income for income and employment tax purposes (sec. 120). The exclusion also applied to any services received by an employee or any amounts paid to an employee under such a plan as reimbursement for the cost of legal services for the employee (or the employee's spouse or dependents). In order to be a qualified plan under which employees were entitled to tax-free benefits, a group legal services plan was required to fulfill several requirements. An employer maintaining a group legal services plan was required to file an information return with respect to the program at the time and in the manner required by Treasury regulations.

The exclusion for group legal services benefits expired for taxable years ending after December 31, 1985.

In addition, under prior law, an organization, the exclusive function of which was to provide legal services or indemnification against costs of legal services

---

[21]For legislative background of the provision, see: H.R. 3838, as reported by the House Committee on Ways and Means on December 7, 1985, sec. 1161; H. Rep. 99-426, pp. 779–781; H.R. 3838, as reported by the Senate Committee on Finance on May 29, 1986, sec. 1262; S.Rep. 99-313, pp. 667-670; and H.Rep. 99-841, Vol. II (September 18, 1986), pp. 539–542 (Conference Report).

as part of a qualified group legal services plan, was entitled to tax-exempt status (sec. 501(c)(20)). The tax exemption for such an organization expired for years ending after December 31, 1985.

Dependent care assistance

Under prior and present law, amounts paid or incurred by an employer for dependent care assistance provided to an employee through a dependent care assistance program are excludable from gross income (sec. 129). The amount excludable was limited, under prior law, to the employee's earned income for the year or, in the case of married couples, the lesser of the employee's earned income and the earned income of the employee's spouse. A dependent care assistance program must be a written plan for the exclusive benefit of employees, must not discriminate in favor of certain employees and must meet certain other requirements.

Reasons for Change

Educational assistance and group legal services

The exclusions for educational assistance and group legal services were originally enacted in 1978 for a temporary period in order to provide Congress with an opportunity to evaluate the use and effectiveness of the exclusions. However, the absence of any information reporting prior to 1985 made it difficult to obtain information concerning the operation of the exclusions.

Congress recognized that the Treasury Department was conducting a comprehensive examination of the effect of the exclusions for educational assistance and group legal services on the income, wage, and benefit bases. Congress believed that it was appropriate to extend the educational assistance and group legal services exclusion for an additional 2 years to permit Treasury to complete its evaluation of the effect of these exclusions based on the information reports that employers are now required to file.

Dependent care assistance

Congress was concerned about the relationship under prior law of the exclusion for employer-provided dependent care assistance and the child care credit. Congress recognized that the prior-law exclusion was more valuable to higher-income taxpayers than the child care credit. Moreover, Congress believed that it was inequitable to provide an unlimited exclusion to individuals whose employers provide dependent care assistance, but a limited tax credit to individuals who were required to pay their own child care expenses.

Consequently, Congress concluded that it was desirable to place a dollar limit on the annual exclusion for employer-provided dependent care assistance benefits to coordinate the exclusion with the tax incentives provided to individuals through the child care credit.

Explanation of Provisions

Educational assistance

The Act retroactively extends the educational assistance exclusion for 2 years. In addition, the Act increases the cap on annual excludable educational assistance benefits to $5,250 from $5,000.

The exclusion is scheduled to expire for taxable years beginning after December 31, 1987.

Group legal services

The Act retroactively extends the group legal services exclusion for 2 years. This provision also extends the tax-exempt status of group legal services organizations (sec. 501(c)(20)). The exclusion is scheduled to expire for taxable years ending after December 31, 1987.

The Act provides a transition rule for group legal services benefits provided under a cafeteria plan. Under this transition rule, an employee will be permitted to revoke an election to take cash or a qualified benefit other than group legal services and to make a new election to take group legal services instead. Such revocation and new election is required to be made no later than 60 days after October 22, 1986, and may relate to any period after December 31, 1985. This transition rule is limited to cafeteria plans that, prior to August 16, 1986, did not allow employees to elect group legal services benefits with respect to a period after December 31, 1985.

Dependent care assistance

The Act limits the exclusion for dependent care assistance to $5,000 a year ($2,500 for a married individual filing separately).

In addition, the Act clarifies the amount of dependent care assistance provided with respect to any employee in the case of an onsite facility maintained by the employer. In the case of an onsite facility, the amount excluded with respect to any dependent is to be based on utilization of the facility by a dependent of the employee and the value of the services provided.

Effective Dates

The provision relating to educational assistance programs is effective for taxable years beginning after December 31, 1985.

The provision relating to group legal services is effective for taxable years ending after December 31, 1985.

The modifications relating to dependent care assistance apply to taxable years beginning after December 31, 1986.

Revenue Effect

The provision is estimated to decrease fiscal year budget receipts by $408 million in 1987, $71 million in 1988, and to increase fiscal year budget receipts by less than $5 million in 1989, 1990, and 1991.

4. Treatment of certain full-time life insurance salespersons (sec. 1166 of the Act and sec. 7701(a)(20) of the Code)[22]

Prior Law

Under a cafeteria plan, an employee is offered a choice between cash and one or more employee benefits. If certain requirements are met, then the mere availability of cash or certain permitted taxable benefits under a cafeteria plan

---

[22]For legislative background of the provision, see: H.R. 3838, as reported by the House Committee on Ways and Means on December 7, 1985, sec. 1162; H.Rep. 99-426, pp. 781–782; and H.Rep. 99-841, Vol. II (September 18, 1986), p. 542 (Conference Report).

does not cause an employee to be treated as having received the available cash or taxable benefits for income tax purposes.

Under prior and present law, a full-time life insurance salesperson is treated as an employee for purposes of eligibility for certain enumerated employee benefit exclusions (sec. 7701(a)(20)). However, although such a salesperson was eligible to receive certain excludable employee benefits that may be provided under a cafeteria plan under prior law, the salesperson was not treated as an employee for purposes of the cafeteria plan provisions.

Reasons for Change

Congress believed it was inconsistent to treat full-time life insurance salespersons as employees for certain employee benefit exclusions, yet limit the ability of such salespersons to elect to receive the same benefits under a cafeteria plan.

Explanation of Provision

The Act permits a full-time life insurance salesperson to be treated as an employee for purposes of the cafeteria plan provisions with respect to benefits that the salesperson is otherwise permitted to exclude from income.[23]

Effective Date

The provision applies for years beginning after December 31, 1985.

Revenue Effect

The provision is estimated to have a negligible effect on fiscal year budget receipts.

5. Exclusion of cafeteria plan elective contributions from wages for purposes of employment taxes (sec. 1151(g) of the Act, sec. 209(e) of the Social Security Act, and secs. 3121(a)(5) and 3306(b)(5) of the Code)[24]

Prior Law

Under prior and present law, no amount is included in the gross income of a participant in a cafeteria plan meeting certain requirements solely because, under the plan, the participant may choose among the benefits of the plan. However, the fact that remuneration is not subject to income tax withholding does not necessarily mean that such remuneration is not subject to tax under the Federal Insurance Contributions Act (FICA) or under the Federal Unemployment Tax Act (FUTA). Both the FICA and FUTA taxes apply to all remuneration for employment, with certain exceptions. There was no provision under prior law with respect to either the FICA or the FUTA that would render inapplicable the principles of constructive receipt of benefits under a cafeteria plan or any other flexible choice plan.

---

[23]A technical correction may be needed so that the statute reflects this intent.

[24]For legislative background of the provision, see: H.Rep. 99-841, Vol. II (September 18, 1986), pp. 542–543 (Conference Report).

Reasons for Change

Congress found it appropriate to clarify the employment tax status of benefits provided under a cafeteria plan.

Explanation of Provision

The Act clarifies that the cafeteria plan exception from the principles of constructive receipt also applies for purposes of the FICA and FUTA taxes. This clarification does not apply to elective contributions under a qualified cash or deferred arrangement that is part of a cafeteria plan.

Effective Date

The provision is effective with respect to years beginning before, on, or after October 22, 1986.

Revenue Effect

The provision is estimated to have no effect on fiscal year budget receipts.

6. Exclusion for post-retirement group-term life insurance under a cafeteria plan (sec. 1151(d) of the Act and sec. 125(c)(2)(C) of the Code)[25]

Prior Law

Under prior and present law, the cost of permanent benefits under a life insurance policy provided by an employer to an employee is includible in income. In general, a permanent benefit is a benefit with an economic value extending beyond one policy year, such as a paid-up policy for future years.

No amount is includible in the gross income of a participant in a cafeteria plan meeting certain requirements solely because, under the plan, the participant may choose among the benefits. Except with respect to elective contributions under a qualified cash or deferred arrangement, the term "cafeteria plan" does not include any plan that provides for deferred compensation.

Reasons for Change

Congress believed that a limited exception to the definition of group-term life insurance and to the deferred compensation rule for cafeteria plans should be provided in the case of nondiscriminatory programs maintained by educational institutions.

Explanation of Provision

As under prior law, the term "cafeteria plan" does not include any plan that provides for deferred compensation, except for a qualified cash and deferred arrangement (as defined in sec. 401(k)(2)). However, new section 125(c)(2)(C) provides an additional exception from the prohibition against deferred compensation for certain post-retirement life insurance for cafeteria plans maintained by educational organizations described in section 170(b)(1)(A)(ii).

Specifically, the prohibition against deferred compensation within a cafeteria plan does not apply to a plan of an educational organization to the extent of

[25]For legislative background of the provision, see: H.Rep. 99-841, Vol. II (September 18, 1986), p. 543 (Conference Report).

amounts that a covered employee may elect to have the employer pay as contributions for post-retirement group life insurance if (1) all contributions for such insurance are to be made before retirement, and (2) such life insurance does not have a cash surrender value at any time. The provision also provides that, for purposes of section 79, any such life insurance is to be treated as group-term life insurance.

Under this provision, Congress intended to allow employees of educational organizations to pre-fund post-retirement life insurance coverage on an individualized basis. Although the insurance coverage might be offered on a group basis to the employees of the educational organization through the cafeteria plan, amounts paid for each electing employee can be credited to individual employee accounts so that the post-retirement life insurance coverage will be fully paid up upon retirement. Under such a plan, the right to the post-retirement life insurance coverage may even vest upon payment of amounts for the electing employee (that is, prior to retirement). However, apart from the paid-up character of the post-retirement coverage, the employee may not have the right to a cash surrender value at any time.

Although the post-retirement life insurance coverage may be guaranteed by a commercial insurer, the employee receives only current life insurance protection after retirement because the employee has no right to a cash surrender value. This guarantee of current life insurance protection under a paid-up insurance policy is similar to that which a retired employee could receive from an actuarially funded group-term life insurance plan. Thus, the provision treats the described post-retirement life insurance benefit as group-term life insurance for purposes of section 79. Accordingly, the value of coverage in excess of $50,000 will be taxable to the retired employee under section 79(c) as it is received annually by the retired employee; section 83 will not apply and the employee will not be taxed on the contributions to fund the post-retirement insurance.

Likewise, the post-retirement life insurance described under section 125(c)(2)(C), as group-term life insurance, will be subject to the nondiscrimination rules under section 89 as well as the rules specifically applicable to cafeteria plans.

Effective Date

The provision is effective for years beginning after the later of (1) December 31, 1987, or (2) 3 months following the issuance of final regulations, but no later than December 31, 1988. An employer may elect to have the provision apply with respect to any plan year beginning after the date of enactment (October 22, 1986), as long as the employer also elects the application of the modifications made by the Act to the employee benefit nondiscrimination rules.[26]

Revenue Effect

The provision is estimated to have a negligible effect on fiscal year budget receipts.

---

[26]A technical correction may be needed so that the statute reflects this intent. Such a correction was included in the versions of H.Con.Res. which passed the House and Senate in the 99th Congress.

Part Three

Design

Six

Coverage and Eligibility

The purpose of Part III is to provide a benefit-by-benefit guide to the design of a flexible compensation program. Regardless of the components of the structure, however, an organization ultimately will need to determine which employee groups are to be covered under the program and what, if any, special requirements should apply for certain groups.

For many organizations, the coverage and eligibility determination will represent largely an extension of current practices. For example, if all employees currently are covered under a common benefit program, the flexible program typically would cover the same employee group, subject to any eligibility or other requirements currently in place. Similarly, groups presently excluded from coverage (such as part-time employees) or covered under separate arrangements (such as members of a collective-bargaining unit, or retired employees) might remain outside the flexible program.

For other organizations, different issues may arise. Large or diverse organizations may already operate multiple employee-benefit programs based on cost or other considerations relating to the different business units or operating entities. In these instances, coverage decisions might be influenced by the type of benefits or the financing structure already in place or by other considerations such as the employee relations environment or the compatibility of administrative systems and procedures.

A separate issue for flexible programs is coverage of new employees—those who join a company sometime before the next annual enrollment. Organizations often establish a waiting period before eligibility for flexible program participation begins, but practices vary in terms of the types of coverage offered in the interim.

The purpose of this material is to examine the issues relating to coverage of different employee groups under a flexible program.

§ 6.1   TYPES OF COVERAGE CATEGORIES

(a)   SALARIED EMPLOYEES

Flexible compensation programs originated within the salaried employee population. As a result, the vast majority of flexible programs (96 percent) cover all full-time salaried employees. In general, few employers impose eligibility restrictions on active employees other than designation as a regular, full-time salaried employee. (See also later discussion of coverage for new employees.)

Occasionally, however, organizations impose eligibility requirements by employee group or by benefit area. For example, a one- to three-year waiting period might apply for long-term disability coverage for certain employees (e.g., nonmanagement). All other flexible program choices are currently in effect, but disability coverage as an option is not available until satisfaction of the service requirement. (Alternatively, the employee might receive no employer credits for disability but still could purchase the coverage.) Under the new nondiscrimination requirements scheduled to take effect in 1989 (and depending on the proportion of employees excluded from coverage), these types of eligibility restrictions most likely will diminish. (This particular example is somewhat misleading in that the new nondiscrimination requirements generally apply to all benefits except disability. See also Chapter Five for discussion of the 1989 nondiscrimination requirements.)

(b)   HOURLY EMPLOYEES

To date, flexible compensation programs have emerged more slowly within the hourly workforce, particularly among union members. Of flexible compensation programs in effect, 62 percent cover nonunion hourly employees, typically in situations where nonunion employees previously were covered under the same program as salaried employees. Only 16 percent of programs cover union employees, either under a separate flexible program or the same one as for salaried employees. (Note, however, that of the remaining 84 percent of employers, 76 percent do not have union employees.)

The emergence of flexible programs for hourly employees has trailed salaried employee practices for several reasons. One is the strong influence of the collective-bargaining process on the determination (or shaping) of benefits for hourly employees. Until recently, flexible compensation has been pegged within the labor environment as essentially a technique for shifting a greater proportion of the cost of benefits (particularly medical) to employees. The vast majority of union hourly medical plans offer first-dollar coverage, so any retreat from essentially full medical protection is perceived as a concession. Recognition that the primary thrust of flexible programs among salaried employees is to permit the tailoring of benefits to individual needs (not necessarily with an increase in cost sharing) has been slow to gain acceptance.

Another factor frequently is deep-seated union concern about the ability of members to make benefit decisions. A perception often exists that benefit decisions somehow are "more complicated" than other personal financial decisions an employee might make, and that the penalty for a "wrong" election is severe (for example, catastrophic medical expenses should the employee waive coverage). In general, familiarity with risk-reducing features such as stop-loss limits and core coverages is low.

To some extent, the concept of flexible compensation with its emphasis on individual determination of benefit needs also runs counter to the basic principle of collective bargaining. Providing choices to individual members has the potential to diminish the role of the union. While certainly not an overt consideration, shades of this reasoning may underlie general labor reaction to choice-making approaches. (In reality, bargaining on employer contributions to a flexible program, in terms of credits and prices, would be little different from negotiating benefit schedules and flat-dollar amounts for which a union currently is able to "take credit" with constituents.)

Since the early 1980s, circumstances have fostered the beginnings of a reevaluation of flexible compensation. Many companies have been unable to recoup labor cost increases through higher prices. The pattern-setting industries—steel, auto, rubber—have experienced declining employment. A greater majority of people accept the simple fact that the cost of medical care is rising too fast and solutions need to be found to curtail unnecessary utilization. Against this backdrop, some union organizations have accepted flexible compensation programs.

Figures vary but to date it appears that about two dozen organizations have negotiated some form of flexible program with various unions. These include Alcoa (1984), Armco (1984), Carpenter Technology (1983–84), Quaker Oats (1984 + based on contract expiration), and Xerox (1984). All of the situations have been unique. In general, however, the bargaining situations included the following kinds of elements:

- The company demonstrated to the union that an active effort was under way to control health care costs beyond introducing a flexible program, such as second opinion surgery, preadmission testing, greater reliance on HMOs, Preferred Provider Organizations (PPOs), and so forth
- The flexible program retained a high-value indemnity option, with employer-contributed credits sufficient to purchase the highest-valued option, at least in the first year
- The flexible program provided union employees the same benefits as salaried employees for the first time
- A particularly attractive option (such as Section 401(k) savings) was "bundled" with the flexible program
- Some "equitable" solution was agreed to for the sharing of any company cost reductions due to lower utilization in subsequent years.

(c) PART-TIME EMPLOYEES

Part-time employees represent the fastest growing segment of the workforce, with part-time employment participation doubling since 1980. Part-time employees currently represent about one-fifth of the total workforce, with higher concentrations in service industries, financial institutions, and hospitals.

Part-time benefits vary substantially among employers. In industries where part-time employees comprise a significant portion of the regular workforce, part-timers generally are extended benefit coverage, but only infrequently at the same level of employer subsidy as the full-time employee population. In other industries where part-time employment is less common, few (if any) benefits are provided. Other employers base benefit coverage on the number of hours worked.

Table 6.1 illustrates coverage of part-time employees under flexible

Table 6.1
Eligibility Requirements for Part-Time Employees

Eligibility	Percent of Programs
All part-time employees	5
20-hours of employment (weekly)	33
30-hours of employment (weekly)	7
Other restrictions	13
No part-time coverage	42

Source: Hewitt Associates 1987 Survey of Flexible Compensation Programs and Practices.

programs. In brief, 42 percent of employers exclude part-timers from the program. Of the balance, the majority base coverage on hours worked. Only 5 percent of employers include all part-time employees under the flexible program.

Of those including part-time employees under the program, 50 percent provide the same benefits and employer subsidy, regardless of employment status. Where distinctions exist, 23 percent provide fewer credits to part-time employees, and 14 percent charge higher price tags for benefit options. Another 23 percent offer fewer benefit areas to part-time employees. (Some of these employers also provide fewer credits, which is the reason the figures add to more than 100 percent.)

Where the level of employer subsidy is based on hours of employment, an issue sometimes arises over the determination of hours worked. Most employers use scheduled rather than actual hours for determination of the employer subsidy. However, inequities could result when actual hours vary substantially from scheduled hours of employment (either significantly higher or lower). Some employers have remedied the problem by using an alternative definition (such as actual hours of employment during the previous quarter).

Another issue arises with the Section 415 limits on use of salary reduction for benefit purchases when the employer also maintains a Section 401(k) plan (and part-time employees are eligible to participate in that plan as well). Because of the way the tests operate, part-time employees (with their reduced hours of employment and therefore usually lower pay levels) are the most affected by the limitations when using salary reduction. (This issue is treated more fully in Chapter Eleven on retirement.)

Finally, a separate issue arises with the application of the new nondiscrimination requirements. In 1989 and after, employers will need to include all employees working over 17 1/2 hours per week in the nondiscrimination tests. Depending on the concentration of part-time employees in an employer's workforce, part-time employees currently excluded from coverage may need to be covered for the company to pass the tests. (See also Chapter Five for discussion of the new rules.)

(d) RETIRED EMPLOYEES

A Section 125 flexible compensation program may continue to cover employees who retire, but an employer is precluded from establishing a program predominantly for former employees. However, even if some retired employees are allowed to remain in the same program as for active employees, only constructive receipt protection is available. Salary reduction is not permissible in that the retiree is no longer receiving salary from the employer. (Pension payments are considered as flowing from the pension trust rather than the employer, and as such they cannot be converted to a pretax basis.)

As a result, the majority of flexible programs (92 percent) cover retired employees under a separate (nonflexible) retiree arrangement. Other options include constructing a comparable flexible program (usually for health benefits or health and death benefits only) outside of Section 125. Another approach might be to permit the employee to make a one-time election of a pre-retirement flexible program option and allow that coverage to remain in force throughout retirement. (Any employee contributions, however, would be paid on an after-tax basis.)

As is the case with retiree welfare benefits in general, special care needs to be taken in drafting and communicating plans for retirees. The courts have begun to address the issue of whether an employer has an implied "contract" with retirees for provision of welfare benefits, the existence of which would greatly reduce a company's flexibility in modifying or terminating a plan. The accounting treatment of post-employment benefits other than pensions is also under review. The manner in which these issues ultimately are decided will have major bearing on the nature and structure of retiree welfare plans, whether or not they are provided through a flexible program structure.

§ 6.2 COVERAGE FOR NEW EMPLOYEES

Most organizations take considerable care to communicate flexible compensation programs so employees will have enough information to be able to evaluate their choices and make decisions. A new employee must make the same kinds of decisions—but often without the same level of support from the communication effort. Although the company can share the same communication materials with new employees and provide resources to answer any questions, most employers still are uncomfortable with new employees making decisions immediately upon employment—especially changes that are irrevocable until the next enrollment (or a change in family status). Only 32 percent of flexible programs permit immediate participation in a full choice making program, while another 10 percent allow immediate participation in only certain benefit areas. For stand-alone flexible spending accounts, only 38 percent of employers permit immediate enrollment.

Instead, majority practice is to impose a waiting period on flexible program participation. Duration of the waiting period varies as demonstrated in Table 6.2.

For the 58 percent of employers with a waiting period for enrollment in the choice-making program, provision of coverage in the interim varies. Some (32 percent) provide no coverage until the end of the waiting period (usually organizations with shorter waiting periods). Others (26 percent) provide standard (nonflexible) coverage in the interim. (The other coverage issue applies mainly to choice-making programs, as stand-alone flexible spending accounts supplement an employer's other benefit coverages.)

Table 6.2
Duration of Waiting Period for New Employees
by Type of Flexible Program

	Type of Program	
Waiting Period	Choicemaking* (%)	Flexible Spending Account (%)
To next annual enrollment	20	38
First of month:		
• After 30 days of service	18	16
• After 90 days of service	15	16
• Following date of hire	13	9
Other waiting period	34	21

*Includes choicemaking programs that also contain flexible spending accounts because the waiting period for both elements is almost always identical.

§ 6.3 COVERAGE BY BUSINESS UNIT

In general, most organizations cover all employees under a common flexible program structure, except where it is most appropriate to develop separate programs (e.g., union-negotiated arrangements). In addition, the culture of an organization most likely will influence the appropriateness of developing different flexible programs for separate employee groups, or excluding certain groups from coverage. (See also Chapter Five for discussion of coverage by line of business.)

In some organizations, a flexible approach provides the opportunity to unify benefit structures across business units or entities, thereby reducing or minimizing the cost and administrative effort involved in operating separate programs or enhancing the ability to transfer employees among operations. Care needs to be taken to assure that the combination of choices makes sense. (For example, offering one group's first-dollar medical plan might allow other employees to increase their coverage beyond what the organization believes necessary for competitive reasons.) In addition, coverage decisions occasionally hinge on the compatibility and flexibility of administrative systems and procedures. (For example, where employees are on different payroll systems, the administrative system for the flexible program needs to be able to accept multiple sources of employee data and produce output for these same employee groups.)

Conceptually, however, what the employer is doing is creating a common flexible program "umbrella" for all employee groups. Within the umbrella program, certain design specifics may vary—such as the availability of HMOs in a particular location or the inclusion of vacation choices in all but those states with special restrictions. The credit formula and option price tags might be set to reflect geographical differences or the cost structure of the business unit. The essential framework, however, is in place to house all employees across the organization under a common benefit structure.

Seven

Health Care

§ 7.1 INTRODUCTION

Choice in health care benefits is usually a cornerstone of a flexible compensation program—a "natural" for employee choice making. Health benefits are among the most visible, highly perceived, and frequently used of all employee benefits. The high cost (and value) of health care benefits, as well as concern over the potential for large unexpected expenses, means that employees will seriously consider which choices are best for them. The frequent availability of coverage through alternative sources, particularly the spouse's employer, dramatically increases employee interest in choice.

All of the attention paid to health care in the last several years reflects the dramatic state of transition within the industry and in the approaches employers are utilizing to provide health care benefits to employees. Evidence of the transition occurring includes:

- Alternative health care delivery systems such as HMOs and PPOs now are significant market forces within many areas of the country.
- Consistently high cost increases over the last decade have grabbed the attention of employers and forced more active involvement in attempting to improve the management of medical costs.
- The National Association of Insurance Commissioners (NAIC) issued —and subsequently reversed—guidelines that would have permitted less-than-full reimbursement of medical claims in situations where dual-income households have duplicate sources of coverage.

These and other factors highlight the fact that a great deal is happening in the health care benefit arena apart from the trend toward flexibility. Often it is very difficult to separate the design of health care choices from many of the other design challenges facing employers. In fact, introduction of a flexible program is usually viewed as an opportunity for an organization to step back from day-to-day operations and rethink overall employee benefit strategy (whether specific to flexibility or not) in health care. Frequently, a number of changes unrelated to a flexible approach are packaged with the introduction of choice making in health care.

§ 7.2 OBJECTIVES FOR CHOICE MAKING IN HEALTH CARE

The objectives an employer has for health care choices typically are consistent with those that apply to the overall flexible compensation program. Frequently, the major objectives relate to appealing to diverse employee needs and controlling benefit costs. Although these and other objectives were discussed in Chapter One, some aspects of each are particularly applicable to health care benefits.

- **Appeal to employees.** Providing an employee with choices in health care recognizes that a single plan cannot best meet everyone's needs. There is a diversity of needs within any workforce—due to the number and characteristics of dependents, the availability of coverage from other sources, anticipated utilization, financial resources (to pay premiums and claims), tolerance for risk, and so forth. Moreover, the needs of an individual are likely to change over time. Providing choices to employees responds to this diversity and gives employees greater control with the net result being enhanced awareness and perhaps greater appreciation of the coverage.

- **Control benefit costs.** The employer's objective to better control or manage benefit costs is usually strongest in health care— because costs are often the highest of any benefit area and typically have escalated much more rapidly than in other benefits. In addition to seeking greater control over the increases in future costs, an organization may wish to find ways to encourage more cost-efficient employee utilization of health care services (either less expensive providers or fewer unnecessary services). In other cases, there may also be an immediate need to reduce health care costs, and the introduction of choice making in conjunction with certain "cutbacks" may be viewed as more palatable than unilateral benefit reductions.

- **Deliver tax effectiveness.** Within the health care portion of a flexible compensation program, tax efficiencies for the employee arise primarily through the use of Section 125 salary reduction. Salary reduction may be used for converting employee contributions from an after-tax to a pretax basis and for establishing flexible spending accounts for tax-favored payment of health-related expenses. If current employee contributions for health care benefits are quite high, the benefit to the employee of using salary reduction can be substantial.

- **Merge different programs.** When two companies or two programs within a single company are being merged, it is sometimes very sensitive to require one group to give up their medical plan and move to the other group's plan. Under a flexible program, both plans may be left as options (at least for the first year or two) as a way of smoothing the transition.

- **Emphasize value.** Many employers believe that employees do not fully understand or appreciate the real value (cost) of their health care benefits. Through giving employees choices and presenting them with the prices of each option, it is possible to enhance employee appreciation of the true value of these benefits.

§ 7.3 TYPES OF HEALTH CARE CHOICES

Choices can be provided in any health care benefit. However, it is almost universal to introduce employee choice in medical benefits and only slightly less common to allow choices in dental benefits (although the range of choice usually is not as great). It is relatively rare to provide options in vision or hearing benefits. Although the subject is covered in depth in a later chapter, it should be noted that the substantial majority of flexible compensation programs also include a health care flexible spending account allowing for pretax reimbursement of medical, dental, and vision and hearing expenses not covered by an employer's other plans.

Among those organizations included in a recent survey of choice making programs, the following percentages allowed choices in company-sponsored health care plans:

Benefit Area	Percent of Companies
Medical	98
Dental	83
Vision	17

(a) MEDICAL

As the preceding table indicated, medical is the single most common area for choice in flexible programs. It is often the most expensive employer-provided benefit, is highly visible, and usually a substantial percentage of employees have the opportunity to be covered under a working spouse's medical plan.

In terms of design characteristics, a choice of three or four medical indemnity plans (i.e., sponsored by the employer) generally is offered to employees. The primary variations in the options are the size of deductible, the amount of any out-of-pocket (stop-loss) limit, and possibly the coinsurance level. Employees may be allowed to select "no coverage" as an option, although often a minimum level of coverage is required. HMO options are often available as alternatives to the indemnity plans, at least in certain geographic areas. A PPO alternative (encouraging use of specific providers through a lower deductible or higher percentage payment by the plan) is occasionally available—either as a specific option or as an element of each indemnity plan option.

(b) DENTAL

Less of a pattern exists in the design of dental options. Most frequently, the employee is offered a "yes or no" choice—either to elect dental or take no dental coverage at all. In other situations, there is a choice of two different indemnity plans: one plan providing lower coverage across all types of expenses (diagnostic and preventive, restorative, reconstructive, orthodontic, etc.) or one plan having a different emphasis in coverage (e.g., substantial coverage for diagnostic and preventive services but little or no coverage for major services).

(c) VISION AND HEARING

It is relatively infrequent to have vision benefits, hearing benefits, or both within a flexible program, and it is even more unusual to provide a stand-alone option. Typically, these relatively predictable expenses are covered only through a flexible spending account. When provided as an option under a program, they are most often combined with a medical or dental selection, primarily to minimize the potential for substantial adverse selection.

§ 7.4 GENERAL HEALTH CARE DESIGN CONSIDERATIONS

Many design considerations relate specifically to medical, dental, or vision and hearing. However a number of design issues cross the full spectrum of health care benefits. Such issues include the determination of the sources of coverage, the coverage tiers, whether employees should be allowed to opt out of coverage, the sources of funds to pay for the benefits, the relationship with a health care flexible spending account, and the overall appeal or attractiveness of the options to employees. The general considerations that cross health care areas are addressed in this section, with greater detail provided in each of the specific benefit design sections.

(a) SOURCES OF COVERAGE

The four principal sources of health care coverage are discussed below.

- **Indemnity plans.** Traditional employer-sponsored indemnity plans are the primary source of medical, dental, and vision and hearing coverage for most organizations. These plans may be fully insured, partially insured, or self-insured, but the company determines the coverage levels to be provided, and the participant generally determines which service providers (doctors, hospitals, dentists, etc.) are to be utilized.
- **Health Maintenance Organizations.** An HMO is an organization that for a fixed prepaid monthly fee will provide a broad range of health care services as needed by the participant. These services are provided by a specified group of physicians, clinics, hospitals, and other service providers. Although HMOs are generally thought of as providing only medical services, some HMOs also include dental or vision and hearing services in their agreements. And some HMO-like organizations, dental maintenance organizations (DMOs), provide dental services only.

- **Preferred Provider Organizations.** A PPO is a service provider or a network of providers that have agreed to discount their normal fees in return for an anticipated increase in volume. Often the PPO represents a hospital plus a panel of physicians, but it can also include other specialists such as dentists. The agreed-upon discount often ranges between five and fifteen percent of the normal fee.

- **Flexible Spending Accounts.** FSAs will be discussed exclusively in Chapter Nine, but they should be considered as a fourth source of health care coverage because a health care FSA reimburses the participating employee for certain health care expenses. Moreover, an employee's decisions on health care options are likely to be influenced by the existence of an FSA as a pretax source of reimbursement for out-of-pocket expenditures.

In most cases, indemnity plans and an FSA will be incorporated as sources of coverage within a flexible compensation program. Decisions as to whether to include HMOs or PPOs are oftentimes more difficult. The employer's considerations regarding these decisions include:

- Does the prior health care program include HMO or PPO coverages? If employees are accustomed to these options and they are working well, there is little related to the introduction of more employee choice which would suggest dropping or modifying these choices.

- What advantages do alternative providers create for participating employees or the organization sponsoring the flexible program? The level of protection and the cost of the coverage should be compared to the indemnity plans to determine if adding HMO or PPO options is attractive.

- What service providers are included in the arrangement? The providers should be recognized as providing high-quality care and should be accessible to a significant portion of the workforce.

- What is the track record of the provider? To be attractive, an HMO or PPO should be financially sound, produce relatively stable costs, have a history of honoring commitments, and be able to attract and retain quality physicians and hospitals.

- Does the HMO or PPO have adequate administrative capabilities? Day-to-day operations should be handled efficiently, and the organization should be able to respond adequately to the employer's requests for information.

(b) COVERAGE TIERS

The majority of health care plans have some features that reflect the number or types of individuals covered under the plan—either in program design or in pricing or in both. When designing health care options, it is important to consider these features and whether each option should use the same approach.

The most common plan design features that relate to the number of individuals covered under an employee's election are family maximums on deductibles and stop-loss limits. For example, a medical plan may have a $200 annual deductible for an individual, but may provide that after three members of a family have each incurred their $200 individual deductible (or, alternatively, after all family members in total have incurred $600 in deductibles), no more deductibles will be charged the family in that year. Such a plan may also have a family stop-loss limit (the maximum paid by the employee in a year) which is three times the individual stop-loss limit. For example, once the individual or family has satisfied the deductible, coinsurance charges on remaining expenses will not exceed $1,000 per person or $3,000 per family.

Family maximums on deductibles and stop-loss limits—especially those that are three or more times the individual amounts—usually add very little to the cost of an option (e.g., less than one or two percent). Oftentimes the added security provided through these family limits will significantly exceed the incremental cost. This "comfort factor" may be particularly important in a flexible option with a large deductible and a high stop-loss limit. Even though the advantage is more significant in high-deductible plans, typically all medical options within a flexible program will have parallel features in this area.

On the pricing side, the family-coverage issue is of greater significance. Although it is rare for a contributory plan to use a one-tier pricing approach, a completely noncontributory plan effectively has a one-tier price structure—the same price regardless of number or type of dependents. Plans with very low employee contributions have often utilized a two-tier pricing approach—one cost for employee-only coverage and a higher cost for family coverage, regardless of the number of dependents. As employee contributions for family coverage increase, the incentive grows to subdivide the family category to reflect the expected cost impact of varying the numbers or types of dependents. Subdividing by size of the family unit also helps minimize equity concerns in terms of the employee covering only one dependent paying the same amount as an employee covering several dependents. In these situations, three- and four-tier pricing approaches are most common. The most typical breakdowns include:

- Employee only, family
- Employee only, employee plus one, employee plus two or more dependents
- Employee only, employee plus spouse or children, employee plus spouse and children
- Employee only, employee plus spouse, employee plus children, employee plus spouse and children, or
- Employee only, employee plus one, employee plus two, employee plus three or more dependents.

The approaches which distinguish between types of dependents (spouse versus children) rather than simply number of dependents, tend to favor single parents with more than one child by allowing them to pay less than the full-family rate. This approach may also be somewhat more equitable in that an average child tends to generate significantly lower claims than an adult—especially for medical benefits.

A more extensive discussion of pricing and credit allocation issues by family status is included in Chapter Twelve.

(c) OPT-OUT CHOICE

The issue of whether employees should be permitted to opt out of health care coverage has the potential of being one of the most emotionally charged subjects in the design of a flexible compensation program. Whether or not it actually becomes a major issue is often more related to pre-flexible program practice than to an organization's underlying philosophies.

For instance, many organizations currently have contributory medical plans with a small monthly contribution for employee coverage and a higher contribution level if dependents are covered. In such an environment, a small percentage of employees typically decide not to pay the contribution, however modest, and therefore have effectively opted out of medical coverage. Presumably these employees—or almost all of them—have medical coverage from another source, although the employer usually has no verification of other coverage. An employer with this type of situation may be uncomfortable with employees foregoing coverage under a flexible program, but in reality, that "bridge has already been crossed" and minimum medical coverage usually is not required.

In other situations, waivers of coverage may not be permissible. This occurs frequently when the prior medical plan was noncontributory for all employees and their dependents. In such a case, neither employee nor employer is accustomed to choice and may be particularly wary of an opt-out alternative.

While the concern over an employee electing to forego medical coverage is usually related to the potential for a large uninsured claim, different issues arise in the area of dental because the likelihood of a catastrophic dental claim is extremely minor. If an organization has a significant concern over employees opting out of dental coverage, it usually is related to the potential for adverse selection and the ability of an individual to defer necessary dental treatment from a period without coverage to a period with coverage. This type of manipulation will lead to higher rates for all plan participants. Most employees and plan sponsors view this as unfair to participants who remain in the plan year after year. Requiring a minimum level of coverage may reduce the individual's ability or incentive to select against the plan. (See Chapter Thirteen for a fuller discussion of adverse selection issues.)

If, under a flexible compensation program, an employee is allowed to opt out of health care coverage, three significant issues need to be addressed. First, should the employee be required to provide some evidence of other coverage, particularly for medical? Based on a recent survey of flexible programs, 60 percent allowed opting out of medical but over one-third of those required some proof or certification of other coverage. Sometimes this process is as simple as signing a statement on the annual enrollment form, while in other cases, more extensive documentation is required.

Second, should some restrictions be placed on the options that are available during subsequent enrollment? About one-half of flexible program employers include restrictions for both medical and dental reenrollment. While reenrollment restrictions reduce the potential for adverse selection, they also diminish the attractiveness of the "no coverage" choice for an employee who is uncertain about future years' needs.

Third, if the flexible program provides credits to employees, how many credits should be given to an employee opting out of medical? Out of dental? Out of vision and hearing? The amount should be sufficient to make it worth considering for employees with other coverage but not so high as to exceed the expected reduction in claims for those who opt out. (In general, those who are in a position to consider dropping health coverage are likely to generate lower-than-average claims cost. For more complete discussion of credit determination, see Chapter Twelve on Prices and Credits.)

(d)   SOURCES OF FUNDS

It is quite rare for health care options to be paid either fully by the plan sponsor or completely by the employees. Generally the employer will provide a significant subsidy, and the participating employee will pay the additional cost required to select the desired options. The employer's subsidy may differ for medical, dental, and vision and hearing benefits; it may vary by the number of family members covered (either explicitly in the credits or implicitly in subsidized prices); and it may be the same as or different from the subsidy in the pre-flexible program. Determining the plan sponsor's subsidy and how that subsidy is reflected in the pricing and credit structure is covered in Chapter Twelve.

In nearly nine out of ten flexible programs, any employee contributions for health care benefits are paid on a pretax basis using Section 125 salary reduction. Paying for health care benefits in this manner reduces an employee's taxes in that year but without the constraints of generating imputed income (as in group life insurance on amounts exceeding $50,000) or changing the tax treatment of benefit payments (as in long-term disability benefits paid for by the employer or on a pretax basis by the employee).

(e)   FLEXIBLE SPENDING ACCOUNTS

A health care flexible spending account will allow for reimbursement of health care expenses not paid by an employee's choice of medical, dental, or vision and hearing options. The existence of a health care FSA may not have a dramatic effect on the design of the health care options, but there may be certain decisions which are influenced by the FSA.

The most dramatic example might be the complete elimination of a stand-alone scheduled vision plan and its replacement by a credit allocation (equal to the company cost of the vision plan) which, along with employee salary reduction, can be deposited in an FSA for vision and other health care expenses. This might be appropriate in a situation where the vision benefits are so low as to be viewed by employees as more of an irritant than a significant benefit and where the administrative expenses are disproportionately high relative to the benefits provided.

In other situations, employee pressure for increases in certain special benefits may be better handled by adding an FSA than by increasing benefits under the health care options. This is particularly true for quite predictable benefits that are very important to a subgroup of employees but of minimal interest to the vast majority of employees. Examples include: orthodontia benefits (usually paid at 50 percent up to a specified dollar limit); outpatient psychiatric benefits (often covered at 50 percent with a "per visit" or annual maximum); and well-baby care (typically not covered at all).

(f)   OPTION ATTRACTIVENESS

The detailed design considerations relating to each type of health care benefit will be covered in the next sections of this chapter. However, after all of the individual health care options are designed, it usually makes sense to review the overall design from the employee's perspective.

For example, the options should be attractive to employees. In general, simplicity in option design strengthens a positive employee response. There are sufficient complexities within a flexible program without introducing health care options that have a great number of minor and difficult-to-understand differences. A parallel structure among the options with only two or three key elements varying (such as deductibles and stop-loss limits) enhances employee understanding and appeal. If practical, it is also beneficial to have this parallelism apply not only within a benefit area such as medical but across all health care options. For example, it may be appropriate for a program with a four-tier pricing structure in medical also to use a four-tier structure in dental, even though the dental prices alone might not seem to justify so fine a breakdown of employee contributions.

The options also should be reviewed to ensure a reasonable spread of employee value and cost. If there are many options with only minor differences in provisions and prices, employees may struggle with adequately differentiating between the options. If there are few options with wide gaps between them, employees may feel uncomfortable with moving away from their "comfort zone" of current benefits. A reasonable middle ground should be struck.

An organization may have an objective of encouraging employees to select certain options—for example, a comprehensive medical option over the prior basic-plus-major-medical option. This can be aided by adding certain attractive features to the preferred option (e.g., higher maximum plan payments), by subsidizing the prices of that option, or by the manner in which the program is communicated (including how the options are named).

Although certain options may not appeal to a broad group of employees and, therefore, participation is anticipated to be low, keeping these options may be very appropriate. Some options may be important because they meet the needs of a small but significant subgroup of employees (e.g., a large deductible catastrophic medical plan may be just the right "fit" for employees covered under their spouse's medical plan). Another may be useful for filling in the gaps in a series of options.

During the election process, employees will, to varying degrees, scrutinize the option features and the price differentials to determine which option best meets their needs. The employer should anticipate this employee scrutiny and test the design and pricing to ensure that the options make sense. Options with higher price tags should provide extra coverage commensurate with the added cost.

§ 7.5 DESIGN OF MEDICAL

(a) IN GENERAL

For the same reasons that medical is usually considered to be the best candidate for choice making within a flexible compensation program, the design of medical choices is typically the most time-consuming aspect of developing the flexible program. There are numerous challenging issues surrounding the development of medical choices (e.g., how many and in what ways should they differ), and decisions are most often complicated by other types of medical design changes also under consideration (e.g., coordination with other plans, addition of certain cost management features). The pages that follow address the considerations applicable to these design issues with an emphasis on those aspects that are unique to or accentuated by the introduction of medical choice making.

(b) STRUCTURE OF OPTIONS

Detailing the design features of each medical option usually begins with an outline of the basic structure of medical choices. How many options should be made available to employees? Will the current plan be offered as an option? What will be the lowest option? How will the medical options differ?

(1)   High Option

Employees often have a "love-hate" relationship with their medical coverage. While they may sometimes complain about what the plan fails to cover and how long it takes to get a claim paid, they tend to react with great concern if the plan is cut back or restructured. And if the current plan is seen by management as being inefficient or encouraging over-utilization of medical services, one objective of the flexible program may be to move away from that plan. This has often been the case, particularly when the prior medical plan provided substantial first-dollar medical coverage as in a basic-plus-major-medical arrangement. However, as more and more organizations have already moved to providing medical benefits under a comprehensive approach with an initial deductible and most often 20 percent employee coinsurance, concern over retaining the prior plan under the flexible program has tended to diminish.

If the existing medical plan is not viewed as an appropriate long-term choice, the issue of whether it should be maintained as a flexible option can be difficult. On the one hand, keeping the plan as the high option can help smooth the transition to the flexible program and "soften" any employee concerns that might arise. This may be especially important for an organization that has undergone a great deal of turmoil or whose employees are particularly suspicious or where other employee groups (e.g., union employees) are covered under a rich medical plan.

On the other hand, if the claims experience of each option is to be tracked separately and the prices in future years adjusted to reflect this experience, it is quite likely that the high option will become more and more expensive relative to the other options, thereby eventually pricing itself out of existence. However, this may simply serve to defer employee concern that might have been dealt with satisfactorily in the first year. Deciding which approach is preferable (immediate elimination or gradual elimination through pricing) is fundamentally a judgment call that needs to be made by each organization.

The presence of an attractive HMO alternative may make it somewhat easier to drop a rich indemnity plan because employees may see the HMO as a place to turn for the high coverage they are losing. Whether this is an acceptable alternative will depend upon the HMO service providers, their quality and location(s), the prices for the HMO coverage, and other factors.

If the existing medical plan is viewed as an acceptable long-term choice, it will typically be offered as an option (usually the high option) under the flexible program, although occasionally with some "tinkering" to make it more parallel to the other options or to modify certain features for cost management purposes.

Often employees would welcome an option that is even richer than the existing plan, perhaps even being willing to pay the added cost. Only rarely will an organization introduce such an option, however, because it usually runs counter to the objective of lowering health care utilization. Moreover, if offered, such an option typically will result in high claims experience and ultimately higher prices in subsequent years.

Determination of the level of coverage which is appropriate for the high medical option will usually be based on a number of considerations, including:

- Provisions of the pre-flexible medical plan
- Medical benefits for other employee groups within the organization
- Employee relations environment
- Employer financial objectives
- Competitive practice, and
- Characteristics of employees (particularly compensation levels and resulting ability to cover deductibles).

(2)   Low Option

In many situations, the low medical option is defined by whether employees should be allowed to opt out of medical coverage. If employees are allowed to waive coverage, the lowest option is no coverage. If not, the provisions of the low option need to be established.

Most often, the lowest indemnity plan option is viewed as a catastrophic-protection or "safety-net" option. An individual covered under this option would have virtually no protection from the higher-frequency, lower-cost claims. But in the event of a major unexpected medical problem generating a large claim, this option would serve to protect the individual from financial ruin.

Defining the level of expense which a typical employee could absorb in this type of situation is quite subjective. However, the considerations include:

- What portion of the employee group is likely to have coverage available through a working spouse? This is probably the subgroup with the lowest need for protection.
- How much can the typical employee afford to pay in medical expenses in a particular year? Although this may be difficult to define, the answer is largely a function of pay level. An investment banking firm with an average income of $60,000 will likely come to a very different conclusion from a retailer with an average pay of $15,000.
- What responsibility does the organization assume to protect employees from the risk of making poor decisions? If concern is high, the spread between the highest and the lowest options should be narrowed.

Typically, the lowest available indemnity option is a comprehensive type of plan with a substantial upfront deductible (often $1,000), 70–80 percent payment of remaining expenses, and a stop-loss limit (sometimes as high as $5,000). In some cases, the deductible may be significantly lower (e.g., $500 for a relatively low-paying organization) or substantially higher (e.g., $5,000 for a high-paying organization that almost decided to allow employees to opt out completely).

Most often the option has family deductible and stop-loss limits of two or three times the individual amounts. However, as the individual deductible and stop-loss limits become larger, organizations sometimes reduce the family maximum to minimize some of the risk involved. At the extreme, for a very large deductible option (e.g., $2,500), the only deductible and stop-loss limit may be per family amounts. This adds very little extra cost to the option because it is unlikely that a family selecting such a low option would have more than one individual with very major expenses in a single year.

(3)   Other Indemnity Options

Once the highest and the lowest medical options are defined, other options can be created to fill in between the extremes. How much filling in is appropriate depends a great deal on how wide the gap is. If the richest plan is the prior high-value basic-plus-major-medical plan and the lowest option is no coverage, there is a wide gap. Therefore, a greater need exists for intermediate options. In contrast, if the richest and the lowest options both provide 80 percent coverage with deductibles of $100 and $500, respectively, less need exists for intermediate options.

Today most medical plans for salaried employees are structured around a comprehensive approach. In a typical situation, employees are offered three or four indemnity plan choices, with all of the options structured in a fairly parallel manner in terms of reasonable progression in deductible amounts, coinsurance percentages, and stop-loss limits. Sometimes, however, an employer must combine "unlike" plans (i.e., basic-plus-major-medical and comprehensive plan options). Combining two plan types has the potential of complicating the employee's understanding and decision-making process, but a "no takeaway" objective may necessitate this approach in some cases.

If the prior medical plan is maintained as the high option, but the organization wishes to encourage employees to select or at least seriously consider the lower plan options, placing higher lifetime maximums or lower stop-loss limits on the lower options could help to accomplish that result. In practice, however, different lifetime maximums on the options may not be particularly meaningful under a program in which employees have the opportunity to make annual changes in their coverage choices.

Two examples of fairly common medical option structures are illustrated in Example 7.1.

(c) COORDINATION WITH OTHER PLANS

All medical plans whether flexible or not need to have clearly defined rules that outline what is paid in the event an individual incurring medical claims is covered by two employer plans. One of the plans will be primary (i.e., paying first) and the other will be secondary (i.e., paying second). When only one plan is involved (or the plan is the primary payer), the benefits to be paid are clear—that is, whatever the primary (or only) plan normally would provide. With two employer plans involved, the issues become more complicated. Which plan is the primary versus the secondary payer? And what benefits will the plan pay if it is determined to be secondary?

New guidance on these issues recently has been provided by the National Association of Insurance Commissioners, an advisory body empowered to recommend policies and procedures to state insurance

Example 7.1

Company A

Option	Deductible (Individual/ Family)	Plan Payments	Stop-Loss (Individual/ Family)	Lifetime Maximum
Premium	$100/$200	80%	$1,000/$2,000	$500,000
Standard	$250/$500	80%	$1,250/$2,500	$500,000
Catastrophic	$1,000/$2,000	80%	$1,500/$3,000	$500,000

Company B

Option	Deductible (Individual/ Family)	Plan Payments	Stop-Loss (Individual/ Family)	Lifetime Maximum
A	$50/$150*	100% basic 80% major medical	None	$250,000
B	$150/$300	80%	$1,000/$2,000	$500,000
C	$400/$800	75%	$1,500/$3,000	$500,000
D	$1,000/$2,000	70%	$2,000/$4,000	$500,000

*On major medical expenses only.

authorities. (Technically, state rules apply to insured plans only, although uninsured plans generally follow insured plan conventions.) One of the revised NAIC guidelines already adopted in most states moves employers away from an approach that automatically designated the father's plan as primary payer for a child (when plans of both the father and the mother covered the child). Under the revised approach, the sex of the parent is ignored, and instead, the plan covering the parent with the earliest birthday in the calendar year becomes the primary payer.

Another NAIC recommendation (introduced but subsequently withdrawn) would have permitted employers to provide less-than-full reimbursement of medical claims for employees with duplicate coverage. Traditionally, "coordination" has meant that employees with dual coverage could receive *no less* than 100 percent payment of covered expenses. A secondary plan was required to pay its regular benefits but to no more than the amount necessary to pay the full amount of the claim in combination with the primary plan. The situation is in direct conflict with the goals most employers have for encouraging employees to reduce medical utilization, and often believed to be unfair to other employees with only one source of coverage. As a result, some self-insured plans ignored the traditional approach to coordination of benefits and provided less-than-full payment in duplicate coverage situations through alternate methods of coordinating payments between plans. The revised NAIC guidelines would have given this same flexibility to insured plans.

One of the most common alternative coordination techniques is known as "maintenance of benefits" or "benefits less benefits." Under this approach, the deductibles and copayment amounts are preserved when the plan is secondary because the secondary plan defines its payment as the *difference* between what it would normally pay if it were the sole plan, and what the other plan actually pays. Thus the covered individual does not receive full payment from the combination of the two plans.

Consideration of a maintenance of benefits (or some other intermediate) approach to handling two-plan coverage is particularly appropriate when introducing a flexible program with choices in medical. Under the traditional coordination of benefits method, the individual covered under two plans would often receive full payment of any claim, regardless of the option selected. Using the maintenance of benefits approach would retain a difference in payments between the options when the flexible program is secondary (as is the case in the absence of another plan) and avoid providing full payment of the total claim (as is also the case in the absence of another plan).

(d)   COST MANAGEMENT FEATURES

Other medical design changes are often made at the same time as a flexible program introduction. This is especially true in the medical area where cost management features—such as precertification of hospital admissions or mandatory second opinions on specified surgeries—are frequently added under the umbrella of a flexible program.

This "bundling" of cost management features with a flexible program introduction may be very appropriate given the substantial employee communication involved in a flexible program, the frequent focus on health care benefits, and the common objective of making the employee a better informed consumer of employee benefits—particularly medical.

(e)   SPECIAL CONSIDERATIONS

- **Employment of Couples.**   Sometimes, a significant number of married couples work for the same organization. When both the husband

and the wife are employed at the same organization, the medical and other health care plans need to specify any special rules. For example, can an employee be covered both as an employee and as a dependent? Should one employee elect family coverage and the other elect no coverage? Do the same coordination of benefits provisions apply to an individual covered twice under the plan as would apply to an individual covered by different employer plans?

These issues have typically been resolved under the prior medical plan, and often parallel decisions are appropriate when moving into a flexible program. The subject should be readdressed, however, particularly if there are significant changes in pricing (either level or structure of employee contributions) or coordination of benefit provisions (which may eliminate any incentive to be covered twice by the same plan).

If the flexible program specifically identifies credits for employees from the medical plan, and these credits vary by family status or number of covered dependents, this issue becomes more complex. Do both employees receive the same credits they would have received had their spouse been employed elsewhere? This may seem to be the most equitable (especially to employees) but could significantly increase the organization's cost because both employees do not receive the full medical value in a traditional plan. Should each employee be allowed to cover himself or herself and only one be allowed to cover the children? Can the organization even adequately identify where these situations exist?

- **Hospitals as Medical Providers and Employers.** Unless a hospital provides only very specialized care (for example, a psychiatric hospital), employees and their dependents usually are encouraged to use the employer's own hospital rather than one of a competitor. In addition to the employee showing support for and confidence in the employer, the employer comes out ahead financially. A day in another hospital may cost $800 in medical benefits, but a day in the employer's hospital may really "cost" only $200 (even though the regular rate would be $800). This $200 cost would reflect the marginal cost of supplies, medicines, food, and so forth, under the assumption that having the hospital bed occupied for the day did not actually require any additional staff, equipment, and so on.

The issues then facing a hospital in designing a flexible program are two-fold. First, should the hospital add (or keep or modify) an incentive to encourage employees and their dependents to use the hospital's facilities? The incentive could be a discounted rate, a forgiven employee copayment, or some other arrangement. Second, how does the hospital determine costs for pricing and credit allocation purposes, that is, using the full stated cost or a discounted cost that only reflects the marginal impact for those individuals using the employer's facilities?

- **Default coverages.** In the initial year of a flexible program, all employees are encouraged and expected to submit a completed enrollment form, indicating their coverage choices. Reminder notices and contact with supervisors should produce close to a 100 percent response. However, it may be necessary to assign default coverages to some employees who simply fail to complete and return the form.

  The default coverage could be any option but might be determined as the option closest to the employee's prior coverage, the noncontributory option (if one is available), the lowest option, or no coverage. The default with respect to the family members covered might be the coverage category in effect most recently or employee-only coverage. In subsequent years, the default coverages most often duplicate the prior year's election (both regarding type of option and covered dependents).

  Decisions as to default coverages (what they should be and whether they should be explicitly communicated to employees) typically reflect the employer's attitudes on responsibility for protecting employees.

§ 7.6   DESIGN OF DENTAL

(a)   IN GENERAL

Over three-quarters of the organizations with flexible compensation programs include dental choices as an element of the program. The attractions for the employer and for the employee are quite similar to those which make medical the most prevalent area for choice making. However, the plan design process is typically much less complex for dental benefits than for medical benefits. A number of reasons for this include:

- Employer costs are much lower (often only 10 to 20 percent of medical) and the year-to-year increases have generally been less rapid.

- Alternative delivery systems such as HMOs and PPOs are less prevalent.
- Duplicate dental coverage (from two employer plans) occurs less frequently.
- The risk of a financially catastrophic dental bill is dramatically less (and if one occurs due to an accident, the medical plan would usually provide coverage).

(b) STRUCTURE OF OPTIONS

The design decisions in dental relate primarily to the number and type of options to be made available to employees.

(1) Types of Options

As discussed earlier, employees are most frequently allowed to opt out of dental coverage within flexible programs because the risk to the employee of doing so is modest (at least compared with the risk of opting out of medical). In such a program, the lowest option has already been defined as no coverage.

Usually the organization introducing the flexible program already has a dental plan in place which is operating reasonably successfully, and the employer is experiencing little pressure to modify it. When this is the case, it is often an easy decision to maintain the existing dental plan as an option.

In many cases, the employer provides two options in dental, the current plan or no coverage. This is essentially a "yes or no" choice. However, if there are concerns about the current dental plan, these might be addressed in one of three ways under the flexible program:

- **Modify the existing plan.** For example, the existing plan might be quite satisfactory except that the annual maximum is less than competitive or the deductible might require updating. Either change could be made with essentially the same plan offered under the flexible program.
- **Add an option.** Possibly the existing plan provides scheduled benefits that have not been updated in some time or simply pays benefits that are lower than many employees believe is competitive. In such a case, the current plan could be maintained as an option and a new plan introduced which meets the needs for increased coverage. Or

the current plan might require a high level of employee contributions and a lower coverage option (either free or with lower employee contributions) might prove attractive.

- **Drop dental coverage.** If a plan has generated a great deal of employee dissatisfaction (either due to low benefit levels or poor claims handling), and if the plan sponsor is concerned over the level of administrative cost and effort to maintain the plan, one alternative might be to terminate the dental plan, convert the prior company cost into credits for employees, and simply allow employees who expect to have dental expenses to use these credits (plus their own pretax salary reduction money) in a flexible spending account for health care. Those who do not expect significant dental expenses could use their credits for other purposes.

There are both broad and detailed design issues which need to be addressed when designing a new dental plan or creating additional options. These include structure of the program (scheduled benefits versus comprehensive benefits); size and type of deductible; whether the deductible should be waived for certain types of expenses; plan payment levels for various types of expenses (diagnostic and preventive, restorative, major, orthodontic, etc.); and maximums (annual and lifetime). These are important subjects for the design of dental plans generally, but they will be addressed here only in the context of choice making programs.

If alternative dental indemnity plans are to be offered, the alternatives can be designed to provide higher (or lower) coverage across most types of expenses, for example, richer scheduled benefits or higher coverage for each category of expense. The differences in benefits and prices should be sufficient to provide employees meaningful choices.

Often the "across-the-board" difference in benefit levels does not apply to orthodontic benefits. Orthodontic expenses are very substantial, generally quite predictable, and typically somewhat deferrable. Plan benefits for orthodontic are also usually subject to a separate lifetime maximum, such as $750 or $1,000. To reduce the potential for employee manipulation (i.e., making a selection based on what is known to be an upcoming expense) and because of the problems associated with differing lifetime maximums under a program with choices, each dental option will usually have the same lifetime orthodontia maximum.

Alternatively, one option may be designed to emphasize diagnostic and preventive expenses with marginal (or no coverage) for major expenses. This may be a replacement for the no coverage option in order to encourage continuing visits to the dentist for exams, X rays, and cleanings.

(2)   Number of Options

The generally lower cost of dental and the resulting smaller differential in cost between options makes it difficult to justify the offering of more than two dental indemnity plan options. Also, the greater predictability of dental expenses makes it more important to achieve a high level of participation in each indemnity plan option to minimize adverse selection concerns. Adequate participation is achieved partially by minimizing the number of indemnity plans, but also by pricing approaches and restrictions on changes in coverage. (See also Chapter Thirteen for discussion of approaches to minimizing adverse selection.)

(c)   COORDINATION WITH OTHER PLANS

As is the case with medical, dental plans need to be structured to coordinate with other employers' plans. But the scope of the issue is much narrower in dental for several reasons. First, situations with duplicate coverage are less frequent. Many employers (especially smaller employers) do not provide dental insurance to their employees, and those that do often require contributions for participation. Second, the dollars involved are not nearly as great. Third, for many claims, each plan may pay less than 50 percent of the submitted claim due to deductibles, employee copayments (which may be as high as 50 percent for major expenses), and reductions for expenses exceeding "reasonable and customary" levels. So the total usually does not exceed 100 percent—the point at which most traditional coordination of benefits provisions become effective.

(d)   SPECIAL CONSIDERATIONS

- **"Anticipatory" Behavior.** Under a flexible program, the communication with employees usually starts at least three months before the new coverages become effective. Changes in benefits being provided by the plans may encourage an acceleration (if benefits are being reduced) or a deferral (if benefits are being increased) of visits to the dentist. This may not be a significant problem, but probably merits consideration both when designing the options and when discussing the timing of the communication steps.

- **Adverse selection.** The opportunity for an employee to select against the plan is much greater in dental than in medical. The impact of this adverse selection can be moderated by effective plan design, pricing, and restrictions on changes. This subject is dealt with extensively in a separate chapter.

§ 7.7   DESIGN OF VISION AND HEARING

Only a minority of the organizations with flexible programs include any vision and/or hearing choices under the program. Where a choice does occur, it is almost universally a simple "yes or no" choice—sometimes as a stand-alone option and sometimes as part of another health care plan (medical or dental). Also, the benefit available is usually a continuation of the plan which was provided prior to the introduction of flexibility.

If there is currently no vision or hearing plan and employees are interested in such coverage, the typical decision is to include vision and hearing as an eligible flexible spending account expense but not to create a separate option to provide such benefits.

If there is an existing plan that is generating problems or concerns over the value provided relative to the expense and administrative effort, an alternative often considered is to terminate the vision or hearing plan, convert the employer contribution into flexible credits, and position the flexible spending account as an alternative means of covering these expenses.

Eight

Death and Disability

§ 8.1 INTRODUCTION

Death and disability coverages often are included as choice areas within flexible programs. These benefits may not be as highly utilized or as visible as medical benefits, for example, but they do serve a most valued function: providing protection to employees and their dependents from the loss of income due to accident, injury, or illness. Because death and disability coverages are relatively inexpensive compared with medical, cost control usually is not as major a design consideration. However, a host of other factors create different kinds of design challenges for the structuring of death and disability benefit options.

Designing choices in death benefit coverage can become complex because of the many types of group life insurance available. In addition to deciding what form or forms of death benefits to offer, an employer will need to address various other issues. For example, what levels of coverage should be made available? How should the options be priced? Who should pay for the coverage? Should salary reduction be used to allow pretax premium payment? Answers to these questions are not always easy or obvious. The design of death benefit choices must take into account the employer's objectives and employee needs as well as legal requirements at both the federal and state levels.

Although the design of disability benefit choices often is viewed as less complex than that of other benefits, there are a number of issues unique only to disability. For example, in the area of short-term disability, the primary issue is whether to offer choices at all, given the extent of coverage already provided through an employer's underlying sick leave or salary continuation program. In long-term disability benefits, a major design issue relates to determining the appropriate level(s) of pay replacement to ensure that the choices are distinct and different, and yet provide an adequate but not excessive benefit amount to employees. Another consideration is whether to use salary reduction for pretax premium payment in light of benefit taxation rules.

§ 8.2   DEATH BENEFITS

Group life insurance is a natural benefit area to include in a choice making program because death benefit needs vary dramatically over an employee's lifetime. For example, the needs of a middle-aged employee with a nonemployed spouse, children, and a mortgaged home will be much greater than those of a young, single employee. In contrast, an older employee nearing retirement with neither children to support nor mortgage payments—but drawing a career-high income—will have still other needs.

In addition, an employee may have various sources of death benefits outside the group life plan such as social security, retirement plans, or individual life insurance policies. Providing choices in group life enables employees to select the level of coverage that best meets individual needs and coordinates with other sources of coverage.

(a)   TYPES OF GROUP LIFE INSURANCE

Group-*term* life insurance is the only form of life insurance permitted in a Section 125 flexible program. Whole life and universal life policies cannot be included as these forms of insurance allow cash value buildup. Some employers, however, offer whole life or universal life (on a group or individual basis) within the flexible program, but outside the Section 125 plan (i.e., coverage is purchased with after-tax payroll deductions—not flexible credits or salary reduction dollars).

(1)   Employee Life Insurance

Employee life insurance provides a lump-sum benefit to a designated beneficiary upon the death of the employee. The primary intent is to ease the financial strain on a family resulting from the loss of an income provider. Employers may provide a maximum of $50,000 of coverage to employees on a nontaxable basis. The cost of amounts in excess of $50,000 must be imputed as taxable income to the employee.

In a typical flexible program structure, an employer provides a certain core level of coverage and offers various options to supplement basic coverage amounts. Levels of coverage typically are based on multiples of pay (e.g., one times pay, two times pay, etc.), although occasionally flat-dollar amounts (e.g., $10,000, $20,000, etc.) are offered. Some companies place a dollar cap on the total benefit payable.

Employers may charge all employees a flat rate per thousand dollars of coverage or assign age-graded rates, which reflect the true cost of the coverage (i.e., older, higher-risk employees pay more than younger, lower-risk employees).

(2) Accidental Death and Dismemberment

Accidental death and dismemberment (AD&D) coverage provides additional benefits if an employee's death occurs as the result of an accident. The plan also may pay benefits—usually stated as a fraction of the policy's face value—in the event of accidental dismemberment.

Some employers structure AD&D coverage exactly the same as employee life insurance, so the benefit for an accidental death simply would be double the benefit paid for death by other causes. In these cases, the cost of employee life and AD&D coverage usually is bundled into a combined rate. Other employers construct a separate AD&D plan with different levels of coverage and separate premiums. AD&D coverage is typically quite inexpensive, and the cost usually does not vary by age. So unless AD&D is tied to employee life (and the combined rate is age-graded), AD&D typically is priced as a flat amount per thousand dollars of coverage, applicable to all ages.

(3) Dependent Life Insurance

Dependent life insurance provides a lump-sum benefit to a beneficiary (typically the employee) upon the death of a spouse or child. Coverage for a spouse and children may be packaged as one election or offered separately as independent options. The coverage usually is offered in flat-dollar amounts, typically providing higher benefits for a spouse (e.g., $5,000) than for a child (e.g., $2,000). In combination, however, the coverage amounts available for dependent life generally are much lower than for employee life. This is partially due to statutory plan maximums on dependent life that have been established by the majority of states. A more fundamental reason, however, is that the death of a dependent generally has less impact on a family's financial status than the death of the employee.

Dependent life usually is available on a contributory basis only. The cost may be either a flat-dollar amount or an age-graded rate (often based on the age of the employee) per thousand dollars of coverage.

(4) Survivor Income

Survivor income plans are designed to provide a continuing stream of payments (usually paid monthly) to an employee's surviving spouse and/or child(ren). Survivor income benefits may be based on a percentage of the employee's pay (e.g., 25 percent of salary) or may provide a flat-dollar amount (e.g., $250 per month). The plan often provides one amount for a surviving spouse plus another amount for children.

Employers offering survivor income benefits are fairly evenly split on provision of the coverage on a company-paid versus contributory basis. Where the employee is required to contribute, premiums usually are based on pay, age, or a combination of pay and age.

(b) DESIGN CONSIDERATIONS

Designing group life insurance options within a flexible program requires consideration and analysis of various factors—including an employer's objectives, the needs of employees, and various legal requirements. Coverage provided under the prior plan also is a consideration in terms of evaluating whether to continue or modify current practice.

(1) Areas of Choice

A fundamental design decision is whether to offer group life insurance in a flexible program. Since employers typically offer some degree of choice in existing employee life plans, most flexible programs (77 percent) include employee life insurance as a choice-making area. In cases where employee life insurance choices did not previously exist, many employers view introduction of a flexible program as an opportunity to offer group life choices because employees generally perceive choice making as a benefit enhancement. Many employers also offer choices in AD&D (56 percent) and dependent life (59 percent). These benefits are popular with employees and often can be included as options in a flexible program at little or no company cost.

Inclusion of AD&D within a Section 125 program touches on a moderately gray area within the tax code. AD&D is not specifically referenced as an "includable" benefit within Section 125 programs. However, longstanding practice among employers is to treat AD&D as a nontaxable benefit, excluding the value of the coverage from the employee's taxable income. Because it is an unclear area, some employers offer AD&D choices on an after-tax basis outside the Section 125 plan to avoid any potentially negative ramifications to the flexible program.

The amount of dependent life coverage that may be provided on a nontaxable basis is another area open to interpretation. As a result, some employers offer dependent life coverage choices outside the Section 125 plan on an after-tax basis only.

Very few flexible programs (8 percent) offer survivor income choices. (Even among nonflexible programs, survivor income plans are relatively rare.) These plans tend to be moderately expensive and often difficult to price because benefits usually are payable for an indefinite period of time (e.g., until the spouse's death or remarriage). Moreover, survivor income plans have not been as popular with employees as other types of life insurance, probably because the payment mechanism (a portion of the employee's earnings paid-out over a period of time) is more difficult to understand and holds less appeal than a lump-sum payment (as is the case with life insurance).

Some employers altogether exclude group life choices from a flexible program. When this occurs, it is typically due to a desire to focus employee attention on a single objective, such as cost containment in health care, or for reasons that relate to administrative constraints.

(2) Structure of Options

Following are some of the key issues employers need to address in determining the structure of death benefit options.

(i) High Option. Determining the high death benefit option usually is a function of various factors. These include employee needs, state and local law limitations, and imputed income tax considerations. In addition, nondiscrimination requirements and underwriting considerations will affect the maximum benefits permissible in a flexible

program. (For more complete discussion of these latter issues, see Chapters Five and Fourteen.)

For employee life and AD&D a high-end option of four or five times pay is usually considered adequate to meet almost all employees' needs. Separately, some employers impose an overall plan maximum (in terms of a dollar limit), usually for underwriting reasons.

Another influence on high-option employee life benefits is statutory requirements in a few localities. (These include the state of Texas, the Commonwealth of Puerto Rico, and the District of Columbia.) Generally, state or local insurance laws apply only to insured plans. Although most larger employers self-insure group life plans, the majority still run the plan through an insurance carrier to preserve the federal tax exclusion for the first $50,000 of employee life insurance. Thus self-insured employers typically must comply with these state and local insurance laws as well.

For dependent life, employers usually limit the "richest" option to $10,000 or $20,000 for spouse coverage, and $5,000 or $10,000 for children. Companies that elect to treat dependent life as a nontaxable benefit within the flexible program usually set the maximum at a lower level (e.g., $2,000 to $5,000 for the spouse, $1,000 to $2,000 per child). However, high-option benefits in dependent life are heavily influenced by state and local limits.

In the area of dependent life, the majority of states and certain localities impose maximum limits. These limits are either: (1) a flat-dollar amount, (2) a percent of employee coverage, or (3) a combination of a flat-dollar amount and a percent of employee coverage (e.g., lesser of $5,000 and 50 percent of employee coverage). Separate limits usually exist for spouse and child coverage.

Based on a 1985 survey of state insurance department personnel, the following states and localities have established some form of maximum on dependent life insurance amounts.

- Arizona
- Arkansas
- California
- Connecticut
- Delaware
- Washington, D.C.
- Florida
- Georgia
- Hawaii
- Indiana
- Kansas
- Kentucky
- Louisiana
- Maine
- Maryland
- Missouri

- New Jersey
- New Mexico
- New York
- North Carolina
- Ohio
- Oklahoma
- Pennsylvania
- Puerto Rico

- South Carolina
- Texas
- Utah
- Vermont
- Virginia
- Washington
- West Virginia
- Wyoming

(Because this information is based on survey information rather than on legal research, employers are advised to check with legal counsel to confirm the current law in states where they have employees or insurance contracts.)

For survivor income, the high-end option usually is no greater than 50 percent of the employee's pay for the surviving spouse plus an incremental amount such as 5 percent of pay per child to a maximum of 15 percent of pay for children.

(ii) *Low Option.*   The fundamental issue related to the lowest death benefit option is whether to require employees to take a minimum level of protection—or to allow employees to opt out of coverage completely. Most employers (70 percent) feel a sense of obligation to ensure that all employees have at least a core level of life insurance. The most common minimum benefit amount is one times pay. Minimums also may be based on estimated burial expenses, competitive practice, past benefit levels, or a combination of these factors.

Since AD&D, survivor income, and dependent life generally are supplemental death benefits (with little or no company subsidy), employees typically have the option to decline coverage.

(iii) *Increments of Coverage.*   Common practice for employee life and usually AD&D is to establish incremental levels of coverage based on multiples of pay rather than flat-dollar amounts. Tying coverage to pay is based on the premise that life insurance is generally intended to replace the breadwinner's income, so the level of coverage should bear some reasonable relationship to an employee's earnings. Among employers with options offered as multiples of pay, the most common increment of coverage is a full multiple of pay (e.g., one times pay, two times pay, and so forth). In some cases, employers also offer half multiples (e.g., 0.5 times pay, 1.5 times pay, and so forth).

Only a minority of employers base levels of employee coverage on flat-dollar amounts, with the most common increments being $10,000 or $20,000. Offering employees coverage choices based on flat-dollar amounts raises a potential conflict with certain federal and state laws that prohibit employees having discretion over the choice of coverage. Employers with flat-dollar amounts, however, have often successfully maintained that flat-dollar amounts are acceptable because employees are not able to select a specific amount of coverage—rather they are limited to choosing one of several options offered by the employer.

Dependent life is almost always offered in flat-dollar increments, usually at modest levels relative to employee life. Survivor income typically is offered in increments of the employee's pay (e.g., 10 percent to 50 percent) sometimes to a flat-dollar maximum on the monthly benefit payable. Less frequently, the increment is a flat-dollar amount (e.g., $100 to $1,000) payable monthly.

(iv) Number of Options. An employer may offer any number of options to employees. But among employers who provide choices in the various group life areas, the average is four options in employee life, six in AD&D, two in survivor income, and three in dependent life. Conceptually, the employer's goal is to offer enough choices to provide a reasonable degree of flexibility to employees, but not so many choices as to cause confusion or unnecessary administrative complexity.

Generally, the number of options offered is a function of other decisions concerning the range of options (i.e., the spread between the highest and lowest levels of coverage), the increments of coverage, and the ease of plan administration.

(3)   Sources of Funds

(i) Employee Life Insurance. The funding of employee group life options in a flexible program often mirrors the funding approach used for the prior basic-plus-supplemental group life plan. In other words, under a flexible program, an employer typically funds a basic level of coverage—either by attaching a $0 price tag or by providing employees with enough credits to purchase the basic coverage. Employees have the option of purchasing additional levels of coverage using remaining flexible credits or their own contributions.

Another design issue related to funding is whether to permit pretax or after-tax premium payment. Under Code Section 79, the value of employer-provided group life insurance in excess of $50,000 is taxable income to the employee. Coverage paid for with employee salary reduction contributions is considered employer-provided. Thus allowing employees to pay for amounts in excess of $50,000 with salary reduction creates additional imputed income. However, most employers (76 percent) use pretax premium payment, recognizing that for most employees the impact of additional imputed income is offset (or in some cases, more than offset) by the tax savings available through salary reduction.

Employers are required to determine the amount of imputed income based on IRS age-graded tables that approximate the cost of coverage. Effective in 1989 (when certain provisions of the 1986 Tax Reform Act take effect), employers are required to use the IRS rates to calculate imputed income on nondiscriminatory benefit amounts above $50,000. For discriminatory benefit amounts, employers must use the greater of the IRS table rates and the actual rates. (Prior to 1989, employers are generally required to use the IRS tables for all benefit amounts in excess of $50,000.) (See Table 8.1.)

(The $50,000 limit on nontaxable benefits has the greatest impact on employee life insurance. However, it is presently unclear whether the value of AD&D and survivor income benefits in excess of $50,000 is subject to imputed income. Since there presently is no clear-cut method for determining what portion of the benefit should be attributed to death—versus dismemberment—most employers do not calculate imputed income on AD&D. Similarly, it is relatively unusual to impute income on survivor income benefits since no established rules exist for calculating the survivor benefit equivalent of $50,000.)

While employers could offer employees a choice between pretax and after-tax premium payment, most do not do so because of additional

Table 8.1
IRS Imputed Income Tables

Age	Cost Per $1,000 of Coverage Per Month
Under 30	$ .08
30–34	.09
35–39	.11
40–44	.17
45–49	.29
50–54	.48
55–59	.75
60–64	1.17

administration and communication requirements. Moreover, while pre-tax premium payment will subject more employees to imputed income (and greater amounts of imputed income), the tax break on salary reduction contributions almost always is sufficient to offset the additional imputed income tax amounts.

(ii) Dependent Life Insurance. Dependent life typically is paid for solely by the employee. Here again the issue is whether to require after-tax premium payment or allow pretax payment.

Dependent life falls under Code Section 61, so the $50,000 income tax exclusion under Section 79 for employee life insurance does not apply. Amendments to Section 61, effective in 1985, suggest that the value of all employer-provided dependent life (which would include coverage paid for with employee pretax contributions) is taxable to employees. Also, regulations issued prior to the amendments state that if employers provide dependent life in excess of "incidental" amounts (often interpreted as $2,000 per dependent), the value of the entire amount is taxable to employees. Since the cost of dependent life is relatively inexpensive and the law is not entirely clear on the limit for nontaxable dependent life benefits, many employers (42 percent) simply require employees to pay the contributions in after-tax dollars.

(4) Option Pricing/Credit Allocation

The primary design issue facing employers in the area of pricing group life options is whether to charge a flat rate to all employees or graduated rates based on age. Although prior practice will have some bearing on the decision, other design objectives may make it appropriate to consider a change.

For employee life, age-graded rates are much more consistent with actual cost than flat rates for all employees, considering the relationship between age and the probability of a claim. Moreover, employers run the risk of adverse selection under a flat-rate scheme since a flat-rate typically is less expensive for older employees (which encourages plan participation), and more expensive for younger employees (which provides an incentive to seek coverage elsewhere).

In situations where age-graded rates represent a departure from prior practice, employers need to be sensitive to what might be perceived as a "take-away" by older employees. In these cases, employers may want to consider offering the lowest level of coverage (e.g., one times pay) to all employees at a flat rate, and price higher coverage options on an age-graded basis. This dual price structure adds an element of complexity from both a communication and an administration perspective but may be appropriate in some situations.

Credit allocation for an age-graded pricing structure is another design issue when credits are based on a cutback from prior coverage levels. Employers who provide all employees the same percent-of-pay credit allocation, in essence, make younger employees (who pay less for coverage) "winners," and older employees (who pay more) "losers." Another alternative is to age-grade the credit allocation structure so it correlates directly with the pricing structure. This approach may raise a question about equity (since older employees receive more credits than younger employees), but it does eliminate the concern over winners and losers. Some employers partially address the equity issue by narrowing the "spread"—making age differences in the credit allocation less extreme than age differences in the prices.

In general, age-graded rates based on the dependent's age are impractical for dependent life—especially covering children. Some employers, however, age-grade the rates for spouse coverage based on the employee's age. This is most common when substantial amounts of coverage are available.

(5)   Enrollment/Reenrollment Restrictions

Some employers attempt to limit the potential for adverse selection in life insurance by implementing enrollment and/or reenrollment restrictions. About one-third of employers (34 percent) place restrictions on first-year elections if employees elect higher than previous levels of coverage. For subsequent enrollments, most employers (76 percent) place some restrictions on an employee's ability to elect up more than one level of coverage at a time. Most often, the restriction is in the form of requiring the employee to provide proof of insurability. (See also Chapter Fourteen on Insurance Considerations.)

§ 8.3   DISABILITY BENEFITS

Disability income plans protect employees against the loss of income due to illness or injury. Disability benefits—particularly short-term disability—are not as commonly included under flexible programs as many other group benefits (e.g., medical, dental, even life insurance). Employee needs in the area of disability usually do not vary dramatically from one individual to the next. Nor do disability benefit needs change significantly over an employee's lifetime. Still, a number of employers offer limited choices in disability to expand the scope of choices offered under a flexible program, to provide benefits on a more cost-efficient basis, or to fill in any gaps in other employer-provided coverages.

(a) TYPES OF DISABILITY COVERAGE

Both short- and long-term disability income benefits may be offered under Section 125 flexible programs.

(1) Short-Term Disability

Short-term disability (STD) options are designed to replace a portion of a sick or injured employee's income after expiration of a company's underlying sick leave or salary continuation benefits (e.g., 30 or 60 days) but before commencement of long-term disability benefits (usually five or six months). Many sick leave or salary continuation plans provide full or partial pay replacement for an extended period of time, often related to the employee's length of service. For shorter-service employees, however, a gap in coverage may exist.

Options in the short-term disability area often are intended to allow employees to fill in the gap, usually on an employee-pay-all basis. Benefit amounts typically match the levels of pay replacement offered under options in the long-term disability area.

(2) Long-Term Disability

Long-term disability (LTD) plans provide income to employees unable to work for an extended period of time due to illness or injury. LTD benefits typically commence after a five- or six-month waiting period, and continue until retirement age or until the employee recovers. LTD benefits are designed to replace a portion of an employee's income—typically 50 percent to 70 percent generally integrated with benefits from other sources (e.g., social security, worker's compensation).

(b) DESIGN CONSIDERATIONS

As with other benefit areas, offering disability choices in a flexible program requires consideration of a variety of factors based on employer objectives and employee needs.

(1) Areas of Choice

A fundamental decision in the design of a flexible program is whether to include choices in disability.

Short-term disability represents an emerging coverage area under flexible programs. Only about 14 percent of flexible programs offer STD choices. Typically, the chief design consideration on whether to include short-term disability choices under the flexible program relates to the employer's existing sick leave or salary continuation practices. If the employer already provides full or partial pay replacement to employees for the entire LTD waiting period, the need for STD choices may be absent. However, if salary continuation or sick leave benefits are service related or dependent upon an employee's employment classification (e.g., exempt salaried), STD choices may represent an appropriate choice area under a flexible program.

Long-term disability benefit choices are offered in slightly under half (48 percent) of flexible programs. For employers with previously contributory coverage (which employees could decline to take), inclusion of LTD under a flexible program represents an extension of current practice. For other employers with noncontributory coverage, inclusion of LTD under the flexible program may provide employees an opportunity to upgrade existing benefits on an elective (versus company-paid) basis. As an alternative, they may elect lower coverage or none at all and use the savings for other choices.

(2) Structure of Options

Following are key issues employers need to address in determining the structure of options in the area of disability.

(i) High Option.   The high-end options for STD and LTD are usually the same. Generally 70 percent pay replacement is the highest benefit option made available. Replacement of more than 70 percent of pay may create insufficient incentive for an employee to seek rehabilitation and return to work.

Underwriting restrictions may dictate a maximum on monthly benefits payable—which may cap the benefit received by employees at higher pay levels.

(ii) Low Option.   An employee's choice in STD benefits often is simply whether to purchase coverage to fill any gap between the end of sick leave or salary continuation and the beginning of LTD coverage. Thus the low-end option is, in essence, no coverage. A few states or

localities sponsor mandatory short-term disability plans that specify minimum requirements for the percentage of pay to be replaced and the duration of benefits payable. Minimum requirements are specified in California, Hawaii, New Jersey, New York, Rhode Island, and Puerto Rico.

Among flexible programs offering LTD choices, 62 percent offer no coverage as the low-end option. An employer's decision about whether to allow employees to waive LTD coverage is often influenced by various factors. One is that social security disability benefits provide, in a sense, a core level of protection. So employees waiving coverage have available at least one alternate source of protection if a disability is serious enough to satisfy social security criteria. Another factor is an employer's sense of responsibility to provide all employees with some level of additional protection. In addition, concern over adverse selection (i.e., the likelihood that high-risk employees will be more inclined to elect coverage) also may cause an employer to require at least a minimum level of disability coverage.

Generally, 40 percent to 50 percent of pay replacement is the minimum benefit option offered. Less than 40 percent of pay replacement typically is viewed as too low to allow the employee to maintain an adequate standard of living. Moreover, at that level of pay replacement, any company-provided benefit typically would be eliminated through integration with social security, particularly at lower income levels. (This would be of particular concern where employees had been contributing for coverage and then received no benefit from the plan due to integration with social security or other plans.)

(iii) Number of Options.   Unlike many other benefit areas included in a flexible program, most employers with disability options limit the number of choices, offering an average of one option in short-term disability and two options in long-term disability.

The typical objective of disability benefits is to allow an employee to maintain an adequate standard of living during a period of disablement. The range of pay replacement generally considered appropriate for this purpose is relatively narrow.

For long-term disability, 50 percent to 70 percent pay replacement is usually considered adequate. While employers could offer multiple options within that range, the difference in cost (and benefit dollars) is fairly small. Some employers provide two clear-cut choices in LTD—options of half or two-thirds pay replacement. Other employers might provide a noncontributory core benefit with a relatively modest dollar maximum (e.g., $1,500/month) or a low limit on covered pay (e.g., $2,000/month) and allow employees who are impacted by these limits to select higher options (at their cost).

Where STD is included in a flexible program, an employee's choices often parallel the pay replacement amounts available under the LTD plan. On the other hand, the choice may be to extend the duration of benefits to fill any gap between STD and LTD. Choices of this nature are especially important to short-service employees who may not have accrued enough days to cover the LTD waiting period.

(3) Sources of Funds

Funding approaches for disability benefits vary.

For short-term disability, most employers continue to provide salary continuation to currently eligible employees on a fully company-paid basis. However, inside the flexible program, the options for employees with a gap in coverage usually are provided on an employee-pay-all basis.

For long-term disability, funding approaches differ. Basically, the approaches available include continuing to provide fully company-paid coverage, providing a core level of coverage and allowing employees to purchase higher coverage levels, or requiring employees to bear the full cost of coverage. Many employers choose to fund LTD under the flexible program at the same level as was the case under the prior program.

A decision on whether to use salary reduction in the program is often more complicated. Under Section 105 of the Tax Code, benefits paid for on an after-tax basis are nontaxable to an employee who becomes disabled. Benefits attributable to pretax contributions are treated as employer provided and, therefore, are taxable when paid. Still, the majority of employers (63 percent) require pretax premium payment on the grounds that salary reduction represents a more cost-efficient means of paying for the coverage, since the probability of disability occurring is relatively low and, therefore, the tax consequences of receiving disability benefits will affect relatively few employees. Moreover, in most cases, the marginal tax rate for employees receiving disability benefits is considerably lower than for active employees making contributions. This is due to the reduction in income from full salary to partial pay replacement, including also (generally) nontaxable social security benefits.

For administrative and communication reasons, few employers offer employees the choice of paying plan premiums on a pretax or post-tax basis. Also, those employers offering employees a choice of payment method typically have found that employees elect to make pretax contributions.

(4) Option Pricing/Credit Allocation

Under a flexible approach, employers must decide how to price options and allocate credits. Typically, the credit allocation and price tags are expressed as a percentage of pay (e.g., one-half of one percent of pay) since the benefits are based on pay. Employers who fund one or all disability option(s), usually attach a $0 price tag to the option(s) or provide flexible credits equal to the cost of the coverage. Option price tags usually represent the expected true cost of disability coverage based on insurance carrier rates. Since the range of coverage is limited to 50 percent to 70 percent pay replacement, the difference in the cost of various options is usually modest. Although not a common practice, some employers use age-graded prices since the probability of a long-term disability varies substantially by age.

Nine

Flexible Spending Accounts

§ 9.1 INTRODUCTION

The flexible spending account concept provides considerable versatility to both employer and employee. Through a flexible spending account, a special tax-favored pool of funds is created that the employee draws from to pay certain expenses. Unlike indemnity plans in which the employee is purchasing protection in case an event occurs, a flexible spending account exists to be used. The uses for a spending account include payment of almost any health-related expense, child care or other dependent care, and personal legal expenses. Sometimes educational expenses of the employee are also payable through an arrangement similar to a spending account.

The versatility of flexible spending accounts has led to their widespread adoption in recent years. Among a survey group of employers sponsoring flexible compensation programs in 1987, 89 percent offered flexible spending accounts. Of these, 70 percent were attached to a broader choice-making program offering options in other benefit areas, and 19 percent represented stand-alone arrangements. Only 11 percent of employers adopted flexible compensation programs without a flexible spending account feature.

Why are flexible spending accounts popular? For some employers, flexible spending accounts represent a way to test the appeal of flexible compensation without committing to an across-the-board, full-choice arrangement. For others, a flexible spending account provides a way to soften the impact of higher employee cost sharing through deductibles and copayment amounts. Finally, a flexible spending account provides a relatively simple way to offer new benefits to employees. Reimbursement of dental, preventive, or other health-related expenses, as well as child care or legal expenses, can occur through a spending account. Yet, the employer is neither locked in to a potentially expensive coverage area, nor is the company committed to offering a benefit that might appeal to only a small segment of the employee population.

§ 9.2 TYPES OF FLEXIBLE SPENDING ACCOUNTS

A Section 125 flexible spending account may cover three different categories of expenses: health care, child or other dependent care, and personal legal expenses. (Even though other kinds of expenses could be reimbursed to the employee on a nontaxable basis—namely, education—these may not be included under a flexible spending account subject to the Section 125 rules. See also the later discussion in this chapter of the special rules for reimbursement of education expenses.)

All three types of flexible spending accounts need not be offered. To date, the most popular arrangement is a combined offering of health care and dependent care expense accounts. Personal legal expense reimbursement is offered by relatively few programs, largely because of uncertainty over the future tax status of employer payments for legal. (The tax exclusion for group legal services was allowed to expire at the end of 1987 and to date has not been reinstated.)

(a) HEALTH CARE

(1) In General

By far the most widely available option among existing flexible spending accounts is the health care spending account. In most plans, a much greater proportion of employees make use of the health care spending account than any other type of account. The primary reason is that most employees or their families will incur some type of health care expense during the course of a year which is not covered by an employer's underlying health plan. Moreover, the opportunity to deduct unreimbursed medical expenses on an individual basis has been sharply limited by the new minimum threshold for total medical expenses needed to claim an income tax deduction. For 1987 and future years, that minimum level has been increased to 7.5 percent (up from 5 percent) of a taxpayer's adjusted gross income (AGI), meaning that the likelihood of reaching the initial threshold is slimmer than ever before for most taxpayers.

A flexible spending account gives back to participants the opportunity to pay for health care expenses with nontaxable dollars. In an account funded solely by employee salary reduction contributions, a participant also realizes tax savings on deferred pay that is used as reimbursement for health care expenses. Without the flexible spending account, the employee must pay for medical care expenses with after-tax dollars unless the 7.5 percent of AGI threshold is met.

Many employers view the health care option in a flexible spending account as a way to offer new benefits to employees without the problems of adding another insured program. For example, the absence of a dental program can be the focus of employee dissatisfaction, yet the employer may shy away from sponsoring a dental plan out of concern over costs.

Rather than add a potentially costly new health benefit, an employer could offer employees the opportunity to have dental expenses reimbursed through a flexible spending account. Employees without dental expenses would be able to use their flexible spending account for other health care needs, such as the purchase of contact lenses or preventive care. And, the employer's contribution may be kept at whatever level the company is comfortable with rather than varying with plan experience.

Another important objective for offering a health care option in a flexible spending account is to ease the bite of introducing cost-sharing measures under an organization's health care plans. The introduction of a comprehensive medical plan featuring front-end deductibles and co-payment amounts for all expenses, combined with introduction of a flexible spending account, has enabled cost-conscious employers to adopt a less expensive medical plan while providing employees the opportunity to reduce the increased share of expenses they must bear. Reimbursement of deductibles and copayment amounts through the employee's flexible spending account eases the pain of new or increased employee cost sharing under the employer-sponsored medical plan.

(2)   Eligible Expenses

The usefulness of health care expense reimbursement under a flexible spending account is as broad as the range of expenses that would be tax deductible if the threshold level of 7.5 percent of AGI were met. In addition to deductibles and copayment amounts, the expenses covered by the account could include the following items. (Note, however, that the employer need not permit reimbursement for all of the eligible expenses.)

- Dental expenses, including preventive, diagnostic, restorative, orthodontic, and therapeutic care
- Vision expenses, including examinations, eyeglasses, contact lenses, and seeing-eye dogs
- Hearing expenses, including examinations and hearing aids
- Artificial limbs
- Physical examinations
- Psychoanalysis and psychologist fees
- Psychiatrist fees and psychiatric care, including the cost of supporting a mentally ill dependent at a specially equipped medical center
- Chiropractic expenses
- Christian Science practitioner expenses
- Acupuncture
- Surgical hair transplant performed by a physician
- Cosmetic surgery
- Electrolysis or hair removal performed by a licensed technician
- Weight-loss or stop-smoking program prescribed by a doctor for a specific ailment
- Alcoholism or drug addiction treatment center, including meals and lodging
- Medicine and other drugs (prescription or otherwise), including birth control pills
- Transportation essential to obtaining medical care, including mileage, tolls, parking, taxi, bus, etc.

Expenses incurred by an employee's spouse and dependents are also eligible for reimbursement from the flexible spending account. The definition of "dependent" follows the rules outlined for a dependent medical expense tax deduction. That is, there must be a "relationship" of the dependent to the employee and the employee must "support" the dependent. Except in the case of a multiple support agreement or a custodial agreement in connection with a divorce or separation, the law requires that the employee provide over one-half of the individual's support.

The relationship test would include any person related by blood, marriage, or adoption to the employee or who is a member of the employee's household and whose principal abode is the employee's home. The support test looks at the actual dollars or the fair market equivalent provided for food, shelter, clothing, medical care, education, and other services and goods.

Medical expenses also may be reimbursable in certain situations where the individual cannot be claimed as a dependent on the employee's tax return. For example, if a married child receives more than one-half his or her support from the employee-parent, then despite the fact that the married child and his or her spouse file a joint tax return and cannot be claimed as a deduction on the employee-parent's tax return, the employee may still be reimbursed for eligible medical expenses paid on the child's behalf.

Another example would be if several people contributed to the support of one individual under a multiple support agreement. Assuming the relationship test is satisfied, if this individual earns more than the allowable amount to be claimed as a tax deduction ($1,950 in 1988), amounts paid by the employee for the individual's medical care may be reimbursed through the flexible spending account even though the individual would not be considered the employee's dependent for tax purposes.

The rules on when medical expenses may be reimbursed from a flexible spending account are not new or unique. They are identical to the rules applied in determining whether a tax deduction for medical expenses is available. The major difference, though, is the ability to utilize the tax-advantageous flexible spending account on the first dollar expended for medical care. For many people who will never reach the 7.5 percent of AGI threshold for a medical expense tax deduction, the flexible spending account is one of the few tax-saving opportunities still available.

(3)   Nondiscrimination Rules

The health care expense portion of a flexible spending account is considered a company-sponsored self-insured medical expense reimbursement plan. This is true even if the plan is fully employee-funded, since pretax salary reduction contributions technically are considered to be employer contributions made at the employee's election in lieu of receiving cash.

There is a trade-off for permitting reimbursement of an employee's medical expenses without causing income to the employee. As in most employee benefit programs, that trade-off is proof that the health care spending account as a separate plan is nondiscriminatory. Until the revised nondiscrimination rules of the Tax Reform Act of 1986 become effective, the nondiscrimination rules for a health care spending account contain three tests. The health care account must benefit 70 percent or more of all employees; 80 percent or more of all eligible employees must benefit if 70 percent or more are eligible; the benefits must meet a reasonable cross-section test.

In addition, all health benefits available to highly compensated employees (those in the highest-paid one-quarter of employees) must be available to all other employees. In the flexible spending account environment, this means that all participants must be able to dedicate the same amount of dollars to health care expense reimbursement.

New uniform nondiscrimination rules for most welfare benefit plans including health care expense accounts have been introduced, effective for plan years beginning in 1989 or earlier if regulations are released. (See also Chapter Five.) The new tests include both an eligibility test and a benefits test.

The three prongs of the *eligibility* test are based on (1) the percentage of nonhighly compensated employees eligible to participate in the plan, (2) the percentage of employees eligible for a benefit that is at least 50 percent of the value of the highest-value benefit for a highly compensated employee, and (3) the nondiscriminatory provision rule. The *benefits* test compares the average value of benefits provided to nonhighly compensated employees with the average value of benefits provided to highly compensated employees.

At the present time, it is uncertain how the *value* of a benefit will be measured for the nondiscrimination tests. Where employee contributions are made by salary reduction, such as to fund a flexible spending account, they will be treated as employer contributions in determining value. If a health care spending account is funded fully or partially by employee salary reduction, the new nondiscrimination rules *may* require some limits on how much a highly compensated employee could contribute without violating the rules.

The penalty for failure to satisfy the nondiscrimination rules will be income to the highly compensated employee equal to the value in excess of the amount that could be provided on a nondiscriminatory basis. If pretax salary reduction contributions made by a highly compensated employee to a health care expense account exceed the amount allowable on a nondiscriminatory basis, then the excess might be convertible to an after-tax contribution.

(b) DEPENDENT CARE

(1) In General

A dependent care expense account is offered as an option under most flexible spending accounts. In 1987, 92 percent of flexible spending account programs allowed for reimbursement of dependent care expenses.

Fewer employees take advantage of dependent care reimbursement than those who use the health care expense account. However, because of the high cost of dependent care and the predictable nature of the expense, the average contribution to dependent care expense accounts tends to be much higher than the average contribution to medical expense accounts.

In 1987, for example, contributions to dependent care expense accounts averaged $1,960, based on an average participation rate of 4 percent of eligible employees. This compared to an average medical expense account contribution of $490 based on an average participation rate of 25 percent of eligible employees.

(2) Eligible Expenses

Eligibility of dependent care expenses for reimbursement under a flexible spending account is determined by the guidelines of Internal Revenue Code Section 129 for an employer-sponsored dependent care assistance program. The major requirements are that the *expense must be "employment related,"* paid to an *eligible dependent-care provider* for care of an *eligible dependent.*

Household expenses and expenses for care of the dependent that enable the employee to work are employment-related expenses. The cost of a nighttime babysitter allowing the parents to get away for an evening out would not be an employment-related dependent care expense.

Payments made to one's own child under age 19 or to any person who is considered a dependent for tax purposes, are not reimbursable dependent care expenses. If services are provided by a dependent-care center, the center must meet all applicable state and local laws and provide care for more than six persons.

The category of eligible dependents includes children and disabled adult dependents. A child must be under age 15 or disabled and considered a dependent for tax purposes. If a custodial agreement in connection with a divorce or separation is in effect, the custodial parent may be entitled to deduct child care expenses even though the noncustodial parent claims the child as a dependent. Physically or mentally disabled adults, including spouse or parents, who are incapable of taking care of themselves and who are considered dependents for tax purposes are also eligible dependents.

Beginning in 1987, a new dollar limit applied to reimbursable dependent care expenses. For single individuals and married individuals who file a joint return, the limit is the lesser of each individual's earned income or $5,000. For married individuals filing separate returns, the lesser of $2,500 or the individual's earned income applies. The $5,000 maximum must be reflected in the plan. However, whether the employer goes further and imposes a $2,500 limit or requires proof that a married person is filing a joint return will depend upon the employer's policy toward policing eligible expenses.

(3) Nondiscrimination Rules

A dependent care expense reimbursement account within a flexible spending account is subject to its own nondiscrimination rules. Prior to the 1986 Tax Act, these rules required the employer to show that an adequate cross section of employees across all pay levels was covered. The plan could not discriminate in favor of "officers, owners, or highly compensated" employees. Higher utilization rates by the latter group, however, would not mean the plan was discriminatory.

Effective in 1988 or 1989, depending upon when regulations are issued, employers will be able to choose to qualify a dependent care expense account as a "statutory" employee benefit plan or a "nonstatutory" benefit. In order to be a statutory benefit, the new uniform nondiscrimination rules would be applied to the dependent care expense account. There would be an opportunity to combine dependent care with health, life insurance, group legal, and educational reimbursement plans to help pass the tests.

The employer may choose, instead, to apply a modified form of the prior discrimination test. Under this approach, the plan would be called a nonstatutory employee benefit plan but would still be a qualified benefit, includable in a Section 125 flexible spending account. The modified test requires proof of nondiscrimination for eligibility by showing a reasonable cross section of eligible employees at all pay levels. In addition, a new benefits test will require proof that the average benefit to lower-paid employees constitutes at least 55 percent of the average benefit to the highly paid. If employee salary reduction is permitted to fund the dependent care expense account, employees earning less than $25,000 may be excluded in determining average benefit value. However, if the employer chooses to consider dependent care a nonstatutory benefit, dependent care may not be aggregated with other benefits to help pass the tests, and the penalty for discrimination will be imputed income to *all* employees, not just the highly compensated.

(4)   Tax Credit versus Spending Account Reimbursement

Taxpayers may take a tax credit on dependent care expenses up to $2,400 per dependent or $4,800 for two or more dependents. The amount of the tax credit is a function of income—for example, 30 percent of eligible expenses at $10,000 of adjusted gross income, scaling down in 1 percentage point increments for each $2,000 of income, to a minimum credit of 20 percent at $28,000 or more. An important consideration for employees is whether it is more advantageous to take the tax credit for dependent care expenses or to pay for these expenses through a dependent care expense account. The same expenses cannot be covered both ways, although the employee may proportion some to each category.

The dependent care tax credit is designed to become less valuable to employees as income increases. At the same time, payment of dependent care expenses with salary reduction amounts through a spending account becomes more valuable as income increases. The crossover income level where the advantages of both methods are approximately equal (in terms of federal taxes) occurs at about $24,000 of adjusted gross income for 1988. Above the crossover level, salary reduction contributions to a dependent care expense account usually are more advantageous. Below the $24,000 family income level, an employee generally would be in a better tax position by taking the tax credit.

(Note, however, that the $24,000 crossover level is useful only as a rule of thumb. Individual situations can produce markedly different tax results. A chief exception to the general rule, for example, may occur when family income is under $17,000. In 1988, an earned income credit is available to families with income below $17,000. For some employees, a salary reduction that lowers income below the $17,000 threshold in 1988 may be more tax advantageous than using the tax credit for the same dependent care expenses.)

Separately, employees with substantial dependent care expenses may use both the tax credit and salary reduction, although the same expenses may not be covered both ways. For example, an employee with $7,000 of dependent care expenses may establish a flexible spending account for $5,000 of eligible expenses and take a tax credit on the balance of $2,000. Or an employee may exhaust the tax credit available for dependent care and use a spending account for costs that exceed the limits for which a tax credit may be taken.

Employers that sponsor a dependent care expense account are not expected to give tax advice. However, they are required by law to provide employees with a description of the dependent care tax credit and the tax exclusion for an employer-provided dependent care expense account. This information must explain that the tax credit may be more advantageous than the exclusion of reimbursed dependent care expenses through a spending account, depending on the employee's tax situation.

(c) LEGAL EXPENSES

A legal expense reimbursement account offers employees the opportunity to have their own and their dependents' personal legal expenses paid on a pre-tax basis. This flexible spending account option has been offered less frequently than health care and dependent care options, due in part to the uncertainty of future extensions in the tax law. While the Tax Reform Act of 1986 continued the provision through 1987, as of this writing, no further extension has been accorded personal legal expenses.

Participation in a legal expense account also has been lower than participation in other accounts—averaging under 2 percent of eligible employees in 1987. However, average contributions by employees who choose to use a legal expense account are relatively substantial— averaging around $443 in 1987.

The rules for an employer-provided legal services reimbursement plan are set forth in Internal Revenue Code Section 120. Reimbursable legal expenses for services performed by, or under the supervision of, a lawyer must be for services of a *personal* nature. This includes expenses for:

- Divorce
- Sale and purchase of a personal residence
- Will preparation
- Adoption
- Personal bankruptcy.

Legal fees connected with operating a business or with property held for commercial purposes would not be reimbursable through the account.

The nondiscrimination rules applicable to a legal expense reimbursement account require that an adequate cross section of employees across pay levels be covered. In addition, the plan must not discriminate in favor of the highly compensated group. When the new uniform nondiscrimination requirements become effective (and provided the exclusion of legal expense reimbursement is extended beyond the end of 1987), employers will have a choice between applying the current nondiscrimination rules or the new rules. The choice is similar to that allowed for dependent care expense reimbursement plans. That is, if the new rules are applied, the plan will be a statutory benefit plan, and aggregation with other plans to help pass discrimination tests is permitted. However, the employer may choose to apply the current rules, treating the plan as a nonstatutory benefit plan.

Some special implementation steps are necessary for a legal expense account. Reimbursement must be made through a separate qualified trust that meets the requirements of Internal Revenue Code Section 501(c)(20). A separate legal plan document is required, and the plan must be submitted for IRS approval.

(d) EDUCATION EXPENSES

Strictly speaking, there are only three categories of reimbursable expenses for a Section 125 flexible spending account: health care, dependent care, and personal legal. The proposed Section 125 regulations and later the Tax Reform Act of 1986, precluded use of a Section 125 flexible spending account for other expenses that may be provided on a tax-free basis to employees.

Yet use of the flexible spending account concept for reimbursement of other nontaxed benefits, particularly education expenses, has been possible—under certain conditions. Essentially, two plans are required although this need not be obvious to employees. Under one plan, which is a typical flexible spending account, employer contributions and employee salary reduction contributions may be directed to health care, dependent care, and legal expense accounts. A separate plan would need to be set up to allow employees to choose to apply some or all of the available employer dollars to education expenses. However, no employee salary reduction contributions (or any other taxable choices) would be permitted to the education reimbursement plan, since only a Section 125 plan may allow a choice between taxable and nontaxable benefits, or pretax salary reduction.

Reimbursable education expenses are defined in IRS Section 127. A year-by-year extension of Section 127 has put educational expenses on the same uncertain footing as reimbursement of personal legal expenses. Both benefits were allowed to expire at the end of 1987. As of this writing, however, it is unclear whether the personal legal and educational expense benefits will be extended retroactively. As the provision currently exists, Section 127 provides that the education received need not be job-related or part of a degree program; rather, any form of education that improves or develops the individual is permissible. However, sports, games, or hobby instruction are specifically excluded. The cost of tuition and books is reimbursable. However, tools or supplies that might be kept after the course of instruction, and meals, lodging, and transportation are not reimbursable education expenses. The maximum annual amount that may be reimbursed is $5,250.

The trade-off of requiring nondiscrimination rules in order to have a nontaxable benefit applies to employer reimbursement of education expenses. If the scheduled December 31, 1987, expiration date for education expense reimbursement is extended, an employer will be able to choose between application of the new uniform nondiscrimination rules and the current rules.

The current nondiscrimination test for eligibility is the same as described for dependent care and legal expense reimbursement: The employer must be able to show that the plan benefits employees across a reasonable cross section by pay levels. A special rule restricts education expense reimbursement paid to employees or their dependents who are 5 percent or more shareholders or owners, to not more than 5 percent of the total annual amount of reimbursement paid by the plan. Also, the plan must be described in a written plan document.

§ 9.3   REQUIREMENTS FOR FLEXIBLE SPENDING ACCOUNTS

The long-awaited proposed regulations to Section 125, released in 1984, acknowledged the flexible spending account as a way for employers to provide benefit choices to employees. The regulations also imposed new limitations designed to clamp down on perceived abuses.

As described in the proposed regulations, the intent was to add an element of risk to the operation of flexible spending accounts.

Employees should not have the opportunity to recoup unused funds during the year or roll over those funds for use in a subsequent year. Instead, funds held in a flexible spending account should be subject to a risk of loss, just as premiums paid for insurance coverage might never be recovered if the insured risk never occurs.

The proposed regulations imposed two major restrictions on flexible spending accounts to incorporate the insurance risk idea and restrict abuses of the accounts. First, an account must allow no more frequent than annual elections to designate how much money will be contributed. Moreover, the annual election must include a designation of funds to the three permitted categories—health, dependent care, or personal legal. Finally, the proposed regulations created a concept known as "use-it-or-lose-it." Money designated to a category under a flexible spending account must be exhausted for expenses incurred during the calendar year, or funds will be forfeited.

(a)   ANNUAL ELECTIONS

Some expenses are generally predictable for the coming year. For example, the amount that will be needed for dependent care or the price of a new pair of eyeglasses can be determined quite easily. Certain other expenses that may occur during the year, though, may be difficult to foresee when the employee makes the annual election.

Through effective communication and planning tools to help employees predict expenses in a coming year, however, the annual election requirement has proven to be less onerous than it first appeared. In fact, for some employers, the annual election requirement has been an administrative boost since practically all account changes are now legally restricted to once per year.

Once made, an election to designate funds to any of the three permitted uses is irrevocable unless there is a change in the employee's family status. This could be a marriage or divorce, the birth or death of a family member, or the spouse's loss of employment.

(b)   FORFEITURE

The term use-it-or-lose-it describes the insurance risk element imposed on flexible spending accounts by the proposed Section 125 regulations. The phrase reflects the requirement that funds allocated to each of the allowable expense accounts must be used to reimburse expenses incurred during the year, or the funds will be lost. The money allocated to each expense type must be depleted for that expense; no shifting of funds from one type of expense category to another is permitted. Also, no distinction is made between an employee's salary reduction contributions and employer contributions. *Any* amounts remaining in the flexible spending account after all of the year's expenses are paid must be forfeited by the employee.

Regarding forfeitures, the employer has discretion to determine use of forfeited funds. Use-it-or-lose-it prohibits reallocation to the individual employee who forfeited unused funds. However, all forfeitures may be accumulated and reallocated on a *per capita* basis to participants and treated as additional flexible spending account credits in the following year. Forfeited funds may also revert to the employer with no obligation to use forfeited amounts for benefit purposes. Some employers have also donated forfeited funds to a charitable organization, either chosen by the employer or selected on the basis of an employee vote.

In practice, the use-it-or-lose-it requirement has turned out to be less burdensome than originally anticipated for several reasons. One is that many flexible spending account expenses are determinable in advance (e.g., dependent care, eyeglasses, or contact lenses). Another is that employers, concerned about the impact of forfeiture on spending account participation, have made efforts to provide employees with tools for budgeting upcoming expenses. As part of the annual enrollment, many companies provide worksheets or other budgeting aids to assist employees in calculating how much should be designated to each expense category. Some also recap the employee's prior year's expenditures as a basis for planning upcoming expenses. Finally, for many employees the opportunity to pay for certain expenses on a tax-deferred basis outweighs the risk of miscalculating and losing some (and usually a small amount) of funds.

§ 9.4   DESIGN CONSIDERATIONS

(a)   TYPE OF APPROACH

Flexible spending accounts may serve as the cornerstone of a flexible compensation program or exist as another option within a broader choice-making arrangement. The appropriate flexible spending account design will depend on an organization's objectives. Also, internal administrative capabilities may be a consideration although the importance of administration as an issue is diminishing with the increased availability of outside recordkeeping firms and computerized administration packages.

The introduction of a flexible spending account as a stand-alone benefit is becoming less common as employers and employees become more comfortable with choice in all benefit areas. Yet for some organizations, a stand-alone flexible spending account provides an attractive means of providing new benefits in a tax-effective way without disturbing an existing benefit structure.

Few organizations offer a broad choice-making program without also offering a flexible spending account. Absent a flexible spending account, choice-making-only plans would allow employees to trade off among different levels of benefits with different price tags, or permit an election to receive cash if the options selected cost less than the available employer credits. But the tax-effective advantage of paying for deductibles, copayment amounts, and other nonreimbursed expenses on a pretax basis exists only through a flexible spending account.

In addition, employees who expect to have few expenses in a particular coverage area may be encouraged to choose a lower-cost option or opt out of a benefit entirely if they know the expenses they do incur can be reimbursed from their flexible spending account. For example, employees who anticipate minimal routine dental expenses may choose to opt out of a dental program entirely, using freed-up credits for another benefit purchase. Meanwhile, dental expenses that do occur during the year would be reimbursed through the flexible spending account. Other employees may decide that by choosing a low-value medical plan, released credits could apply to purchasing additional life insurance. Medical expenses toward the higher deductible in the lower-value plan can be reimbursed through the flexible spending account.

(b)   SOURCES OF FUNDS

Two sets of decisions must be made in determining how to fund flexible spending accounts—the employer's and the employee's. The employer must decide where the money to fund accounts should come from, how much is available, and whether any limits should be set within the flexible spending account. Deciding how to handle forfeitures at the end of the plan year will impact the employer's funding decision. Employees must decide how much they should contribute if salary deferral is allowed and where to allocate the available funds based on anticipated expenses during the year.

There are many possible sources of company contributions to a flexible spending account program. If flexible spending accounts are being offered as a new benefit in addition to the existing program, an employer may have the resources to channel new money into the accounts.

The more common scenario during the battle against medical cost inflation has been introduction of a flexible spending account as a way to ease the blow of reduced medical benefits. Part of the employer's savings from adopting a less-valuable plan might be contributed to employees' flexible spending accounts. A reduced medical plan with effective cost-management features should enable the employer to benefit from a slower rate of medical cost inflation and in some cases, may result in immediate savings. In future years, the employer could review the level of medical contributions, including the fixed contribution to the flexible spending account, to see if an increase or a decrease in the amount spent is appropriate.

If the flexible spending account is part of a full-choice medical program, part of the plan's design generally dictates how many "credits" each employee will be able to spend for the whole program. By choosing lower-cost options where available, flexible credits are freed-up and could be directed to the flexible spending account. The employer need not make a specific allocation of funds to the account; each employee is expected to be able to determine the mix of benefits and flexible spending account amounts that best fit his or her particular needs.

How the employer contribution is communicated to employees is an important consideration in implementing a flexible spending account. If there is no guarantee that employer contributions will continue at the same level, or if the first contribution is "seed money" not to be repeated in future years, this should be made clear in initial communications. If the contribution is tied to savings in other parts of the benefit program, employees may expect information on how well costs have been controlled.

(c) LIMITS ON CONTRIBUTIONS

Another important decision for plan design is determining the limits on how much an employee can dedicate to the flexible spending account. With the exception of dependent care, many plans have imposed individual limits.

One reason for placing a ceiling on spending account contributions is to help assure compliance with the nondiscrimination requirements. Having a specific dollar limit set at a level which is attainable by all employees provides everyone with equal availability to spending accounts and reduces the potential that highly paid employees make prohibitively greater use of the accounts than lower-paid employees.

Another reason for an upper limit on employee contributions is to minimize the likelihood that employees will reach the Section 415 limits. This is of particular concern in organizations with Section 401(k) salary deferral and a significant company contribution to the plan. Because of the requirement that compensation after salary reduction (both Sections 401(k) and 125) be used to determine maximum and annual account additions to defined contribution arrangements, it is *lower*-paid employees who run a greater risk of reaching the Section 415 limits. (See also Chapter Eleven for a complete discussion and examples of the interaction between the Section 415 limits and the use of salary reduction.)

In addition, upper limits on employee contributions may also help reduce the possibility that employees will over use salary reduction to the point of risking substantial forfeitures.

(d)   TIMING OF REIMBURSEMENTS

Another factor in flexible spending account design is the incorporation of features that will facilitate administration. Generally, a limit on how often reimbursement may be received (for instance, once per month) and a minimum total of expenses that should be submitted for reimbursement ($25 or $50) will ease the task of the plan's administrator.

Ten

Time Off with Pay

§ 10.1 INTRODUCTION

Benefit programs include several different variations of time off with pay from vacation through holidays and sick leave to a variety of leaves of absence (e.g., jury duty and military service). Some of these types of time off, such as vacation, tend to be taken largely at the employee's election. Most holidays are "fixed" on particular dates, although employers frequently allow a few holidays to "float," permitting the employee discretion over when to take the day(s). Sick leave is intended to be used only when the employee is legitimately ill. Leaves of absence, on the other hand, while technically a type of time off, usually are excluded from a flexible program, largely because leaves tend to last an extended period of time and typically require management approval.

An emerging development in the area of time off with pay is the combining of all the different types of paid time off (excluding leaves) into a single umbrella category, "personal days" or "personal time." The employee receives a specified allotment of days and determines how to use the time—whether for vacation and sometimes holidays or for illness. The umbrella category also helps minimize the burden to employers of having to "police" the separate types of time off. The employee recognizes that excessive sick days erode the time available for vacation and vice versa.

§ 10.2 OBJECTIVES FOR CHOICE MAKING IN TIME OFF

Time off with pay is becoming an increasingly popular option within flexible programs. Today over one-quarter (27 percent) of flexible programs offer vacation buying, vacation selling, or both. Among these companies, 47 percent permit both buying and selling, while 42 percent permit buying only and 11 percent permit only the selling of vacation days.

One of the chief reasons employers include time off in a flexible program is that the trading of vacation time is popular with employees. In fact, time off typically ranks at (or near) the top of the list of benefit changes employees would like to see incorporated under a flexible approach.

For example, buying usually holds considerable appeal for younger employees with shorter service since vacation schedules usually relate to length of employment. Also, shorter-service employees are more likely to be part of a dual-income household where flexibility in matching vacation schedules is likely to be important (e.g., the employee might be eligible for one to two weeks, while the spouse may receive three to four weeks elsewhere). These employees tend to be interested in trading other benefits (e.g., medical when coverage is available through the spouse's employer) for additional time off. Buying of vacation time also may appeal to some longer-service employees who have sufficient vacation for normal needs, but periodically might be interested in an extended vacation.

The opportunity to sell time off tends to appeal to older, longer-service employees, and often higher-paid employees. Frequently, these employees currently may be using only a portion of their scheduled vacation time and may be forfeiting the rest in organizations without carry-over provisions. Also, these employees tend to place greater priority on security coverages and may want to use the dollars freed from vacation time to pay for coverages in other areas, particularly in organizations implementing age-related premiums (e.g., for life insurance).

As Table 10.1 illustrates, among organizations that permit both buying and selling, about 40 percent of employees will trade days— usually to buy more time. Nearly one-third of employees, when given the chance, will spend real dollars for time off. The buyers tend to be younger, shorter-service and lower-paid employees. Only about 12 percent will cash in vacation time. However, the sellers tend to be somewhat higher-paid employees, most likely those with sufficient seniority to have extra unused days. The net effect of buying and selling between

Table 10.1
Time Off Election Results

	Buyers	Mean	Sellers
Percent electing	29%	—	12%
Average age	34	36	46
Average pay	$20,000	$23,000	$42,000
Number of days	4	14 available	4

Source: Hewitt Associates data base on employee elections under flexible compensation programs.

these two groups tends to come close to a "wash" from the standpoint of cost.

Beyond offering a popular option to employees, employers often have other reasons for including time off in a flexible program. Other objectives include:

- **Expand vacation schedules.** When competitive or other pressures cause an employer to consider extending vacation (or other time-off programs), a flexible approach can enable liberalization without commensurate cost to the employer. An organization may offer employees the option to buy more time without a blanket increase in vacation days for everyone. If an employer wants to pay a portion of the cost, an extra contribution for all employees can be added to the flexible dollar pool.

- **Increase flexible credits.** Vacation selling can be used to enrich the credit pool for a flexible program. Selling five days of vacation time ($1/52$ of a year) can add almost 2 percent of pay to the credit total. This may be an attractive way to allow employees to expand the credit formula on an optional basis for purchase of other benefits without a blanket increase in employer contributions.

- **Transition from a "banking" system.** Historically, many employers have allowed employees to "bank" unused vacation time for use at a later date. However, the potential for large, unfunded liabilities to accumulate on a company's books often makes vacation banking an unattractive system. Moreover, recent tax rules narrowed employer deductibility of accrued but unused vacation time, which further limits the appeal of vacation banking systems. To some extent, introduction of a flexible program, including the opportunity to buy or sell vacation days, may provide the motivation or rationale for cutting back or eliminating an existing banking system. As will be discussed later, the carrying forward of unused vacation time is considerably more difficult to accommodate under a choice-making program.

§ 10.3 TYPES OF TIME-OFF CHOICES

Conceptually, an employer could allow choice making in any time-off area. In practice, however, the buying and selling of time off is most common in the vacation area. Inclusion of holidays as a choice area usually is more prevalent in industries that operate each day of the year (e.g., hospitals, airlines). Sick leave is only rarely included under a flexible program, except to the extent an employer has consolidated (or intends to) the various types of time off into a personal leave or paid time-off umbrella. (See also Chapter Eight on disability for discussion of short-term disability under flexible programs.) Other special-purpose types of time off (such as leaves of absence) almost always are left outside flexible program structures.

(a) VACATION

Vacation is the type of time off most frequently included in flexible programs. Typically, employers retain the pre-flexible vacation schedule and permit the buying of additional days beyond that point or the selling of days within the existing schedule. Key issues relating to designing a vacation option include:

- **Number of Days.** Companies tend to limit the number of days that may be traded for several reasons. One reason is to limit the magnitude of the amount of "soft-dollar" expense from time off that can be converted into "hard-dollar" cost (i.e., converting unused days to cash, Section 401(k), or spending account deposits). Another reason is that limiting the number of days that can be bought or sold to a set number helps ensure that the program will meet nondiscrimination standards. In effect, all employees have access to the same percentage of pay. Finally, capping the number of days available for buying helps minimize potential scheduling problems, particularly in situations where the employee would need to be replaced during the vacation.
- **Units of Time.** Conceivably, organizations could permit the buying or selling of vacation in any increment of time. In practice, most

organizations use either days or weeks. Denominating time off in days—rather than a block of time such as a week—tends to provide employees greater flexibility, especially with the fairly high price of purchasing a full week of vacation (usually about two percent of annual pay). On the other hand, blocks of time may be easier to track, particularly in organizations with nonstandard work weeks (e.g., 10- or 12-hour shifts). Denominating time off in units of less than a day tends to be relatively rare.

- **Pricing of Time.** The pricing of time off raises issues relating to economics versus perception. From an economic standpoint, a case could be made that the value of a day (or week) of time is higher than the actual daily (or weekly) rate for buying purposes and lower for selling purposes. That is, both the cost of employee benefits and the value of unused vacation time currently "donated" to the employer (that does not allow vacation banking) should be factored into the arithmetic. Only rarely, however, are employers able to calculate the "true" value of time off with such precision—or convince employees of the logic of such an approach. As a result, most flexible programs price time off at 100 percent of the daily or weekly rate of pay.

    Occasionally, a dollar maximum is placed on the price assigned to a day of vacation, especially for selling days, in order to limit the hard-dollar exposure for highly paid employees.

(b) HOLIDAYS

The inclusion of holidays in a choice-making program usually is based on the employer's business. Some organizations operate every day of the year (e.g., hospitals), so the buying or selling of holidays can be treated much the same as vacation time. In fact, at these organizations, vacation and holiday time frequently are treated as like entities and continue as such under a choice-making program.

At most organizations, however, practical barriers prohibit the inclusion of holidays. If an organization is closed on designated holidays (e.g., national or local holidays), allowing sale of the day makes little sense. Many organizations make available additional floating days that employees may take largely at their discretion (much like vacation). It is the floating rather than fixed holidays that become eligible for trade under the choice-making program.

Floating days also may work well as options in an organization that wants to provide time-off flexibility but is constrained by a vacation banking system. Floating days usually are not subject to banking in the same way as vacation days. Outside the flexible program, the employer might retain banking of vacation days, while inside the program, only the floating days are permissible as a choice area.

(c) PERSONAL DAYS

In general, few organizations include sick leave or initial illness days as a choice area within a flexible program. (Typically, sick leave policies provide full or partial salary continuation for a period of time such as 30 days or a period related to the employee's length of service.) Companies tend to have more difficulty with the abuse of sick leave than almost any other benefit area. It is a difficult management problem to control with major cost implications when employees treat accrued sick time as though it were vacation. (See also Chapter Eight on disability for discussion of options in short-term disability, which usually commences after expiration of an initial period of salary continuation.)

Instead, some organizations have opted to consolidate vacation, holidays (all or only the floating days), and sick leave into an umbrella of paid time off. The idea is to move away from the traditional concept of special-purpose types of time off and into an environment that delineates a total number of days off with pay and permits employees to determine how to use those days—whether for vacation or illness. The total number of days off may remain the same, or the sick days may be reduced, but the point is to create awareness that only a certain number of personal days will be allotted each year. A flexible approach simply allows employees to buy or sell days above or below their specified allotment.

§ 10.4   RESTRICTIONS ON TIME-OFF CHOICES

Time off is unlike almost any other benefit area that could be included under a flexible program. Outside a flexible program, an employee who has earned time off often has a choice to take that vacation now or later or to carry over unused time, generally without application of any special rules. Inside a flexible program, however, that same time-off choice triggers special rules, namely, the prohibition against deferral of compensation except as allowed under Section 401(k). Separately, an emerging (and as yet unresolved) issue is federal preemption of state laws prohibiting forfeiture of unused vacation time.

(a) FORFEITURE

The proposed regulations on Section 125 specifically addressed the buying and selling of vacation time. Under the regulations, time off generally cannot be carried forward from one year to the next. (The reason is that the only "deferral" permissible under Section 125 is a Section 401(k) cash-or-deferred option.) Further, the proposed regulations separate purchased days into "elective" and "nonelective" days.

Elective days are considered to be all days in excess of a minimum and over which an employee may exercise some choice. For example, assume a pre-flexible program entitled an employee to four weeks of vacation, but the new flexible program permits the employee to buy or sell up to five days. If that employee elects to keep four weeks of vacation, the employee's elective days are those in excess of three weeks. That is because the employee has the option to sell the fourth week of vacation, if desired. Further, vacation days are assumed to be used in an order that exhausts the nonelective days (the first three weeks) *before* the elective days (one week). (The employee does not have the option to determine which days are elective or nonelective.) If the employee uses all four weeks of vacation, no days are forfeited. But if the employee uses only three weeks, the five elective days cannot be banked.

The rules are different for nonelective days. From the preceding example, suppose the employee elects at the beginning of the year to sell the five elective days. During the year, the employee uses only two weeks of the three weeks of nonelective time. These nonelective days (only) would be eligible to be carried forward for use in the subsequent year.

Most companies encourage employees to use vacation days—whether elective or nonelective—in the current year to avoid loss of unused vacation time. Alternatively, some organizations will cash out any unused elective days (only) before the end of the year. That way, the employee avoids being in the position of deferring compensation to a subsequent tax year.

(b) STATE REQUIREMENTS

Recently, several states have become active in passing legislation requiring an employer to pay employees for accrued vacation time. In particular, California has one of the more aggressive statutes, treating vacation as a form of wages earned by pay period and requiring cash out of accrued but unused time at the date of termination. This requirement is potentially in conflict with the prohibition of deferred compensation applied to vacation time under Section 125 arrangements (unless unused days are cashed out each year).

Under recent court decisions, if a vacation arrangement is "funded," ERISA preempts state jurisdiction in this area. However, most vacation plans (Section 125 or otherwise) are not funded arrangements, so it is less clear that the federal statute supercedes state laws. Until the issue is resolved, either through court cases or federal enactment, employers should seek legal counsel on the applicability of specific state requirements.

(c) NONDISCRIMINATION

To date, vacation or time off is not governed by any specific section within the Internal Revenue Code, and therefore has no special nondiscrimination requirements other than the general rules that apply to Section 125 programs. In fact, nondiscrimination is effectively easier to accomplish in the vacation area. As a pay-related benefit, assuring that all employees have equal access to the same percentage of pay (i.e., the same number of days available for buying or selling) is considered sufficient for satisfying nondiscrimination requirements. If all employees may trade five days beyond the current vacation, for example, the program generally would be viewed as acceptable.

§ 10.5 DESIGN CONSIDERATIONS

(a) TYPE OF APPROACH

One key consideration is whether to allow choices in the area of time off. For all practical purposes, the banking of time off under a Section 125 program is prohibited. Therefore, organizations with extensive banking arrangements already in place, either would need to modify current practices or retain vacation banking outside the flexible program, while permitting more limited choices (such as floating holidays or purchase of additional nonbankable vacation days) within the flexible program.

Other considerations relate to the areas of scheduling (for buying) and hard-dollar cost (for selling). Allowing employees to buy extra time off raises the potential for scheduling conflicts—or greater costs if the employee who buys extra vacation must be replaced at a higher rate. As a result, most organizations are careful to communicate that purchased time off requires the same scheduling and coordination with management or supervisory staff as regular vacation. (In fact, some organizations require a supervisor's approval before the employee may even purchase additional days.)

The selling of time involves conversion of soft-dollar expense to hard-dollar cost, particularly among employees who previously failed to use their entire allotment. In practice, however, most companies find that even among senior (higher-paid) employees, vacation remains a valuable benefit, so the amount of time actually sold has a relatively modest impact on costs. Further, where vacation buying is also allowed, more employees tend to purchase vacation time, so the net cost effect tends to be minimal.

For employers interested in offering flexibility in time off, the trend in recent years has been to combine opportunities, rather than allow only buying or selling. The combined offering tends to mitigate the cost effect of allowing selling only and provides the broadest flexibility to employees.

(b) AREAS OF CHOICE

Majority practice is to restrict time off choices to vacation only. Sometimes employers will include holidays—usually only the days that float. The exception is industries that operate each day of the year so that the trading of holidays represents a practical option. Sick leave is eligible for trading only to the extent that an organization already has converted to an umbrella time-off program that treats all time off as personal days, regardless of reason.

(c) LIMITS ON CHOICE

Most programs place some limits on the trading of time off. Usually the limits take the form of a maximum number of days that may be bought or sold—typically five days either way. Most organizations set a price for days bought or sold at 100 percent of pay. Only a minority of organizations limit their exposure by capping the dollar amount on days sold (e.g., actual pay to no more than $200 per day). Separately, most organizations require employees to take some vacation time (e.g., minimum of one or two weeks) at least partly to restrict the potential for abuse in terms of allowing employees to cash out vacation and then use the time anyway.

(d)   ADMINISTRATION OF CHOICES

To some extent, an organization's level of comfort with vacation choices may hinge on the systems and procedures already in place to monitor time-off recording. At issue is the potential for abuse—allowing employees either to cash out a portion of time off and use the days anyway or to take more time than even an additional purchased allotment. Different organizations decide the issue in different ways. Some have adequate controls in place to monitor time reporting accurately. Others have only limited concern over the potential of employees abusing time-off policies, irrespective of controls. In any event, administration may loom as an issue that inclines an organization one way or the other on inclusion of time-off choices in a flexible program.

Eleven

Retirement

§ 11.1 INTRODUCTION

To date, few employers have included retirement choices as specific options within flexible programs. One reason is the nature and structure of defined benefit pension plans—the primary source of retirement income for the majority of employees. Most pension plans are geared to providing benefits based on the employee's final-average earnings and years of service at retirement, which makes it difficult to set an accurate price tag on increments of pension very far in advance of the employee's actual retirement date (or at least without knowledge of the intended retirement date).

Another reason is that the rising stock and bond markets have boosted pension fund investments in recent years, thereby reducing (or even eliminating) current pension cost for many employers. In effect, employer attention to cost control has been diverted from pensions to other benefit areas (primarily medical).

Finally, the availability of individual salary reduction under Section 401(k) arrangements has provided employers a comparatively simpler way to meet employee needs for additional retirement income as well as a tax-favored vehicle for employee contributions. (In contrast, employee contributions to a pension plan must be made on an after-tax basis.)

The types of retirement plans under consideration here include defined benefit pension plans and defined contribution arrangements (mainly savings and profit sharing plans), including a Section 401(k) salary reduction feature. Note that most of the discussion is oriented toward Section 401(k), as this is the vehicle most organizations use to accomplish the delivery of flexibility in the retirement area—the only type of retirement plan that may be offered directly under a Section 125 flexible program. A few employers have implemented a form of choice making in the pension area although through a separate arrangement constructed outside the Section 125 program. In effect, employees are permitted to purchase increments of pension, "pension equivalents," at the same time they make their other flexible program elections. However, the pension amounts are purchased in after-tax dollars usually with little or no employer subsidy.

Separately, many employers already maintain stand-alone Section 401(k) plans. However, a major focus of this chapter is on coordination of Section 401(k) with flexible compensation programs—not on use of Section 401(k) as a separate vehicle for retirement savings. The rules for these plans are quite complex, particularly after the 1986 tax act which imposed new limits on contributions and expanded the nondiscrimination requirements. Section 401(k) rules are discussed here only to the extent they bear on the design of a flexible program. (See also Chapter Four for a summary of the legislative origins and nondiscrimination requirements for Section 401(k) plans.)

§ 11.2 OBJECTIVES FOR CHOICE MAKING IN RETIREMENT

The reasons for wanting to include retirement choices in a flexible program generally parallel the motivations for offering choice in other benefit areas, with a few differences. As is the case in other benefits, one reason for offering choice is to meet diverse employee needs and preferences, particularly in cases where the employer is unwilling (or unable) to raise retirement benefits on a company-paid basis. Retirement may also be an area that holds significant appeal to only a minority of the employee population, while the majority has greater interest in other benefit areas. Providing choices enables employees to meet their own special needs (e.g., permitting earlier retirement, making up for a short career with the current employer, or otherwise supplementing existing retirement benefits).

Another motivation for including retirement as a choice area is to provide an additional option for unused flexible credits (amounts remaining after the purchase of medical, dental, life insurance, and so forth). Some employers are concerned about employees cashing out employer-provided benefit dollars, yet they recognize that cash represents an attractive flexible program option to employees. A Section 401(k) plan can serve as the repository for unused credits.

A different motivation for reviewing the retirement area on design of a flexible program is as a means of opening up a potential source of credits for the flexible program. In the period before salary reduction was available, several flexible programs were structured around a cutback in future service pension benefits, using the savings as a source of credits for the flexible program. (However, in most of these early cases, the existing pension provided very high benefits, so the majority of employees gained more from the introduction of choice making in other benefit areas than they lost through a reduction in future pension amounts.) Although this approach has been used only infrequently in recent years, it may have merit in situations where an employer has limited alternatives for generating a sufficient credit pool for the flexible program, and trimming a high-value pension plan would do little to diminish either employee security or the employer's competitive position.

Alternatively, a few employers have begun to explore using a Section 401(k) plan as an additional funding source for a flexible program. Under this approach, a portion of employer monies (either the matching funds in a savings plan or the annual allocation in a profit sharing plan) would be made subject to employee election for use in the flexible program. This type of approach tends to have appeal in situations where an employer's objective is to focus employee attention on the total compensation aspect of pay and benefits or where the Section 401(k) plan is very "rich" and employer credits in the flexible program may be insufficient for employees to cover their benefit needs. However, whether Section 401(k) monies should be used as a funding source for "consumption" in the flexible program (versus saving in the Section 401(k) plan) depends on employer objectives in the retirement area and the level of retirement income already provided through that and other plans.

§ 11.3 SECTION 401(k) WITHIN FLEXIBLE PROGRAMS

Basically, a Section 401(k) plan is a defined contribution retirement vehicle (e.g., a savings, profit sharing, stock bonus, or pre-ERISA money purchase pension plan) with an employee option to take certain amounts in cash (which is currently taxable) or to defer these amounts (with deferral of taxation) into the plan. Most Section 401(k) plans accept salary reduction contributions, thereby allowing employees to forego a portion of their currently taxable compensation (e.g., salary or bonus) to have that same amount deposited as a nontaxable employer contribution in the defined contribution plan. (As mentioned earlier, the cash-or-deferred compensation feature can be incorporated only within defined contribution vehicles—not defined benefit pension plans.) Further, Section 401(k) plans are the only form of deferred compensation that can be linked directly with Section 125 plans, which creates the three-way trade-off—choices among cash, deferred compensation (retirement), and welfare benefits. It is through this linkage that funds (including unused flexible credits) may flow directly between the two types of choice-making approaches.

Note that the direct linkage need not occur. Many organizations design flexible programs independent of a Section 401(k) plan. In these cases, employees make two-way choices under each choice-making arrangement. That is, under the flexible program, employees decide between purchasing benefits or receiving unused flexible credits in cash (if cash is an option). Under the Section 401(k) plan, employees decide between receiving salary or bonus amounts currently or deferring that amount into the Section 401(k) plan. An employee interested in moving unused flexible credits into the Section 401(k) plan simply makes two elections: first, to take unused credits in cash and second, to reduce salary by a comparable amount as a Section 401(k) contribution.

Separately, note that many "not-for-profit" employers (such as hospitals) and government organizations maintain defined contribution vehicles qualified under Section 403(b) or Section 457 of the Internal Revenue Code, which generally function much like Section 401(k) in terms of accepting salary deferral amounts and occasionally matching on employee funds contributed (although there are some important differences). Since passage of the 1986 tax act, which prohibited these types of organizations from offering new Section 401(k) plans, Section 403(b) and Section 457 arrangements remain the predominant forms of defined contribution plans available to nonprofit employers. However, neither vehicle may be linked directly to a Section 125 flexible program. Instead, employers interested in permitting the deposit of unused flexible program funds in the retirement vehicle must follow the two-step process outlined earlier.

(a)   IN GENERAL

Since 1981, when the IRS sanctioned individual elections to defer compensation, Section 401(k) salary reduction arrangements have experienced explosive growth. Today over 80 percent of major U.S. employers include a salary reduction feature in savings or profit sharing plans. Moreover, the popularity of these types of retirement savings arrangements most likely has been further enhanced by the 1986 tax act which limited the use of Individual Retirement Accounts (IRAs). For many employees, Section 401(k) still represents the most tax-effective way to save for retirement, even though the limits are lower than was the case before the 1986 tax act. (See Chapter Four for a summary of the contribution limits.)

In addition to the tax advantages, however, many companies provide an incentive for employees to participate in the plan: employer matching on employee funds contributed. In fact, matched savings plans comprise the majority of Section 401(k) arrangements—offered by over three-quarters of major companies with a salary deferral feature. Moreover, the rate of matching often is most attractive—over half of the plans match at a rate of 50 cents on each dollar contributed by the employee, while nearly one-quarter match employee contributions dollar for dollar. (Usually, employer matching occurs on only the first five or six percent of pay contributed by the employee.)

As a further inducement for employee participation, the majority of employers with Section 401(k) plans allow employees to have early access to monies contributed under the plan. Over 90 percent of employers permit withdrawal of employee contributions in the event of financial hardship, while over half allow employees to take a loan on Section 401(k) funds.

(b)   TAX CONSIDERATIONS

As is the case with salary reduction under Section 125, monies deferred into a Section 401(k) plan escape federal and most state income taxes. (Currently, the only exception is the state of Pennsylvania.) However, a number of municipalities tax Section 401(k) deferrals—this list of municipalities generally differs from those taxing Section 125 salary reduction amounts. (For comparison, see also the listing in Chapter Two.) The municipalities taxing Section 401(k) salary deferral amounts include:

- Birmingham, Alabama
- Wilmington, Delaware
- Jefferson County, Kentucky
- Louisville, Kentucky
- Owensboro, Kentucky
- Kansas City, Missouri
- St. Louis, Missouri
- Akron, Ohio
- Canton, Ohio
- Cincinnati, Ohio

- Cleveland, Ohio
- Columbus, Ohio
- Dayton, Ohio
- Toledo, Ohio
- Youngstown, Ohio
- Erie, Pennsylvania
- Philadelphia, Pennsylvania
- Pittsburgh, Pennsylvania
- Scranton, Pennsylvania

However, unlike salary reduction amounts under Section 125, salary deferrals under Section 401(k) are subject to social security taxation. Thus salary reductions under Section 401(k) have no impact on future social security benefits. (For the impact of Section 125 salary reduction on social security benefits, see also the illustration contained in Chapter Two.)

(c) COORDINATION WITH SECTION 125

Almost 60 percent of flexible programs treat Section 401(k) as part of the flexible program. That is, the opportunity to save for retirement (or other purposes) is communicated as another flexible program option. (Among the balance of employers, the majority consider Section 401(k) unrelated to the flexible program.) However, in terms of the flow of funds between plans, only 50 percent of those with employer credits permit employees to deposit unused flexible credits directly into the Section 401(k) plan. (In particular, financial institutions, where cash-or-deferred profit sharing is especially prevalent, more frequently include Section 401(k) as an option for unused credits.) In contrast, 84 percent of programs allow employees to take unused credits in cash.

To date, few employers have harnessed the two types of choice-making arrangements to allow the flow of funds in the opposite direction—from Section 401(k) to Section 125 as an additional source of credits. But this type of approach might hold considerable appeal, particularly in situations where an employer has a "rich" profit sharing formula, relatively low-valued medical benefits, and limited alternatives for generating sufficient credits in the flexible program (other than through the addition of new employer money). In these instances, the employer might mandate that some portion of the profit sharing allocation (for example, 8 percent from a 12 percent contribution in a given year) remain in the Section 401(k) plan, while the balance is made available for use in the flexible program, at employee election.

One determinant of linking the two types of choice making may be compatibility of the employer's payroll and recordkeeping systems. Most Section 401(k) plans are designed to accept employee contributions in the form of a percentage of pay. Under a flexible program, unused credits usually would be dispersed to employees as a specific-dollar amount (paid out each pay period or on a one-time basis). The recordkeeping system for the Section 401(k) plan needs to be able to accept specific-dollar amounts—a modification which may not be worth the administrative effort involved if both the number and dollar amount of deposits are expected to be low. (On the other hand, funds flowing in the opposite direction usually are easier to accommodate in the flexible program in that credit allocations to employees typically are based on a combination of a percentage of pay plus a flat-dollar amount.)

Another consideration that arises on linking the two forms of choice making is treatment of unused credits in the Section 401(k) plan. That is, will excess credits be eligible for employer matching funds if a match is part of the Section 401(k) plan design? Should matching still occur if unused credits represent the employee's only contribution in the plan? Finally, will unused credits be made available under the same terms and conditions that apply for loan or withdrawal of other Section 401(k) funds?

(d)   EFFECT OF SECTION 415 LIMITS

As noted in Chapter Nine on Flexible Spending Accounts (and elsewhere in the book), the Section 415 limits may pose special problems for lower-paid employees when an employer sponsors both a Section 401(k) plan and a flexible program using salary reduction. The effect of these limits is felt most significantly when the salary reduction amounts are quite high, and it occurs whether or not the Section 125 and Section 401(k) plans are linked. (Separately, note that the Section 415 issue also arises for nonprofit and government employers using salary reduction under both Section 125 and alternative defined contribution vehicles.)

In general, Section 415 of the Internal Revenue Code limits contributions to (and payments from) qualified retirement plans. One of the limits within Section 415 caps the total annual addition that may be made to a defined contribution plan on behalf of an employee to the lesser of $30,000 or 25 percent of pay. It is the 25 percent of pay limit on the annual addition that may create the problem for lower-paid employees. For purposes of determining the annual addition, Section 415 generally defines pay as W-2 compensation. Thus all salary reduction amounts—whether used to make contributions to the Section 401(k) plan or for the purchase of benefits in the Section 125 program—are subtracted from the employee's pay before determining the maximum annual addition permitted to defined contribution retirement vehicles.

Separately, the annual addition counts all amounts contributed to the Section 401(k) plan, including employee salary deferrals (which are treated as an employer contribution); any amounts the employee contributes on an after-tax basis; actual employer contributions, including matching contributions; and any forfeitures which are allocated to employees. (In some plans, forfeitures arising from unvested amounts are allocated to remaining participants. In most plans, forfeitures are used to reduce the employer's matching or profit sharing contribution.)

The effect of this interaction between Sections 415, 401(k), and 125 is best illustrated through example. (For simplicity, the following examples concentrate solely on the effects of salary reduction and ignore any other factors such as employer contributions, employee after-tax contributions, and forfeitures which generally would worsen the Section 415 problem for lower-paid employees.)

Assume an employee earns $20,000 per year and contributes 16 percent of pay to the Section 401(k) plan through salary reduction.

Example 1:

Gross pay	= $20,000
Section 401(k) salary reduction	= 16% of $20,000, or $3,200
W-2 pay	= $16,800
Maximum annual addition under Section 415	= 25% of W-2 pay = .25 × $16,800, or $4,200
$3,200 ≤ $4,200	PASS 415 TEST

This deferral is within the Section 415 limit, being less than $30,000 or 25 percent of pay.

If the employee, however, also wants to use salary reduction to contribute $5,000 to a flexible spending account, a different circumstance results.

Example 2:

Gross pay	= $20,000
Section 401(k) salary reduction	= 16% of $20,000, or $3,200
Section 125 salary reduction	= $ 5,000
W-2 pay	$20,000
	− 3,200
	− 5,000
	= $11,800
Maximum annual addition under Section 415	= 25% of W-2 pay
	= .25 × $11,800, or $2,950
$3,200 > $2,950	FAIL 415 TEST

Therefore, this employee's use of salary reduction under both Sections 401(k) and 125 would violate the Section 415 limits. As a result, the employee would have to reduce salary reduction contributions under either Section 401(k) or Section 125 to meet the constraints of the Section 415 limits.

The effect of the Section 415 limits diminishes as pay increases. This can be illustrated using the facts in the second example but assuming gross pay of $30,000.

Example 3:

Gross pay	= $30,000
Section 401(k) salary reduction	= 16% of $30,000, or $4,800
Section 125 salary reduction	= $ 5,000
W-2 pay	$30,000
	− 4,800
	− 5,000
	= $20,200
Maximum annual addition under Section 415	= 25% of W-2 pay
	= .25 × $20,200, or $5,050
$4,800 ≤ $5,050	PASS 415 TEST

Absent large salary reduction amounts under Section 125, employers generally would encounter the Section 415 limits only in the context of very high-paid employees. Until involved with the design of a flexible program using salary reduction, few employers might have reason to suspect that the Section 415 limits may create special problems for lower-paid employees. But the interaction of salary reduction with the Section 415 limits needs to be examined whether or not retirement is included as a direct choice area under the flexible program.

§ 11.4   PENSION OPTIONS OUTSIDE THE FLEXIBLE PROGRAM

Conceptually, for an employer to offer true choice making in the pension area, the goal would be to allow employees to (1) reduce pension benefits in exchange for cash or credits that could be used for other benefit purchases or (2) apply credits from other areas to the purchase of additional pension benefits. However, for a host of technical (and practical) reasons, few employers structure pension options in this manner. Defined benefit pension plans are not one of the permissible choice areas that may be offered within a Section 125 program. Moreover, pension rules largely prohibit the selling (or other reduction) of accrued pension rights.

Instead, the few employers (4 percent) who include pension as a choice area under the flexible program (but not under the Section 125 plan) do so through alternative means. Although approaches vary, the choice offered employees is generally the purchase (only) of supplemental amounts. In effect, the concept is similar to a contributory pension plan except that both the amount and the cost of the pension increment are known in advance. (For this reason, the concept is referred to as pension equivalents.) Generally, the funding source is solely employee after-tax contributions, although the employer may choose to subsidize the cost of the options.

Consider, for example, a design that allows employees to buy an annuity of $10 to $100 per month, in $10 increments, payable from age 60. (The amount purchased is actuarially decreased or increased for earlier or later commencement.) Employees pay an annual premium based on their current age and the amount of supplement they want to purchase. For example, an employee might purchase an additional $50 per month, commencing at age 60, for an annual price tag based on the employee's current age.

The pricing and funding of the pension equivalents can occur through either of two instruments. One instrument might be the employer's existing qualified pension trust. This approach would offer the most latitude for design and pricing of the options because the employer would stand behind the benefit promise. For example, if the employer wanted to price the options in a low-cost manner for employees, aggressive actuarial assumptions could be used to determine the price tags. However, if the aggressive assumptions were not realized by the pension trust, the employer would have to make up for any shortfall. (On the other hand, conservative actuarial assumptions could be used to minimize the potential for such a shortfall.)

The other alternative might be an insurance contract. This alternative provides the greatest financial protection to the employer, but it occurs at the expense of flexibility in pricing the options for employees. The benefits are fully insured so the potential need for additional employer contributions is eliminated. Another potential concern, however, is that design may be limited by underwriting restrictions of the carrier.

Table 11.1 illustrates the differences that might arise in the prices charged to employees under the two types of funding instruments. The table shows the single premium for an annuity of $10 per month beginning at age 60, based on an insured contract and employer pension funding that uses relatively aggressive actuarial assumptions (9.5 percent interest). (Note that the figures are shown for illustrative purposes only; actual rates would vary based on current market conditions, employer funding assumptions, and so forth.)

Thus an employee currently age 25 interested in purchasing an additional pension amount of $50 per month beginning at age 60 would be charged either $700 (5 × $140) or $225 (5 × $45), depending on the financing instrument adopted by the employer. This type of pricing effect will have considerable impact on an employer's decision of whether to include pension options under a flexible program, as well as on the appeal of these options to employees.

Table 11.1
Relative Price Tags for Pension Equivalent of
$10 Per Month Commencing at Age 60
(Insured vs. Funded Arrangement)

Current Age of Employee	Annual Pricetag	
	Insured	Funded
25	$140	$ 45
35	230	110
45	430	270
55	890	670

The preceding discussion presumes that the employer is interested in applying the principles of choice making to the retirement area for purposes of allowing employees to supplement future retirement income. An alternative motivation for examining retirement on design of a flexible program may be as a means of releasing credits as a funding source for the flexible program. Although used infrequently in recent years, this approach could have merit in situations where the employer already is considering the consolidation of different pension plans (e.g., after a merger or acquisition) or generally reevaluating the structure of a pension plan that provides higher benefits than may be necessary for competitive reasons.

Although a cutback in previously accrued benefits cannot occur, a different strategy may be to reduce the accrual rate for future service only. All or a portion of the savings attributable to the reduction in future service benefits may be used as a credit generator within the flexible program. Employees would have the option to use those funds inside the flexible program, possibly with an option to retain the retirement aspect of those funds through deposit in a companion Section 401(k) plan.

§ 11.5   DESIGN CONSIDERATIONS

(a)   TYPE OF APPROACH

In contrast to other benefit areas, fewer employers have designed flexible programs to offer choices in retirement. Defined benefit pension plans in particular only rarely are incorporated under a flexible approach, and that is usually only to allow employees to buy supplemental pension amounts through a design constructed outside the Section 125 plan (typically outside the pension plan as well). Instead, most employers have regarded Section 401(k) as the vehicle through which to accomplish choice making in the retirement area whether or not that plan is directly linked to the flexible program.

For most employers, the level and structure of existing retirement plans will exert primary influence on any decisions relating to the flexible program. For example, an employer with an already "rich" defined benefit pension plan may have little incentive to offer even more under a flexible approach. Instead (depending on other considerations), introduction of a flexible program may provide the impetus for a cutback in that plan—assuming a substantial portion of the cost savings would flow through to employees in the form of higher credits or expanded benefit options under the flexible program. Similarly, an employer with generous matching or profit sharing allocations in a Section 401(k) plan might find that linkage with the flexible program (for deposit of unused credits) accentuates the number of employees reaching the maximum deferral or Section 415 limits.

However, the majority of employers may find themselves in other situations—namely, recognizing that employees would welcome an additional opportunity to supplement pension income, having enough room in the Section 401(k) plan to accept unused credits, and (perhaps) seeking an additional source of credits for the flexible program. In these situations, the following checklist of considerations may prove helpful.

- Would enough employees elect retirement choices to justify any added administrative expense involved in developing pension options or modifying recordkeeping systems to accept the flow of funds between Sections 401(k) and 125, or both?
- Given the expected flexible program credit structure, what is the likely amount of deposits—to either arrangement?
- How much room exists in the Section 401(k) plan to accept an additional source of contributions?
- How important is a cash option to employees?
- Where does the pension plan rank relative to competitive norms?
- How well understood is the existing pension plan?
- What parallelism (if any) in terms of matching, withdrawal, and so forth, will be accorded unused credits deposited in the Section 401(k) plan—versus salary deferral amounts?
- How would pension options be funded? How much risk is the employer willing to bear in terms of the potential for future subsidization?

(b) LIMITS ON CONTRIBUTIONS

As explained earlier, the combined use of salary reduction under Sections 401(k) and 125 can create the situation where some lower-paid employees may reach the Section 415 defined contribution plan limits. Most of the potential for this occurring can be contained through adjusting the caps on use of salary reduction—percent-of-pay deferral limits in the Section 401(k) plan and dollar maximums on flexible spending accounts. However, designing a fail-safe solution—one in which every employee who elects the absolute maximum in each area will still satisfy the Section 415 limits—may require the placement of caps so low as to be unduly restrictive for the majority of other employees. Therefore, it is usually necessary to test for the limits and develop a contingency plan for those who make excess elections.

Basically, the options include unilaterally mandating which excess salary reductions will be scaled back (Section 125 or Section 401(k)) or counseling with the employees to determine which reductions will have the least effect in their situation. For example, trimming salary reduction contributions to a flexible spending account generally makes more sense than scaling back Section 401(k) deferrals which are eligible for an employer match. (A dependent care spending account in particular may be the most likely area for reduction because the employees so affected generally will be eligible for an alternative tax credit on all or a portion of dependent care expenses.) However, pinpointing precisely where the cutbacks should occur is difficult to generalize, given the wide variety in benefit programs and employee demographics. Each employer's program and each employee's own unique circumstances will influence the setting of priorities for scaling back excess contributions.

Part Four

Structure and Financing

Twelve

Prices and Credits

§ 12.1 INTRODUCTION

If flexible compensation were viewed as a car, the pricing and credit structure would be recognized as the engine. It is the pricing and credit structure that puts the program in motion—or brings it to a standstill. Employees choose from their "menu" of options by comparing the prices for the benefit choices to the dollars available to spend and matching the various alternatives to their individual needs. If the pricing and credit structure is not well thought through, excessive employer costs or too many employees electing the same option could result. These types of results defeat the purposes of a flexible compensation program. Employer costs should be controlled, not unbridled. Employee selections should be those which best meet individual needs. The typical employee workforce has diverse needs, and those needs should manifest themselves by members selecting a wide variety of benefit options.

The two components of the structure—prices of the options and credits (or benefit dollars) available to employees—often are considered the same thing. In reality, they are like two sides of a coin, different but closely interrelated. For example, program prices may actually encompass a portion of the credit allocation in terms of a price subsidy. Nonetheless, a company will find the task of developing a pricing and credit structure more manageable if the two components are viewed separately.

Accordingly, this chapter discusses the two components separately, but not without frequent reference to their interdependence. The chapter is organized as follows.

The first section examines the setting of objectives for the financial structure of a flexible program and demonstrates how objectives influence the pricing of options and the allocation of credits. The next section explores the pricing of program options, focusing first on pricing short-term benefits (medical, dental, and vision) and next on pricing long-term benefits (life insurance and long-term disability). (See also the separate chapters within Part III for a brief discussion of pricing and credit generation for other benefits—namely, vacation, retirement, and other types of death and disability coverage.) Subsequently, the discussion moves on to the derivation and allocation of credits under a flexible program. The chapter concludes with ways to analyze the total structure for purposes of determining feasibility.

It should be noted that while the focus of the chapter is on first-year pricing and credit allocation, the same processes and procedures apply for subsequent-year changes in the financial structure of a flexible program. (See also Chapter Twenty on financial analysis for additional discussion of subsequent-year pricing.)

§ 12.2   SETTING OBJECTIVES

(a)   FOUR PRICING AND CREDIT OBJECTIVES

After an organization has developed the basic design of a flexible compensation program, the next phase is to price the options and determine the sources, amount, and allocation of credits. Neither of these steps can be accomplished, however, without examination of employer objectives for the financial structure of a flexible program. Experience shows that employers frequently have four goals or objectives they want to accomplish through the pricing and credit structure. These objectives may be summarized as follows:

- **Option prices should be set realistically, based on anticipated experience.**   That is, the prices of the benefit options should fully support the claims those options are expected to experience. Using realistic prices will enhance employee understanding and appreciation of program costs and allow benefit choices to be made freely without the influence of incentives or disincentives.

- **Flexible credits should be allocated equally.**   That is, each employee should receive an equal dollar amount or percentage of pay in flexible credits. If benefit dollars are to be considered another form of compensation, allocating credits based on age, number of dependents, and so forth, represents an inappropriate allocation of employer dollars—akin to awarding pay increases on factors other than merit.

- **There should be no losers under the program.**   That is, to prevent negative employee perceptions of the new program, each employee should be able to repurchase prior coverage (or if unavailable, the most comparable coverage) with no increase in costs.
- **There should be no additional employer cost.**   That is, a reason for adopting a flexible compensation program is to enhance the organization's ability to control costs. In keeping with this goal, the employer should not incur additional cost for benefits due to implementation of the flexible compensation program.

(b)   FOUR PRICING AND CREDIT APPROACHES

As desirable as each of these four objectives might be, it is generally impossible to achieve all four simultaneously under a flexible program. The primary reason is that most organizations currently do not allocate employer dollars for benefits equally to all employees. That is, most benefit programs today contain subsidies. One example appears in life insurance, where all employees may be charged a flat rate per $1,000 of insurance regardless of age, resulting in a subsidy of older employees by younger employees. Another area is medical coverage, where employees with dependents may not pay the full value of the dependent coverage, resulting in a subsidy of employees with families by the employer.

Consider an example of the pressures created for a flexible program structure when medical benefits for dependents currently are heavily subsidized. In a typical situation, an employer might have medical claims costs that average $1,000 for a single employee, and $2,500 for an employee with dependents. As illustrated in Example 12.1, the

Example 12.1
Current Medical Plan Claim Costs (Per Employee)

| | Employee Coverage Status | |
	Single	Family
Annual medical claims cost	$1,000	$2,500
Employee contributions	0	(500)
Employer cost	$1,000	$2,000
Percent of employees in status group	50%	50%
Average cost	$1,500	

employer might require contributions from the family employee, but employer cost still would amount to $1,000 for the single employee and $2,000 for the family employee, even though average cost for the covered group might be $1,500.

The employer wants to implement a flexible program offering options in medical. One option will be the current plan (Option A), but the two new options will be lesser-valued plans—Option B which is valued at 80 percent of the current plan and Option C which carries 70 percent of the current plan's value. Claims cost under each of the options is expected to be as follows:

Expected Medical Claims under Flexible Program Options (Per Employee)

	Single	Family
Option A (current plan)	$1,000	$2,500
Option B		
(valued at 80% of Option A)	$ 800	$2,000
Option C		
(valued at 70% of Option A)	$ 700	$1,750

The issue for the employer is how to structure the pricing of the options and allocate credits to employees for the purchase of those options, but in a manner that achieves all four of the objectives cited earlier—realistic option pricing, equal allocation of credits, no losers under the program, and no additional employer cost. In general, an organization has four basic approaches or alternatives to choose from for the structuring of prices and credits. These include allocating credits on the basis of (1) family coverage costs, (2) average cost for all employees, (3) an actuarially determined amount, or (4) the cost of single employee coverage. But as is explained next, each approach will achieve only three of the four employer objectives—none will achieve all four objectives.

(1) Family Credits

The first approach is the family credit allocation (see Table 12.1). This approach involves allocating enough credits so the most costly employee (in this case, the employee covering a family) will incur no additional cost.

Table 12.1
The Family Credit Approach

	Single	Family
Option A (current plan)	$1,000	$2,500
Option B	$ 800	$2,000
Option C	$ 700	$1,750
Credits	$2,000	$2,000
Average cost per employee	$2,000	

Objectives Achieved

1. **Experience-based (realistic prices)**
2. **Equal credits**
3. **No losers**
4. No additional employer cost

With this approach, the first three objectives are attained. Prices are based on expected claims. Each employee receives an equal amount of credits—$2,000 worth. No employee need incur any additional cost.

The employee covering a family under this approach must pay $500 for Option A—which is no change from the prior plan. However, the single coverage employee experiences a windfall of $1,000 at the expense of the employer, raising average employee cost from $1,500 to $2,000 per employee. Objective 4 is not achieved.

(2)   Average Credits

The second approach simply calculates average cost of the current plan per covered employee and allocates that amount in credits to each employee (see Table 12.2).

Table 12.2
The Average Credit Approach

	Single	Family
Option A (current plan)	$1,000	$2,500
Option B	$ 800	$2,000
Option C	$ 700	$1,750
Credits	$1,500	$1,500
Average cost per employee	$1,500	

Objectives Achieved

1. **Experience-based (realistic prices)**
2. **Equal credits**
3. No losers
4. **No additional employer cost**

Again, prices are based on expected claims, and the credit allocation is equal for all employees. Also, by definition, this approach produces no additional employer cost—the credits equal the average cost of the prior plan. However, the approach produces both winners and losers. That is, there are employees who are better off *and* employees who are worse off relative to the coverage they had under the prior plan. For instance, the employee covering a family under Option A will now pay $1,000 versus $500 under the prior plan. Objective 3 is not reached.

(3) Actuarial Credits

The third alternative is referred to as the actuarial approach (see Table 12.3). This method allocates credits based on the average cost of each employee to the employer prior to the flexible compensation program. The allocation takes into account the differing cost of employees based on whether or not they cover dependents.

Objectives Achieved

1. **Experience-based (realistic prices)**
2. Equal credits
3. **No losers**
4. **No additional employer cost**

Table 12.3
The Actuarial Approach

	Single	Family
Option A (current plan)	$1,000	$2,500
Option B	$ 800	$2,000
Option C	$ 700	$1,750
Credits	$1,000	$2,000
Average cost per employee	$1,500	

There are no winners and losers because employees can choose Option A and receive the same coverage at the same cost as under the prior plan. However, some employees (i.e., those not covering dependents) may feel it is inappropriate that those covering dependents receive an additional $1,000 in benefit value from the employer. Benefit pay equity (Objective 2) is not achieved.

(4) Single Coverage Credits

The fourth alternative is the single coverage credit approach (see Table 12.4). Credits are allocated to all employees at a level equal to the average cost of the employee-only (single) coverage.

Objectives Achieved

1. Experience-based (realistic prices)
2. **Equal credits**
3. **No losers**
4. **No additional employer cost**

In order to meet the objective of no losers, prices for family coverage are adjusted downward so the out-of-pocket cost to employees remains the same. This, of course, is in contradiction to Objective 1. Prices for family coverage now are unrealistically low, with each option priced at $1,000 less than the expected cost. Also, relationships between the options are misleading for family coverage. Option C is valued at 70 percent of Option A, but it now appears to be worth 50 percent of Option A ($750/$1500 = 50 percent). Finally, the relationship between coverage levels is inaccurate. For instance, Option C for family coverage costs

Table 12.4
The Single Credit Approach

	Single	Family
Option A (current plan)	$1,000	$1,500
Option B	$ 800	$1,000
Option C	$ 700	$ 750
Credits	$1,000	$1,000
Average cost per employee	$1,500	

$50 more than Option C for single coverage. In reality, the option is worth $1,050 more. Thus it is more difficult for employees to make reasonable decisions when prices are unreflective of true cost or value.

(c) Adopting a Strategy

The pricing and credit structure for a flexible program creates the potential for a dilemma although it is one that can be remedied by setting priorities. Addressing key issues such as those that follow can help an organization establish a strategy for the structure of a flexible program.

- What broad organizational goals should be reflected in the pricing and credit structure?

    Addressing this question will surface organizational attitudes toward pay equity (Objective 2) and its appropriateness within an organization's culture. That is, are benefits viewed primarily as protection for employees, which may indicate that differing credits may be appropriate for employees with greater need for protection? Or do benefits represent a portion of an employee's total compensation, which may argue against differentiation by family status or age? Concerns about competitive position may also arise, both in terms of employee recruitment and cost control. Moreover, how this question is answered will lead to decisions on the importance of each of the other objectives.

- What are the objectives for the flexible compensation program?

    If future cost management is a goal, the employer may insist on experienced-based prices (Objective 1) where the cost is effectively severed from the form of benefits, and no hidden costs exist in the form of price subsidies. The use of realistic prices effectively forces the employer's cost to be equal to the credits allocated to employees. Thus the employer cost is more easily identified and managed. If immediate cost containment is a goal, no additional cost (Objective 4) at the program's genesis would likely be a requirement.

    If immediate cost reduction is a goal, by definition, some employees will be losers (Objective 3) either through reduced coverage or increased employee contributions. The employer may also want to enhance the employee's appreciation of benefit value which would incline the organization toward a realistic pricing structure (Objective 1) to give employees the most accurate indication of that value.

The preceding discussion focuses on only a few of the possible program objectives and their implications for pricing and credit allocation. The point is that these objectives should be considered when adopting a strategy for the structure of a flexible program.

- What is the current employee mood or morale?

The success of a flexible compensation program will vary depending on employee reaction to the organization's pricing and credit strategy. For example, the idea of benefit losers (Objective 3) may or may not be acceptable, depending upon the organization's financial situation and the benefit programs of competitors. On the other hand pay equity in benefits (Objective 2) may not be an issue. The current employee mood should be taken into account when the organization develops its price/credit strategy.

After considering questions such as these and setting priorities, an organization's strategy will begin to form. The strategy may include all four of the basic approaches discussed earlier, a combination of several, or some variation as will be discussed later in this chapter. What the objective-setting process will certainly do, though, is crystallize a price/credit strategy that is consistent with the organization's desires and set the stage for the making of decisions on prices and credits.

§ 12.3   PRICING PLAN OPTIONS

When pricing options in a flexible program, it is helpful to separate benefits into two categories: short-term benefits and long-term benefits. Short-term benefits are those where claim frequency is high and per claim amount is relatively low. Benefits in this category include medical, dental, and vision. The plans are heavily utilized because of their nature, and plan costs are evaluated in terms of annual claims. For those many employees who do incur claims, the average claim size is typically small compared to long-term benefits.

Long-term benefits are those where claim frequency is low and per claim amount is high. Benefits in this category include life insurance and long-term disability. Most employees will never incur a claim for these benefits, but if they do, the claim is large. Claim costs can fluctuate dramatically from year to year. Costs are not evaluated in terms of annual claims but in terms of the probabilities of claims and the expected annual costs based largely on actuarial data. The long-term contingencies being protected against are severe in nature, typically ending an employee's active working career.

The following discussion covers the pricing of short-term benefits. Although the focus is on medical benefits specifically, the methodology is appropriate for all short-term benefits. The next section covers the pricing of long-term benefits.

(a) SHORT-TERM BENEFITS

The pricing of benefit options can vary dramatically, depending on the organization's objectives for prices and the program in general. No matter what the objectives are and what pricing scheme is desired, actual or realistic prices for the benefit options should be determined first.

Realistic prices are those prices which could reasonably be expected to support the claim costs. This may be true for each option individually or for all the options under one type of benefit. Basically, the pricing process can be divided into six steps: (1) Data Collection and Analysis, (2) Option Pricing, (3) Subgroup Pricing, (4) Anticipation of Change, (5) Pricing Scheme Adjustments, and (6) No Coverage Option Pricing. The first four steps are used to determine the realistic prices.

(1) Data Collection and Analysis

The first step in pricing involves collecting data on the current plan over the last few years. This includes claims data for the covered group, administration fees, premium costs for an insured plan, and participation data (by dependent coverage category). The short-term nature of these benefits makes annual claims of the plan a reasonably good indicator of the true future cost of the plan.

For pricing decisions, it is preferable to use "claims incurred" for a given year rather than "claims paid." Claims incurred represent all the claims attributable to a given year, including those actually incurred in one year but paid in the succeeding year. Since "covered employee" data is usually tracked for the plan year, a more accurate "claims per covered employee" can be calculated from this amount. Also, incurred claims experience will reflect more accurately the impact of plan changes because changes tend to be made at the beginning of a year. (If available, this data also should be broken down by subgroups, as will be discussed later.)

The collection of data serves two purposes. One is that the data will serve as the basis for pricing all of the options in a benefit category. The other is that the data should provide some indication of past cost trends and which factors to use to anticipate cost increases for the coming year.

During this process the organization should review the data which is already available and determine what additional data should be collected in the future. The employer will want to set up data-tracking mechanisms now as data will be crucial to future-year pricing, to determining the program's financial position, and to managing the program's costs.

Organizations should recognize that the reflection of a plan's claims experience in prices for future years might very well lag by one year. New prices will need to be developed at least two to three months prior to the beginning of the next plan year. Data will be available for only seven or eight months of the current year when the pricing analysis for the next year needs to be performed. Employers will be forced either to allow the reflection of experience in pricing to lag by a year or to attempt to project the experience based on partial-year data.

(2)   Preliminary Option Pricing

After claims data has been gathered and a per-covered-employee cost determined, the next step is option pricing. Option pricing consists of determining a fair price for each benefit option, based on covered employee claims experience in the current plan.

Option pricing requires that a "relative value" for each option be determined, usually based on the current plan. Using these relative values and current claims data, preliminary option prices can be calculated. For example, if the employer calculates that the current plan (Option A) is worth $1,000 per employee, and two new options, B and C, are worth 80 percent and 70 percent (respectively) of the current plan, the preliminary prices would be set as shown in Table 12.5.

So far, the prices are preliminary because they are based on claims data that is one or possibly two years old, and adjustments have not yet been made for plan changes, adverse selection, or different employee utilization patterns. A later step will involve adjusting the preliminary prices for these and other changes.

Relative values are usually calculated using insurance underwriting methodology. A value is determined for the base plan according to the characteristics (e.g., deductibles, out-of-pocket maximums, coinsurance

Table 12.5

Option	Relative Value	Base Plan Claims Per Employee	Price
A (current plan)	100%	$1,000	$1,000
B	80%	$1,000	$ 800
C	70%	$1,000	$ 700

percentages) of the plan. Values are then calculated for the options, and a relative value is determined by dividing the option value by the base plan value. Relative values usually are most easily calculated by the employer's insurer or consulting actuary.

(3) Preliminary Subgroup Pricing

Subgroup pricing is a method of dividing the pricing structure into smaller groups with similar characteristics. Subgroup pricing helps minimize adverse selection by creating more equitable prices for different groups of employees. The most common category is dependent coverage. The range of alternative dependent categories includes:

- Employee only, family
- Employee only, employee plus one, employee plus two or more dependents
- Employee only, employee plus spouse, employee plus children, family, or
- Employee only, employee plus one, employee plus two, employee plus three dependents, and so forth.

Other pricing subgroups might include location for organizations with employees in multiple locations or might be based on age of the employee. Geographical (location) pricing is becoming more common for medical benefits, particularly when the claims experience varies dramatically by location due to underlying differences in the cost of medical services. Age pricing (for example, in 5- or 10-year age brackets) is utilized very infrequently but is likely to become somewhat more common in the future. The differences in dental and vision costs have not been large enough to warrant making these distinctions.

Subgroup pricing is based in part on an organization's own experience if the claims data is available. However, even if the data is available, it typically is not used exclusively. This is because the number of covered employees in each subgroup may be small, and consequently the claims data may not be as reliable as the data for the entire plan. Therefore, prices should be checked for reasonableness based on related data from outside sources.

(4)   Anticipation of Changes

After the preliminary prices have been derived, some adjustment will be required. The preliminary prices are based on claims data a year or two old. Annual claim costs, especially medical claims, cannot be expected to remain static. There are many reasons why claims experience will likely change:

- **Medical Inflation.**   General increases in the cost of health care services are to be expected. One measure of medical inflation is the medical component of the Consumer Price Index. In a recent five-year period (1983-1987), the compound average increase measured 7 percent—versus only half that level for general inflation.
- **Technological Improvements.**   The cost of medical care may increase at a faster rate than medical inflation alone because of the expense of new technology to improve diagnosis and treatment.
- **Employer Cost Leverage.**   If features such as deductibles and out-of-pocket maximums are not indexed or periodically adjusted for inflation, the percentage of each medical claim paid for by the employer will increase over time. The effect of fixed schedules and maximums is in the opposite direction.
- **Plan Changes.**   Claims data from earlier periods require adjusting for any recent plan changes which affect benefit levels.
- **Health Care Utilization.**   As changes emerge in the design of plan benefits and in the way health care is being provided, utilization of health care services may change (either positively or negatively).
- **Adverse Selection.** In a flexible compensation program, employees are given a financial incentive to choose a plan which best fits their needs. However, if the probability of their need is too predictable, adverse selection will result. (See also Chapter Thirteen on adverse selection.)

In the late-1980s, a typical range for estimates of employer cost increases has been 12 percent to 18 percent per year, excluding changes due to plan design, utilization, and adverse selection. For consistency, such an estimate should be compared to the current plan's historical cost increases.

If plan design changes were made, the cost impact can be reasonably estimated through the relative-value pricing methodology. As for utilization changes and adverse selection, their expected impact is generally not included in the prices until subsequent years when the actual results of the program can be measured. Changes in utilization after introducing a flexible program usually produce reductions in cost (because employees are often moving to medical plans with greater cost sharing through deductibles and coinsurance levels), and predicting the amount of this change is exceedingly difficult. Estimating expected adverse selection is also very speculative, and reflecting an estimate in the pricing could actually exacerbate the adverse selection problem, so adverse selection estimates are also typically excluded.

(5) Pricing Scheme Adjustments

The preceding material describes how realistic prices are developed. If these are not the prices the organization prefers to use, there are alternatives. The alternatives are generally in one of two categories: "carve-out" pricing and subsidized pricing.

- **Carve-Out Pricing.** This pricing scheme is essentially a different way to communicate realistic prices. For instance, if the program is designed with a core or required minimum option, the employer may prefer to have employees see a price of $0 for this option. Alternatively, the employer may want to use this scheme to minimize the visible difference in credits (or prices) by coverage category (family versus single). For example, assume the realistic prices for medical options in a flexible compensation program are as follows:

	Price	
Option	Single	Family
A	$1,000	$2,500
B	$ 800	$2,000
C	$ 600	$1,500

If the employer believes a core option should be implied, a pricing scheme (called core carve-out) can subtract the price of Option C from Options A and B as follows:

	Price	
Option	Single	Family
A	$400	$1,000
B	$200	$ 500
C	$ 0	$ 0

(Alternatively, the core could be single coverage under Option C with the result that all of the realistic prices—single and family—are simply reduced by $600.)

If the employer wishes to make it clear beyond a shadow of a doubt that the flexible compensation program is not a benefit reduction, the carve-out price will be Option A instead of C as follows:

	Price	
Option	Single	Family
A	$ 0	$ 0
B	$(200)	$ (500)
C	$(400)	$(1,000)

This second scheme is referred to as negative pricing because the prices represent additional credits the employee receives for choosing a certain option. Because prices are really credits in disguise, negative pricing is considered an appealing way to encourage employees to select a lower-valued option.

Carve-out pricing does include drawbacks. The employee will not have as full an appreciation of the total cost of the different options, and it is often difficult to explain to employees what the prices represent. Future price increases may also be more difficult to explain because they will be larger relative to the price shown. For example, if the prices for Option A rise 12 percent in one year and the prices for Option C rise 4 percent, the realistic prices for single coverage move to $1,120 ($1,000 × 1.12) for Option A and $624 ($600 × 1.04) for Option C. These may look quite reasonable to employees, but if the core carve-out approach is utilized, the price for Option A rises from $400 ($1,000 – $600) to $496 ($1,120 – $624), a full 24 percent.

The question of what to do with the $0 option will also surface. (That is, should the option always be free to the employee? When does the employer start charging for the option?) Finally, the carve-out pricing scheme is a less flexible cost-management tool because the approach tends to bind the company to cost increases in the $0 option instead of breaking the automatic escalation with a separation of prices and credits.

- **Subsidized Pricing.** Subsidized pricing represents an indirect form of credit allocation. "True prices" ultimately are equivalent to claims experience (or premiums charged by an insurance company in an insured situation). Prices that differ substantially from true prices are another form of credits being allocated to employees on a subsidized basis. The subsidies can take the form of across-the-board percentage subsidies (e.g., prices are 80 percent of realistic prices); constant flat-dollar subsidies (e.g., the price for covering dependents is $500 less than the actual cost); or simple price reductions. Whether subsidized prices reflect an added company cost will depend upon the interrelationship of prices and credits.

There are several reasons why an employer may opt for price subsidies. The employer may want to encourage the selection of certain options because of cost savings expected from that option. In other words, the employer may want to provide an incentive for employees to choose one option over another. Conversely, the employer may want to limit the potential for adverse selection in an option by encouraging more employees to select it (e.g., dental coverage). Subsidies may also be necessary if the first three objectives discussed earlier have priority.

Some companies try to avoid extensive price subsidies. One reason is that subsidies tend to skew employee selection decisions by masking the value of the benefit options. Subsidies also can restrict the ability of a flexible program to serve as a cost-management tool, because some of the costs are hidden and thus more difficult to exert control over. In addition, it can be difficult to reprice consistently in future years if prices are artificially derived from the start.

Many employers will utilize price subsidies initially although intending to eliminate them gradually over time. This strategy allows employees to adapt and accept the loss of subsidy, but not all in one year. However, in these cases, it may be advantageous to explicitly communicate the strategy to employees, so they recognize and accept increases from the previously subsidized levels when required.

(6) No Coverage Option Pricing

The issue of whether to allow employees to waive coverage, especially in medical, is an area for considerable debate within an organization. One area of concern is philosophical. What is the company's responsibility to ensure that employees are protected? Another concern is adverse selection—the fear that only the healthiest employees will choose no coverage and, therefore, receive significantly more in credits than the program would have paid in claims. This result would increase total employer costs. As discussed in Chapter Thirteen, adverse selection concern can usually be managed through design and pricing decisions. Moreover, employees cannot know their own health situation sufficiently to risk a year without coverage. Employees who choose no coverage almost always have coverage available under another medical plan (e.g., that of the spouse's employer), and there is no evidence these employees are healthier than other covered employees.

No coverage pricing is really a variation of negative pricing. The employer is trying to determine how many credits to give to someone opting out of coverage. In theory, the issue is a straightforward claims-cost question. Knowing what the average employer-paid claims would have been for these no coverage employees (assuming they had remained in the plan), would indicate exactly what the no coverage "price" should be. In practice the cost is unknowable.

Another issue relates to the generosity of the rebate for opting out of coverage. The claims cost of these employees is no longer left to chance occurrence during the year; it is fixed by the dollars given to these employees for selecting no coverage. Moreover, the dollars are hard dollars, not the soft-dollar exchange of prices and credits evident for employees who remain in the plan. Because of the lack of margin for error, the credits given for the no coverage option often are conservatively estimated at less than the expected value.

(b) LONG-TERM BENEFITS

Pricing long-term benefits bears some relation to short-term benefit pricing, but there are also striking differences. For instance, prices are rarely based on annual claims experience, the benefits are more often insured, and the benefits are designed to cover the employee and only minimally cover dependents, if at all. However, the pricing process for long-term benefits still involves consideration of the four pricing objectives and their priority (i.e., realistic prices, equal credits, no losers, and no additional employer cost). Here the equal credits objective typically relates to avoiding age-based differences, however, rather than coverage-category based differences. Setting objectives for long-term benefits will help guide the organization in the pricing process.

The long-term pricing process will also follow the same six steps as pricing short-term benefits although the manner in which these steps are addressed is quite different.

(1)   Data Collection and Analysis

Although collection and analysis of employer data is usually done, the information is almost always too sketchy to be sufficient for pricing purposes. For pricing long-term benefit plans, general actuarial data considered in conjunction with the characteristics of the employer's workforce is more appropriate. Also, if the benefits are insured, the employer's cost may be predetermined by insurance company rates.

(2)   Preliminary Option Pricing

Long-term benefits are typically expressed as a dollar amount of coverage or a percent of pay. Therefore, prices are expressed either on a per thousand basis or as a percent of pay, with the price of additional coverage relatively easy to calculate. LTD may represent an exception. In LTD, benefits are usually offset by social security or other disability benefits. The relative value of option prices will not be as directly related to the pay replaced. For example:

Option	Benefit Formula	Pay Replacement by Social Security	Actual Plan Pay Replacement
A	50% of pay less social security	30%	20%
B	60% of pay less social security	30%	30%

Cost of Option A = .5% of pay

Cost of Option $B \neq \dfrac{60\%}{50\%} \times .5\%$ of pay or .6% of pay

Cost of Option $B = \dfrac{30\%}{20\%} \times .5\%$ of pay or .75% of pay

The basis for these types of calculations tends to be more actuarial in nature and, therefore, may be more readily available from the employer's insurer or consulting actuary.

(3)   Preliminary Subgroup Pricing

Long-term benefits have fewer subgroup categories which are truly applicable for pricing (dependent coverage is very limited, geographic differences tend to be insignificant, and so forth). The one category that is very applicable, however, is age. Long-term benefits are significantly age related. Life insurance is the most obvious example, but the same is true for LTD.

Because of the close relationship between age and need for these long-term benefits, age-graded rates tend to be considered more equitable. Age-graded rates also decrease the potential for adverse selection by being more competitive with market rates, particularly for life insurance. For example, if a flat rate per $1,000 of coverage were charged for life insurance, younger employees could probably buy it cheaper on the open market. Older employees, however, would recognize the low price and purchase the coverage. The true cost of the benefit would then be much more than the flat rate being charged. Age-graded rates help eliminate this potential problem.

Age-graded life insurance rates can be acquired from the employer's insurance company or actuary. However, an even simpler solution for many organizations is to use the imputed income rates expressed in Revenue Code Section 79 for life insurance. The rates are reasonable and also eliminate imputed income calculations if amounts over $50,000 are paid with after-tax dollars. The current Section 79 rates vary by age from $.08 to $1.17 per month per $1,000 of coverage.

There are some considerations that relate to age-grading long-term benefit prices. Historically, if a flat rate has been charged, the new rate for older employees will be considerably higher. Older employees may not be able to purchase their previous coverage without a significant increase in contributions. Conversely, if the credit allocation is tied to the price of the coverage, large amounts of benefit dollars may be "given away" to older employees. In general, however, most organizations still use age-graded rates in their pricing structure for life insurance. Although the true cost of LTD coverage is also highly age related, the majority of companies do not vary LTD prices by age. It is not believed to be as critical an issue for LTD due to the lack of a large market of competitively priced individual policies (as is the case in life insurance).

(4) Anticipation of Changes

Unlike short-term benefit prices, which are adjusted for a variety of anticipated changes, long-term benefits are susceptible to only one primary influence—adverse selection. However, pricing for adverse selection in long-term benefits is extremely difficult. Adverse selection is better addressed by age-grading prices, limiting maximum benefits, limiting benefit increases from year to year, or including underwriting restrictions. Typically, prices are not adjusted for anticipated changes.

(5) Pricing Scheme Adjustments

Pricing scheme adjustments are also limited in scope. Price subsidies are one possibility. Subsidies are still common for LTD benefits but less so for life insurance. Some employers view LTD coverage as especially important and wish to encourage participation through subsidized prices. Employers also recognize that insurers are less anxious to cover LTD if participation is low, so they are more likely to feel compelled to support the benefit financially.

Some form of carve-out pricing is another possible pricing scheme. For example, if minimal LTD coverage is required as part of core benefits, the employer will often pay the cost. The employer could pay for the minimal LTD coverage by simply giving employees enough additional credits to purchase the coverage. Alternatively, the employer could price the minimal coverage at $0, implicitly paying for it. This $0 price tag makés it very clear to employees that the benefit is employer paid. The cost of options offering more LTD coverage would then be the incremental cost of the additional coverage.

In the life insurance area, a company may wish to introduce rates which vary by age group, but the increase in costs for older employers who had previously paid a flat rate (e.g., $.40/month/$1,000) may be unacceptable. As an intermediate position, the company may elect to introduce a modified age-related pricing scheme, for example $.15 to $.80 by age rather than the full Section 79 rates of $.08 to $1.17 by age.

As part of this step in the process, some preliminary financial analysis should be done, especially if prices are not directly related to costs. The most obvious example is when benefits are fully insured. If the rate charged by the insurance company is different from the option price tags, calculations can be made to determine if the prices are supporting benefit costs in the aggregate. If life insurance options are currently available, testing can be performed based on current selections by employees. A simple alternative method of testing is to assume all employees select one times pay. Similar methods can be used for LTD testing.

(6) No Coverage Option Pricing

No coverage option pricing is not nearly the financial issue it is for short-term benefits, especially medical plans. Claims are neither as frequent nor as predictable, so permitting no coverage is less of an invitation for adverse selection. However, the issue can be an emotional one. Considering that the contingency being covered (death or total and permanent disability) is a devastating one, employers are often reluctant to allow employees to go without coverage. Also, if credits are being allocated based on the age-related prices of the benefit, a large amount of benefit dollars can be generated for older employees. Employers may be unwilling to allow all of these dollars to be used for other purposes, especially when a lack of coverage can be very detrimental to employees and their beneficiaries. Therefore, no coverage credits are often "scaled back" to minimize the incentive to opt out and, in many cases, some minimal core coverage is required for long-term benefits.

§ 12.4 DETERMINING FLEXIBLE COMPENSATION CREDITS

Closely related to the setting of option prices is the generation of credits used to purchase the benefits. In one sense, credits are simply the other half of the equation. For instance, prices and credits can be manipulated to "net out" to the desired result for each employee. However, an approach such as this which only considers the net effect and not what prices and credits represent independently, fails to utilize the full potential of a flexible compensation program. Conversely, if prices represent the true expectation of the total cost of the benefits, employer-allocated credits represent the employer's expected cost. This approach, which fully separates the employer cost of benefits from the form of benefits provided, tends to be a highly effective means of cost management in that costs have been explicitly identified. This approach can also be readily communicated to employees because prices and credits represent easily understandable concepts. The separation of option prices and credits (or related variations) forms the basis of the following discussion.

Three key elements must be developed to form a credit structure for a flexible compensation program. These include the sources, the amount, and the allocation of credits.

When developing credits, the points discussed next apply to the second and later years as well as the first year of program operation. The flexible compensation program can serve as a long-term planning tool as well as a short-term solution.

(a) SOURCES OF CREDITS

Where does the money come from? Conceptually, the sources of funds for a flexible program originate with either the employer or the employee. Practically, how those funds are derived is somewhat more complicated. The employer usually is not making an arbitrary decision about the flexible credits and their origin. Rather, credits are generated from a combination of identified sources.

(1) Current Benefits

Current benefits that will become part of the flexible compensation program all have costs associated with them, net of any employee contributions. The fact that a benefit is included under the new flexible program creates a credit pool equal to the cost of those current benefits. This cost can be cut back, added to, or held constant depending on the cost strategy of the organization. In any event, prior plan costs represent a source of credits. Although this credit pool is created, the amount explicitly allocated to employees will usually take into account the pricing scheme. (This concept is discussed in more detail in a later section on allocation of credits.)

(2) Benefit Reductions

Another source of credits is benefit reductions—not necessarily reduction of the benefits included in the flexible program, but from reductions in other benefit areas. For example, an organization may conclude that retirement plan benefits (and resulting contributions) are too high and that a reduction is in order. Instead of absorbing all of the savings from cutting back future accruals to a retirement plan, some portion of the future savings may be passed on to employees in the form of credits. On the other hand, a benefit plan may be eliminated for one reason or another (e.g., a minimal vision plan may be dropped), and the cost savings may flow into the credit pool.

(3)   Additional Employer Money

A third source is simply additional employer money. The employer may want to add to the credit pool to provide dollars for a new benefit plan, to make the overall program more attractive, to reward employees for an especially profitable year, and so forth. Of course, this avenue only applies to those employers not wishing to reduce benefit costs.

(4)   Employee Salary Reduction

Depending on the coverages employees select, their credit allocation may not be sufficient to cover all benefit needs. To make up the shortfall, employees can use salary reduction to add dollars to the credit pool. The opportunity for employees to use salary reduction to increase credits is common practice. In fact, it is rarer in today's environment to have a flexible program that is fully employer-paid.

(b)   AMOUNT OF CREDITS

Defining the sources does not necessarily define the size of the credit pool, although identifying the sources helps set parameters for the amount. For instance, one source will be the cost of the current plans, such as medical. The employer, however, may not want to incur the same cost as at present for medical coverage, or the company may want to "take credit" for some of the tax savings that employees might realize if their contributions to medical are being changed to a pretax basis at the time the flexible program is being introduced. As the employer examines each of the benefit plans to be included in the flexible program, the company will want to evaluate current cost levels to see how much should be used to generate credits. Using this component approach, the employer can identify how many dollars from current benefits will be available for credits.

The employer will also be identifying the amount of additional dollars from possible reductions in other benefit areas or simply how much additional benefit cost the organization is willing to support. The fourth source, salary reduction, is largely an independent decision as employees determine whether to use salary reduction, if made available.

After the amount of credits generated from different sources has been identified, the employer needs to view the result in terms of what the credit pool actually represents: the employer cost of the benefit program. Ultimately, equating the total credit pool to benefit costs is the concept that makes flexible compensation an efficient benefit cost-management tool.

The decision on the amount of available employer credits should be considered for future years as well as the current year, at least in a strategic sense. Conceptually, a strategy should be developed for how the credit pool is intended to increase in future years. The decision may be as flexible as a totally discretionary decision every year, or it may be as structured as the amount necessary to support a specified level of benefits. The strategy may tie credit-pool increases to salary increases, company profitability, or even some outside index. The point is to bring future strategy into focus so that the flexible compensation program has some direction for managing benefit costs.

(c) ALLOCATION OF CREDITS

The third and final task of developing the credit structure is to determine how to allocate credits to employees. There are almost as many variations in credit allocation structures as there are flexible compensation programs. However, these structures generally flow directly from only a few key considerations: the concept of pay equity in benefits, the employee's ability to repurchase current (or equivalent) benefits, and organizational objectives.

(1) Pay Equity in Benefits

From the outset, if an employer wants to achieve pay equity in benefits (Objective 2 from the earlier discussion), prices for benefit options will be set realistically, and credits allocated on a per capita basis. Some organizations have adopted this structure in the first year. However, they have also accepted the consequences of this structure. Employees will be either better or worse off compared to their prior program. Many employers who agree with the concept of benefit pay equity cannot accept these consequences, at least not all in one year. Instead, many prefer to phase in the concept over a number of years.

Some organizations also have attempted to achieve apparent benefit pay equity by allocating equal credits and changing the prices to achieve the desired net result. However, a limitation of this approach is that it merely disguises in the prices the portion of the credit allocation that is not equal for all employees.

(2) Repurchase of Current Program

Ensuring each employee's ability to repurchase the current program or some other stated level of benefits was also discussed earlier as Objective 3—no losers under a flexible program. If this objective is a high priority, it will be a major factor in the design of the credit allocation structure. The most straightforward method of guaranteeing that each employee will be able to purchase a given level of benefits is through a component allocation structure.

Component allocation is a structure whereby credits are allocated to employees for each type of benefit, and the sum of the components is the employee's total credit allocation. A certain number of credits is provided for medical, dental, life insurance, vision, LTD, and so forth. In so doing, it is readily apparent where the credit shortfalls or excesses exist for each type of benefit. Component allocation is also consistent with credit source determination because the cost of the current benefit program is determined on a component basis. A component allocation method also lends itself better to a financial analysis of each of the types of benefits individually. Expected employer cost (credits) and expected total cost (prices) are available for each benefit to compare to actual employer cost and actual total cost.

Component credit allocation can be refined beyond benefit type to subgroups of employees in much the same manner as subgroup pricing. Credits can be allocated based on dependent status, either actual number of dependents or by coverage chosen. In addition, the credit allocation may vary by age or geography. An age or geography structure may be appropriate if prices are grouped on that basis. The component credit structure with a subgroup allocation does not necessarily mean employees will be able to purchase a given level of coverage, but it will be easier to measure and ensure the desired result for each employee.

Component credit allocation often leads to a formula type of allocation. Because of the different nature of benefits (some being pay-related and some not), the ultimate allocation may be based on a formula with a flat-dollar component and a percentage-of-pay component. For example, assume the credits allocated for each type of benefit are as shown in Example 12.2 for a given employee, age 45, and earning $40,000 per year.

Example 12.2
Component Credit Allocation

Benefit	Credits
Medical	$1,200
Dental	$ 200
Vision	$ 50
Death	1% of pay
LTD	.5% of pay

Formula:
$$\$1,450 + 1.5\% = \$1,450 +$$
$$(.015 \times \$40,000) = \$2,050$$

Depending on the subgroup breakdown, employees will have a formula fitting their own characteristics and situation.

Component credit allocation can also be accomplished implicitly through the pricing mechanism. The carve-out pricing method can actually be a component credit allocation method. To illustrate, consider some alternatives of a simple flexible medical plan that can be priced in different ways—using realistic prices, a core carve-out method, and negative prices—shown in Example 12.3.

Example 12.3
Component Credit Allocations through
Different Pricing Structures

	Option	Single	Family
Alternative 1:		*Realistic Prices*	
	A	$1,000	$2,500
	B	800	2,000
	C	600	1,500
Alternative 2:		*Core Carve-Out*	
	A	$ 400	$1,000
	B	200	500
	C	0	0
Alternative 3:		*Negative Pricing*	
	A	$ 0	$ 0
	B	(200)	(500)
	C	(400)	(1,000)

Using the core carve-out pricing scheme, each employee selecting single coverage implicitly receives $600 in credits, and each employee selecting family coverage implicitly receives $1,500 in addition to any direct credit allocation. Also, in the negative pricing scheme, the employee selecting family coverage receives $2,500. These examples should also help illustrate that unrealistic prices are really a variation of a credit allocation scheme. Some employers feel it is advantageous to provide credits implicitly through the prices, especially if credits are not allocated equally. In addition, implicit credit allocation tends to reduce an employer's concern over the cost of an employee selecting no coverage and taking the credits in cash. An "implicit" scheme locks some of the credits into the benefit selections, preventing employees from cashing in the options.

Component credit allocation is also useful for an explicit benefit-by-benefit recognition of an employer subsidy. This structure can be useful for an employer attempting to achieve an equal credit allocation in the medical plan, but doing so over a number of years. For example, an explicit subsidy can be provided which allows all employees to purchase the most valuable medical option in the first year. In future years, as prices and credits increase, however, the subsidy is held constant or even eliminated. To illustrate using the facts from the previous example:

	Realistic Prices	
Option	Single	Family
A	$1,000	$2,500
B	800	2,000
C	600	1,500
First year credits:		
All employees	$1,000	$1,000
Subsidy		
(Explicit)	0	1,500
Total credits	$1,000	$2,500

After the first year, the subsidy could be held constant or reduced, with the reduction either reallocated to employees on a per capita basis or used to reduce the cost of the benefit.

(3) Organizational Objectives

Because of their significance, employee benefit costs cannot be considered in a vacuum, and neither should the credit allocation formula for a flexible program. The organization's allocation of credits, be it an explicit allocation or implicit in the prices of the benefit options, is really an allocation of employer benefit dollars. Organizational objectives, then, will have an impact on the method of allocating those benefit dollars. Examination of organizational objectives will help illustrate this concept.

- **Cost Management.** An organization may feel management of benefit costs is a top priority. This objective would lead the organization to a very explicit credit allocation structure in which credits are equivalent to employer costs and no costs are hidden in the prices.
- **Profit Sharing.** Some organizations feel strongly that the sharing of successes and profits should permeate all aspects of the employee's relationship with the company, including benefits. This can be accomplished in the flexible compensation program by allocating more or less credits based on the profitability of a division or the company as a whole.
- **Service Recognition.** Employers may want to recognize and reward employees who are loyal to the organization. Credits may then vary by years of service.
- **Social Responsibility.** Some employers consider it a social responsibility to provide benefits to employees, independent of other benefit-related objectives. This responsibility may lead the employer to (1) support a selected level of benefits, (2) require employees to select a minimum level of coverage, (3) limit the employee's ability to cash out credits, (4) subsidize certain benefits that should be encouraged, (5) vary credits by neither profitability nor service, or (6) limit aggressiveness in managing costs.
- **Pay Equity.** Employers who believe pay equity in benefits is as important as in other forms of compensation may eventually want to allocate credits on a per capita basis.

The objectives an organization has for the allocation of credits will almost always have some internal inconsistencies. Identifying the priorities and finding the right mix of objectives can be a difficult step within the design of a flexible program.

§ 12.5 TESTING FOR FEASIBILITY OF THE PRICE/CREDIT STRUCTURE

Although the discussion has treated prices and credits as two independent components, both are intertwined. To determine the feasibility of the total structure, prices and credits must be viewed in combination. A key determinant of how the components fit together is the way employees are affected. In this regard, a winners and losers analysis can be extremely valuable.

In addition, an analysis of employer cost should be performed. The analysis will entail accumulating the credits explicitly allocated to employees, the expected value of the implicit credits (price subsidies), the hidden costs not recognized in the realistic prices, and the changes in costs due to employee selection patterns.

Finally, the structure should be reviewed with a broader perspective. Getting too close to all the "numbers" can obscure a primary purpose for a flexible program—meeting the needs of employees. Reviewing the structure for reasonableness can bring the program back into focus.

(a) WINNERS AND LOSERS ANALYSIS

Winners and losers analysis is simply comparing an employee's situation before and after implementation of the flexible compensation program. What were the benefits each employee was receiving prior to the new program? What was the employee's cost? How does this compare to the employee's cost for similar benefits purchased under the flexible approach? How many dollars are available for other uses if the employee chooses a different combination of benefits? What will the result be if the organization follows a different price/credit strategy in the future? To illustrate, a very simple first-year winners and losers analysis of a medical plan is provided in Example 12.4.

The analysis shows the additional cost (or dollars available) for employees relative to their cost for medical benefits under the prior plan. For example, the employee who selects family coverage must either pay an *additional* $500 to receive the same coverage as in the prior year or select a reduced coverage option and pay the same amount as in the prior year with Option B or less with Option C. Winners and losers analysis is an attempt to outline in dollars the employee's perspective of choices compared to the prior year. The analysis may surface flaws in the price/credit structure in terms of unintended impact on employees.

If the employee contributions are changed from an after-tax to a before-tax basis at the time the flexible program is introduced, the tax benefit received by the employee might be taken into account in a winners and losers analysis.

Example 12.4
Employee and Employer Cost in Prior Plan

	Single	Family
Prior medical plan cost	$1,000	$2,500
Employee contribution	0	500
Employer cost	$1,000	$2,000

Flexible Compensation
Medical Plan Price/Credit Structure

	Prices	
Option	Single	Family
A (prior plan)	$1,000	$2,500
B	800	2,000
C	600	1,500
Employee credits	$1,500	$1,500

Winners/Losers Analysis

Option	Single	Family
A	$(500)	$500
B	(700)	0
C	(900)	(500)

(b)   EMPLOYER COST ANALYSIS

Some analysis should be performed to determine expected employer cost, especially if cost management is a goal of the flexible program. This analysis involves identifying the obvious employer costs, credits plus price subsidies, and also the not-so-obvious costs. These not-so-obvious costs include:

- Adverse selection: Will the plan costs rise if employees are allowed to choose their own benefits? If so, how much?
- Dependent coverage: Will the program likely cause employees to change their decisions on where to cover their dependents? If so, what is the likely cost impact?
- Benefit utilization: If employees change their benefit elections, will that change likely affect their propensity to use the services the benefits cover? If so, what might be the impact?

Although these areas of cost are somewhat nebulous, attempting to identify them and calculating an expected employer cost of the plan is an important exercise in determining the appropriateness of the price/ credit structure and the ultimate success of the program. (See also Chapter Twenty for a broader discussion of employer financial analysis.)

(c) REASONABLENESS

It is difficult to define exactly what this final step may include for each employer. Basically, it is reviewing the program as the average employee will. The employer should be asking the same kinds of questions an employee will ask such as:

- Do I understand the options?
- Do the prices make sense?
- How does the price for one option compare to another?
- Are the choices clear, or are the options and their prices so close together as to be indistinguishable?
- Is one option an obvious choice over all others, no matter what my situation?
- Are the credits adequate for my needs?
- Is the employer paying a fair share of the cost?

At times the employer may become too close to the plan to remain fully aware of the employee's perspective. An alternative is to test the flexible compensation program with a sample group of employees. (See also Chapter Seventeen.) Pretesting the plan with employees could bring to light subtle problems with the price/credit structure that otherwise may be difficult to identify. Pretesting may also provide a necessary measure of confidence in the program prior to implementation.

Thirteen

Adverse Selection

§ 13.1 INTRODUCTION

Few concepts are more feared—or misunderstood—in the field of flexible compensation than adverse selection. The concern arises in that any offering of choice, whether inside a flexible program or otherwise, increases the potential that "bad risks" will be drawn to certain options, thereby driving up the cost of the coverage and producing negative financial results. The misunderstanding occurs for various reasons.

One reason is the relative newness of flexible compensation arrangements. Until embarking on a flexible compensation project, few employers (or their underwriters) might anticipate the leverage that exists for controlling experience through plan design and option pricing. In effect, design and pricing operate as levers within a flexible program to contain the potential for adverse selection.

Another reason is that adverse selection within flexible programs is often confused with higher claims costs. In practice, the risk of higher claims resulting from a move to choice making is often nonexistent due to the structure of most flexible programs. In medical, for example, the pre-flexible plan (or a lesser variation) typically is offered as the highest-valued option in the program. Some proportion of employees will opt down in coverage from that level, thereby lowering aggregate claims cost. Instead, the adverse selection issue in flexible programs relates more to the level of "reward" or "incentive" provided to employees (through credits or lower prices) to elect lesser-valued coverages or to opt out of the program altogether.

Finally, the adverse selection issue presumes that employees are able to predict benefit plan utilization—both for themselves and their families—with a high degree of accuracy. Except in unusual situations (such as an employee already in poor health anticipating major surgery), experience shows that the types of calamities covered by most benefit plans are "unknowable" in advance, particularly in family-coverage situations. Further, emotion often clouds what otherwise might be strictly economic decisions in the benefit area. In effect, security and budgeting often are more powerful influences on employee benefit plan elections than the profit motive.

The purpose of this chapter is to discuss the concept of adverse selection as it relates to flexible programs and to explain the types of approaches used to minimize the potential for unfavorable financial experience. Note that most of the discussion concentrates on the potential for adverse selection to occur in medical plans, paying limited attention to other benefit areas. Typically, employers are most concerned about medical because the majority of benefit dollars within a flexible program flow through this benefit plan area.

§ 13.2 ABOUT ADVERSE SELECTION

To understand *adverse* selection, it may be helpful to review the general principles underlying the concept of insurance. True insurance occurs when the likelihood of a claim is completely unknown or random, but the potential consequences are so great that few people would forego paying a modest amount to gain the coverage. Consider an illustration.

Example 13.1 shows a hypothetical distribution of claims in a given year for a medical plan covering a group of 100 employees. The price of

Example 13.1
Illustration of "Winners" and "Losers" in Medical

Annual Claim Range	Number of Employees	Average Claim	Total Claims	Total Premiums	Claims Less Premiums
$0–$499	50	$ 200	$ 10,000	$100,000	$(90,000)
$500–$1,999	30	1,200	36,000	60,000	(24,000)
Over $2,000	20	7,700	154,000	40,000	114,000
	100	$2,000	$200,000	$200,000	$ 0

the coverage equals $2,000—or the same amount as the average employee's claims. (In order to simplify, retention, reserves, administrative, and other costs are excluded from the example.)

The majority of the members in the group incur claims that are lower than the price of the coverage. In effect, these employees are "losers" under the plan (shown in italics) in that their cost exceeded what they received in terms of benefits. A few employees are "winners" under the plan (shown in bold typeface) in that their claims exceeded the price of the coverage. Still, all of the members of the group are willing to pay the average price to protect against the risk of incurring a large medical claim. This is the principle of insurance—the risk of an event occurring is spread over a group of people with none of the members able to predict individual (or family-unit) experience.

Adverse selection is created when employees know or can reasonably predict the probability of an occurrence. For example, based on the previous illustration, if all the participants could predict their medical claims, only employees with claims in excess of $2,000 would purchase the insurance. Those with claims below that amount would be better off without the coverage. So the provider of the insurance would experience a shortfall in revenue to pay the cost of the claims. In the jargon of the insurance industry, employees would have "selected against" the plan.

Another way to illustrate the concern over adverse selection is in the area of vision coverage. Assume that an employer wants to cover vision expenses on an insured basis. Further, assume that the price of the insurance is $50 and the cost of lenses, for example, is $200. As the need for vision care is relatively predictable, only those employees who expect to use the benefit will elect the coverage. In time, the plan will be covering only the bad risks (i.e., those who need lenses), so eventually the price of the insurance will equal the cost of the lenses—$200. The principles of insurance will fail to operate.

Vision represents one of the most extreme examples of the potential for adverse selection to occur. (The other area with significant potential is dental.) The chief reason is that the risk the insurance is intended to cover is almost totally predictable. If the event the insurance protects against is less predictable, the potential for adverse selection diminishes proportionately. For example, at the opposite end of the spectrum in terms of predictability would be death and AD&D coverages. The incidence of either of these two events occurring is considerably more difficult to predict, so the potential for adverse selection to arise to such an extent as to influence plan costs is relatively minimal.

In the middle of the spectrum in terms of the potential for adverse selection is medical. One of the reasons medical represents a medium rather than extreme possibility for adverse selection is the relative unpredictability of most claims, particularly for a full family. Few employees know with certainty what their level of medical plan utilization will be in a given year. Further, decisions on medical (as well as other benefit areas) often are clouded by emotion. Many employees want the "best" medical protection for themselves and their families, whether or not the coverage represents a "good deal" financially. Finally, medical plan elections often are based on factors unrelated to the specific options offered—namely, the availability of coverage through a spouse's employer. For these kinds of reasons, adverse selection often turns out not to be the nemesis it first appears simply because employees cannot make fully rational economic decisions in every case.

Another reason that the impact of adverse selection can be reasonably contained is that proper program design and option pricing further shrink its potential for occurring. For example, offering coverage for the most predictable types of expenses (e.g., vision, hearing, sometimes dental) through flexible spending accounts—rather than on an insured-plan basis—effectively avoids any potential for adverse selection. But this type of "easy" solution is not always available (or practical). Instead, adverse selection needs to be controlled through other means. The purpose of the next section is to explore the range of solutions available to employers for controlling adverse selection through restricting choice (design) and varying costs (pricing).

§ 13.3 CONTROLLING ADVERSE SELECTION

Adverse selection is dependent on two variables. One is the availability of choice, and the other is the predictability of the occurrence. Influencing one factor influences the other. For example, if a benefit is predictable but choice is unavailable, no adverse selection will occur (because of the absence of choice). On the other hand, if a benefit is available for selection in numerous forms and amounts, but occurrence of the benefit need is completely unpredictable (or random), again, no adverse selection will result (because of the absence of predictability). Therefore, the freer employees are to choose and the more accurate their ability to predict, the greater will be the concern over adverse selection.

If an employer's goal is to eradicate any potential for adverse selection, that objective can be achieved. But the means would involve radically restricting the choices available to employees or prohibitively inflating the prices of the options. Instead, most employers elect to tolerate some amount of adverse selection almost as a "necessary evil" in flexible compensation programs. That is, they will use the levers of design and pricing to control the magnitude of the potential for adverse selection, but they will otherwise accept the risk of some (modest) increase in costs because of the advantages to be gained from choice making and the potential for savings in other aspects of the program. In medical, for example, reduced utilization by employees electing options with higher deductibles and copayment amounts often offsets all or most of any cost increases resulting purely from unfavorable experience.

The following material examines the control that can be exerted over adverse selection through the design and pricing of specific benefit options.

(a) DESIGN APPROACHES

As discussed previously, restricting choice reduces the effect of predictability and therefore limits the potential for adverse selection to arise. Numerous design approaches can be used to contain the potential for unfavorable experience, some of which are used more frequently in certain benefit areas than others. In general, however, these types of design approaches include the following:

- **Limit the frequency of choice.** Some employers limit the frequency under which employees may move in or out of specific benefit options (e.g., every two or three years instead of annually). This type of design restriction is particularly effective in the more predictable benefit areas such as vision or dental. In effect, the longer the period of coverage (or no coverage), the more difficult it is for the employee to predict expenses or specifically influence the timing of incurring those expenses.
- **Level the spread between options.** In some coverage areas (such as medical or long-term disability), it may be appropriate to minimize the difference between high and low options to avoid extremes in employee elections. Many employers offer a core coverage specifically for this reason. Core coverage promotes a larger covered employee group, thereby spreading the financial risk over a wider population. Another

variation used most frequently in life insurance is including maximum benefit limitations (e.g., fixed-dollar amounts or percent-of-pay multiples). These types of restrictions serve to moderate the impact of adverse selection.

- **Require proof of insurability.** Some programs require proof of insurability before employees may increase coverage in medical or life insurance.

    This type of restriction may apply to any increase in coverage or may be limited to increases of more than one level of coverage.

- **Group certain coverages together.** Some flexible programs package certain options; for example, dental or vision coverage with medical. This has the effect of reducing the employee's ability to predict specific benefit plan utilization, and it also causes elections to be based on factors in addition to the employee's expectation of incurring a claim. Another variation is to require interdependent elections; for example, the most valuable dental option is available only on choosing a lower level of medical. The popularity of these types of restrictions, however, has waned in recent years because the trade-off for minimizing adverse selection is reduced flexibility to employees.

- **Delay full payment.** Another approach is to delay or restrict full payment of benefits. In dental, for example, lower benefits might be paid in the first six months (or one year) following a period of no coverage. In the disability area, delayed enrollment might make benefits effective only one year after the date of the election or subject to a shorter maximum duration for a disability which occurs in the first year of coverage. These types of design restrictions help prevent the possibility of a "windfall" accruing to employees inclined to move in and out of coverage—and also discourage such patterns of election.

- **Offer flexible spending accounts.** As mentioned earlier, many employers cover certain health-related expenses (e.g., vision, hearing, occasionally dental) only through flexible spending accounts. This strategy removes the insurance element from these types of coverages, thereby fixing the benefit cost and eliminating any potential for adverse selection.

- **Maintain parallel design.** Consistency in option design helps avoid differences in coverage that employees may be able to manipulate. For example, orthodontia coverage might be offered with each dental option and at the same level of plan payment. Similarly, outpatient psychiatric, prescription drug coverage, and so forth might be attached to each medical plan option. If the specific coverage pertains to a predictable benefit, it typically makes sense to include it consistently throughout all like options.

• **Test the program with employees.**   Although not a design restriction, many employers test preliminary program design with employees. Testing may bring to light any potential weaknesses in the design that later could produce adverse selection. Any shortcomings in the proposed program then can be corrected prior to implementation. Separately, testing also can provide a firmer basis for the actual pricing of flexible program options.

Well-designed plan restrictions can be tremendously effective in controlling the potential for adverse selection. Since adverse selection is predicated on the choice and predictability of benefits, employers can selectively restrict choice and thereby reduce the potential for additional costs. However, design restrictions need to be used judiciously so as not to reduce excessively the flexibility and, therefore, the usefulness of choice-making programs to employees.

Unfortunately, there are many times when design restrictions either are inappropriate or insufficient as a defense against adverse selection. The other available lever is pricing.

(b)   PRICING ALTERNATIVES

As a general rule, anticipating adverse selection in the pricing of plan options is difficult to accomplish. In many respects, *pricing, employee elections,* and *experience* are interconnected to such an extent as to form almost a circular chain. That is, pricing decisions influence selection patterns which in turn affect experience. Using experience to set prices influences employee elections so that prices are affected yet again. The circular flow—almost akin to a dog chasing its tail—is almost impossible to interrupt. However, some measure of relief can be achieved through a number of pricing strategies designed to limit the magnitude of the cost impact that may be produced by adverse selection.

One approach is to price options in a way that reflects the expected risk or cost of the benefit. Consider, for example, age-related pricing in life insurance. Life insurance coverage is often charged to employees at the same flat rate, regardless of age. However, the value of life insurance is distinctly age related (because the risk of death increases with age). If a flat rate is charged to everyone, older employees will recognize that the price for the coverage represents a bargain, while younger employees will find the rates inflated. As a result, a disproportionate number of older employees will select higher levels of coverage which will increase the plan costs and eventually increase the price the company needs to charge employees. Younger employees will seek coverage outside the benefit program because better deals exist elsewhere. Age grading the prices can help minimize the potential for adverse selection costs (if having older employees elect large amounts of life insurance because of an artificially low price is viewed as adverse selection).

A similar risk-related pricing structure can be adopted in medical through tiered pricing of the coverage. For example, employees covering several dependents typically would be inclined to select the richer plan options because of the greater probability of claims being incurred for a full family. To draw a cross section of lower risks (e.g., employee only, or employee plus spouse) will require some differential in the pricing of the options. This is the reason many organizations use three or four (sometimes more) coverage tiers for option pricing, rather than only one or two. Tiered pricing causes the relationships between options to be more realistic and, therefore, it reduces the potential for employees to select against a particular plan based on family size.

Another relatively straightforward strategy for mitigating the effects of adverse selection is employer subsidization of the option prices. For example, an employer with two dental options (coverage or no coverage) may want to encourage broad participation in the plan. Subsidized pricing can make the coverage a "better deal" for more employees, thus encouraging participation. Higher participation will help spread the risk, thereby diminishing the potential for adverse selection.

However, even with age- or risk-related pricing or employer subsidies, an underlying difficulty with adverse selection is *anticipating* actual experience. Only rarely does "expected" experience precisely match actual utilization, especially in medical and dental. This problem is not unique to flexible programs, but it is heightened by the ability of the employee to choose levels of coverage

Consider an example. Assume the employer offers three medical plan options: the current plan (now costing $100 per month) plus two lesser-valued coverages worth 90 percent and 75 percent, respectively, of the current plan. Pure actuarial pricing might suggest that the option price tags be set at $100, $90, and $75. One decision the employer will face is whether to anticipate the potential variance in claims experience and adjust the price tags accordingly or to operate the flexible program in the first year using these unadjusted price tags.

Adjustment of the price tags for anticipated experience can be accomplished in several ways. One approach is to reduce the reward to employees for opting down by loading the prices of the lesser-valued options. That is, instead of charging $90 and $75 for the lower coverages, the prices might be set at $100 (same as actuarial pricing), $95, and $85. This solution would diminish the potential for over-rewarding the presumably good risks who elect lesser coverage although at the expense of reduced flexibility to employees. Moreover, in practice, what is likely to happen under this approach is that more employees will remain clustered in the rich current plan (because the incentive to consider the other options is diminished) rather than moving to plans with more cost-efficient designs, thereby thwarting cost-management objectives for the program.

A second alternative would be to push all of the cost of expected adverse selection (say, 2 percent of medical cost) into the highest-valued option, but keep the prices for the other options at the same level. If half the employees are expected to remain in the high option, this might require about a 4 percent increase in the high-option prices to recoup a 2 percent total medical program cost. Prices under this strategy would be set at $104 for the current plan, and $90 and $75 for the other options. All of the cost of adverse selection has been added to the price of the highest-valued option—so employees effectively cannot buy back their prior coverage without paying significantly more (unless the employer increases credits by a like amount for all employees).

Further, to avoid paying more for the prior plan, a greater-than-expected number of employees will likely be driven to the lower-valued options, thereby escalating the price for those options. However, the net effect most likely will be positive in that these are the options with higher deductibles and copayment amounts. Ironically, some added cost savings is likely to have been achieved as an unintended result of the concern over adverse selection—but at the risk of employee dissatisfaction over the increased cost to purchase the prior plan.

A variation on this strategy would be to spread the cost of the anticipated adverse selection over the price of all the options (for example, increasing the price of each option by 2 percent). Here the original relative relationships between the plans have been maintained and

greater equity achieved by spreading the cost of adverse selection produced by offering choice to all employees, but a similar (although di-
minished) problem exists with the ability of employees to buy back the
former coverage.

The practical difficulties with anticipating adverse selection incline
many employers to use of unadjusted pricing—at least in the first year
of a flexible program's operation. The prices are set at the pure actuarial level and adjusted only after the combined effect of adverse selection
costs and utilization savings are better known. Under this type of scenario, it would not be unusual to see expected versus actual experience
on the order of magnitude shown in Example 13.2.

This example also illustrates another issue that arises with adverse
selection. That is, the effect of adverse selection will be felt disproportionately across options, producing both positive and negative results.
The actual claims experience under any one option (particularly in
medical) will likely vary (and perhaps dramatically) from that expected
under a completely random election process. But unfavorable experience in one option (typically the highest option) will usually be offset
(in full or in part) by favorable experience in other options, so the impact on the aggregate experience of the program is likely to be modest.

It should be noted also that unfavorable experience may not always
be negative. That is, on occasion an employer may want to encourage
(or allow) adverse selection to occur naturally as a means of phasing
out an option. This might be the case in situations where the highest-
valued option is considered too rich, but the employer is concerned
about the employee relations impact of eliminating the option by de-
cree. Instead, the employer might allow "option suicide" to occur by
keeping the pricing of each option on a self-supporting basis. Over
time, migration of the heaviest users to the option will cause the price
to rise prohibitively, in which case the option will have priced itself
out of the market.

Example 13.2

Option	Percent of Employees Electing	Actuarial Value	Actual Experience	Effect of Adverse Selection
High	60	$100	$110	+ 10%
Intermediate	25	90	85	− 6%
Low	15	75	50	−33%
Average Cost		$ 94	$ 95	+ 1%

To summarize, adverse selection in choice-making programs does not represent a benign influence on plan costs. It is an issue that requires careful attention and consideration. The point is, however, that numerous strategies and techniques can be employed to limit its potentially damaging effects. In combination, the levers of program design and option pricing can be activated in such a manner as to shrink most of the potential for adverse selection to a manageable level.

Fourteen

Insurance Considerations

A typical flexible compensation program is laced with benefit options that may require some involvement by an insurance carrier. Life insurance, short-term disability, long-term disability, medical, and dental options often will be underwritten for the smaller employer or administered by a carrier for the larger organization.

§ 14.1 THE INSURER'S PERSPECTIVE

(a) INSURANCE RISK CONCERNS

To understand the insurer's perspective of flexible compensation programs, some appreciation of the carrier's financial risk is helpful. To a carrier, an employer who designs a benefit program (whether flexible or otherwise) and then tells someone else to insure it, is attempting to play poker with a stranger's money. The "player" organization risks little, while the stakes are high for the strangers. Although this may not be an issue for very large employers (who typically self-fund many of their benefits), it is a concern for smaller employers who insure most or all benefits.

As background, it may be helpful to discuss the three universal methods of insuring programs: pooled, conventional, and partial insurance.

Pooled insurance is the most familiar concept. Auto insurance is pooled. A driver is placed in a pool with others sharing similar characteristics. The experience of the pool influences the rates the individual is charged. At year-end, no premium is returned even if a particular driver avoided having an accident, and neither are any deficits applied to the policies of the drivers who have an accident. So the slate is wiped clean each year. In the next year, however, rates might increase if the driver is reassigned to the pool with the "one-accident" drivers. Pooled group insurance of this kind is typically used for organizations of 200 or fewer employees.

Conventional insurance requires a full financial accounting at the end of each plan year. If any premium is left after the carrier deducts all claims, reserves, and expenses, the employer receives that difference. Conversely, if a deficit occurs, that amount is charged interest, carried forward, and collected by the carrier in lieu of premium rebates in future years. Although all deficits potentially can be recovered, a carrier will have two incentives to avoid deficit situations: (1) initial loss of cash flow, and (2) possible termination by the employer of the policy prior to full recovery. This kind of conventional insurance is the most common group benefits financing method.

Partial insurance is a generic term for any arrangement where the employer self-funds the coverage up to a predetermined limit, after which the carrier's liability begins. The limit might be by claim, by employee, by total claims expected per year, or some other variation. The risk to an insurance carrier under a partial insurance arrangement is very similar to the risk under any other insured arrangement. Large or excessive claims will trigger deficits. Under partial insurance arrangements, the deficits may or may not be recoverable in future years, depending on the terms of the policy.

In each case involving insurance then, the carrier is at risk to some degree and will seek to protect itself by influencing plan design, requiring evidence of insurability for especially risky benefits, or increasing rates to avoid deficit positions.

The three primary influences on risk are:

- Volume, or number of participants in the benefit plan
- Liability, or size of potential claim reimbursement
- Selection patterns, namely, the potential that high utilizers will tend to select the plan.

For example, a $200,000 life insurance benefit is not a high risk for a carrier insuring a 5,000-employee organization where only 100 employees are eligible for this benefit based on pay. The total annual life insurance premium from this organization will easily absorb the one or two large claims that might occur in a year. The same benefit for a 50-employee organization with a much smaller annual premium would be considered risky.

To explain the influence of selection patterns, consider the 5,000-employee organization with a flexible compensation program under which all employees are eligible to purchase a $200,000 benefit. If only ten people do so—who are all 64 years old and perhaps not in the best of health—and the other employees take little or no coverage, the total annual premium is far less than $200,000. This is an extreme example, but it serves to illustrate what a carrier will recognize as adverse selection and, therefore, potential risk. These and other more subtle variations are types of risk potential that appear in various aspects of flexible programs. (See also Chapter Thirteen for ways to minimize this type of risk.)

(b)   ADMINISTRATIVE CONCERNS

Insurance carriers provide most employers with a substantial number of administrative services: (1) participant eligibility maintenance and benefit verification, (2) life and health claims processing, (3) premium/fee statement preparation, (4) COBRA coverage administration, (5) conversion policy maintenance, and (6) cost containment program administration. Administrative concerns that might result from flexible compensation programs typically would arise from the *eligibility maintenance* and *claims processing* functions.

Over a decade ago, insurance carriers began to install sophisticated computerized claims processing systems that accept eligibility information on computer tape, process claims with a minimum of manual intervention, and generate meaningful claims reports. Insurance carriers have been refining these programs continually to adapt to the changing benefit environment (preferred provider organizations, COBRA, cost management, etc.).

As a result, most major carriers have systems in place that can readily process almost any medical or dental claims that may be generated by a flexible compensation program. The function of processing claims for multiple-option medical programs, for example, does not even require a systems change. Carriers simply use the same procedures required to process different plans for different divisions of the same company—a capability built into all systems years ago.

The carrier's systems specialists are generally cooperative in making some changes to adapt to unusual plan features. Of course, the size of an organization will influence the carrier's interest in customizing systems and procedures. The 100-employee organization, for example, probably will have to accept the limitations of their carrier, simplify the plan, or attempt to select an alternate carrier with a more flexible system.

Inflexibility of a computer program, however, does not in itself void a carrier's ability to administer a particular program. Since manual intervention may be required for any client's unusual program features, this approach is available at least as a backup measure to the carrier.

A good flexible compensation program should be designed to meet a company's specific needs and objectives and should not be unduly restricted by systems limitations. However, some preliminary planning regarding possible administrative snags might reduce the amount of time-consuming carrier negotiations or the number of manual intervention situations that might be required of a carrier with a less sophisticated claims payment system. (Later in this chapter, the types of possible administrative stumbling blocks are addressed.)

(c) STATE INSURANCE LAWS

Each state has adopted laws that apply to group insurance policies executed in that state regardless of the state of residence of employees. Some states have written laws to apply also to residents of their states who might be insured under policies executed in other states. Recent court decisions have confirmed that state insurance laws do not govern self-funded plans.

State legislation governs insurance carriers, so it is generally the insurer's responsibility to inform policyholders of any proposed options that might conflict with state law. Typically, however, most organizations also research state laws during the design phase of flexible compensation program development to avoid any last minute surprises.

Although state insurance laws typically do not specifically address flexible compensation programs, they can often influence an employer's plan design decisions. Flexible compensation creates the situation where substantially expanded or reduced benefits would be available through employee selection. However, state laws typically view each benefit option separately and may restrict the level of benefits that can be offered within the framework of an insured or partially insured flexible program.

Examples of the types of state rules which sometimes impact the design of flexible program options include:

- Limits on the amount of employee group life insurance (e.g., four times pay)
- Limits on the amount of dependent group life insurance (e.g., one-half of the employee insurance amount)
- Prohibition of certain methods of coordination with other employers' medical plans (e.g., no maintenance of benefits).

Although special state insurance laws can be readily identified and dealt with in most cases, the issues can be more complex for a large multidivision employer with employees (and possibly insurance contracts) in multiple states.

§ 14.2   AVOIDING POSSIBLE STUMBLING BLOCKS

Although an employer designs a flexible compensation program to meet organizational objectives, designing around some touchy carrier concerns can often be accomplished without major compromises. Creativity in plan design can ameliorate insurance carrier concerns in a number of areas. The following design discussion is organized by major benefit area.

(a)   MEDICAL

(1)   Adverse Selection

In an insured or partially insured situation, the insurance carrier's objective in underwriting medical coverage is to rate the benefit plan options to anticipate any adverse selection that might occur. That is, the high utilizers may tend to pick the highest coverage possible, and the low utilizers may tend to opt out or choose the least coverage possible. If this occurs, it results in less spreading of the risk and a higher cost per employee than in a situation where all employees participate in a single plan. The carrier will typically reflect some expectation of adverse selection in the rates charged to the employer.

Methods available to the plan sponsor to minimize adverse selection are outlined in Chapter Thirteen. In addition, that chapter discusses alternative ways of developing the option prices that are communicated to employees—which may be different from those developed by the carrier.

(2)   Core versus Opt-Out Provision

Insurers typically will be much more comfortable in underwriting risk when employees are provided a minimum level of coverage. Core coverage promotes a larger covered employee population, thereby allowing the insurer to spread the risk over a larger financial base. Allowing an opt-out provision in a plan could increase an underwriter's concern over adverse selection. However, if an employer's current nonflexible program requires employees to pay for coverage, introduction of an opt-out provision will probably not dramatically change employee participation under the flexible compensation program.

The core versus opt-out concern also arises in other benefit areas, but it is most pronounced in health care (medical, dental, vision).

(3)   Evidence of Insurability

Evidence of insurability refers to a process requiring employees and dependents to complete a health statement to initially enroll in or move up to certain options. Coverage can be denied to employees or dependents based on their health statement responses, or a physical may be required before coverage is approved. Although this approach is an effective safeguard against adverse selection, it also restricts employee choice making and results in some administrative difficulties. A more palatable approach (and a reasonable compromise) might be allowing the employee to elect the next higher level of coverage without evidence of insurability, but requiring evidence of insurability for greater increases in coverage.

(4)   Claims Administration

Stumbling blocks might arise in claims administration if the employer designs an unusual option that cannot be easily programmed into the insurer's claims processing computer system. These snags are not directly related to the introduction of medical choices, but they might occur because specific medical plan provisions were changed in the flexible program design process. Simple changes made to an employer's plan in order to create options (e.g., deductibles, out-of-pocket amounts) typically do not affect the insurer's ability to process claims electronically.

However, other less typical changes that might require manual intervention include:

- Multiple coinsurance levels within the same plan
- Penalties or incentives applicable to certain cost containment features (e.g., hospital preadmission review, second surgical opinion) which are not standard for the insurer
- Implementation of a nonstandard (for that insurer) preferred provider organization
- Nonstandard benefits or benefit limits for expenses such as home health or hospice care.

These administrative difficulties should not discourage employers from adopting these provisions, but employers should be aware that some slight changes in design might enable insurers to avoid manual intervention. Audits of insurance carrier claim payments show that errors are significantly greater in situations where manual intervention is used.

(5) Preferred Provider Organizations

PPOs have become the new medical plan cost containment feature of the late 1980s. Many insurance carriers have negotiated special contracts involving strict utilization review requirements and discounted fees with hospitals and physicians, and they offer these "panels" to their employer clients. Participating employers encourage employees to use the panels by creating special incentives (e.g., higher coinsurance, lower deductibles) when these providers are utilized.

Insurance carriers offer PPOs in two formats. An insurer might sell to an employer an insured PPO package that has preestablished sets of benefits for panel versus nonpanel providers, and allows employees to select either type of provider at the time of service. Offering attractive rates, the carrier designs the program so that a certain percentage of all expenses is likely to be incurred at the panel providers. The employer can offer this plan as an option to the standard medical plan or as one of the medical choices under the flexible compensation program.

In the other, more popular variation, the insurer offers its panel to the employer who builds the preferred provider incentives into the already existing medical plan. If this approach were used in a flexible compensation program, the PPO incentives would be included in each medical plan option. The disadvantage of this approach is that the insurance carrier will be less likely to underwrite aggressive rates because the carrier typically has little or no control over plan design, and it is difficult to estimate the level of PPO utilization. The advantage is that all employees are eligible for these special benefits regardless of the medical plan selected.

(6)   Health Maintenance Organizations

Some employers are concerned that their medical plans are losing too many employees to HMOs where the level of benefits provided is typically higher than most employer programs. The concern is that healthier employees will pick HMOs because of the wide range of benefits offered, despite the limitations on choice of providers. In this scenario, the standard medical plan would harbor the high utilizers, resulting in increased costs per employee in that plan. Because HMOs are typically "community-rated," the employer receives virtually no financial gain when low utilizers participate in the HMO.

This issue is not unique to flexible compensation programs, and it may in fact be moderated under a flexible approach. As another option within a flexible program, the employer might also construct what looks like an HMO in terms of providing a high level of benefits, but what is actually more of a PPO with incentives to promote employee selection and also with utilization review to help reduce costs. The presence of these (and other) attractive alternatives in medical can help stem any flow of good risks into HMOs.

(7)   Triple-Option Programs

Insurers have recently begun to offer several variations of "triple-option programs" in which a standard medical plan, an HMO, and a PPO are all underwritten by one insurer. The rates are developed based on the employer's experience under all three plans. The HMO included in such an option is not federally qualified, however, because of the community-rating requirement presently in the federal HMO law.

These arrangements can be built into flexible compensation programs much like the PPO approach. The choices might look like Table 14.1.

In this program, Options A through D will be experience-rated together, although the experience of each option would be tracked separately for purposes of experience analysis, internal cost allocation, and potential use in developing employee option prices.

Table 14.1

Option	Type	Deductible	Coinsurance
A	Standard/PPO	$ 50	Preferred providers = 100% with some small copayments; Others = 80% to $1,000 out-of-pocket
B	Standard/PPO	$200	Same
C	Standard/PPO	$750	Same
D	HMO (Experience-rated)	None	100% with some small copayments
E	Other HMOs	None	Same

(b)   DENTAL

(1)   Adverse Selection

Although the total dollar effects of adverse selection on medical plans can be large, the financial effects on dental plans can be greater when measured as a percentage of plan costs.

(For a discussion of adverse selection in the dental area and ways in which an employer can minimize its effect through plan design and pricing, refer to Chapter Thirteen.)

(2)   Claims Administration

Like flexible medical options, the mere offering of choices in dental creates few inherent claims administration problems. Only in adding a unique plan provision might a stumbling block be created.

One provision that might cause administrative concern to a carrier involves a "preexisting condition" exclusion. Some employers have attempted to limit adverse selection by requiring coverage under the flexible program for a certain period of time (e.g., one year) before a bridge is replaced, for example. Many carriers' systems must view this dental option as two separate benefit plans—one for pre-year one participants and one for post-year one participants. The employer, then, would need to submit eligibility information distinguishing between these two groups.

Employers might find alternative approaches to control adverse selection which are as effective (or more effective) than this type of limitation, but without the administrative difficulties.

(3)   Prepaid Dental Plans

Some organizations offer prepaid dental plans that act much like medical HMOs. These organizations have negotiated reduced fees with selected panels of dentists. Expenses are usually reimbursed in full except for small copayments.

A prepaid dental plan can be an attractive addition to choices in dental, especially in a situation where the employer has chosen to offer only one standard dental option. The prepaid dental plan can result in substantially higher benefits to employees.

(c)   VISION

(1)   Adverse Selection

Because vision care expenses are even more predictable and discretionary than dental expenses, the risk of adverse selection is greater. As a result, most employers choose to provide employees with vision care reimbursement only through flexible spending accounts.

Alternatively, employers who prefer to offer a vision care benefit may create a core vision plan or include a vision benefit in all of the medical options. Another alternative would be to include examinations under the medical plans but leave the purchase of lenses and frames to the flexible spending account. The vision options could also be packaged with dental options to restrict movement in and out of the plans.

(2)   Prepaid Vision Plans

Employers who plan to include prepaid vision plans as a part of their flexible compensation program should be aware that providers offering these arrangements are especially sensitive to adverse selection. They will often decline to offer their arrangements as a part of a flexible compensation program without two- to three-year enrollment requirements unless a minimum participation level can be guaranteed.

(d)   LIFE INSURANCE

(1)   Adverse Selection

Insurers are not typically as concerned about adverse selection in life insurance as they are in health care benefits. The total costs are usually much less, the predictability of claims much smaller, and the experience they have in dealing with choice making plans in life insurance is much higher. (See also Chapter Thirteen for discussion of common ways to minimize adverse selection in the life insurance area.)

(2) Evidence of Insurability

Insurance carrier underwriters will have some concerns, although modest, in the area of life benefit selection. The employee is no longer provided with employer-paid basic life and given the opportunity to buy additional coverage. Instead, credits are allotted by the employer, and the employee is permitted to select as much coverage as he or she needs. This potential volatility in coverage may promote conservative underwriting practices unless the program is properly presented.

In particular, a carrier usually will wish to impose evidence-of-insurability requirements for benefits exceeding a certain level. This level is typically based on employer size or total anticipated life volume. In a 1,000-employee company with a maximum $400,000 lifetime benefit, employees might be required to submit evidence of insurability for amounts exceeding $250,000.

If possible, it is often preferable to avoid such an evidence-of-insurability approach. A denial of benefits may result in a reselection of choices by the employee. The final denial might not be communicated by the carrier until after the program has gone into effect, resulting in a reprocessing of that employee's election form and possibly retroactive adjustment to payroll reductions. With some discussion, carriers are often willing to "grandfather" any large benefits being carried by employees under the current program without evidence of insurability.

(3) Dependent Life

Several states have maximum dependent life benefit allowances, often at flat-dollar levels of $5,000 or $10,000. Some states require that dependent benefits not exceed a certain percentage (e.g., 50 percent) of the employee's life benefit. Some carriers offer out-of-state life insurance trusts to avoid these limitations and to offer employers greater flexibility in providing dependent life coverage.

(e) LONG-TERM DISABILITY

As in other benefit areas, insurers will want to spread the risk associated with long-term disability benefits among as large a population as possible. A typical stumbling block that occurs with disability is misunderstanding of a flexible program's credit allocation method. Without a full understanding of the overall flexible program structure, a carrier's underwriter might see a completely voluntary long-term disability plan and rate it using large adverse selection margins assuming the high risks will be more likely to choose the coverage. In reality, the program may be designed to provide each employee with enough credits to purchase at least a minimum level of long-term disability coverage. This mechanism does not guarantee the underwriter that all employees will opt for the coverage, but participation in the option will be substantially greater than enrollment in a purely voluntary plan where the employee pays the full cost of the coverage. (See also Chapter Thirteen for more complete discussion of approaches to controlling adverse selection.)

§ 14.3 WORKING WITH THE INSURER

In order to work effectively with an insurance carrier on installation of a flexible compensation program, the employer needs to consider issues related to communication, negotiation, and implementation.

(a) COMMUNICATING WITH THE INSURER

Early notification to an insurer that flexible compensation is being considered could help avoid future complications. Carriers who have had some experience with flexible compensation programs should have insights regarding the interaction of flexible options with their own systems, procedures, and underwriting guidelines. During this initial notification and discussion, an employer might recognize the need to solicit proposals from other carriers if the existing carrier's capabilities are insufficient.

Another objective of early notification is to create an atmosphere of openness where carrier input is sought and fostered. The carrier representatives—underwriters, systems analysts, claim supervisors, contract specialists—will begin to share in the team approach to flexible compensation, enhancing the chances for a smooth implementation.

In some situations, the line between the insurer's constructive input and negative inflexibility may be unclear. Employers should design flexible compensation programs to meet their needs, while recognizing that some concessions to insurance carrier underwriting or administration limitations might be necessary, particularly for the smaller employer.

(b) NEGOTIATING WITH THE CARRIER

Carrier negotiations on flexible compensation programs typically involve one or more of the following issues:

- Insurance rates
- Benefit limitations
- Administrative procedures.

As discussed earlier, insurers might view the flexible compensation program as a risk, resulting in conservative underwriting (i.e., high rates). To temper the risk, the carrier might wish to limit the maximum benefits available or require evidence of insurability for some benefits. Also, carrier systems limitations or standard procedures might inhibit the flexible compensation program design or administration.

All of these issues are negotiable—to some degree. Prior to negotiating any issue, the employer should estimate the size of the "bargaining chips" involved. That is, how motivated is the carrier to accommodate the employer and retain the account? Any or all of the following factors can influence the insurer's perspective:

- **Size of organization.** A "large" client represents lower risks and higher profitability to an insurer. However, the employer's size might be viewed differently based on the company's geographic location and on the carrier's current book of business in the office that would be handling the account.
- **Life insurance volume.** Life insurance continues to be a profit leader for insurance companies, so substantial life benefits make any package extremely attractive to a carrier.
- **Employer prestige.** An insurance carrier may enhance its image in a community by including as current clients the most respected local organization(s).
- **Market share.** The size of a carrier's market share is gaining increased importance as insurers negotiate discounts with local hospitals and physicians.

With this understanding of the carrier's perspective, the employer can discuss issues openly and honestly, recognizing that some concessions might be necessary.

(c) SELECTING A NEW CARRIER

Most employers can maintain their existing insurers when a flexible compensation program is adopted. However, sometimes, "irreconcilable differences" require that an employer's existing carrier be replaced. These circumstances can arise in the following kinds of situations:

- The insurer's services or rates have been uncompetitive, and a change in carriers would have been considered regardless of the proposed program design.
- After some preliminary discussions with the insurer, the employer finds that the insurer's systems or services are unable to adapt to flexible compensation.
- The employer uses two or more insurers to underwrite the current benefit package and determines that consolidation of all benefits under one carrier will simplify flexible compensation administration.

Definitions and assumptions change from carrier to carrier. The employer must ensure that the carrier representatives have a clear understanding of the program as designed by the employer. The search for a replacement occurring in conjunction with a flexible program implementation may not be the best timing for the employer—but in certain situations may be warranted.

(d) IMPLEMENTING THE PROGRAM

Insurers have had considerable experience implementing new benefit plans under traditional benefit programs, both for existing and new clients. Except for any unusual flexible program details created by the addition of choice, the administrative work will be handled by the insurer as any other new program. Assuming that the employer and the carrier have adequately planned the implementation process and assigned project completion dates, the implementation will proceed smoothly.

However, to increase the potential for a smooth transition, following is a short checklist of carrier administrative responsibilities that need to be addressed.

Systems:

- Adapt employee eligibility data to include new benefit choices.
- Program claims payment system with new benefit options and plan provisions.
- Establish the appropriate breakdowns for maintaining and reporting claims experience.

Employee Communication:

- Prepare any required explanatory and enrollment materials and new identification cards.
- Deliver claim forms to the employer for any new benefits being offered.

Contracts:

- Amend policies to reflect new benefits.

Final rates must be established by the insurer prior to communication of the program to employees. This timing is sometimes an issue. Because of communication, enrollment, and systems requirements, an employer might need final rates three to four months (or more) prior to the effective date. Underwriters sometimes do not have data adequate to calculate realistic rates so far in advance of the effective date, especially for coverages where claims experience can fluctuate significantly from month to month. This issue of rate delivery timing should be addressed in preliminary discussions with the insurer. Rates for self-funded coverages, of course, can be developed at any time since insurer involvement is not an issue.

Part Five

Communication

Fifteen

Communicating with Employees

§ 15.1 INTRODUCTION

Even with the most carefully crafted design and the most efficient administration system, the level of success of a flexible compensation program at last depends on one uncontrollable element: people. Benefits, after all, are for *employees*. Eventually, employees will be the judges of how well the program meets their protection needs, motivates their behavior, or encourages them to join or remain with the company.

The reaction of employees, therefore, can determine how well a flexible program meets its objectives, and that reaction will be shaped during the implementation process. Today most employees are aware of the concept of benefit choice making and in some environments have even lobbied employers for a flexible program. Still, when actually faced with making decisions in areas they may never even have thought about before, the mere fact of the change can trigger all the emotions associated with protecting the status quo: fear, uncertainty, suspicion, anxiety. If such potential employee concerns are not dealt with adequately, all the time, money, and effort spent designing the program might just as well never have been spent.

Flexible programs really work best when employees use them well—when their benefit choices change as their life situations change, when they use the spending accounts with minimum forfeitures, when they associate the value of their benefits with the cost of providing them. But flexible programs are used in this way only when employees have confidence in and enthusiasm for the process. Companies achieve the best results when employees are satisfied with the benefit protection available, accepting of the reasons for any cutbacks, comfortable that reasonable cost sharing is fair, and convinced that choice making increases the usefulness of benefits.

However, these results are not achieved automatically with the implementation of a flexible program. Employee satisfaction with flexible compensation cannot be created or controlled by an act of will, but it can be significantly influenced. Communication in a variety of forms can be used effectively to motivate, educate, persuade, and satisfy employees as to the value of the flexible program and their ability to make the decisions they will need to make.

(a) STEPS IN IMPLEMENTATION

Flexible compensation requires a substantial commitment in time and effort from both the employer and the employee. While it is just one part of the implementation task, communication can represent the single largest hard-dollar cost, particularly for employers with few internal design or production resources. And money aside, the sheer size of the communication task can appear overwhelming before the task has even begun. Therefore, communicating a flexible program requires a strategy—a strategy designed to achieve the best results for the time and dollars spent, recognizing that employees have a significant role to play in the final success or failure of the program.

While each flexible compensation program is unique, experience reveals there is a logical order to the information flow:

- **Step One: Developing a plan.** The company should identify an overall communication approach consistent with the organizational environment.
- **Step Two: Announcing the program.** The program must be announced to employees in a way that will maximize positive emotions and minimize negative ones.
- **Step Three: Educating employees.** Employees need additional information to better understand the concepts and get a handle on the facts and figures.

- **Step Four: Enrolling employees in the program.** Enrollment forms, worksheets, workbooks, instructions, and other enrollment-related communication must be clear and easy-to-follow.
- **Step Five: Following up.** Follow-up communication must be considered to help keep the level of benefit understanding high for claims filing and reenrollment.

The remainder of this chapter examines these steps in more detail.

§ 15.2   DEVELOPING A PLAN

Flexible compensation communication is almost always more extensive, more technical, and broader in scope than other employee benefit communication undertakings. If a company is not used to communicating on this scale, the prospect can be daunting. However, organizations implementing a flexible program also see the potential in being able to capitalize on the communication effort as an opportunity—a chance perhaps for the first time to create significant employee interest in benefits, to strengthen awareness and appreciation of employer expenditures for benefits, and to promote greater understanding and ownership of benefit coverages.

Employees' initial reaction to change, the significant impact their decisions could have on their own personal financial security, and the diversity of viewpoints present in any workforce make a substantial communication effort almost mandatory. The investment in time, money, and effort can be significant, but planning the process carefully helps save not only time and money, but considerable effort down the road.

The result of a careful, coordinated planning effort is often a written document—a blueprint that can be followed as the communication campaign unfolds. While such a document is often changed and updated as implementation proceeds, it never fails to keep the campaign on track.

(a)   ANALYZING THE ENVIRONMENT

To get the planning started, assemble a small team including plan designers or administrators and those responsible for the communication effort.

Remember that field representatives can bring a different perspective. Once the team is assembled, invest some time in reviewing the task ahead and analyzing the communications environment at the company. In short, make sure all team members are starting from the same place. To a large extent, designing the appropriate communication campaign depends on the team's conclusions on environmental issues such as:

- **Scope of the program**—which benefits are involved and what is the level of employee risk if a "wrong" decision is made; which parts of the program will change the most and require more explanation; which benefit areas have been historically "sensitive" for employees
- **Audience**—which employee groups will be included in the program; the profile of the audience (age, sex, marital status, length of service, level of education, etc.); the need for translation to a foreign language; how important/unimportant communicating to families might be
- **Employee relations climate**—how employees are feeling about the company *before* flexible compensation; field morale versus morale at company headquarters; relations with unions or groups lobbying for unionization; recent history of benefit or compensation increases or cutbacks
- **Current business environment**—both inside the company and among competitors—how the company is faring economically; how employees have seen the results (e.g., layoffs, bonuses); how the flexible program reflects the company's business strategy; any good news or bad news likely to break during the implementation of the flexible program
- **Existing communication channels**—benefit communication that worked well and not so well in the past; other internal communication channels typically not used for benefit communication but which might be considered; any new equipment or technology recently available to the company.

And finally, consider any particular "trouble spots" which may not be reflective of the company as a whole but may affect how the program is received by a particular group or division, for example, rumors of a plant closing at one location. Once the planning team has a shared understanding of the communications *environment*, the focus can narrow to the communication campaign.

(b) SETTING OBJECTIVES AND CHOOSING MESSAGES

The most effective communication campaigns are designed to meet very specific objectives. "Let's just tell employees about it" is certainly a straightforward approach, but one that quickly gets mired down in a mass of detail and contradictory messages. Furthermore, it is all but impossible to communicate just the facts. Facts are always colored by the viewpoint of the communicator; words carry connotative as well as denotative messages. One of the first tasks in the planning process, therefore, is for the team to decide just what they want to tell employees and how they want the message told. This is done by setting objectives, by establishing parameters that will guide the communication effort.

For example, one company may want to emphasize the value and competitiveness of the flexible program. For another company, the priority might be to introduce the concept of total compensation—tying benefits and pay together. Other broad objectives could include:

- Explaining the concept and rationale behind flexible compensation
- Educating employees so they can make informed decisions
- Conveying the concept of managing or controlling benefit costs for the future
- Introducing the concept of an employer/employee partnership in providing protection and security
- Establishing a company identity in a merger, spinoff, or reorganization environment.

Once overall objectives have been agreed upon, the planning team should list the most important messages—the central issues or ideas to convey to employees through the communication effort. Such messages might include:

- "You can tailor coverages to your own needs."
- "You and the company can manage costs better."
- "You can choose (not choose) your old plans."
- "You can take advantage of important tax benefits."
- "Choice is a good thing."
- "The program is unique."
- "Nobody loses."
- "The company is spending the same amount of dollars as before."

The unique character and environment of the organization should lead naturally to the right objectives and specific messages for the communication campaign. The planning team's study of the background and climate should inform the objective-setting process, just as the chosen objectives and messages will be the raw material from which the communication pieces finally will be developed.

(c) DEFINING MEDIA AND APPROACH

Once the planning team has identified *what* they want to say, they need to turn their attention to *how* they want the message delivered—the media for getting the message from the company to the employee. Clearly, every known medium for human communication can be considered from the simplest (face-to-face) to the most complex (satellite transmission to a company cable system or interactive video presentations using laser disks). The task of the planning team is to determine which vehicles make the most sense given what they know about the company's environment.

Despite the vast array of possibilities, most flexible programs are communicated using multiple combinations of generally available types of media—employee meetings as well as print and audiovisual presentations. According to a recent survey, employers with flexible programs in place identified the media they used in the first year and subsequent years as shown in Table 15.1.

Determining the media, however, is only half the battle. Most people (particularly in office environments) receive a blizzard of paper every day. Employees must have some means to identify which information is related to the flexible program and which is not. In other words, a "communication campaign" is not a "campaign" unless it contains some unifying elements. Those elements typically fall into two categories: vocabulary and design.

Choosing a vocabulary for the flexible program can seem relatively simple. First, the planning team must decide what the program is to be called. Now that flexible compensation programs have been around for several years, it is not surprising that most, if not all, of the generic names have been devised and are in use. Here is a representative list:

Flexplan '88 ('89, '90, etc.)	ChoiceSystem
FlexAccount	FlexComp
Flex Fund	FlexChoice

Table 15.1
Communication Media

	First Year (%)	Subsequent Years (%)
Employee meetings	97	78
Newsletters	79	54
Highlights brochure	79	46
Personalized enrollment material	71	58
Election confirmation report	68	52
Bulletin board notices, memos	63	48
Enrollment workbook	63	39
Summary plan descriptions (SPDs)	49	50
Hotline and/or information center	54	36
Sound/slide show	48	21
Videotape presentation	47	16
Benefit statements	39	44
Payroll inserts	23	13
Claim kit	18	9
Interactive computer software	5	3

Source: Hewitt Associates 1987 Survey of Flexible Compensation Programs and Practices.

(Continued)

SelectPay	BeneTrade
PlusPay	Flexpay
Benefits Plus	BenePlus
FlexSecurity	Beneflex

In certain circumstances, a new and unusual name readily presents itself. A prominent brokerage house uses "FlexFolio" and a major utility company uses "FlexPower." However, more and more today, employers are turning away from coining a name for their flexible program and simply referring to it as "Flexible Benefits" or "Flexible Compensation." An obvious reason is the dwindling supply of names not already in use. An alternative is to tie the campaign together with a theme or tagline, such as these being used by companies today:

". . . The Right Combination"
". . . Benefits You Can Count On"
". . . The Choice for Your Future"

Once a name or theme has been chosen and other vocabulary decisions have been made (such as what to call option prices, flexible credits, etc.), graphic designers can be called in to unify the look of the campaign with color, type style, paper, illustrations, and other graphic design elements. Again, make sure the approach chosen is appropriate for the environment. It is probably unwise to adorn communication materials with expensive looking graphics if the flexible program is accompanied by significant benefit cutbacks. On the other hand, in a different environment, bright, interesting graphics can send a message to employees that the new program is valuable and a high priority to the company.

(d) ESTABLISHING SCHEDULES, RESPONSIBILITIES, AND BUDGETS

The planning process is incomplete until a schedule for implementation has been established, responsibilities have been assigned, and budgets have been approved. Typically an employer will need more time, more people, and more money in the first year flexible compensation is communicated than in later years.

Communication planning needs to occur well in advance of the targeted implementation date. As a general rule, the average number of months required for planning the campaign and preparing the materials is six months. Interestingly, the lead time for getting a campaign underway tends to vary little by the size of the organization. (For example, companies with 10,000 or more employees require on average about 6.7 months of preparation time, while smaller organizations take a little over five months for preparation.) In effect, the planning process involves about the same magnitude of effort, regardless of the number of employees eligible for the program. A typical timetable for communication is shown in Example 15.1.

To assign responsibilities, the planning team must first consider any internal resources the organization can bring to bear, including the corporate communication staff, training department, print shop and mail room, and even graphic designers from the marketing department, if appropriate. In some companies, the staffing requirements will have been included in the prior year's budgeting process. However, the vast majority of companies must try to staff the communication effort with internal people already committed to other projects. The corporate communication staff will have the bimonthly company magazine to release, the training department will be committed to the annual sales meeting, and so on. However, once the planning team

Example 15.1
Sample Communication Timetable

Activity	1988									1989	
	Apr	May	Jun	Jul	Aug	Sep	Oct	Nov	Dec	Jan	Feb
Develop communication plan		■									
Present to management			■								
Present to human resources staff			■								
Distribute announcement materials				■							
Publish articles in company newspaper					■		■		■		■
Issue newsletter (twice monthly)					■		■				
Pretest enrollment materials					■						
Train meeting leaders/counselors						■					
Conduct employee meetings/distribute election kits							■	■			
Staff benefits hotline							■	■	■		
Election deadline								■			
Send confirmation reports									■		
Effective date									■		

knows how much talent and time is available internally, it can fill the gaps with outside resources, up to the budget available.

It is difficult to generalize about budgets for flexible compensation communication. So many elements will vary from company to company and campaign to campaign. However, there seems to be one almost-universal truth: it is more extensive and will cost more than any other benefit communication the company has ever undertaken. During the implementation year, communication costs are driven up by the sheer volume of information and the number of individual communication pieces required to carry the communication effectively in a relatively short period of time.

When budgeting, the planning team must consider these issues:

- The internal resources (soft dollars) available and the external support (hard dollars) that will be needed
- The complexity of the flexible program or the company environment (some companies simply have more information to send than others)
- The size of the population and the quantity of the materials needed
- The media included in the plan, including any design elements which will affect costs (colors, paper quality, illustrations or photographs, etc.)
- The availability and efficiency of the distribution network in place at the company for shipping and receiving materials.

As might be expected, communication costs vary by type of flexible program. For example, the numerous moveable parts within a choice-making-plus-flexible-spending-account arrangement would require a more extensive first-year communication effort than a stand-alone spending account. Figure 15.2 shows the average internal (soft dollar), external (hard dollar), and total costs associated with each type of program.

On a per capita basis, however, costs decrease with the size of the organization as shown in Figure 15.3.

These are significant dollars. But when compared to the cost employers pay every year to provide benefits to employees, and considering the value to be gained when employees understand and appreciate a flexible program, the numbers begin to appear less overwhelming. When setting communication budgets for a flexible program implementation, therefore, it is helpful to understand upfront that the numbers will be

Figure 15.2
First Year Average Communication Costs

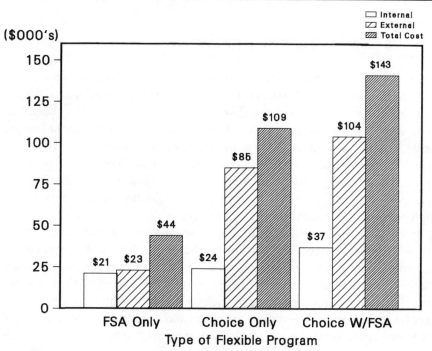

Source: Hewitt Associates 1987 Survey of Flexible Compensation Programs and Practices.

Figure 15.3
Average Communication Costs Per Employee

| | Per Employee Total Cost | |
| | Flexible Spending | Choicemaking with Flexible |
Eligible Population	Account	Spending Account
Less than 1,000	$25.75	$49.40
1,001 to 5,000	16.70	28.00
5,001 to 10,000	*	23.50
10,000 or more	2.95	15.80
Average:	$ 5.05	$20.80

Source: Hewitt Associates 1987 Survey of Flexible Compensation Programs and Practices.
*Too small a sample size for reliable cost data.

large. But they do not have to be unreasonable; with proper planning, costs can be controlled and managed.

§ 15.3   ANNOUNCING THE PROGRAM

Once the communication plan has been completed and approved, the campaign can begin. A successful announcement phase starts where employees are and recognizes that the company will seldom have the first word. The grapevine often has taken care of that. In hallways, break rooms, and plant floors, on telephones, telexes, and assembly lines, the news about flexible compensation may be out and possibly inaccurately so. By the time the employer is ready with the big announcement, employee reactions already might have been kicked into high gear by half-truths and sheer conjecture.

In this environment, announcing a flexible compensation program can sometimes be seen as a marketing challenge. The company needs to get employees' attention and convince them that official channels are the best, most reliable sources of information. Starting with many details is usually a mistake; instead, acknowledge the turmoil employees may be in and begin there. Get managers and the human resources staff on board first, for this group will later support the communication effort with employees.

To the extent possible, announcement communication should be:

- **Straightforward.** In a general way, let employees know what they are winning and what they are losing.
- **Reassuring.** Provide evidence of management support and assure employees that more communication (more details) will follow.
- **Attention-getting.** Keep it short and simple.

Employee acceptance can pay large dividends to an employer, so many companies have chosen innovative approaches to announcement materials, approaches they would not have considered before flexible compensation. These include highly creative campaign themes; novelty items such as buttons, T-shirts, and posters; and a wide variety of other nontraditional media. This type of unusual media blitz can be very effective, depending on the environment, but it is not always necessary. A letter from the Vice-President of Human Resources or a memo from the CEO can work just as well. What is needed is good, clear, reassuring, simple, and straightforward communication.

§ 15.4   EDUCATING EMPLOYEES

Once employees have tuned in to the company as a source of information, the channel cannot go off the air and still expect to keep the audience enthralled. A steady flow of information will not only keep employees' interest but will begin to provide the misinformed with consistent, accurate information.

Education is an important step in achieving employee acceptance of the program, but do not give too much education at one time. If we are honest in remembering our worst educational experiences, they would probably include the nonstop lecture packed with details and the all-night study sessions before exams. Usually, we passed the exams but forgot the content within a week. The concepts behind flexible compensation and the details of how the individual plans work need to be stored more permanently. Employees need to make this information part of their working knowledge, to build on in the months and years ahead. Employers can help by developing educational materials that:

- **Arrive in small doses.**   Build understanding in the employee group by adding one piece of knowledge to another. Employees may not take the time to read a book about their benefits, but they likely will read four pages once every couple of weeks.

- **Focus on what is important.**   Providing all the details during implementation is probably not only unnecessary, but self-defeating. Employees cast adrift on a sea of information will pick and choose the messages they receive (or choose none at all). Focus on what employees *must* know to enroll; save the fine print for later.

- **Offer diversity.**   Different people are attracted by different media. Some read newspapers; others do not. Different company locations may have very different media needs. Communicate in different ways, at different times, and remember to provide a forum for getting questions answered.

- **Encourage learning over time.**   With flexible compensation, employees are required to understand benefit messages in more than a general way. Experience indicates that for a typical full-flexible program, employees will need to devote several hours to their decision process. The volume of details alone, not to mention the importance of the decisions being required, indicates that reinforcement of the messages is critical. Communicate simply, but often.

Newsletters or regular articles in the company newspaper can be very effective vehicles for time-releasing details about the program in specific environments. One large health care company used newsletters to good effect because employees had been trained to receive company financial information in that format. On the other hand, a large manufacturing company had less success with this method because many employees had no workspace to keep such materials, and the company was unwilling to incur the cost to send materials home.

The key is to take the audience into account when choosing the media for the education phase. If newsletters will not work, maybe a highlights brochure sent to the home will. Or try an audiocassette. One Midwest power company mounted a sales-like campaign to encourage employees to read the education materials. Local sports figures were enlisted to make 60-second "commercials" for the flexible program on audiotape. For example, a catcher from the local American League baseball team talked about how he needed more protection than his teammates and compared his situation to an employee with several dependents. The audiotapes were played over the public address system in cafeterias and throughout company buildings at the end of each day. An unusual approach, certainly, but tailor-made for an employee audience unaccustomed or hesitant to read benefit materials.

Most organizations also conduct employee meetings near the end of the print communication campaign. This is usually the time when a company unveils a sound-slide show or audiovisual presentation encapsulating and to some extent "selling" the merits of the new program. In addition, employees have the opportunity for face-to-face interaction with meeting leaders who are well-versed in the program, familiar with the organization's reasons for "going fexible," and available to field any questions about the new program.

§ 15.5 ENROLLING EMPLOYEES

By the time employees have reached this stage, they should have received enough information (in small doses) to have a basic understanding of the concepts and important details of the program. They should feel satisfied that they understand how they will be affected by flexible compensation and the company's motives for implementing the program.

Enrollment communication has two goals. First, from the company's perspective, enrollment forms must be completed and returned on time and as accurately as possible. And second, from the employees' perspective, the enrollment process must be relatively easy and nonthreatening. These goals are not necessarily mutually exclusive, but they often seem as if they are. In fact, the entire implementation effort can flourish or founder on this issue.

Enrollment materials must represent the joint efforts of computer systems, administration, and communication professionals. If systems issues drive the development of materials, the result is often too technical for administrators or employees to use easily. If administration issues take over, the often cumbersome result is not only complex for employees, but impossible for keypunchers to follow.

Communicators can cause problems, too. When communication issues are allowed to override systems and administration concerns, the materials may not provide enough information to allow systems and administration people to do their jobs.

Effective enrollment communication builds on the foundation laid during the education process and takes into account the needs of other disciplines. It is effective when it is:

- **Clear and easy to follow.**   If enrollment is the "final exam," make sure the test is easy to understand. Provide examples and simple instructions, directing employees from one piece to another or from one part of the form to another. Clearly identify space used only by administrators.

- **Consistent.**   Keep the anxiety level low by using terms and phrases made familiar by earlier communication. There should be no surprises here, no last minute changes in terminology to confuse employees.

- **Complete.**   Tell employees what they need to think about and what they can ignore for now.

- **Positive.**   This is the chance to revisit the big picture, to look at the overall goals of the program and to define a future direction for benefits and compensation at the company. After concentrating on the details for a period of time, employees will welcome the opportunity to put the pieces together.

If there is a secret to a successful enrollment phase, it can be summed up in one word: personalization. Employees learn the value of flexible compensation more quickly and completely when they see the effects on their own situations before choosing coverage. Communication materials can be personalized to varying degrees. Here are some common approaches, listed in order of increasing personalization:

- **Role-modeling** uses a number of fictional examples and allows employees to identify the ones most closely resembling their personal situations. Typically included in overview materials or audiovisual presentations, role-modeling establishes a set of demographics and life circumstances, then outlines why the fictional people chose the benefits they did. While technically not a true personalization, role-modeling does help employees become aware of the different issues they may have to think about when making their own decisions.

- **Worksheets, workbooks, and calculators** allow employees to learn something about how benefits affect them personally by entering personal information manually and doing calculations. For example, a worksheet for a spending account might ask employees to write down eligible expenses they had in the previous year (glasses, physical exams, dental work, dependent day care, etc.), then estimate how much they expect those expenses to be in the coming twelve months. An additional calculation with the help of tables will show the employee the tax savings expected by using the spending account for those expenses.

- **Computerized reports, worksheets, and election forms** provide some basic personalized information for each employee from the company's data base. If there are restrictions on certain benefit options—HMO eligibility, for example—these personalized materials can show just those options for which the employee is actually eligible. When benefit amounts or option prices differ by pay, family status, or years of service, computer-printed materials can show employees the precise value of the benefit and what it will cost them to choose it. Not only is this information clearly useful to the employee when making decisions, but it can prevent a multitude of errors on election forms by limiting the number of mathematical steps the employee must take.

- **Interactive software and interactive video** are beginning to emerge as an effective new medium for employers to communicate with employees during the enrollment phase, and for good reason. Interactive materials offer the highest degree of personalization. Employees with access to such a system can not only find their individual benefit amounts and prices, but they can create new scenarios again and again before finally completing the enrollment form. They can watch as each change in option affects not only their coverage but their overall cost and their tax situation. They can project account balances into the future and look at the effect of choice making on their take-home pay with the push of a button.

All the goodwill earned through the announcement and education stages can reap rewards for the employer now. If enrollment materials are personalized to some degree, usable, and easy to understand, employee confidence and appreciation for the program will grow, and the enrollment process will meet with fewer errors overall.

§ 15.6   FOLLOWING UP

Are employees satisfied with flexible compensation? At the time of enrollment, the final answer to that question is still probably nine to twelve months away. If the enrollment process has gone well, most employees will be fairly satisfied with the *idea* of choice making. However, the true test will come when they actually start to *use* the new program or when they reenroll. That is when follow-up communication can make a major difference.

Unfortunately, at too many companies, the implementation team disbands—officially or unofficially—after enrollment. Each discipline goes its own way, usually on to other concerns or new projects. This feeling of closure at enrollment time is natural. But if a concerted effort is not made to keep up the flow of information, companies run the risk of abandoning the field just as the game is nearly won. Ultimately, employees will judge the program by how well they remember the elections they made, how easily they can get a question answered, how efficiently claims are processed, and how willing they are to "play the game" when reenrollment rolls around.

The follow-up communication stage is really never over, but it is probably most critical in the first twelve months after implementation. To be effective, follow-up communication should be confirming, consistent, and complete.

To be confirming, find ways to report to employees about the benefit coverage they elected individually and as a group. A computerized confirmation or benefit statement is a clear communication to employees that the "system" understood and recorded their elections accurately. It will also serve as a reminder of the coverage they have when they need to use their plans months down the road.

Use the newsletter or company newspaper to reinforce the election patterns which meet the program's objectives. And find out how employees felt about the enrollment process by the most direct approach: ask them. Do a follow-up focus-group study or ask a random sample of employees to complete a questionnaire and report the results to the employee group.

To be consistent, simply keep up the good work. If the communication approach used for implementation worked (graphics, theme, terminology, etc.), do not abandon it now. Build on what has gone before as claim forms, status-change forms, reimbursement forms, account statements, summary plan descriptions, and other communication materials are developed.

To be complete, think about filling in the gaps. Now is the time for summary plan descriptions and all the detail employees could not have used effectively during enrollment. Take some time to repackage or reorganize reference materials. There may be a more logical approach for the flexible compensation environment.

Perhaps the most important job in the follow-up phase is the communication leading up to and surrounding second year enrollments. "Reflex" provides an opportunity for the company to make things better, to learn from any mistakes made during implementation and broaden the base of employee satisfaction. Taking time to evaluate first-year communication efforts can help immeasurably when year two appears on the horizon.

§ 15.7 SPECIAL CONSIDERATIONS

Ideally, this five-step approach to communication will lead to a successful implementation. Particularly if the company is offering a good news benefit package, the communication effort, while extensive, can be fairly straightforward.

However, not all companies will be serving up unleavened good news. In many cases, flexible compensation is accompanied by cutbacks. In others, employers must approach a workforce mindful of past economic or organizational problems. Even at companies where almost everything lines up in the good news column, pockets of employees may have reactions different from the population as a whole. For these companies, communication can be seen as the most unpredictable factor in

a flexible compensation implementation. Many of the particular communication problems such companies will face are emotional in nature, while others are simply related to getting the job done. Either way,
the successful solving of these communication problems is not only essential, but it can have a major positive effect on employee acceptance
of the flexible program.

(a) EMPLOYEE UNCERTAINTY

Whether they believe flexible compensation is a good idea or a bad idea,
the secondary reaction of most employees hearing about it for the first
time is uncertainty. They are being asked to make decisions in an area
that could have a significant effect on their financial security, but also
one they know little or nothing about as yet. "The Company" has always
made those decisions before. Suddenly, it seems, they have to learn a
whole new language, and the risk of failure seems high.

Disarming employee uncertainty is a gradual process. It starts with
the confidence projected by company representatives as they announce
the program, and it usually ends once the employee has successfully
enrolled and used the new benefits. The communication campaign can
encourage this process by including some basic strategies:

- **Focus on personalized communication.** Provide materials that
  will help employees understand how their decisions affect their personal situation. Find ways to demonstrate the balance between benefit cost and risk in a *personal* way. Any opportunity employees have
  to try different scenarios with real numbers will help them make
  decisions they can feel good about.
- **Provide real life examples.** The new program will not operate in
  a vacuum. It is designed for *people* to use, so provide employees with
  examples of how real people might elect and use their benefits.
- **Emphasize the implications.** To be comfortable with choice making, employees need to know more than the facts and figures. They
  also need to understand the implications of what they are doing, the
  reasons why one employee might choose differently from another.
  While a line must be drawn between informing and giving employees
  advice, even a list of issues employees should consider can help.
- **Provide an effective question and answer network.** Employees
  should know about and feel comfortable approaching a designated
  person for answers to their questions. An effective network of this

type can be crucial in resolving misunderstandings, clearing up complaints, and facilitating decision making.

(b) EMPLOYEE SUSPICION

In some environments, employees can view a flexible program as management's attempt to "sneak something past" them. One company was surprised at the high level of employee suspicion their new program caused, even though the program was announced shortly after the company reorganized and laid off 5,000 people. An unstable business or employee relations environment is the best breeding ground for employee suspicions. This type of negative organizational background will affect *any* changes the employer makes—flexible or not. And when flexible compensation is being used as an opportunity for increased cost sharing or other perceived cutbacks, negative employee perceptions can develop very quickly.

However, of all the communication problems, employee suspicion succumbs most easily to the right communication strategy. It depends, in part, on having realistic goals. It may be impossible to get all employees to embrace the program completely, but it *is* possible to help many of them understand the reasons behind the changes and to accept the business decisions as necessary, no matter how unpleasant.

The best way is to be straightforward. For employees to support the program, they must have the whole story. Companies should have confidence in their benefit design and address any trade-offs openly. Tell both sides of the story and, importantly, give employees the *reasons* behind the decisions. A high degree of management and supervisory support for the program can help here. And finally, rely on the value of choice making to help sweeten the pot. While employers should not market the program beyond its merits, experience shows that a substantial number of employees will see cost sharing as a fair trade for the benefit of flexibility.

§ 15.8 SUMMING UP

Communication is one of the most important aspects of the implementation process. The employer simply has no other choice but to communicate and communicate well. Therefore, companies considering a flexible program might as well bite the bullet and realize it will take a major commitment of resources—both money and people—to do the communication job right. Since those resources will be required any-way—whether the communication is effective or just mediocre—companies should take this opportunity to at least think differently about how the task might be approached. Look at new media possibili-ties. Identify new strategies. And most importantly, plan the communi-cation effort in detail so both time and money can be used wisely.

Experience shows that all of the resources it takes to communicate a flexible program are worth it in the end. When the communication job is done well, when employees are comfortable with the program and trust the process, the company's other objectives for flexible compensa-tion—even cost management—are more easily attainable.

Sixteen

Training the Human Resources Staff

§ 16.1 INTRODUCTION

While often seen as two separate disciplines, employee communication and the training of the human resources staff are inextricably linked when introducing flexible compensation. Without the enthusiasm, understanding, and support of these professionals, it is unlikely employees will receive the kind of education and personal attention they need during the implementation phase.

In many ways, the human resources staff can be considered part of the media for communicating flexible compensation. Regardless of the title they use—personnel representatives, benefit administrators, human resources professionals—their potential for influencing employee behavior (positively or negatively) is far greater than for any other vehicle in the communication campaign. These are the meeting leaders who will be the first to put a "human face" on all the printed communication employees have been reading about the new flexible program. These are the administrators who will be staffing benefit hotlines and otherwise answering questions employees might have about enrollment or their specific coverages under the new flexible program. These might also be the people who will be helping employees file claims under the new flexible program.

Still, most companies spend more time, money, and effort preparing booklets and videotapes than they do preparing this most effective communication resource. While the level of success of the flexible program is highly dependent on the ability of these people to communicate, training them to do their job well is often an afterthought.

If personnel representatives are media, however, they are also audience. First and foremost, they are employees—with the same personal questions and concerns as the rest of the employee population. Furthermore, the satisfaction an organization hopes to generate in employees over a period of time must be achieved in them much more quickly. They have a job to do—a job critical to a successful implementation.

That job further defines the personnel representatives as audience. To meet their personal needs, they must have similar types of information as employees. But to meet their professional needs, they must have more in-depth knowledge of the program. They must have specific skills in leadership, counseling, and administration. They must have positive, realistic attitudes. And they must have it all sooner, before they become the focus of the program for employees.

For this reason, organizations implementing flexible compensation are really facing *two* communication campaigns: one for employees and one, less elaborate but nevertheless complete, for the human resources staff. The campaigns must be integrated and compatible although unfolding along separate time lines and using different media plans.

§ 16.2 TRAINING THE TRAINER

Besides their usual administrative function, personnel representatives can be thought of as trainers—people who teach or direct the understanding and attitudes of the employee group. As trainers, they will be considered the experts by employees looking for answers, but the level of knowledge, experience, and competency will vary by role and level of experience. Managers and members of the implementation team are likely to bring more experience and skill to the training task. Local benefits representatives, on the other hand, may be less comfortable representing the program to employees.

Some representatives are newcomers who inherited whatever knowledge they have from the person who occupied the job before them. Others are old hands who may have a good grasp of how the current plans work, but they may lack a broad outlook as to why the plans function as they do. Still others have been at their jobs so long that the fundamental changes required by flexible compensation will seem almost bewildering. The larger the company, the wider the range will be.

A common mistake is for implementation teams (who typically have been studying and working on the program design for several months) to assume that other benefits professionals in the company will approach implementation with the same knowledge base. Organizations must recognize that people other than those who have been intimately involved with benefit design will be responsible for administering flexible compensation and telling employees about the program. In short, the trainers must first be trained.

The goal of training is to develop personnel representatives who are both competent to carry out the new requirements of their jobs and confident in their ability to do so. While there are no hard and fast rules for designing a training program, it is usually helpful to follow the same five steps involved in employee communication: planning, announcement, education, enrollment, and follow up.

(a)   DEVELOPING A PLAN

The training program for personnel representatives will depend in large measure on the roles they will ultimately play in the implementation and ongoing administration of flexible compensation. Like employee communication, a training program should be planned in advance to take into account the scope of the flexible program, the employee relations climate, and the current business environment. But the type of training needed will also depend on the:

- Background and experience of those being trained, including the current state of morale of the human resources staff locally and company-wide
- Roles they will be called upon to perform—the administrative function of the benefit administrator, the employee relations function of meeting leaders or election counselors, or the coordination function of managers
- Specific knowledge, skills, and attitudes required for the implementation
- Other duties they perform on a regular basis and the time they will have available to train for and carry out their implementation roles
- Geographic dispersion and local backup available, and
- Commitment of the organization to training, in terms of time, money, and effort.

(b) ANNOUNCING THE PROGRAM

Too often, personnel representatives learn about the flexible compensation implementation at the same time employees do. Or they receive a cursory memo from the Vice-President of Human Resources a few days before the "big announcement"—time enough for them to worry about all the questions they will get but not time enough to prepare themselves or ask for additional details. Considering that the attitudes of these professionals will be critical to employee acceptance of the program, this type of announcement is a major tactical error. Organizations taking this approach set themselves up for problems by antagonizing the very people they must have on their side.

The solution is relatively simple. Inform and *train* personnel representatives before sending them into the line of fire. A memo from the Vice-President of Human Resources is not a bad start if it explains the roles human resources staff members will play, arrives well before the announcement to employees, describes the training they will receive, and provides the name and phone number of a person who can answer questions. Allay their initial concerns by providing case histories of successful implementations at other, similar organizations. If possible, involve them in testing employee communication materials and help them feel some ownership in the change by encouraging participation in the decision-making process.

By preparing the human resources staff early in the process, some information will start leaking to employees before the official announcement, but the grapevine will always be ahead of official communication channels anyway. At least the organization can head off some potential concerns by preparing personnel representatives in advance. Moreover, with an informed staff participating, chances are the information on the grapevine will be more accurate than otherwise might be the case.

(c) EDUCATING THE HUMAN RESOURCES STAFF

Whether the communication is for employees or personnel representatives, it is important to provide the details in small doses. It is unrealistic for a company to bring together its human resources staff just before the election process starts and force them to learn everything they need to know in two days. Confronted with this scenario, they probably will not even *look* at the massive resource binders they receive, let alone *read* them.

Information should begin flowing shortly after the plan design is completed. Again, consider the time personnel representatives have available to devote to their education. Chances are, this new information will have to be absorbed in addition to the work they already are handling. Phasing in their education respects the demands on their time and increases the likelihood that they will learn what they need to know.

By the time the program is announced to employees, personnel representatives must have a working knowledge of the concepts behind the flexible program, how the plans work, and what will be required of them and of employees. As information is released to employees, the trainers need an ever-deepening level of knowledge to keep up with the questions they will be getting. When planning how to provide this information, keep in mind:

- **Variety.**   Communicate in different ways, at different times. Some learn better by reading, others through face-to-face discussion, and still others from lectures. This does not necessarily mean high-cost production values (art, color, and other design elements). Simple, black and white memos can be effective as long as they are not the only communication vehicle used.
- **Overload.**   Too much at one time is never a good thing. If a groundwork of plan knowledge is laid over a period of time, formal training meetings can be used to better advantage by concentrating on skills development.
- **Examples.**   Build on the benefits knowledge administrators already have. Start with the most familiar aspects, then add more information. Use examples common in their work, then illustrate the new situation. Better still, ask them to share examples of employees' questions in a formal or informal network as the program unfolds.
- **Recap and review.**   Do not forget to tie it all together. Understanding the "whys" will be just as critical as knowing the "whats" and "hows."
- **Role definition.**   Help the personnel representatives understand what they have to do and when they have to do it. Make them feel part of the team. Even sending tidbits of "fun" information, like how the Vice-President of Human Resources forgot to sign her election form, can reinforce the feeling of teamwork.

Finally, determine exactly how much information will be useful. People serving in different functional disciplines may need different amounts or types of information in order to be competent and confident in the roles they will play.

(d) ENROLLING EMPLOYEES

While employee questions will add to the workload of the human resources staff throughout the flexible compensation introduction, the actual enrollment phase "turns up the heat." Their normal workload must be set aside completely for anywhere from two weeks to two months, depending on the situation. Furthermore, personnel representatives must suddenly become more *proactive.* Instead of responding to employees' initiatives, they will be required to lead meetings, counsel elections, work with new administration procedures or software, or manage these activities.

To that anxiety, add the fact that they will be making their own benefit elections. They will be going through the same process as employees—discerning their protection needs, evaluating their family situations, weighing cost versus risk. All in all, enrollment time is a high-stress period for administrative staff, so the better prepared they are (in advance) the more successful they will be.

One simple but considerate approach might be to allow them to dispose of their personal elections before the actual enrollment period, if possible. Let them make their elections early. If that is not feasible, at least provide copies of the enrollment materials and structure exercises so they can do all the thinking and decision making in advance, leaving only the form to complete during their busy period.

With their personal situations taken care of, the next step is to help increase the confidence level of personnel representatives. In formal training sessions, provide ways for them to test their knowledge of the program and to practice specific skills needed in the final weeks before implementation. Allow representatives to practice leading meetings, handling questions, dealing with confrontational behavior, correcting election errors, or running new administration programs, for example.

(e) FOLLOWING UP

Once all the elections are entered and confirmed, the real, everyday work begins. While the administrative processes will continue to be fine-tuned over a period of time, three specific types of follow up are extremely valuable but often overlooked:

- **Debrief them.** The human resources staff is in the best position to describe what went right and what went wrong with the implementation. They can explain how the employee communication materials should be improved and how smoothly the enrollment process went. For an organization looking ahead to second year enrollments, this resource is invaluable and relatively easy to tap.
- **Say thank you.** Personnel representatives have stretched beyond their former limits to help the organization implement flexible compensation. A simple "thank you"—unassociated with any other task-related communication—will speak volumes.
- **Keep them informed of what is ahead.** Implementation-related issues will continue to be important for six to twelve months after the actual effective date. Keep personnel representatives up-to-date on enrollment patterns, status changes, and other information that could have an effect on how they do their jobs.

§ 16.3 TYPES OF TRAINING

The effectiveness of any training program will finally be judged by how successfully the personnel representatives do their implementation jobs. Success usually depends on the mastery of certain knowledge and skills used to carry out various roles. When designing a training program, then, the organization should spend some time identifying the specific knowledge, skills, and roles needed, based on the current environment and company objectives.

(a) TRAINING FOR KNOWLEDGE

Much of the earlier discussion on education applies to building knowledge. Knowledge includes the "facts and figures," plan provisions, election processes, and role definition. But while paper flow and administrative procedures need to be mastered, training for knowledge should also focus on the big picture: how each plan works in the context of the others and the organization's compensation philosophy and objectives.

The first impulse when training for knowledge is to organize a lecture or classroom setting. The classic arrangement is to fill an auditorium, set up a projector, create several hundred overhead transparencies, and watch the audience slowly sink into their chairs with glazed eyes before the first coffee break. There is a better way; in fact, there are many better ways. Time-releasing information gives the organization an opportunity to communicate knowledge in a variety of formats. Newsletter articles, audiotapes, summaries, reviews, opportunities for self-testing or peer discussion, computerized or videotape instruction—all can be effective in helping personnel representatives acquire the knowledge they need.

On the other hand, there is a value to large group meetings. Training meetings are important opportunities for administrators to meet and talk with one another, to ask questions, to get the most up-to-date information, to *build* on the knowledge they already have. But in training for knowledge, large meetings should focus on the *key* issues. The details can be sent out in advance.

(b) TRAINING FOR SKILLS

Besides acquiring a new base of knowledge about flexible compensation, the human resources staff will need to learn or improve certain skills or behaviors. The specific skills needed will depend on the roles each individual will play and will run the gamut from operating the videotape machine in an employee meeting to running a sophisticated new computer program or working one-on-one with participants who may be frustrated. Those who are experienced will already have many of the needed skills. Others will have to brush up on one or two, while still others will never have performed the skill their implementation roles will demand.

When the objective is developing or improving skills, information alone will not do the job. To *own* the skills, the personnel representative will need a chance to *practice* them. Start by providing models, demonstrations, or case studies of the skill needed. Then move on to application projects, that is, experiments the administrators can conduct on their own, in feedback sessions with small groups, or in role playing exercises. If the skill is technical in nature, running equipment, for example, set up the equipment in an environment where they can practice and ask questions in case of trouble.

Because some people are "quicker studies," they will acquire new skills faster than others. Be sure to allow enough time for the majority of personnel representatives to become confident in their ability to use the new skill or behavior. If they feel unsure or unprepared, that uncertainty will be the primary message transmitted to the employee group.

(c) TRAINING FOR ROLES

Everyone who will be involved in the flexible compensation implementation will require training in knowledge and skills. But how much training they need in each area—and the specific types of knowledge and skills—will depend on the actual jobs they will be doing. The most effective training programs are role-specific, providing a basic level of training for everyone with additional efforts tailored to the different roles to be performed.

The first task is to define who will be performing which task, and that is not as easy as it sounds. Depending on the people available, it may not be easy to assign one job to this person and another job to that person. Very often, members of the human resources staff will fill more than one role. Meeting leaders may also be election counselors. Benefit administrators may also be meeting leaders. Where there are limited resources, the human resources manager may wear all of these hats. The specific roles and how they are filled will vary from organization to organization, but there are still some role-specific training issues to consider.

(1) Training Benefit Administrators

Benefit administrators have the responsibility for administering the program over the long term. They may supervise a staff of people who will keypunch employees' benefit elections. They usually process claims and answer employees' day-to-day questions about how the plans work. They are typically identified as professional benefits specialists, the "gurus" with all the answers.

Knowledge-building will be a crucial part of the training for benefit administrators. They will need detailed resources if they are to continue to do their jobs effectively following implementation. Administration manuals (detailed descriptions of administrative procedures) are important tools for them. Benefit administrators will ask questions on the fine points of plan design; they will need enrollment procedures defined down to the form number on the data input sheet. Usually, no one else will need the level of detail that benefit administrators require, so it is important to meet their information needs apart from the general training sessions.

Skill development will also be important, particularly if benefit administrators must use new computer systems or administrative processes. If the training involves new technology, relate the new procedures to the old way of doing things so they can get their bearings. Allow time for hands-on work (reviewing completed forms for errors, working on terminals, etc.), so they feel confident with the process once the "flood" of enrollments begins.

(2)   Training Meeting Leaders

If employee meetings will be held to introduce flexible compensation or answer employee questions, meeting leaders will be needed. Leaders typically call people together, set the tone, pace, and objectives of the meeting, handle questions, distribute information, and generally act as company spokespeople and ambassadors for the new program.

Usually, meeting leaders are assigned from the ranks of benefit administrators or other benefit specialists, but they may not always be the only choice. They do bring a detailed knowledge of how the plans work, but sometimes they do not have the other skills necessary to be effective. Moreover, leading meetings is a significant commitment at the very time their administration workload is heaviest.

Another alternative might be to recruit staff from other departments for the job. Raid the recruiting, training, or communication departments. Line managers are often quite successful as meeting leaders. If it is difficult to find all of the knowledge and skills needed in one person, consider using a team or even a panel to lead meetings.

Meeting leaders do not necessarily have to be experts on the plan. They should have a basic knowledge, understand the concepts, be able to field most typical questions, and know where to send employees for answers to more detailed questions. More importantly, meeting leaders need good presentation and group discussion skills. They should look and feel confident as they welcome employees, present material, handle questions, and facilitate the meeting. They should be able to sympathize with employee concerns or confusion and be realistic about what the program will achieve. But most of all, they should be enthusiastic and *believe* what they say, for the success of the employee communication effort will depend in large part on the meeting leaders' positive attitudes.

Capable people can be found, trained, and put in front of a group of employees with great success. There are exceptions, of course, and the messages from meeting leaders are not always consistent. With reasonably good selection and training, however, there is a consistency of sincerity and enthusiasm that registers well with employees.

(3) Training Enrollment Counselors

Enrollment counselors typically answer questions and work through enrollment issues during the election process. Whether in face-to-face settings or on the telephone, enrollment counselors are the "lifeline" for confused or concerned employees. A single contact with an enrollment counselor can make the difference between an employee's positive or negative reaction to flexible compensation.

Detailed plan knowledge is not really necessary for enrollment counselors to be effective, as long as backup resources are available. Rather, they need to understand clearly how to complete enrollment forms and the issues employees should consider when making elections. Skill development for enrollment counselors should emphasize the techniques of supportive, interpersonal communication—how to ask sensitive questions, how to react responsibly to employee emotions. A counselor must be skilled at coaching employees toward decision making and leading employees to understand how the program can work for them. The counselor must do this without crossing the line into advice-giving—a practice that could later prove inappropriate or damaging to the organization. In short, enrollment counselors must have the skills to *handle* questions and *ask* questions in a way that will lead to a positive conclusion for and by the employee.

(4) Training Human Resources Managers

Most likely, human resources managers will themselves define how much they want to be involved personally in the implementation of a flexible compensation program. At the very least, they will assign the roles to be played by people reporting to them. At the other end of the spectrum, they could choose to be meeting leaders or enrollment counselors or take direct responsibility for deciding how the program is communicated. No matter how involved they become, however, as managers of the human resources function, they will influence the behavior and attitudes of other benefit professionals and employees with whom they come in contact.

Training for human resources managers should be planned with a sensitivity to their specific needs and schedules. Provide training materials in advance. Concentrate on background information, the organization's philosophy and objectives that led to flexible compensation, and the ways implementation will affect their departments.

§ 16.4   SUMMING UP

Experience proves that taking the time, making the effort, and spending the money necessary to thoroughly train the human resources staff makes a significant difference in the implementation process. Enrollments are bound to go more smoothly—not only in the first year but during reenrollments as well. When administrators feel confident about their implementation role, it will infuse their normal daily tasks and continue to influence employees as well as the entire organization in a positive way.

Seventeen

The Role of Employee Listening

No matter what other objectives exist for introducing a flexible compensation program—whether the program involves an increased benefit expenditure, a cutback, or simply rearrangement of existing dollars—maximizing employee appeal will be a critical factor in achieving program success. Employee listening provides valuable guidance for helping to generate maximum employee satisfaction. Employee listening can be used in a variety of ways, including test marketing flexible compensation or fine-tuning design or employee communication materials.

§ 17.1   DEFINITION OF EMPLOYEE LISTENING

Employee listening is a structured process for identifying employee needs and gathering employee perceptions. There are two basic formal listening approaches: quantitative and qualitative.

Quantitative employee listening involves a written survey, typically administered to all employees or a statistically reliable random sample. Quantitative listening is aimed at defining precisely how many employees feel a certain way and whether subgroups feel differently.

Qualitative listening involves face-to-face discussions, either one on one or in group meetings, usually with only a small cross section of employees. Qualitative listening is aimed at probing why various employee attitudes exist, how those attitudes are formed, and how the attitudes can be reinforced or changed.

An analogy may help clarify the difference between the two approaches. Quantitative surveys are similar to a telescope. They provide a broad picture of what is on the horizon. Qualitative interviewing is more like a microscope. It studies the way individual components work together to form a whole. Attitudes toward any issue are the result of a number of factors. Certainly facts play a part, but only a part. Expectations, rumors, trust, misunderstanding, interest, apathy, and personal situations all affect employee attitudes. Quantitative listening identifies the key factors present in a particular environment; qualitative interviewing identifies how the factors work together to shape attitudes.

Neither approach is "best" for studying employee attitudes toward flexible compensation. Whether a quantitative or a qualitative approach, or a combination, should be used depends on:

- The particular information to be gathered
- What kinds of data an organization's management requires to make decisions
- Whether significant variations in attitudes are expected among different employee groups
- How important it is to understand employees' reasons for their answers
- How much attention it is desirable to call to a study
- The time frame for collecting the information.

§ 17.2   USES AND PURPOSES OF EMPLOYEE LISTENING

There are three stages in which employee listening can be of value for studying flexible compensation:

- Before program design, to identify employees' benefit preferences and priorities and to assess employee interest in choice making
- After program design, to assess reaction to the proposed plan and identify information needs
- After implementation, to measure satisfaction with program design and communication and to evaluate any appropriate changes.

(a) BEFORE PROGRAM DESIGN

Employee listening can serve several purposes prior to program design.

First, listening can provide a perspective or context for task-force decision making. As any organization that has worked on a flexible program can attest, there are times when the development process comes to a standstill because agreement cannot be reached on design issues. Often the deadlocks are based on conflicting hypotheses about employee needs, attitudes, and preferences. For example, one person states that employees will not care about more life insurance; another argues that the organization should not communicate the flexible program as being a "big deal" because all that is happening is that employees are being given choices, with no additional company dollars; another holds that only one dental option is needed because all employees will buy the most dental coverage possible. Employee listening provides definitive information to prove or disprove such hypotheses and keep the design process moving.

A second reason for conducting employee listening prior to program development is related to the basic nature of flexible programs—the emphasis is on meeting individual employees' benefit needs. Preliminary employee listening identifies individual benefit preferences and priorities and defines what needs to be done to meet those needs. Consider the guidance provided to three different organizations from separate employee listening surveys.

Employees at each organization were asked to complete a benefit trade-off exercise. They could choose to increase, decrease, or maintain coverage in current benefit areas or choose new coverages not currently offered. But like the organization itself, they had to work within a set benefit budget, so increasing coverage in one area required decreasing coverage elsewhere. The results showed differences as illustrated in Example 17.1.

With this insight, each organization developed a very different type of flexible program. Organization A decided to offer higher-deductible medical options than originally intended since over one-quarter of employees expressed interest in lesser-valued coverage. The company shifted some of the medical plan subsidy to the savings plan in response to employee preferences.

Organization B responded to the listening results by expanding the flexible program design to include an HMO and reallocated some of an

Example 17.1
Employee Benefit Priorities: Sample Results
from Different Organizations

Percentage of Employees Who Want:	Organization A	Organization B	Organization C
Medical coverage:			
Increased	6%	32%	14%
Kept the same	65	54	82
Decreased	25	10	3
Dropped	4	4	1
Dental coverage:			
Increased	29%	34%	24%
Kept the same	46	44	60
Decreased	11	18	8
Dropped	14	4	8
Life insurance coverage:			
Increased	16%	19%	24%
Kept the same	52	52	55
Decreased	19	24	11
Dropped	13	5	10
Savings plan benefits:			
Increased	39%	22%	30%
Kept the same	55	32	54
Decreased	6	42	15
Dropped	0	4	1

existing savings plan contribution to employees in the form of additional flexible credits.

At Organization C, employees' heavy emphasis on current medical and dental benefits alerted management to the need for additional benefit communication. This organization had a history of providing high-value benefits, with employees consistently choosing its coverage over that available through a spouse's employer. A supplemental communication campaign was developed to explain coordination of benefits between different employer plans and to stress that electing lower coverage would generate flexible credits for use in other benefit areas.

A third potential purpose for employee listening prior to program design is the opportunity provided for building employee ownership of a flexible program. Listening to employees conveys that a major change is being considered and that employee input is valued by management as one of the factors that will be used in program-design decisions. Later, as appropriate, communication can capitalize on the employee input and show how it was used to shape plan design.

This consideration may be particularly valuable in programs that will involve a cutback. Some organizations hesitate to ask for employee reaction in such a situation. However, the negative message of a cutback can be significantly offset by permitting employees to identify where a cutback would be most acceptable or least painful.

(b) AFTER PROGRAM DESIGN

After a preliminary design has been developed, employee listening can be used to test reaction to the proposed program and to identify employee information needs. Specifically, listening can answer five important questions about the implementation of a proposed program.

First, listening can assess how employees react to the philosophy underlying the proposed program design. Listening can probe how employees react to key design considerations, such as the equity of benefit-dollar allocations, the need for improved cost control, and so forth. Insights into these overall reactions provide a valuable framework for understanding employee attitudes toward and perceptions of individual program components.

Second, listening for design purposes can determine how employees will react to the particular features proposed and answer such questions as how well the design meets employee needs, whether it has the right number of choices, and what program changes employees would make if given the chance. This information determines the perceived value of each of the various options and helps decide whether the design specifics are right from the employees' perspective.

Third, through a mock enrollment exercise, listening can be used to develop projections of choices the entire employee population might make under the proposed program. Such information on likely elections can also help assure that assumptions made regarding option pricing and adverse selection are appropriate for the particular organization.

Fourth, listening can probe whether the planned content and approach of flexible compensation communication materials are appropriate. Under a flexible approach, decision making responsibility rests with the employee, so there is little room for misunderstanding or omissions. Listening can assess the appropriate approach and quantity of communication.

Finally, listening can determine whether there are differences in understanding and appeal of a flexible program among employee subgroups and help in fine-tuning final program design and communication.

(c) AFTER PROGRAM IMPLEMENTATION

After the program's introduction, employees must prepare for second, third, and subsequent enrollments. They will read and study the communication materials, discuss the various benefit options, review last year's expenses to estimate upcoming flexible spending account deposits, assess whether they should increase their savings plan deposits, and so forth. In subsequent years, listening can be useful in probing such issues as:

- How smoothly did the enrollment process go? Many benefit managers say they hear only about the problems and feel the need for a more realistic and well-rounded picture of how the process worked.
- Are communication pieces effective? Are employees reading them? Should some materials be added or dropped? What questions or confusions still exist? Have new issues arisen?
- Are employees paying as careful attention to the process in subsequent years? Are they actively rethinking their choices each year, or do they become content to "stay" with their prior elections? Probing the reasons for employee elections can become important, particularly in situations where the employer was counting on employees opting for certain coverages in subsequent years.
- Are the enhanced levels of benefit appreciation and understanding initially associated with a flexible approach being maintained? Do employees understand and appreciate benefits more once they have experience with choice making? Or are employees settling back to pre-flexible levels of awareness?

In addition to providing this information, follow-up listening reinforces the employee-oriented nature of the flexible program and reaffirms management's interest in employee preferences and priorities.

§ 17.3   WHEN NOT TO LISTEN

There are two situations in which it may not be appropriate to seek employee input. One involves dangerous questions. The other involves dangerous answers.

An example of a dangerous question is: How will employees react to a reduction in the level of medical benefits? An organization testing this issue will alert the grapevine before it has prepared the full-scale communication campaign explaining the need for the change. If it is imperative to assess employee reaction to such an issue, an indirect method of questioning (such as probing the importance of and satisfaction with current coverage levels) usually will yield better results.

A dangerous answer is one to which an organization is unwilling to respond. Consider this situation: an organization was planning to reduce and eventually eliminate the subsidy for family medical coverage. The change was based upon a philosophical objective of equity as well as upon concern over possible future discrimination challenges. Those with dependents were obviously expected to resist such a change. Since the organization was not willing to maintain the subsidy, asking for employee feedback would have proved an empty process at best.

§ 17.4   HOW TO LISTEN

(a)   PERSPECTIVE

Before deciding to proceed with any employee listening, consideration should be given to environmental issues such as:

- The usual means of communicating with employees, and how employees are likely to react to a listening study given that prior experience
- The prevailing employee relations climate
- Management's willingness to share the study purpose with employees and to respond to the listening results with either action or communication.

Such issues can affect both the validity of the listening results and the impact of the listening exercise on overall company/employee relations.

(b) SETTING OBJECTIVES

To ensure that listening produces the information needed, it is important to consider the way the results are to be used. Is information on satisfaction or dissatisfaction with current benefits needed to help decide the appropriateness and value of a flexible program? Are the results to be used for a "go/no go" decision? Is there already a commitment to introducing a flexible program to improve cost management, seeking employee input only to fine-tune program design? Is plan design set and is the goal to assess communication issues and needs?

Answers to these questions will dictate when the listening should be conducted and whether quantitative or qualitative listening is more appropriate.

(c) TYPES OF APPROACHES

In deciding whether to use a quantitative or qualitative listening approach in a particular situation, the following advantages and disadvantages need to be considered.

(1) Quantitative Listening

The primary advantage of a quantitative survey is that it provides definitive statistics. The results quantify precisely how many employees agree and how many disagree with whatever questions have been asked. For example, the results can quantify how many employees are comfortable with benefit choice making, how many are not, how many express interest in various options, and so forth.

The second advantage is that detailed analyses can be performed to determine whether different groups of employees have different opinions. For example, subgroup analysis can pinpoint whether employees in different family situations have different reactions toward the way a flexible credit allowance is allocated, whether special communication needs exist at different locations, and so on.

If a standardized survey is used, a third advantage is that the results allow for valuable data base comparisons to determine if an organization's employee reactions are typical or atypical. This information can then be used to identify issues unique to that employer's environment that may require special attention.

The fourth advantage is that a written survey is a more efficient, less time-consuming way to reach a large number of employees than face-to-face meetings with the same number of employees. This is of particular benefit for organizations with a widely scattered work-force. In such circumstances, a questionnaire is perhaps the only practical way to involve employees in outlying locations and to reach such locations with a positive message of management's interest in their opinions.

As an example of the efficiencies of the survey questionnaire approach, one southeastern state passed legislation authorizing the establishment of a flexible benefit program for 55,000 public employees scattered to literally every corner of the state. As part of a planning study, the state wanted to gather employee ideas and attitudes toward benefits. However, the task of collecting meaningful input from that many employees proved logistically overwhelming. A further complication was the fact that employee job categories included legislators, social workers, hospital orderlies, and park rangers—groups with widely different educational backgrounds.

Yet the state believed it was crucial to gather employee input to identify the environment they would face on introducing a flexible program. The solution was to use a mail survey, sent to the homes of 10 percent of each state agency's employee population.

Inherent in quantitative surveys, however, are also some disadvantages. Most significant is the limited opportunity provided for employee education. While a minimal problem when testing general employee benefit preferences, this is a particularly critical drawback for testing reaction to a specific flexible program design. For employees to provide well-informed reactions and opinions, in-person education with the opportunity for questions and answers is needed.

A second limitation of a quantitative survey is that the reasons for and feelings behind the opinions identified cannot be probed very well. The data will clearly determine whether employees think their new flexible benefit program is "average," "above average," or "below average," but it will fail to explain *why* employees hold those opinions. What program are employees comparing this one with when they judge benefit quality? Are some of the benefits more prominent in their mind than others when they make that judgment? Are they less concerned about life insurance because medical is their top priority? Inability to track such thought patterns is one of the limitations of a quantitative survey.

Finally, there is an issue that can be an advantage or a disadvantage, depending upon the objectives of the employee listening exercise. A quantitative survey is very high profile; questions are in print, and a large number of employees receive questionnaires. The questionnaire makes it evident that a particular issue or benefit area is being explored. If a benefit improvement is going to be introduced, the advance notice can serve as a "plus." The survey can be the early signal that something is coming and a visible sign that the employee perspective is being taken under advisement. Feedback of the survey results can also serve as a first step in the communication campaign to build excitement about the change.

On the other hand, if there is a cutback under study, the high profile can work to the employer's disadvantage. If management is not prepared to communicate the details and answer employee questions and concerns, a qualitative listening approach is more appropriate.

(2)   Qualitative Listening

The purpose of qualitative listening is to determine why employees feel the way they do, and most importantly, how those feelings developed. For testing interest in choice making, qualitative listening typically takes the form of focus group interviews. This involves gathering together a cross section of employees in groups of 8–10 at a time. A trained focus group facilitator leads the discussion, making sure that the discussion stays on track, that all employees participate, and that no one dominates the discussion. The goal is to tap into or replicate the type of employee discussion that takes place in the hallways, cafeterias, and lounge areas of an organization.

Generally, focus groups are most effective with a diverse mix of participants—employees with different lengths of service, different family situations, and a mix of men and women. Such diversity tends to generate a more lively discussion. As a side benefit, a mixed group also allows participants to see that different needs and opinions exist and that management is facing the challenge of satisfying a variety of needs.

One caution, however, is that mixing focus group participants in terms of grade or pay level may create problems. Benefit discussions often generate comments about family budgets, such as the affordability of an option involving a higher medical deductible or what portion of pay can be contributed to a flexible spending account. In such situations, lower-income employees will feel uncomfortable with others earning more and may refrain from speaking freely. On the other hand, those at a higher-income level may feel reluctant to hurt the feelings of others who are more concerned than they are about an increased deductible. Separating group participants by income or position helps avoid these problems.

What are the advantages and disadvantages of qualitative listening? The primary advantage is that face-to-face interaction provides the opportunity to track how attitudes are formed, indicating ways to reinforce attitudes that are desirable to maintain or strengthen as well as how to change or overcome negative attitudes or employee misperceptions.

Another advantage of qualitative interviewing is that the focus-group-meeting format provides the opportunity for employee education. Employees can be provided with a presentation on a proposed flexible benefit program and have a chance to ask questions. Meeting leaders have a chance for follow-up questioning to be sure employees truly have a good understanding of the information presented and to ensure employee feedback is based on informed opinion.

In terms of disadvantages, the main drawback is that the results are not quantifiable. The emphasis is on what and why, not how many.

A second possible disadvantage is the potential for group dynamics to affect results. Someone with a very negative attitude, for example, may repeatedly voice complaints and try to dominate the group, or participants may voice only polite agreement to avoid confrontation or repercussions. The meeting leader must be well trained to respond to and balance both kinds of participation.

Finally, as is true for quantitative listening, the approach itself can offer either an advantage or disadvantage. Qualitative interviewing is relatively low profile. Only small numbers of employees are involved, relatively little is in print, and the discussion is open-ended. Qualitative listening is less likely to produce negative repercussions within the environment, but it is also less likely to generate significant employee interest.

(3)   Combination Approach

Testing employee attitudes toward a particular design requires in-person education. However, it is also usually desirable to gather statistical data quantifying employee attitudes and determining likely election choices. This result can be achieved through a combination of quantitative and qualitative listening involving three parts as follows:

- An education session to give employees needed information to make decisions about the proposed flexible program.

- A benefit election exercise during which employees record their benefit choices on an election form, using a workbook which shows personalized flexible credit allowances and the pricing for each benefit option.
- A feedback session in which reactions to the proposed flexible program, election process, and communication materials are discussed. At the end of this discussion, employees complete a written questionnaire quantifying their reactions.

(d) SELECTING LISTENING PARTICIPANTS

How many employees should be included in the listening and how they should be selected depend upon two basic issues: statistical precision and employee relations or "face validity."

A random sample of employees may be sufficient to provide statistical reliability, but it may leave other employees feeling their views are being ignored. A statistically sound sample may not be necessary when a few representatives of various departments or locations can clearly articulate the opinions of the employee group.

Following is a description of four typical methods for selecting a sample of listening participants.

- A *random sample* is used if the intention is for everyone in the employee population to have an equal possibility of being selected. A simple example would be selecting every twentieth name from an employee roster arranged in a *nonordered* fashion, with the starting name chosen randomly.
- A *stratified random sample* tends to be more appropriate when there are many important subgroups within the employee population. Stratifying the population by job category, for example, would assure that employees are chosen from each job category in proportion to their distribution in the population. Selection from within each stratified subgroup is made randomly. A disadvantage of a stratified random sample exists for many organizations, however, because of the geographic dispersion of their locations. Selecting a stratified random sample is likely to include only a few employees from each of a large number of locations, resulting in significant costs and difficult logistics.
- To avoid such a scattered sample while maintaining statistical projectability, a *cluster stratified sample* can be used. This involves

randomly selecting a limited number of locations expected to represent many others.

- A *purposive* sample can be used if projectable statistics are not required. Employees are simply hand-selected to represent key subgroups.

In any case, the total number of employees to be sampled and the method of sample selection should be based on consideration of the trade-off involved (i.e., cost versus the degree of statistical precision and certainty required). Issues to be addressed include:

- What degree of precision and certainty about each overall finding is required for the type of decisions to be made?
- Are there specific subgroups of employees for which statistically precise information is required? Are there any subgroups of employees or locations that can be excluded from the listening?
- What proportion of the employee population is at each location? Are different reactions expected from employees at different locations?
- Regardless of statistical considerations, how much face validity or believability will the sample size need to have for the people who will be reviewing the results?
- Regardless of statistical considerations, how many employees at how many locations need to be included for employee relations purposes?

§ 17.5 LISTENING AS COMMUNICATION

The listening process is itself a form of employee communication—an important and visible message that management cares about employee opinions. However, the listening process will raise employee questions. Why is the company asking about benefits? What will be done with the information gathered? How will things change as a result of the study?

It is impossible to avoid raising employee expectations. The key is to raise the *right* expectations. The listening exercise must make clear that, while important, employee input represents only one consideration to be reviewed in making program design decisions. The listening effort needs to include an explanation that legal, administrative, cost considerations, and so forth, will also be taken into account, and in some areas these factors may carry greater weight than employee opinions.

On the positive side, the listening process can capitalize on the employee relations value of seeking input. Even if only a small number of focus group interviews are to be conducted, an announcement of a study can be sent to all employees. After any type of listening, follow-up communication should identify ways in which employee suggestions were addressed or explain why not if that is the case. This turns the process into a two-way communication channel and provides an opportunity to explain both employees' and management's point of view.

An additional communication opportunity presents itself for employee listening on flexible compensation. A key communication message for any flexible compensation program is that a flexible approach responds to individual employee needs. The listening process can help reinforce the broader message of flexible compensation by stressing that employees are being asked to identify their needs to be sure the program suits them.

Part Six

Administration

Eighteen

Managing Administration

§ 18.1 GETTING STARTED

(a) INVOLVING THE ADMINISTRATORS

Administering a flexible compensation program usually is more complicated than administering a traditional benefit program. Administration is a major consideration both from an implementation and an ongoing processing viewpoint. Therefore, it usually makes sense to involve key administrators as soon as possible in the plan design process. The plan design is a major factor in determining the cost and feasibility of flexible program administration.

Departments whose administrative procedures and systems typically are affected most by a flexible program include benefit administration, payroll, and data processing. The individuals who can provide the best input on the impact of a proposed program on these areas are the ones most familiar with the current procedures and systems. These include the administration of current benefit programs, payroll processing, and payroll/personnel computer systems. Without the involvement of these individuals, what may seem like a minor issue to the program designers could make the administrative task considerably more costly or, in the worst case, impossible.

If for some reason it is not possible to involve representatives from each administrative area in the initial plan design, it may be appropriate

429

to refrain from finalizing design until an administrative evaluation can determine the program's full effect on administration.

(b) DEVELOPING A DETAILED PROGRAM DESIGN

Once the basic plan design is complete and approved by management, there likely will be many open design issues affecting administration. To determine which open issues need to be addressed, first look at policies, procedures, and systems associated with the current benefit program. Which existing requirements also must be met by the flexible program? Second, study each aspect of the proposed flexible program and determine its effect on each employee category (full-time, part-time, etc.) and employee status (retired, temporary, leave of absence, etc.). Third, identify new benefit administration requirements created by the flexible program (spending account claims review, annual reenrollment, etc.).

Here are some examples of the kind of questions that may be resolved in the detailed design process:

- What data items are required (e.g., date of birth, hire date, number of dependents)?
- What are the eligibility requirements for each employment category covered under the flexible program?
- How will flexible credits elected as cash be allocated to employees, and what will be the frequency of allocation (i.e., lump sum, per pay period)?
- How will changes in compensation during the plan year affect pay-based coverage amounts and employee costs?
- What coverages, if any, will be given to employees who fail to turn in enrollment elections?
- How will employee coverages and costs change due to changes in employment status? Family status?
- What are the reporting requirements of the flexible program to insurance carriers? Third-party administrators? Accounting? Employees? COBRA beneficiaries?

Finalize specifications for the administrative system(s) only after the detailed program design is complete. Otherwise the system may end up driving the plan design instead of supporting the program.

(c) ADMINISTRATIVE FUNCTIONS

Whether the flexible program is limited in scope including only health care choices or broad in offering choice making in many benefit areas, the same basic administrative activities need to be performed. The administrative functions of most flexible programs include: enrollment in the program, ongoing coverage administration, spending account recordkeeping, and payroll processing.

§ 18.2   ENROLLMENT PROCESSING

(a) TYPES OF ENROLLMENT

Flexible program enrollments can be classified as annual enrollment of all participants (both active employees and COBRA beneficiaries) and periodic or immediate enrollment of newly eligible employees. The difference in the administrative activities involved in each enrollment type is principally one of scale. Annual enrollments usually involve all eligible participants whereas periodic enrollments may involve only a small number of employees.

The first annual enrollment involves all eligible employees. Administering the initial annual enrollment usually begins three or more months prior to the program effective date. In following plan years, all eligible employees may be required to reenroll as options, option prices, and flexible credit allocations change from year to year. Even though all eligible employees are involved in an annual reenrollment, employee understanding of the flexible program is greater than in the first program year. Therefore, the annual reenrollment effort may not require as much time to plan or execute. If no changes occur in either options or prices, annual reenrollment may be limited only to employees wishing to change their elections.

Qualified beneficiaries as defined under COBRA regulations whose coverage periods cross plan years also are eligible to participate in annual enrollment. All health care options offered to active employees also must be offered to COBRA participants during annual enrollment. For this reason, the flexible program's enrollment system often is used to enroll and track COBRA beneficiaries just as it is used to enroll and track active employees.

The frequency of periodic enrollments depends on plan design. Periodic enrollments can occur semiannually, quarterly, monthly, or even daily (i.e., on date of hire).

The more often enrollment takes place, the greater the total administrative effort will be. For most employees, the concept of flexible compensation is new. Therefore, many employers try to allow enough time for employees to understand the program, including discussing options with other family members. Interim coverage in critical benefit areas may be provided to new employees until the employee is eligible for enrollment in the flexible program. This approach provides employees with basic coverage while they are considering their flexible program elections. Enrollment at specified intervals (quarterly, semiannually) concentrates the administrative effort at each enrollment period. Daily or monthly enrollments may distribute the administrative workload more evenly. Interim coverages or longer waiting periods are used frequently by organizations with high employee turnover in the first months following employment.

(b) DATA COLLECTION AND VERIFICATION

The first step in the enrollment process is the collection and verification of participant data required by the plan design and administrative requirements for the program. Limited flexible programs such as a flexible spending account, may require only minimal data such as name, employee identification number or social security number, and work location or home address. Broad programs covering many benefit areas usually require more extensive data such as date of birth, date of hire, number of dependents, family status, pay, and employment category.

Collection of the required data involves the identification of the data source and/or the consolidation of data to a central source depending on the degree to which data are already centralized, and the accessibility of the data to the enrollment system.

Verification of data is very important especially when accuracy can affect the individual's eligibility for the program or the options and option prices available. Such data may include pay, age, length of service, employment category, employment status, and work location.

Clearly, if required data reside in one place and are reasonably accurate, this initial step of the enrollment process requires less time and effort than if data must be collected from several sources or if the accuracy of the data is unreliable.

(c)   IDENTIFICATION OF ELIGIBLE PARTICIPANTS

After required data have been collected and verified, eligible participants can be identified. Eligibility is based on factors such as service, employment status, employment category, location, and possibly age. If required data are accurate, identifying eligible participants may be a simple step. This step can be more complex, however, if all benefits offered under the flexible program do not have the same eligibility requirements.

(d)   PERFORMING CALCULATIONS

Once eligibility has been determined, the next step in the enrollment process is to compute the flexible credit allowance, option availability, and option prices for each eligible participant. For a limited program offering the same flexible credit allowance, options, and option prices to everyone, no individual calculations are necessary. However, a broad flexible program may allocate flexible credits based on individual participant characteristics such as pay or length of service. Prices for some options such as life insurance and paid time off may be based on pay or age. Some prices, such as medical or dental prices, may vary based on an employee's work location or employment status (active employee or COBRA beneficiary).

In addition to computing specific flexible credits and option prices, it may be necessary to determine which options are available to each participant for the year. For example, the plan may require participants to remain in the same medical or dental plan for a minimum number of years. In the case of life insurance, an increase in coverage over the current level may require proof of insurability. If the program includes HMOs, only participants within each HMO's geographic service area are eligible for a particular HMO.

For programs that have variations, each employee's flexible credit allowance, prices, and options will be individually calculated and communicated to the employee. Qualified beneficiaries of COBRA will be notified of their eligibility to reelect health care coverages and the cost of their health care options.

(e)   ENROLLMENT MATERIAL

The scope of the program and the sophistication of the enrollment system will affect the type of enrollment materials used. Enrollment materials for a limited flexible program generally consist of an election form and a booklet describing the program. As the scope of the program broadens, additional communications and personalized enrollment material may be needed. The enrollment material for a broad flexible program usually consists of an election form, an election workbook, and a personalized statement.

The design of the election form is important to ensure easy entry of elections into the enrollment system. If the election forms will be key inscribed, column numbers may be required. If the elections will be entered on a computer terminal, the data items on the form may be designed to match the data items on the entry screen or vice versa.

A computer-posted personalized statement is often used for broad programs. This personalized statement is an individual report of each participant's available options, option prices, and flexible credit allowance. The basic participant data used for calculations may be printed on the report to provide for final verification of this data by the participant. In addition, if the participant currently is participating in the flexible program and is reenrolling, the statement may show the participant's current coverages.

The personalized statement, election form, and workbook may be three separate communication pieces or a single combined packet. The personalized information may be computer posted on the election form. In other cases, the election workbook is computer posted with employee-specific credit allowances, options, and option prices.

Employee enrollment materials usually are packaged for each eligible employee and distributed prior to employee meetings held to discuss the program and allow questions to be answered. Employees are instructed to return their completed election forms to their local or central benefit office. Enrollment materials for COBRA beneficiaries usually are distributed through the mail. Allow plenty of time for editing elections, correcting election errors, producing confirmation statements, and communicating elections to ongoing administration systems when setting the deadline for returning the forms.

(f)   PROCESSING AND EDITING PARTICIPANT ELECTIONS

Editing participant elections is an important step in each enrollment process. Elections may be checked to ensure that the participant's arithmetic is correct, that option prices are correct, and that the participant has elected options that are, in fact, available to the participant.

Editing is relatively straightforward with a limited flexible program. Forms can be designed so that participants simply circle or check the option they want. This simplifies editing to the point of simply checking that the participant made one election in each benefit area. However, in a program offering a variety of benefit options and variable flexible credits and option prices, the editing is more complex and time consuming. For this reason, editing is an automated function in most broad flexible program enrollments.

Some election errors can be corrected by the administrator. Most election errors, however, must be corrected by the participant. For example, transposition errors can occur when elections are key inscribed. Errors of this type can be corrected simply by referring to the participant's election form. If the participant has recorded an incorrect option or option price on the election form, however, it may not be clear what option the participant intended to elect. This type of error requires correction by the participant. If an automated system is used for editing, the edit report produced by the system may be designed for use as a turnaround document and sent to the participant for correction.

The error rate for initial annual enrollment can range from 5 percent to over 30 percent. The complexity of the plan design, the effectiveness of preenrollment communications, and the clarity of the enrollment material all have an effect on the election error rate. The enrollment system may provide statistical information on the types of errors employees are making. This information is helpful in restructuring communication material and enrollment forms for subsequent enrollments.

After elections have been edited and errors have been corrected, elections are recorded on appropriate ongoing administration systems. Employee pretax and after-tax deductions are recorded on the payroll system. If spending account or savings plan elections are included in the flexible program enrollment, required data are reported to and recorded on the appropriate recordkeeping systems. In addition, health care (medical, dental, vision) elections are reported to the appropriate claims processors to ensure proper claim certification.

A status monitoring program is an essential part of the enrollment system where large numbers of participants are involved or where the enrollment process involves multiple locations. Status monitoring reports list participants with missing enrollment forms and participants with elections that have been entered but are invalid. Reports identify the participant's name and location for easy follow up. More sophisticated status monitoring systems may include a finer breakdown of where participants are in the enrollment process. Such systems identify how many participants have had personalized statements produced, valid elections but no signature, confirmation statements produced, and so forth.

(g)   ELECTION CONFIRMATION STATEMENTS

After elections are validated, a confirmation statement may be produced to confirm the participant's elections. The confirmation statement is a personalized statement showing the elections recorded on the enrollment system for the participant.

Confirmation statements are important for several reasons. If employees are allowed to decline certain benefit coverages, the statement serves as a reminder to the employee that he or she does not have coverage during the coming year. In addition, under Section 125 plans, employees are not allowed to change their elections during the year except in the event of a family status change. Therefore, confirming an employee's elections prior to the beginning of the plan year is very important. Confirmation statements also give employees a chance to catch any errors they made during enrollment or administrator errors made during election entry. Finally, if the program assigns default coverages to employees who have not returned their election forms prior to the deadline, the statement notifies the employee of the benefit coverages selected by default.

In its simplest form, the confirmation statement may be a copy of the participant's completed and edited election form. With broad flexible programs, it is desirable to produce a computer-posted confirmation statement showing not only the employee's elections, but also providing information on the pay period withholding rates that will be required to pay for the employee's coverages. A more elaborate statement may show the estimated tax savings which will result from the employee's election to pay for coverages with pretax salary reductions.

Confirmation statements generally are distributed as early as possible in the enrollment period. As a practical matter, some participants will want to make changes or corrections. If changes are made before the first payroll deductions are taken or bills are produced for COBRA beneficiaries, these changes are easier to accommodate.

(h)   POST-ELECTION REPORTING AND ANALYSIS

After annual enrollment is completed, statistical and analytical reports may be produced for use in analyzing the impact of the program. The election analysis reports can be used to determine such things as:

- Is the program meeting the needs of employees?
- Is the program meeting management objectives (e.g., if medical cost containment is an objective, are employees electing the higher-deductible medical options)?
- What changes in the benefit program should be considered for next year?

Election analysis reports have the most value when reports from one year are compared to reports of another year. Election analysis reports typically include summary information on elections in each of the benefit areas as well as on the overall use of flexible credits and salary reduction. Information may be broken down by age, service, pay, family status, location, and so forth.

§ 18.3   ONGOING COVERAGE ADMINISTRATION

Another area of flexible compensation administration is the ongoing administration of coverages after participants are enrolled in the program or prior to their eligibility for the program.

Ongoing coverage administration under a flexible program differs somewhat, although not dramatically, from ongoing administration under a traditional benefit program. In most cases, as an organization moves from traditional benefits to flexible benefits, existing ongoing administration procedures need to be modified. In some broad flexible programs, new procedures or systems need to be developed.

One requirement of ongoing administration may be to process interim coverage for new employees. This requirement depends on the design of the program. If the program does provide employees with some basic levels of coverage prior to eligibility for the flexible program, new employees need to complete enrollment forms to authorize payroll deductions, if any, and to make choices if limited choices are offered. Interim coverage enrollment processing is included as a function of some flexible program enrollment systems. However, interim coverage enrollment often is administered outside the flexible program enrollment system.

Coverage change processing occurs throughout the year. In general, an employee may change coverages if the employee has a family status change (e.g., marriage, divorce, birth/adoption of a child). If an employee terminates or transfers to an employment status which is not eligible for full benefits under the flexible program, for example, from full-time to part-time, the employee's coverage may change. A change in pay may mean that an employee's pay-related coverages such as life or disability insurance are increased or decreased. If this occurs, the employee's cost of coverage may or may not change. Flexible credit allowances solely or partially based on pay or family status also may change.

Enrollment change procedures are established to process these coverage changes. New elections and deduction rates are recorded on the payroll system, and in some cases new flexible spending account contribution rates are recorded on the spending account recordkeeping system.

Another function of ongoing administration is the production of group insurance reports. Periodically, the total coverage costs for each benefit option are computed and reported. For insured plans and HMO options, this entails the calculation and payment of required premiums to the carriers. For self-insured benefits, this involves the calculation of adequate funding levels to cover expenses and maintain reserves.

Periodic health care certification reports or magnetic tapes are produced for the health care claims processor(s). This information includes each participant's health care benefit election, and enables the claims processor to certify coverage. The administrative system produces a coverage certification report or tape for the claims processor at the end of the annual enrollment process and periodically throughout the year.

Ongoing administration often includes notifying qualified beneficiaries of their rights to continue coverage under the provisions of COBRA, tracking and reporting continued coverages, and billing COBRA participants.

§ 18.4   FLEXIBLE SPENDING ACCOUNT ADMINISTRATION

(a)   FLEXIBLE SPENDING ACCOUNT ENROLLMENT

Most flexible compensation programs in existence today include a flexible spending account. If the flexible program offers choice making in a variety of benefit areas, enrollment in the flexible spending account is part of the annual enrollment in the flexible program. If the flexible program consists solely of a spending account, annual enrollment in the program still is required.

Employees enrolling in the flexible spending account complete an enrollment form to elect contributions to one or more of the accounts offered under the plan. This is because Section 125 rules require that separate contribution elections be made for each expense category—health care, dependent care, and legal. (See Chapters Four and Nine.)

If spending account contributions involve salary reduction, contribution elections are recorded on the payroll system. Ideally, the payroll system will be able to record separate contribution reduction amounts for each account offered by the plan. For instance, payroll would take two spending account contribution reductions for an employee electing to participate in both the health care and dependent care accounts.

Some payroll systems cannot easily add new deductions. If this is the case, an employee's contribution elections can be combined and recorded on payroll as one salary reduction amount. The recordkeeping system then maintains the employee's election for each account and allocates the contribution amount received from payroll according to the employee's elections.

The final step in the spending account enrollment process is to establish accounts on the recordkeeping system for each employee electing to participate and if necessary, record each employee's contribution elections on the recordkeeping system.

(b) RECORDING CONTRIBUTIONS

Contributions are periodically posted to each participant's accounts maintained by the recordkeeping system. Where salary conversion is involved, accounts may be updated each time salary reductions are taken by payroll, or payroll may accumulate contributions and report them to the recordkeeping system periodically. If a tape transfer to an outside recordkeeping service is being used, monthly reporting may be more cost effective than pay-period reporting. Quarterly, semiannual, or annual updates are used in some programs where only employer contributions are involved.

Where a link between the payroll system and the spending account recordkeeping system is difficult or impossible or where only employer contributions are involved, the recordkeeping system may be designed to update employee accounts automatically with elected contribution amounts. The administrator then must verify that the correct amount was allocated to each employee's accounts and make adjustments to account balances if necessary. For example, an adjustment may be required if an employee was on an unpaid leave of absence but was still showing a contribution rate on the recordkeeping system.

(c)   PROCESSING REQUESTS FOR REIMBURSEMENT

The employee completes a request-for-reimbursement claim form and attaches the required supporting documents to begin the payment processing cycle. Most programs require employees to submit covered health care expenses to the insurance carrier or claims processor before requesting reimbursement for the unpaid portion of the expense. In this case, the explanation of benefits from the claims processor provides the required documentation. A bill, receipt, or cancelled check may provide the required documentation for uninsured expenses. Claim submittal procedures and a list of eligible expenses are communicated to employees during enrollment in the flexible spending account.

The request for reimbursement form may be designed for easy data entry into the recordkeeping system. Benefit categories may be coded to allow the system to post the expense to the appropriate account. Other information may include the dates expenses were incurred, the amount requested for reimbursement, the name and age of the dependent (dependent care account), and the name of the provider of services. Include space on the form for several expenses and benefit types to reduce claims processing administration.

Other ways to control the administrative effort are to limit the frequency of submissions (e.g., once a month) and to set minimum submission and claim payment amounts (e.g., $50). Usually, these limits are waived during the final processing month of the plan year to accommodate year-end employee submissions.

Spending account claims approval may be done externally by a third-party administrator or internally by program administrators. If done internally, the approval process may be centralized or decentralized. The claims approval process includes the following steps:

- Checking the employee's program eligibility. This step may be aided by an automated recordkeeping system.
- Checking that expenses were incurred during the program year in which contributions were posted. In other words, 1988 contributions can only be used to reimburse expenses which were incurred during 1988 based on dates of service.
- Checking for supporting documentation.

- Determining if expenses qualify as eligible expenses. Claims processors are provided with a detailed list of eligible and ineligible expenses.
- Checking that the form is signed by the participant.

Once the request for reimbursement is approved by the claims processor, it is processed for payment by the recordkeeping system. Usually, requests for reimbursement are authorized for payment to the extent of the employee's account balance for the type of expense benefit. Checks may be produced by the recordkeeping system, by another internal system such as accounts payable, by an external checkwriter (e.g., a bank), or the reimbursement amount may be processed by payroll and included in the employee's regular paycheck as a nontaxable addition to net pay. Payments typically are made to the participant, not to the provider of services.

The frequency of reimbursement generally depends on the recordkeeping system and check-writing system used as well as the plan design. Payment timetables are communicated to employees during enrollment.

A pending feature in the recordkeeping system eliminates the need for employees and claims processors to resubmit claims that exceeded the account balance of a particular benefit type when originally submitted. When an eligible claim is processed for an amount exceeding the employee's account balance for that expense type, the recordkeeping system pays the claim to the extent of the account balance and automatically pends or holds the remaining claim amount for future payment once funds are available.

The recordkeeping system produces an explanation of payment for each participant receiving a reimbursement during the processing period. The statement typically includes paid and pended amounts and the ending account balance by benefit type. Year-to-date contribution and payment information also may be included.

(d) TERMINATED EMPLOYEES

Often during the detailed plan design phase of implementation, the initial reaction of benefit administrators is to terminate an employee's spending account participation on or shortly after termination of employment. Some qualify the decision to terminate participation based on the reason for termination (voluntary termination versus layoff, etc.). Most cite administrative workload as the primary reason for wanting to terminate accounts prior to the end of the plan year.

The majority of employers ultimately decide, for a combination of administrative and design reasons, to leave terminated employee accounts open until the spending accounts for active employees are closed following plan year-end.

In deciding what the differences in administrative effort really are, consider the following questions:

- How will employee terminations be communicated to and recorded on the spending account recordkeeping system?
- If accounts remain open beyond termination but are closed prior to the end of the plan year, how will the recordkeeping system know when to close the account?
- If exceptions to the rule are made, how will these be determined? How will the accounts be reopened?
- If the accounts are left open, how will payments to terminated employees be distributed?
- Can the check-writing system produce checks for terminated employees?

(e) YEAR-END PROCESSING

Because of the use-it-or-lose-it requirement and because employees may not receive all of their year-end bills or explanations of benefits until after the plan year ends, most organizations keep accounts open for a period of time after the end of the plan year. During this period, the recordkeeping system maintains two sets of accounts for each participant: the current year accounts and the prior year accounts. In most cases, the carry-over period is from one to six months after the plan year ends. During this period only claims for expenses incurred during the prior year may be submitted against the prior year's account balance.

Dependent care spending accounts have a special year-end reporting requirement. Each year by January 31, the recordkeeping system must produce a statement for each participant in the account during the prior calendar year. This statement reports the total amount reimbursed to the participant during the prior calendar year. This usually includes payments from two plan years. For example, a statement produced January 1988 for the 1987 plan year must include payments made during the 1986 carry-over period plus payments made during January through December for the 1987 plan year. These statements are distributed to participants only and are not filed with any regulatory agency.

The recordkeeping system reports forfeitures when accounts are closed at the end of the carry-over period. This information is used to update the general ledger.

(f)   REPORTING ACCOUNT ACTIVITY TO PARTICIPANTS

Most spending account recordkeeping systems produce an explanation with each payment. This statement usually includes a breakdown by benefit type of all payment activity for the reporting period including pended amounts as well as paid reimbursements. In addition, periodic account-activity statements are produced for each participant. These statements provide a beginning and ending balance, and a summary of contribution and claims activity. All information is provided on a per account basis (health care, dependent care, legal).

Even if periodic account statements are provided, there will be other occasions when participants will have questions about their spending accounts. These questions may concern overall account balances or specific contribution or claim activity. Administrators need access to up-to-date account information in order to respond to employee questions.

(g)   RECONCILING THE SPENDING ACCOUNT AND THE GENERAL LEDGER

The final flexible spending account requirement is reconciliation to the general ledger. Typically, the reconciliation process occurs with a frequency consistent with an organization's standard accounting cycle.

The funding of a flexible spending account involves the creation of an accrued liability. This liability represents an amount of money set aside by the employer and/or employees to pay for eligible expenses which will be reimbursed in the future. The liability account is increased each time a contribution is made to the spending account, and the account is decreased each time a payment is made or an unused balance is forfeited by an employee.

Basic journal entries are made to the general ledger accounts to correspond to each step in the administrative process. Spending account contributions are accounted for as a benefit expense (the debit) which is offset by an entry to an accrued liability account (the credit). This liability account is a control account which ties to the sum of the account balances for all participating employees. The periodic credit entry usually is picked up from the payroll deduction register. (Note that the employee is an unsecured creditor with respect to the employer for his or her account balance until a reimbursement request has been submitted.)

At the end of the reimbursement processing cycle when payments are issued to participants, the reimbursement amount becomes payable to the employee, and another entry is made. This entry takes the total of all payable amounts, and then debits the liability account and credits accounts payable.

Once reimbursement checks are created and issued to employees, a final payment entry is made. This entry is a debit to accounts payable and an offsetting credit to cash. Note that this credit entry is made to the general cash asset account.

The final transaction to consider is the account closure transaction. When unused funds are forfeited by employees on termination or at year-end, the total forfeiture amount is a debit to the liability account and a credit to the company's general asset account. The spending account recordkeeping system, therefore, aids the accounting process by providing the closing spending account balance and the total reimbursement amount for the accounting period.

§ 18.5   CHANGES TO PAYROLL PROCESSING

Whether the flexible program is broad or limited in scope, implementation of the program involves changes to the payroll system. Deduction fields may need to be added to the payroll system to accommodate Section 125 salary reductions. Separate deduction fields usually are maintained for spending account contributions and group insurance plan premiums.

The net-pay computation must be adjusted to reflect the fact that some payroll taxes are not applicable to Section 125 salary reductions. Under current law, Section 125 reductions are treated similarly to 401(k) reductions with a few exceptions. Like 401(k) reductions, Section 125 reductions are not subject to federal tax. Unlike Section 401(k) reductions, however, Section 125 reductions are exempt from FICA taxes. Both Section 401(k) and Section 125 reductions are exempt from most state and city taxes. However, some states and cities tax Section 401(k) reductions or Section 125 reductions or both. (See also Chapter Two.) Because of the varied tax treatment at the state and local levels, the net pay calculation for payroll systems servicing multiple locations can become very complex.

If a new benefit plan enrollment system is implemented to accommodate the flexible benefit program, or if the existing benefit plan enrollment system is modified significantly, the payroll system will be modified to interface with the enrollment system. Both before-tax and after-tax payroll deductions for the program are reported to payroll by the enrollment system each year following annual enrollment. The enrollment system also reports deductions throughout the year for new employees and for employees who are changing their coverages.

If the flexible program includes a flexible spending account, payroll will be modified to interface with the spending account recordkeeping system. The payroll system periodically reports spending account contribution amounts to the recordkeeping system for each participant in the accounts. Contribution amounts for each participant may be reported to the recordkeeping system by benefit type or as a lump sum if the recordkeeping system can allocate the contribution amount based on the employee elections.

If the payment amounts are included in employee paychecks as an addition to net pay, the payroll system is modified to receive payment amounts from the recordkeeping system for each employee. The pay stub then is modified to show the addition to net pay.

§ 18.6   ADMINISTRATIVE STAFFING REQUIREMENTS

The two areas that have the biggest impact on staffing requirements are annual enrollment election entry and spending account claims processing (if handled in-house).

(a)   ELECTION ENTRY

On the average, three minutes per form are required to enter an election form into an online enrollment system. Entry time may vary widely based on several factors including:

- The enrollment system's online response time, and
- The amount of information being entered.

(b)   CLAIMS PROCESSING

The reviewer normally checks to be sure the expense is an eligible expense under the plan and that the participant has signed the form and provided the required supporting documentation. This effort requires on the average, four minutes per claim request. When determining staffing requirements, consider the following assumptions.

- Participation in the spending accounts typically is 15 percent to 40 percent of the eligible employees.
- If monthly claim submission restrictions are applied, participants will submit on average five to seven claim requests per year.
- If claims are entered into an online system, one full-time administrator is needed per 2,500 to 4,000 participants.

(c)   OTHER STAFFING CONSIDERATIONS

Other functions to be considered when assessing the impact of the flexible program on staffing include:

- Administrator and employee education
- Production and distribution of personalized enrollment reports and election confirmation statements
- New employee enrollments
- Enrollment change processing
- Spending account reimbursement check and account statement distribution
- Employee coverage and spending account status inquiries.

Nineteen

Administration Solutions

§ 19.1 EVALUATING ADMINISTRATIVE ALTERNATIVES

Prior to the early 1980s, implementing a flexible compensation program meant developing an in-house administrative system. In most cases, developing the system was the most complicated and time-consuming part of implementing a flexible program. Today while implementation remains a lengthy and detailed process, many good alternatives to in-house system development are available. The key to the success of the implementation effort is careful evaluation of the range of administrative solutions and selection of the system that best meets the organization's program design and administrative needs.

(a) EVALUATION PROCESS

The evaluation of administration alternatives typically begins immediately following the development of the preliminary program design. While program design is an important factor, other issues affecting the evaluation include:

- The number of eligible participants
- The degree to which administration will be centralized or decentralized

- The timing of program implementation
- The availability of internal data processing and administration resources
- The organization's long-term plans for program enhancements or modifications, and
- The implementation and ongoing processing budgets for the project.

Ideally, an evaluation committee should be formed to discuss each of these factors and use them in an evaluation process. (The factors are described in more detail in the section on selection criteria within this chapter.) The evaluation process may take weeks or months to complete depending on the number of alternatives under consideration and the selection techniques used.

Many different approaches may be used to evaluate administrative alternatives, ranging from very informal to very formal. One of the most common approaches involves issuing a Request for Proposal (RFP), selecting "finalists" based on responses to the RFP, and allowing each finalist to demonstrate capabilities in a subsequent meeting with the evaluation committee. Whether or not an RFP is issued, the committee will want to meet with each of the vendors to ensure a mutual understanding of the needs and constraints of the organization. Actually seeing a demonstration also will help in assuring the committee of the vendor's ability to deliver a suitable system within the required time frame and budgets.

(b) EVALUATION COMMITTEE

As with any decision-making process, the number of people on the evaluation committee likely will have a direct relationship to the length of time needed to make a decision. However, in order to make the right decision, the right people need to participate in the evaluation process. In general, it is usually more efficient in the long run to sacrifice time, rather than short cut the process by eliminating an area that could have significant input into the evaluation process.

A committee to evaluate flexible compensation administration alternatives ideally consists of individuals from each of the following areas:

- Benefit administration,
- Human resource information systems (or benefit systems),

- Management information systems, and
- Finance.

Each of these areas needs to be represented, usually by people with decision-making authority as well as a working knowledge of day-to-day activities in the area. Again, both functional levels need to be represented, whether in the form of one person or more.

(c) ADMINISTRATIVE ALTERNATIVES

Broadly defined, six alternatives exist for administering a flexible compensation program. Specifically the alternatives include:

- Manual administration
- Spreadsheet software
- Personal computer administration software
- Mainframe administration software
- Time-sharing services, and
- Third-party administration.

(1) Manual Administration

Manual administration of a flexible compensation program may be appropriate for small organizations with simple flexible programs. One organization implemented a flexible spending account for 50 participants and administered the program using three-by-five index cards and colored paper clips to designate different levels of account activity. Word processing was used to produce quarterly statements for all participants.

(2) Spreadsheet Software

Smaller organizations that have access to personal computer hardware and software have used commercial spreadsheet software to semi-automate flexible program administration. In some cases, spreadsheet software has been used successfully to administer even a broad flexible program for a small number of participants.

As with manual administration, word processing often is used to produce personalized statements for participants.

(3)   Personal Computer Administrative Software

Flexible program administration systems may be developed or purchased for installation on a personal computer. In many cases, PC-based systems provide all the processing capabilities and functionality of mainframe software.

In a personal computer environment, interfaces with mainframe systems such as payroll may be facilitated through the transferring of data files between systems. Transfers of data files can be accomplished electronically or by using floppy diskettes or magnetic tapes.

Decentralized administration is supported through linking multiple personal computers to the same hard disk storage. While technology in this area is rapidly changing, problems still can arise in many personal computer networks with data transmission speeds, data accuracy, and limited disk storage capacity.

Historically, the printing speed of personal computers discouraged some organizations from using PC-based software for flexible program administration. However, with higher speed and better quality printers increasingly available and the option of transferring high volume print files to mainframe printers, printing is no longer a major concern for most organizations.

Personal computer systems are available from a wide variety of benefit consulting firms and software vendors.

(4)   Mainframe Administrative Software

Like personal computer-based systems, mainframe software for flexible program administration may be developed internally or licensed from a vendor. Mainframe systems are especially advantageous to larger organizations with centralized data processing. In this kind of environment, additional hardware seldom is required to support the flexible program. Existing data communication networks may be used to support decentralized administration. Systems maintenance is performed by the data processing department, along with the ongoing maintenance performed for other administration systems, such as payroll and accounting.

Mainframe administration software will interface with other mainframe systems through the electronic transfer of data. Some mainframe applications can access data directly from the payroll/personnel data base, thus eliminating the need for file transfers.

Most mainframe software is built to maintain a separate participant data base to house only data necessary for administering the flexible program. Some systems, however, operate using the payroll or personnel system's employee data base, and thus have no need to maintain their own participant data bases.

As with PC solutions, mainframe software systems for administering a flexible program are available from a wide range of benefit consulting firms and software vendors.

(5)   Time-Sharing Services

In a time-sharing environment, administrators have online access to software located on a vendor's computer. Access may be limited to certain time periods or may be unlimited depending on the time-sharing service.

An administrator gains access to the system using a terminal, modem, and data communication link between the modem and the host computer. In many cases, the connection is made through a telephone line. Security prohibits the administrator from accessing the accounts of other organizations using the same service. To the administrator, a time-sharing service will provide the same functional capabilities as a mainframe system installed on the company's own computer.

Like personal computer systems and mainframe-based systems, a time-sharing service must interface with the organization's payroll and other administration systems. Interfaces between the administration system and the payroll system take place via magnetic tape or data file transfers over the data communication lines. Reports produced in a time-sharing environment typically are sent to the organization through the mail. Alternatively, print files may be sent over the data communication lines for printing on location. Transferring large files over a data communication line is often a slow process under current technology.

There are not yet many organizations offering time-sharing services for flexible compensation administration. However, time-sharing offers many advantages over installed systems for certain organizations. The pros and cons of each type of administration approach are explored further in the selection criteria section of this chapter.

(6)   Third-Party Processing

A third-party processing approach to administration takes much of the work out of the hands of the organization's administrators. This approach typically is used for spending account administration, but it is

increasingly being offered by various vendors for enrollment processing as well.

Third-party spending account administration differs from a time-
sharing approach in that review and entry of spending account claims
plus payment distribution are handled by the service provider rather
than the plan administrator. Spending account participants typically
send their requests for reimbursement directly to the third-party administrator (TPA). The TPA reviews the request and issues the payment.
Users of the service seldom have online access to account information,
thus all participant questions are directed to the TPA.

Enrollment support offered by TPAs usually is limited to annual or
periodic (quarterly) group enrollments. Individual or more frequent
group enrollments typically cannot be accommodated.

Third-party administration operates similarly to time-sharing in
terms of interfaces between the provider of the service and the user's
mainframe system. Interfaces typically are accomplished via magnetic
tape.

Third-party administration services for flexible spending accounts
are offered primarily by insurance companies. TPA services for enrollment also are offered by benefit consulting firms.

(d) SELECTION CRITERIA

(1) Program Design

The design of the flexible program is an important factor in selecting an
administrative approach. Design will have an impact both on the type
of system selected (manual, spreadsheet, personal computer, etc.) and
the system selected within that system type. For instance, if the plan
calls for minimal choice making and no employee-specific calculations,
the program may be administered by the payroll/personnel system with
minor enhancements. However, if the program is broader in scope with
many employee-specific components, a new administrative system may
be required.

If the program offers employees the choice between paying for benefits with before-tax or after-tax dollars, the administrative system selected will need to track both before- and after-tax elections for each
employee, regardless of whether the system is mainframe, time-sharing,
or personal computer.

All program details need not be determined prior to the selection of
the administration system. However, the system selected needs to have

the flexibility to handle unforeseen changes as the program design is finalized.

(2)   Number of Participants

Manual administration and spreadsheet software may be good alternatives for organizations with less than 500 program participants. Larger groups typically require more sophisticated personal computer, mainframe or time-sharing solutions if in-house administration of the program is desired.

The capacity of personal computer software is a function of the amount of data that will be stored for each participant and the hard-disk storage available on the personal computer system. As a rule of thumb, current and historical data for 1,000 flexible program participants can be stored in ten megabytes of hard disk storage.

As technology advances, faster processing speeds and greater data storage capacities will allow larger organizations to administer their programs using PC solutions.

Size is less of a factor when evaluating time-sharing and mainframe alternatives. The cost of the system, the desire to decentralize administration, and the availability of internal data-processing resources often are more important issues to consider.

(3)   Centralized versus Decentralized Administration

Some approaches lend themselves better to decentralized processing than others. In either time-sharing or mainframe environments, an organization can support decentralized administrator processing and still retain central control and produce summary-level reports. In a personal computing environment, maintaining central control of the system and producing summary-level reports are possible but considerably more difficult to achieve.

(4)   Implementation Timetable

The timing of program implementation has an impact on an organization's "build or buy" decision as well as the type of system to implement. In almost all cases, building a system internally will take more time than buying a comparable system from a vendor.

Once a decision has been made to buy, the type of system chosen will be a factor in the amount of time required for implementation. All other factors being equal, a time-sharing service or third-party administration approach will have the least impact on an organization's internal resources and therefore may be implemented faster than other administrative alternatives. A personal computer system requires less time to implement than a mainframe system because of the impact a mainframe system has on internal data-processing resources and the mainframe operating environment.

(5)   Data Processing and Administration Resources

The availability of internal data-processing resources is an important factor when evaluating administrative alternatives. Not only is data-processing support a key issue during implementation, but it also remains a major factor in ongoing support of the system.

The importance of adequate data-processing resources obviously is key to the decision on whether to build or buy a system. Once the decision is made to buy, however, internal data-processing support is still important. A time-sharing, third-party, or even a personal computer approach to administration requires some ongoing support from data processing. However a mainframe solution has the greatest impact on data-processing resources on an ongoing basis.

The availability of benefit administration resources also is a factor to consider in selecting the best approach.

A personal computer-based system residing in the benefit area usually requires greater administrator support than a mainframe-based system. In a personal computer environment, the administrator often is responsible for monitoring the print process, distributing the system output, and performing system backups and other system housekeeping functions. In a mainframe environment, these functions typically are performed by computer operators.

A time-sharing service may require less administrator involvement than either a personal computer or mainframe-based system, depending on the level of service provided by the time-sharing service. Third-party administration requires the least amount of administration resources.

(6)   Plans for Program Expansion

Just as the initial program design is a consideration in selecting an administrative alternative, plans for future program expansion are also important. For example, a personal computer system may be adequate to support even a large organization's flexible spending account. However, if the program is expanded in a subsequent year to include broad choice making, the revised program may exceed the capacity of the personal computer system. The same problem may occur if the program is expanded to include new employee groups or additional business units.

(7) Budgets

Implementation and ongoing administration budgets are almost always factors in the selection of an administrative solution. Building an administrative system is in most cases more expensive than licensing a software package. However, given the time and internal data-processing resources, some organizations prefer the soft-dollar expense of in-house development to the hard-dollar cost of buying a system or using a time-sharing service or TPA.

When the decision is made to buy a system or service, budget constraints may be a factor in deciding what type of system to implement. When reviewing the cost of each alternative, both implementation and ongoing costs are taken into consideration.

Installable systems, both personal computer and mainframe, typically involve three types of costs: one-time planning and software preparation charges, licensing fees, and ongoing software maintenance charges.

Time-sharing services often use a two-tier fee structure comprised of one-time planning and preparation charges and ongoing charges based on participation in the program.

Third-party administrators may structure their charges similarly to time-sharing services or charge on a per transaction basis. Transaction-based charges are commonly used for spending account administration. In this situation, transactions may include incoming spending account claims or spending account reimbursements or both.

When comparing the cost of administration systems, it is important to look at the overall costs for each system in relation to the services provided by each vendor. Some vendors include administration and payroll consulting services, training, administration manuals, and other consulting services in their product fees. Other vendor's product fees include only the software.

(e)   VENDOR ASSESSMENT

Once the type of administration system is determined and the range of acceptable systems narrowed, how does an organization assess each vendor's ability to deliver as promised?

One of the best ways to assess a vendor's qualifications is to ask for and check references. Ask for references:

- In the same industry
- With a similar program design
- Of a comparable size
- In the same geographical area
- With the same administration alternative
- Who have used the system for more than one year.

When checking references, talk to both administrative and systems personnel. Find out about both the implementation support and the on-going support provided by the vendor. Visit a user of the system if possible. Also meet with the people who will be implementing the system or service. How much experience do they have in similar implementations?

Another factor to consider is the range of services provided by the vendor. During implementation of the flexible program, the design, communication, and administration project teams will be working closely to ensure that the administrative system supports both the plan design and the communication approach. For organizations using consultants for design and/or communication, many implementation difficulties can be reduced if the same consultant is helping with program administration. For instance, the personalized enrollment statement produced by the enrollment system needs to use the same format and terminology as the enrollment form and election workbook designed by the communicators. The format of the enrollment form must support the agreed upon election entry approach. And finally, the administrative system must support the detailed plan design, both during annual enrollment and throughout the plan year.

§ 19.2   IMPLEMENTING THE ADMINISTRATIVE SYSTEM

(a)   DEFINING SYSTEM SPECIFICATIONS

Regardless of whether the administrative system is developed in-house or licensed from a software vendor, the first step in implementation involves defining system specifications. During this step, the implementation project team will work to:

- Develop an implementation workplan.
- Design the functional and technical specifications for the system based on the program design and administrative rules.
- Identify updates to existing administrative support systems and procedures such as payroll, personnel and accounting systems.
- Define the interface requirements between each applicable system, including:

Frequency

Mode (magnetic tape, report, electronic transfer, etc.)

Data requirements

(b) PROGRAMMING AND TESTING

This step is the most difficult and time-consuming phase of implementation. The responsibility for this step depends on whether the system is being developed in-house or licensed from a vendor.

To support the initial annual enrollment in a broad flexible program, the system typically is fully tested and ready to begin enrollment processing at least three to four months prior to the program effective date.

(c) TRAINING ADMINISTRATORS

Administrator training is an important part of the implementation process. Enrollment training takes place prior to the initial enrollment. Spending account and ongoing administration training may be deferred until just prior to the program effective date. Administration or user's manuals typically are distributed to administrators and discussed during training.

The approach to training is tailored to meet the needs of the organization. If administration is going to be decentralized, training may be done at each administrative location. Alternatively, administrators may be assembled at one company location or trained at a neutral site.

Part Seven

Experience

Twenty

Financial Analysis

§ 20.1 CHALLENGE OF FINANCIAL ANALYSIS

Conceptually, financial analysis of a flexible program involves little more than calculating the cost (either historical or projected) of the benefit program. In practice, however, performance of a cost analysis is considerably more complex, in many ways resembling art as much as science. This is true whether the financial analysis is future-oriented (i.e., predicting future costs) or past-oriented (i.e., analyzing actual past costs).

To some extent, financial analysis of a flexible program is hampered by the same limitations that apply to conventional program structures. That is, experience data is often limited or tracked in insufficient detail; exceptional claims experience (either positive or negative) can distort year-to-year comparisons for all but the very largest organizations; and results of certain design features (such as mandatory second surgical opinions or precertification of hospital admissions) are no more reliably quantifiable when introduced under a flexible approach than under a conventional benefit structure.

Still other complications arise directly from the nature of the flexible program structure. For example, a flexible approach typically permits trade-offs among benefits or levels of coverage and the conversion of benefit dollars to other forms of compensation (i.e., cash or tax-deferred savings or flexible spending account deposits). The different uses of these monies as well as the applicable tax consequences need to be reflected in a financial analysis.

Finally, flexible programs are typically launched in concert with other organizational changes, which complicates the financial analysis. Organizations often use flexible programs as a means of integrating benefits for newly acquired divisions or units, changing or strengthening corporate culture, or responding to increased competition for new hires. In addition, companies often upgrade existing administrative systems and procedures or improve employee communication at the same time as introducing the flexible program. When multiple purposes are being served, it is often difficult to determine which portion of the overall implementation expenses should be "charged" against the flexible program.

The purpose of this material is to outline the various types of financial analyses applicable to a flexible program, to discuss the uses of these analyses, and to provide a conceptual framework for performing financial analyses.

§ 20.2   USES AND PURPOSES OF FINANCIAL ANALYSIS

(a)   INITIAL PROGRAM DESIGN

Financial analysis is useful in helping an organization structure the design of a program. This includes deciding which benefit areas to incorporate in the program, the specific design of the options within a benefit area, the prices to charge for each option, and the amount of credits (if any) to allocate to each participant. The objective is to design the program to meet the company's financial objectives and to ensure that the financial impact on employees is reasonable and appropriate. (Financial considerations which are key to these design decisions are covered in earlier chapters on specific benefit areas and pricing and credit allocation.)

(b)   COST/BENEFIT ANALYSIS

While introducing a flexible program may create a number of pluses for an organization and its employees, there are also significant costs involved. Senior management will often require a "dollars and cents" analysis of the impact of a flexible compensation program before approving plans for implementation.

A cost/benefit analysis of the financial impact of a flexible program may focus primarily on the initial year, or it may incorporate a projection of costs over a three- to five-year period.

For example, an energy company hit hard by a drop in oil prices used first-year cost analysis to decide between introducing a flexible program with a variety of cost savings features or making unilaterally deep benefit cuts. The company discovered that by overhauling the existing program, including replacing an expensive medical plan with a choice of three comprehensive options (with deductibles ranging up to $1,500) and introducing changes in health care (and other) cost management features simultaneously, a first- and subsequent-year savings of $2.5 million dollars could be realized. The savings represented about a 25 percent reduction in the cost of the affected benefits. The financial analysis influenced the design of the flexible program in terms of accomplishing the company's cost reduction objective, but it also helped convince management that more severe benefit "take aways" for employees could be avoided.

In other situations, financial analysis shows an increase in costs in the first year of a program (particularly if implementation costs are simply treated as a first-year expense rather than being capitalized), reaching a break-even point in the second or third year and realizing a savings beyond that point.

(c)   CASH FLOW PROJECTIONS

Separate from the issue of whether costs will increase or decrease by introducing a flexible program, an organization's cash flow patterns are likely to be altered. Although this is often overlooked (and may not be important in some organizations), a brief financial analysis of the impact on cash flow may prove to be useful.

Consider the likely impact of a health care flexible spending account funded by salary reduction. In general, health care spending accounts slow down an organization's cash distributions as funds which would have been paid in salary are instead allocated to the accounts for disbursement weeks or months later. Cash distributions out of the accounts may rise significantly near the end of the year (and near the end of any grace period which extends into the next year) as employees attempt to deplete the accounts to avoid forfeiture. Also, if forfeitures are reverted to the company (rather than being contributed to a charity or used for some other purpose), the estimated amount and timing of the reversion should be reflected.

Other aspects of a flexible program may also have a significant impact on cash flow. If employees are able to take cash in lieu of certain benefits, the timing of cash payments may be accelerated. If added vacation days may be purchased but unused elective days are cashed out at year-end, a significant drain on cash flow could occur in December. If medical or dental benefits are reduced as an element of a flexible program, claims costs may be dramatically higher between the announcement and the effective dates.

(d) EXPERIENCE EVALUATION

Some organizations use financial analysis to measure the effectiveness of a flexible program in controlling medical or other benefit plan costs. For example, among the reasons one financial services organization introduced a flexible program was to freeze medical plan costs. The organization offered various levels of medical coverage and found that over time employees gravitated toward the higher-deductible options. At the end of the program's fourth year of operation, employer costs for medical remained at exactly the same level as in the first year of operation. Moreover, the price tag to employees for only one of the options needed to be increased—and then only by rates comparable to inflation. The company stabilized costs without unreasonable cost sharing with employees.

(e) FUTURE PRICING AND REDESIGN

One of the more important reasons for financial analysis is to assist organizations in making option pricing and design decisions for future years. This is especially important in medical, but is relevant in other benefit areas as well.

For example, when alternative medical plans are included in a flexible program, prices need to be assigned for each option and for each coverage category (e.g., employee only, employee plus spouse, etc.) within the options. (See also Chapter Twelve for more complete discussion of initial-pricing decisions.) Development of these prices is important to ensure that the selection process is not biased toward specific choices, that employees are not overcharged as a group, that contributions to HMOs are set appropriately, and so forth. Although the experience of each option may not be the only factor incorporated in a pricing decision, clearly it will be a major determinant of next year's pricing. Even employers who are fully insured need to monitor the financial experience of each option as their insurer will be comparing the program with others it underwrites to evaluate prices for coverage in subsequent years. In either case, therefore, the employer (and employees) will be affected financially, either directly or indirectly.

§ 20.3   COST/BENEFIT ANALYSIS

Perhaps the most important type of financial analysis conducted surrounding the design and implementation of a flexible program is that aimed at determining whether an organization should adopt such a program. In effect, is a flexible program worth the implementation effort and cost? The answer to this question will be easy to arrive at in some situations (clearly "yes" or clearly "no"), but arriving at an answer will be quite complex in other situations. Even after a financial analysis is complete, the degree to which nonfinancial objectives are being accomplished (or alternative problems created) needs to be considered before a final "go/no go" decision can be made.

In the following discussion, it is assumed that the plan design (including determination of prices and allocation of credits) has been finalized and the review of the financial impact on individual employees (evaluating winners and losers) yields satisfactory results.

(a)   IDENTIFICATION OF COST VARIABLES

The first step in analyzing the cost impact of a flexible program is to determine the potential areas of significant cost changes (increases or decreases). Although certainly not a complete list, the following provides an indication of the types of items that might be considered for a broad flexible program:

Cost Savings Areas

- Specific benefit reductions such as an increase in the medical deductible, a change in the coordination of benefits approach, and so forth.
- Increases in employee contributions either initially or in future years.
- Decreases in medical utilization due to higher deductibles and copayment amounts (possibly also including any savings arising from specific cost management features).
- Reduction in payroll taxes (primarily FICA savings related to pretax contributions).
- Decreases arising from employees dropping out of the program in dual-coverage situations.
- Forfeitures from flexible spending accounts (if not donated to charity or allocated for another purpose).
- "Float" within spending accounts (resulting from later payment by the company).

- Potential savings in ongoing administration (due to consolidation of multiple benefit programs or computerizing previously manual processes).

Cost Increase Areas

- Implementation costs (communication, administration, legal documentation, consulting fees, staffing requirements).
- Ongoing operational costs (communication, administration, etc.).
- Increased participation in optional, partially subsidized benefits (due to the increased communication effort or pricing and credit allocation approaches).
- Credits provided on waiver of coverage (if nonparticipating employees previously resulted in no company costs).
- Election experience (adverse selection).
- Improvements in specific benefits (e.g., updating plan maximums) made in conjunction with the introduction of the flexible program.
- Increases in payroll taxes (if benefits can be converted into cash or Section 401(k) contributions).

Not all of these items will apply in each situation, and others which are specific only to that employer may arise. The point is that any cost factor which is significant in magnitude and can be reasonably evaluated should be included in a cost/benefit analysis. Any cost factor which is likely to be significant but cannot be evaluated with reliability should be included as a "best guess" or with a range of results.

(b) COMPUTATION OF COST IMPACT

The objective of this type of financial analysis is to provide the employer with an indication of the anticipated effect of a flexible program on benefit costs. As described earlier, numerous variables will produce either gains or losses, including some that defy precise measurement. At this point in the design or approval process, however, the employer needs to make a decision whether to proceed with implementation of a revised benefit program, so the estimated cost impact needs to be determined on the most reasonable basis available.

In some cases, the computation of the cost impact will be relatively straightforward and can be accomplished with a high level of precision and reliability. Certain changes are very measurable. Some examples are replacing an insured dental plan with a $200 allocation to a flexible spending account, making a 20 percent increase in employee contributions to medical, or increasing a deductible by $50. Other changes may not be measurable by the employer, but the bottom-line result is known (e.g., situations in which a third party has guaranteed cost savings from precertification of hospital admissions).

Often, however, the program will have some elements where the financial impact cannot be confidently predicted—either because of uncertainty about employee elections or about the actual experience for the year under the elections made. Sometimes it may not even be possible to determine whether the effect will produce an increase or a decrease in costs. This difficulty may be illustrated with a feature as relatively straightforward as mandatory second opinions on specific surgical procedures. While a "guesstimate" of the impact will likely be made and an overall savings anticipated due to elimination of some unneeded surgeries, in reality, this feature could increase medical plan costs because of the additional charges for second or even third opinions in cases where the original recommendations for surgery are confirmed.

Regardless of the level of precision, the number of variables, or the length of the measurement period, the general formula in Example 20.1 can be used to compute the cost implications.

This formula might be applied for only one year to determine a first-year cost impact for the revised program versus the projected cost of continuing the prior program, or it may be applied for three to five years to estimate a longer-term impact. (Only rarely is a period longer than five years used to analyze the financial impact of a benefit program change.)

Example 20.1
Computation of Flexible Program Cost Increases (Decreases)

Cost Effect = Increase (decrease) in CLAIMS (self-insured employer), OR
Increase (decrease) in PREMIUMS (insured employer)

− Increase (decrease) in EMPLOYEE CONTRIBUTIONS

+ Employer CREDITS paid in cash or Section 401(k) deposits

+ Increase (decrease) in IMPLEMENTATION or ongoing OPERATIONAL COSTS

+ Miscellaneous OTHER COSTS

− Miscellaneous OTHER SAVINGS

(c) EXAMPLE

To illustrate the operation of the formula (see Example 20.2), consider the following situation.

Assumptions

- There are 1,000 employees
- Average medical cost is projected at $2,000 with the employee paying 25 percent and the company paying 75 percent
- Flexible program consists of:

> Choice of three medical plans (current and two lower options with the lowest option producing "leftover" credits)
> Health care and dependent care flexible spending accounts
> Pretax premium payment for medical plans.

In this case, if the implementation costs of $100,000 had been spread over two years rather than fully allocated to the initial year, the first year would have produced a $35,000 savings, and the second year would have produced a $76,000 savings.

Example 20.2

Year 1 Impact

	Current Program	Flexible Program	Difference
Expected medical claims	$2,000,000	$1,800,000	−$200,000
Employee contributions	−500,000	−600,000	−100,000
Employer credits in cash	0	200,000	+ 200,000
Implementation costs	0	100,000	+ 100,000
Operational costs	0	50,000	+ 50,000
Other costs			
—One part-time benefits clerk	0	15,000	+ 15,000
Other savings			
—FICA taxes on employee contributions and FSA contributions	N/A	−50,000	−50,000
—FSA forfeitures (contributed to charity)	N/A	N/A	0
Year 1 Impact			+ $15,000 (Cost Increase)

Example 20.2 *(continued)*

Year 2 Impact

	Current Program	Flexible Program	Difference
Expected medical claims (+10%)	$2,200,000	$1,980,000	−$220,000
Employee contributions (assuming credits only increased 8% and prices increased 10%)	−550,000	−688,000	−138,000
Employer credits in cash	0	220,000	+ 220,000
Operational costs	0	50,000	+ 50,000
Other costs			
—One part-time benefits clerk	0	16,000	+ 16,000
Other savings			
—FICA tax	N/A	−54,000	−54,000
—FSA forfeitures	N/A	N/A	0
Year 2 Impact			−126,000 (Cost Savings)

In order to prepare such an analysis, certain decisions and assumptions need to be made, such as:

- What time period for the evaluation is appropriate?
- Should one-time implementation expenses be treated as first-year expenses or spread over multiple years?
- What assumptions should be made regarding employee election patterns?
- What experience is likely under self-insured options?
- What strategy will be used for future increases in option prices and credits?
- What levels of future inflation and pay increases are appropriate?

§ 20.4   FUTURE PRICING AND REDESIGN

Once a flexible program is in operation, an employer must readdress option design, option pricing, and credit allocation issues for the next year. An important part of this annual process is financial analysis of the experience for the current year (and possibly past years). This analysis will often form the backdrop for at least the option pricing and credit allocation portions of the process and sometimes also influence option design issues.

The purposes of this financial analysis are to help answer the following kinds of questions:

- Are the actual aggregate program costs consistent with those projected for the year?
- Were the individual options fairly priced? If not, what changes may be appropriate?
- Does the experience under the program or under any specific option suggest particular design changes?
- What level of company credits in conjunction with the option prices will produce the appropriate level of company cost? What level will seem fair/reasonable to employees?

(a) LOOKING BACK

Despite its importance, actually conducting this form of financial analysis can often be very difficult. Often, the most significant problem is lack of reliable and timely experience data. The design, pricing, and credit allocation decisions resulting from this process need to be communicated to employees, and their elections need to be recorded prior to the beginning of the next plan year, so this analysis often needs to occur at least three or four months prior to year end.

However, at this time, the claims experience available in a self-insured situation will at best cover only the first half of the year (especially in the medical and dental areas where there is typically a one to two month lag between the time claims are incurred and the time they are paid by the insurance company or third-party administrator). As a result, pricing decisions usually must be made on the basis of limited data for the prior year, extrapolated forward to a full-year basis.

Employers can minimize the potential for frustration by anticipating upcoming data needs and taking steps to facilitate the early collection and categorization of results—particularly for medical and dental experience. Steps in the data collection process might include:

- Advise insurers, third-party administrators, or internal systems staff of the need for detailed analysis of elections and claims experience.

- Provide parameters for reporting actual experience—by employee group (e.g., active versus retired, hourly versus salaried), location, or division.
- Request itemization of employee data by type of coverage (e.g., Medical Plan A, Medical Plan B, etc.) and coverage category (e.g., employee only, employee plus one dependent, etc.).
- Establish tracking systems to identify and isolate specific large claims that could potentially distort the results, particularly for options elected by a small number of employees.

Extrapolating half-year data to a full-year basis, although necessary, can be complicated by a number of factors which may make simply doubling the half-year results inappropriate. Among these are the claims lag mentioned earlier, the continuing monthly increase in costs due to inflation, and the tendency for claims to be higher in the second half of the year after more participants have met the deductible.

It is typical to see medical experience by option which is quite different from that which would be produced by a fully random selection pattern. (See Chapter Thirteen on adverse selection.) For example, the pattern of actual versus expected claims experience might be on the order of that shown in Example 20.3.

If the actual experience is substantially different in the aggregate from that expected, the data should be reviewed to determine whether the experience is likely to be reliable as a predictor for the future. Perhaps an unusually high (or low) number of major claims occurred during the experience period, but these are unlikely to reoccur. In a small group, for example, the average claims experience under a low option might actually exceed the average claims experience under a high option due to one or two very large unexpected claims of employees who

Example 20.3
Illustration of Variation in Actual vs. Expected Claims Experience

Option	Number of Employees	Option Price Tag	"Expected Claims" Based on Price Tags*	Actual Claims	Actual as Percent of Expected
High	600	$2,000	$1,200,000	$1,330,000	111
Intermediate	300	1,600	480,000	400,000	83
Low	100	1,200	120,000	70,000	58
	1,000		$1,800,000	$1,800,000	100

*Assumes no adjustment for anticipated adverse selection or utilization changes.

selected the low option. This experience should be identified in the analysis, but it is probably inappropriate for full inclusion in the development of future prices.

(b) LOOKING FORWARD

After the historical experience has been accumulated, reviewed, and adjusted (if necessary), decisions need to be made regarding the future year's option prices. Again, this subject is discussed mainly from a medical perspective since medical is more often self-insured, having typically high costs and differences in option experience which can be great. (Also, setting prices for the next year based on the current year's experience will require some estimate of the expected increase in medical or dental claims due to inflation. Estimates of the expected trend factor for the next year are typically available from insurance companies and other sources.)

Assuming the medical experience shown in the earlier illustration (or 111 percent of "expected" for the high option and 83 percent and 58 percent for the other options), the issue arises as to what degree (if any) the individual option experience should be considered in next year's option prices.

One alternative is to ignore the variations from "expected" as long as overall medical program experience is in line with that expected (as is the case in this example). Under this approach, the option prices will maintain the same approximate relative relationships from year to year, thereby achieving a sense of stability from the employee's perspective.

On the other extreme would be a full reflection of the difference actually experienced between the options. In this example, such an approach would nearly double the spread between the high option and the low option prices in a single year. This would quickly drive employees away from the highest option. In some situations, this form of "option suicide" may, in fact, be an objective—to eliminate an unduly inefficient rich medical plan through the mechanism of pricing. In other cases, this may be inappropriately disturbing to those participants who are inclined to select the highest-level medical option.

An intermediate approach is often used which reflects only a portion of the experience-based differences in option costs. This might result in "nudging" employees away from the high option (or at least encouraging them to consider other options) rather than "driving" them away.

As part of this decision, one important (and often overlooked) step should be undertaken. The prices which are to be presented to employees need to make sense relative to the coverage levels being provided. This is particularly true if the full experience difference is to be used and, therefore, the pricing spread between the options is to be dramatically increased. The price differentials between the options should be compared with the differences in benefits payable under the options to ensure that employees are being presented with reasonable choices.

For example, if the difference in deductibles under two medical options (high and intermediate) would produce no more than a $150 gain to employees in coverage, the difference in prices between the options should not exceed that amount. Employees should not be asked to pay more for an option than they could expect to receive in coverage— regardless of the actual experience (which could have been unusual in a given year). In effect, the option choices and price tags need to be reviewed for logic in the eyes of employees as well as reflection of actual experience.

Index